CW00371348

THE COMPLETE BOOK OF
BIRDS

THE COMPLETE BOOK OF
BIRDS

DAVID ALDERTON

This edition is published by Armadillo, an imprint of Anness Publishing Ltd,
Blaby Road, Wigston, Leicestershire LE18 4SE
Email: info@anness.com

Web: www.annesspublishing.com

Anness Publishing has a new picture agency outlet for images for publishing,
promotions or advertising. Please visit our website
www.practicalpictures.com for more information.

© Anness Publishing Ltd 2002, 2011

All rights reserved. No part of this publication may be reproduced,
stored in a retrieval system, or transmitted in any way or by any means,
electronic, mechanical, photocopying, recording or otherwise,
without the prior written permission of the copyright holder.

A CIP catalogue record for this book is available from the British Library.

Publisher: Joanna Lorenz
Managing Editor: Helen Sudell
Editor: Debra Mayhew
Text Editors: Jen Green, Dawn Titmus
Design: Nigel Partridge
Illustrators: see acknowledgements page
Map Illustrators: Anthony Duke, Janos Marffy
Editorial Readers: Jonathan Marshall, Richard McGinlay
Production Controller: Ann Childers

ETHICAL TRADING POLICY
Because of our ongoing ecological investment programme, you, as our customer, can have
the pleasure and reassurance of knowing that a tree is being cultivated on your behalf to
naturally replace the materials used to make the book you are holding. For further
information about this scheme, go to www.annesspublishing.com/trees

Also published as *The World Encyclopedia of Birds & Birdwatching*

Pictures: Endpapers: Ostrich (Struthio camelus); *page 1: Crested quetzal* (Pharomachrus antisianus);
p2: Lauterbach's bowerbird (Chlamydera lauterbach); *p3: Swallow* (Hirundo rustica);*p4: Green broadbill* (Calyptomena viridis);
p5: Blue tit (Parus caeruleus) *(top) and Glossy ibis* (Plegadis falcinellus).

Jacket pictures: Oxford Scientific films: back flap, back (top right and front middle).
Ardea: back (top left, top middle, bottom left, bottom middle, bottom right), spine, front (all four).

PUBLISHER'S NOTE
Although the advice and information in this book are believed to be accurate and true at the time of going to press,
neither the authors nor the publisher can accept any legal responsibility or liability
for any errors or omissions that may have been made.

Manufacturer: Anness Publishing Ltd, Blaby Road, Wigston, Leicestershire LE18 4SE, England
For Product Tracking go to: www.annesspublishing.com/tracking
Batch: 2811-12955-1127

CONTENTS

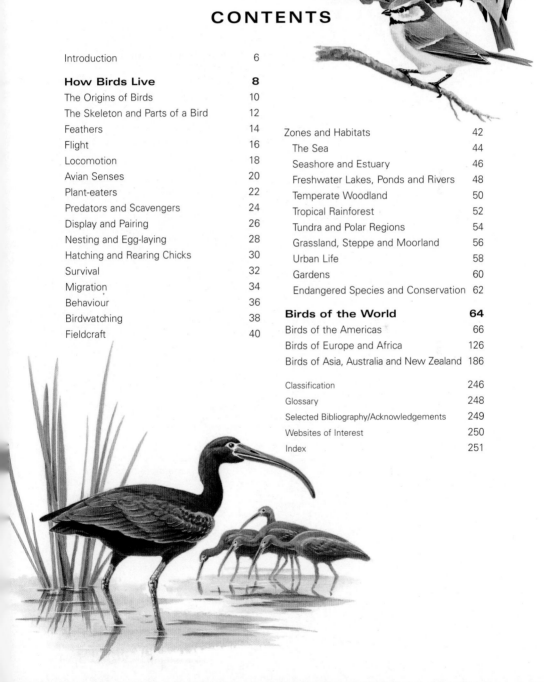

INTRODUCTION

Birds have been a source of fascination and inspiration to people since the dawn of history. Birds' mastery of the skies not only inspired humans to invent flying machines but also helped facilitate the development of modern aircraft, since aeroplane designers borrowed the aerodynamic features of birds to revolutionize aircraft used in intercontinental travel.

Birds have also influenced our cultures in a spiritual sense, as reflected, for example, by the thunderbird legends of the native North Americans and the phoenix featured in Egyptian mythology. In Europe, as elsewhere, birds have become significant in various festivals. The robin (*Erithacus rubecula*) is now inextricably linked with Christmas, while the return of the common cuckoo (*Cuculus canorus*) from its African wintering grounds is eagerly awaited as one of the early signs of spring. The same applies around the world, with cranes (Gruidae), for example, having particular significance in Japanese culture.

It may seem surprising, but there are still new species of birds being discovered every year. Among the most recent is a new bald-headed parrot from the Mato Grosso region of Brazil, reported for the first time

Below: Birds have adapted to live, feed and breed in a wide range of different habitats. Here a puffin (Fratercula arctica) is returning from a successful fishing trip at sea.

Above: Being large in size may make birds more conspicuous, like the Australian cassowary (Casuarius casuarius), but it can mean they are less vulnerable to predators too.

in July 2002. As an approximate guide, there are over 9,000 avian species present on Earth – a total far in excess of the number of mammals. There is virtually no environment on the planet where birds are not to be seen, even in the freezing wasteland of Antarctica, where penguins maintain a remarkable vigil to breed in one of the most inhospitable environments to be found anywhere on Earth.

Birds have spread so widely over the planet's surface not only because of their ability to fly, but also because they are highly adaptable in their feeding habits. Birds eat a wide variety of foods, ranging from microsopic plankton to the carcasses of large mammals, as well as all types of vegetable matter and numerous invertebrates.

In recent years, human activities have had an increasingly harmful impact on numerous avian populations around the world, and are now threatening the very survival of many species. On the bright side, however, technology is being applied as never before to assist the survival of critically endangered species such as the Californian condor (*Gymnogyps californianus*), giving real hope for such birds' survival in what may hopefully become a more enlightened era of human activity.

Birdwatching has also benefited from technological advances, such as the Internet, which enables information about new sightings to be relayed instantly to

enthusiasts. Undoubtedly, webcam opportunities to observe bird sites even on the other side of the world will increase in the years ahead. Yet one of the reasons why birdwatching has become such a popular pastime is that it can be carried out basically anywhere. No special equipment is necessarily required, although binoculars, sketchpads and similar items can add greatly to your enjoyment and understanding of avian life.

This book is a celebration of birds that sets out to reveal the diversity that exists in both their form and lifestyles. The second part features species from around the world, aiding their identification by placing them initially in regions and then in the particular environments in which they are most likely to be seen. Even if you do not have the opportunity to visit far-flung places such as tropical rainforests or Antarctica, you will still be able to marvel at the diversity of avian life that exists on our planet, as portrayed in these pages.

*Below: Secure nesting sites are important for the survival of all birds. This Harris's hawk (*Parabuteo unicinctus*) has bred successfully, with its nest being protected by a thorny cactus.*

HOW BIRDS LIVE

The most obvious thing that distinguishes all birds, from the tiniest hummingbirds (Trochilidae) to the gigantic Californian condor (*Gymnogyps californianus*), is the presence of feathers on their bodies. The need to lighten birds' weight so that they can fly with minimum effort has led to significant changes within their bodies as well, and yet the basic skeletal structure of all birds is remarkably similar, irrespective of their size. In other words, birds are unmistakable.It is instantly clear that even the few groups of flightless birds,such as penguins (Spheniscidae), are descended from ancestors that possessed the power of flight, although these birds have since evolved on different lines to suit their habitat.

The other feature unique to birds is that all species reproduce by means of calcareous eggs. Birds' breeding habits are very diverse, however. Some birds even transfer the task of incubation to other species, by laying in their nests, while others create natural incubators that serve to hatch their chicks and carefully regulate the temperature inside.

There is even greater diversity in the feeding habits of birds, as reflected by differences in their bill structure and also their digestive tracts. Birds' dietary preferences play a critical part in the environment as well. For example, in tropical rainforests, many fruit-eating species help to disperse indigestible seeds through the forest, thus helping to ensure the natural regeneration of the vegetation.

The birds of tropical rainforests are often surprisingly hard to observe, betraying their presence more by their calls than by their bright colours. However, birds can be easily observed in many other localities. Birdwatching itself can develop into an absorbing pastime offering an unparalleled insight into the natural world. Many practical tips to help you enjoy this activity are included in the following pages.

Left: Black-headed gulls (Larus ridibundus). These noisy and conspicuous birds have highly adaptable natures and can sometimes be seen in large groups. They have expanded their range inland from coastal areas in recent years, thanks to human changes affecting the landscape.

THE ORIGINS OF BIRDS

Vertebrates – first flying reptiles called pterosaurs, and later birds – took to the air about 190 million years ago. Adapting to an aerial existence marked a very significant step in vertebrate development, because of the need for a new method of locomotion, and a radically different body design.

The age of *Archaeopteryx*

Back in 1861, workers in a limestone quarry in Bavaria, southern Germany, unearthed a strange fossil that resembled a bird in appearance and was about the size of a modern crow, but also had teeth. The idea that the fossil was a bird was confirmed by the clear evidence of feathers impressed into the stone, as the presence of plumage is one of the characteristic distinguishing features of all birds. The 1860s were a time when the debate surrounding evolution was becoming fierce, and the discovery created huge interest, partly because it suggested that birds may have evolved from dinosaurs. It confirmed that birds had lived on Earth for at least 145 million years, existing even before the age of the dinosaurs came to a close in the Cretaceous period, about 65 million years ago. As the oldest-known bird, it became known as *Archaeopteryx*, meaning "ancient wings".

Pterosaurs

A study of the anatomy of *Archaeopteryx*'s wings revealed that these early birds did not just glide but were capable of using their wings for active flight. Yet they were not the first vertebrate creatures to have taken to the skies. The pterosaurs had already successfully developed approximately 190 million years ago, during the Jurassic period, and even shared the skies with birds for a time. In fact, the remains of one of the later pterosaurs, called *Rhamphorhynchus*, have been found in the same limestone deposits in southern Germany where *Archaeopteryx* was discovered. The pterosaur's wings more closely resembled those of a bat than a bird, consisting simply of a membrane supported by a bony framework, rather than feathers overlying the skin.

Some types of pterosaurs developed huge wingspans, in excess of 7m (23ft), which enabled them to glide almost effortlessly over the surface of the world's oceans, much like albatrosses do today. It appears that they fed primarily on fish and other marine life, scooping their food out of the water in flight. Changes in climate probably doomed the pterosaurs, however, since increasingly turbulent weather patterns meant that gliding became difficult, and they could no longer fly with ease.

Avian giants

In the period immediately after the extinction of the dinosaurs, some groups of birds increased rapidly in physical size, and in so doing, lost the ability to fly. Since their increased size meant that they could cover large distances on foot, and as they faced no predators while large hunting mammals had not yet evolved, these large birds were relatively safe. In New Zealand, home of the large flightless moas, such giants thrived until the start of human settlement about a millennium ago. The exact date of the final extinction of the moas is not recorded, but the group had probably died out entirely by the middle of the 19th century.

Below: The largest species of moa would have dwarfed a man.

Above: An impression of how Archaeopteryx *may have looked. It is impossible to be sure of its coloration from its fossilized remains.*

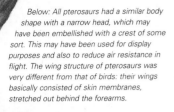

Below: All pterosaurs had a similar body shape with a narrow head, which may have been embellished with a crest of some sort. This may have been used for display purposes and also to reduce air resistance in flight. The wing structure of pterosaurs was very different from that of birds: their wings basically consisted of skin membranes, stretched out behind the forearms.

It was this large surface area that allowed them to glide with little effort, but becoming airborne in the first place required great effort. The lack of body covering over the skin also had the effect of causing greater heat loss from the body. In birds, the feathers provide insulation as well as assisting active flight.

Below: Hoatzin chicks (Opisthocomus hoazin) are unique among today's birds in possessing claws on their wing tips, which help them to climb trees. The claws are lost by the time the birds are old enough to fly.

The spread of birds

After the age of *Archaeopteryx*, it is thought that birds continued to radiate out over the globe and became increasingly specialized. Unfortunately, there is very little fossil evidence to help us understand their early history. This lack of fossils is partly due to the fact that the small carcasses of birds would have been eaten whole by scavengers, and partly because their lightweight, fragile skeletons would not have fossilized easily. In addition, most birds would not have been trapped and died under conditions that were favourable for fossilization.

By the end of the age of the dinosaurs, birds had become far more numerous. Many seabirds still possessed teeth in their jaws, reflecting their reptilian origins. These probably assisted them in catching fish and other aquatic creatures. It was at this

stage that the ancestors of contemporary bird groups such as waterfowl and gulls started to emerge. Most of the forerunners of today's birds had evolved by the Oligocene epoch, some 38 million years ago.

Some groups of birds that existed in these times have since disappeared, notably the phororhacids, which ranged widely over South America and even into parts of the southern United States. These birds were fearsome predators, capable of growing to nearly 3m (10ft) in height. They were equipped with deadly beaks and talons, and probably hunted together in groups.

Recent finds

During the mid-1990s, the discovery of avian fossils in China that were apparently contemporary with those of *Archaeopteryx* aroused considerable interest. Like its German relative, *Confuciusornis* possessed claws on the tips of its wings, which probably helped these early birds to move around. Similar claws are seen today in hoatzin chicks. *Confuciusornis* resembled modern birds more closely than *Archaeopteryx* in one significant respect: it lacked teeth in its jaws. Further study of the recent fossil finds from this part of the world is required however, as some may not be genuine.

THE SKELETON AND PARTS OF A BIRD

The bird's skeleton has evolved to be light yet robust, both characteristics that help with flight. To this end, certain bones, particularly in the skull, have become fused, while others are absent, along with the teeth. The result is that birds' bodies are lightweight compared to those of other vertebrates.

In order to be able to fly, a bird needs a lightweight body so that it can become airborne with minimal difficulty. It is not just teeth that are missing from the bird's skull, but the associated heavy jaw muscles as well. These have been replaced by a light, horn-covered bill that is adapted in shape to the bird's feeding habits. Some of the limb bones, such as the humerus in the shoulder, are hollow, which also cuts down on weight. At the rear of the body, the bones in the vertebral column have become fused, which gives greater stability as well as support for the tail feathers.

The avian skeleton

In birds, the greatest degree of specialization is evident in the limbs. The location of the legs is critical to enable a bird to maintain its balance. The legs are found close to the midline, set slightly back near the bird's centre of gravity. The limbs are powerful, helping to provide lift at take-off and absorb the impact of landing. Strong legs also allow most birds to hop over the ground with relative ease.

There are some differences in the skeleton between different groups of birds. The atlas and axis bones at the start of the vertebral column are fused in the case of hornbills, for example, but in no other family.

Feet and toes

Birds' feet vary in length, and are noticeably extended in waders, which helps them to distribute their weight more evenly. The four toes may be arranged either in a typical 3:1 perching grip, with three toes gripping the front of the perch and one behind, or in a 2:2 configuration, known as zygodactyl, which gives a surer grip. The zygodactyl grip is seen in relatively few groups of birds, notably parrots and toucans. Touracos have flexible toes so they can swap back and forth between these two options.

The zygodactyl arrangement of their toes helps some parrots to use their feet like hands for holding food. Birds generally have claws at the ends of their toes, which have developed into sharp talons in the case of birds of prey, helping them to catch their quarry even in flight. Many birds also use their claws for preening, and they can provide balance for birds that run or climb.

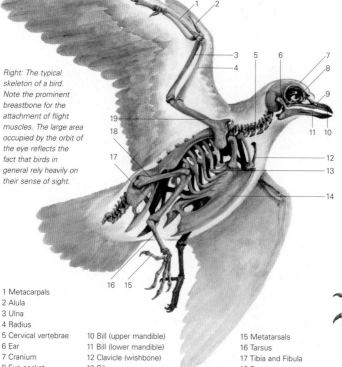

Right: The typical skeleton of a bird. Note the prominent breastbone for the attachment of flight muscles. The large area occupied by the orbit of the eye reflects the fact that birds in general rely heavily on their sense of sight.

Parrot

Above: Parrots use their feet for holding food, rather like human hands.

Bird of prey

Above: In birds of prey, the claws have become talons for grasping prey.

Wader

Above: Long toes make it easier for waders to walk over muddy ground or water plants.

Duck

Above: The webbed feet of ducks provide propulsion in water.

1 Metacarpals
2 Alula
3 Ulna
4 Radius
5 Cervical vertebrae
6 Ear
7 Cranium
8 Eye socket
9 Nostril
10 Bill (upper mandible)
11 Bill (lower mandible)
12 Clavicle (wishbone)
13 Ribs
14 Sternum (breastbone)
15 Metatarsals
16 Tarsus
17 Tibia and Fibula
18 Femur
19 Humerus

Above: The narrow bill of waders such as this curlew (Numenius arquata) *enables these birds to probe for food in sandy or muddy areas.*

Above: Birds of prey such as the golden eagle (Aquila chrysaetos) *rely on a sharp bill with a hooked tip to tear their prey apart.*

Above: Cranes have strong, pointed bills, which they use like daggers to seize prey such as frogs between the upper and lower parts.

Above: Flamingos have bills that enable them to feed with their heads trailing backwards in the water.

Above: The hyacinthine macaw (Anodorhynchus hyacinthinus) *has one of the most powerful bills of any bird.*

Above: Whale-headed storks (Balaeniceps rex) *have large bills that allow them to scoop up quite large vertebrate prey.*

Bills

The bills of birds vary quite widely in shape and size, and reflect their feeding habits. The design of the bill also has an impact on the force that it can generate. The bills of many larger parrots are especially strong, allowing them to crack hard nut shells. In addition, they can move their upper and lower bill independently, which produces a wider gape and, in turn, allows more pressure to be exerted.

Wings

A bird's wing is built around just three digits, which correspond to human fingers. In comparison, bats have five digits supporting their fleshy membranes. The three digits of birds provide a robust structure. The power of the wings is further enhanced by the fusion of the wrist bones and the carpals to create the single bone known as the carpometacarpus, which runs along the rear of the wing.

At the front of the chest, the clavicles are joined together to form what in chickens is called the wishbone. The large, keel-shaped breastbone, or sternum, runs along the underside of the body. It is bound by the ribs to the backbone, which provides stability, especially during flight. In addition, the major flight muscles are located in the lower body when the bird is airborne.

Darwin's finches

In the 1830s, a voyage to the remote Galapagos Islands, off the north-west coast of South America, helped the British naturalist Charles Darwin to formulate his theory of evolution. The finches present on the Galapagos Islands today are all believed to be descended from a single ancestor, but they have evolved in a number of different ways. The changes are most obvious in their bill shapes. For example, some species have stout, crushing beaks for cracking seeds, while others have long, slender beaks to probe for insects. These adaptations have arisen to take full advantage of the range of edible items available on the islands, where food is generally scarce. Some species have even developed the ability to use cactus spines and similar items as tools to extract seeds and invertebrates. In total, there are now 12 recognized species found on these islands, and nowhere else in the world.

Below: The diversity of the finches of the Galapagos is remarkable, being represented here, from top left moving clockwise, by the large insectivorous tree finch (Camarhynchus psittacula); *the woodpecker finch* (Camarhynchus palidus); *the vegetarian tree finch* (Camarhynchus crassirostris); *the cactus ground finch* (Geospiza scandens) *and the large cactus ground finch* (Geospiza conirostris).

FEATHERS

The presence of feathers is one of the main distinguishing characteristics that set birds apart from other groups of creatures on the planet. The number of feathers on a bird's body varies considerably – a swan may have as many as 25,000 feathers, for instance, while a tiny hummingbird has just 1,000 in all.

Aside from the bill, legs and feet, the entire body of the bird is covered in feathers. The plumage does not grow randomly over the bird's body, but develops along lines of so-called feather tracts, or pterylae. These are separated by bald areas known as apteria. The apteria are not conspicuous under normal circumstances, because the contour feathers overlap to cover the entire surface of the body. Plumage may also sometimes extend down over the legs and feet as well, in the case of birds from cold climates, providing extra insulation here.

Feathers are made of a tough protein called keratin, which is also found in our hair and nails. There are three main types of feathers on a bird's body: the body, or contour, feathers, the strong, elongated flight feathers on the wings, and the warm, wispy down feathers next to the bird's skin.

A diet deficient in sulphur-containing amino acids, which are the basic building blocks of protein, will result in poor feathering, creating "nutritional barring" across the flight and tail feathers. Abnormal plumage coloration can also have nutritional causes in some cases. These changes are usually reversible if more favourable environmental conditions precede the next moult.

The functions of feathers

Plumage has a number of functions, not just relating to flight. It provides a barrier that retains warm air close to the bird's body and helps to maintain body temperature, which is higher in birds than mammals – typically between 41 and 43.5°C (106 and 110°F). The down feathering that lies close to the skin, and the overlying contour plumage, are vital for maintaining body warmth. Most birds have a small volume relative to their surface area, which can leave them vulnerable to hypothermia.

A special oil produced by the preen gland, located at the base of the tail, waterproofs the plumage. This oil, which is spread over the feathers as the bird preens itself, prevents water penetrating the feathers, which would cause the bird to become so

Above: A bird's flight feathers are longer and more rigid than the contour feathers that cover the body, or the fluffy down feathers that lie next to the skin. The longest, or primary, flight feathers, which generate most thrust, are located along the outer rear edges of the wings. The tail feathers are often similar in shape to the flight feathers, with the longest being found in the centre. Splaying the tail feathers increases drag and so slows the bird down.

1 Primaries	9 Auricular region
2 Secondaries	(ear)
3 Axillaries	10 Nape
4 Rump	11 Back
5 Lateral tail feathers	12 Greater under-
6 Central tail feathers	wing coverts
7 Breast	13 Lesser under-
8 Cere	wing coverts

Below: Feathering is highly significant for display purposes in some species, particularly members of the Phasanidae family. The cock blue peafowl (Pavo cristatus) has a very elaborate train of feathers, which it fans open to deter rivals and attract mates.

Above: The vulturine guineafowl (Acryllium vulturinum) is so-called because of its bare head and neck, which is a feature of vultures, although it is not a carnivorous species itself.

waterlogged that it could no longer fly. The contour feathers that cover the body are also important for camouflage in many birds. Barring in particular breaks up the outline of the bird's body, helping to conceal it in its natural habitat.

The plumage has become modified in some cases, reflecting the individual lifestyle of the species concerned. Woodpeckers, for example, have tail feathers that are short and rather sharp at their tips, providing additional support for gripping on to the sides of trees. Vultures, on the other hand, have bare heads because plumage here would soon become stained and matted with blood when these birds fed on a carcass.

Social significance of plumage

Plumage can also be important in social interactions between birds. Many species have differences in their feathering that separate males from females, and often juveniles can also be distinguished by their plumage. Cock birds are usually more brightly coloured, which helps them to attract their mates, but this does not apply in every case. The difference between the sexes in terms of their plumage can be quite marked. Cock birds of a number

of species have feathers forming crests as well as magnificent tail plumes, which are seen to greatest effect in peacocks (*Pavo cristatus*), whose display is one of the most remarkable sights in the whole of the avian world.

Recent studies have confirmed that birds that to our eyes appear relatively dull in colour, such as the hill mynah (*Gracula religiosa*) with its blackish plumage, are seen literally in a different light by other birds. They can visualize the ultraviolet component of light, which is normally invisible to us, making these seemingly dull birds appear greener. Ultraviolet coloration may also be significant in helping birds to choose their mates.

Moulting

Birds' feathering is maintained by preening, but it becomes frayed and worn over time. It is therefore replaced by new plumage during the process of moulting, when the old feathers are shed. Moulting is most often an annual event. However, many young birds shed their nest feathers before they are a year old.

Moulting may also be triggered by the onset of the breeding season in some species, as is the case in many whydahs and weavers. These birds resemble sparrows for much of the year, but their appearance is transformed at the onset of the breeding period. Whydah cock birds develop lengthy tail plumes, and the birds also become more strikingly coloured. Hormonal alterations in the body are important in triggering this process, with external factors such as changing day length also playing a part.

Iridescence

Some birds are not brightly coloured, but their plumage literally sparkles in the light, thanks to its structure, which creates an iridescent effect. One of the particular features of iridescence is that the colour of the plumage alters, depending on the angle at which it is viewed, often appearing quite dark, almost black from a side view. This phenomenon is particularly common in some groups of birds, notably members of the starling family (Sturnidae), hummingbirds (Trochilidae) and sunbirds (Nectariniidae), which are described as having metallic feathers as a result.

In some cases, the iridescent feathering is localized, while in others, it is widespread over most of the body. Green and blue iridescence is common, with reddish sheens being seen less often. Iridescence is especially common in cock birds, helping them to attract mates. In some cases, therefore, it is seen only in the breeding plumage, notably on the upperparts of the body and the wings rather than the underparts.

Below: A blue-chinned sapphire hummingbird (Chlorestes notatus) displays its iridescent plumage.

Right: The feather shaft holds the feather in place in the skin. The barbs run off the shaft at regular intervals, rather like the branches of a tree, and divide into smaller branches called barbules. These have tiny hooks attached to them that reinforce the structure of the flight feather, making it more rigid.

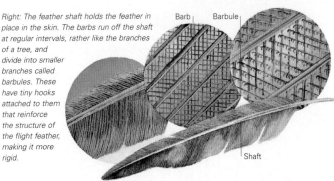

Barb Barbule

Shaft

FLIGHT

Some birds spend much of their lives in the air, whereas others will only fly as a last resort if threatened. A few species are too heavy to take off at all. The mechanics of flight are similar in all birds, but flight patterns vary significantly, which can help to identify the various groups in the air.

In most cases, the whole structure of the bird's body has evolved to facilitate flight. It is important for a bird's body weight to be relatively light, because this lessens the muscular effort required to keep it airborne. The powerful flight muscles, which provide the necessary lift, can account for up to a third of the bird's total body weight. They are attached to the breastbone, or sternum, in the midline of the body, and run along the sides of the body from the clavicle along the breastbone to the top of the legs.

Weight and flight

There is an upper weight limit of just over 18kg (40lb), above which birds would not be able to take off successfully. Some larger birds, notably pelicans and swans, need a run-up in order to gain sufficient momentum to lift off, particularly from water. Smaller birds can dart straight off a perch. Approaching the critical upper weight limit for flight, the male Kori bustard (*Ardeotis kori*) is the world's heaviest flying bird, although it prefers to run rather than fly because of the effort involved in becoming airborne.

Below: A typical take-off, as shown by a Harris's hawk (Parabuteo unicinctus).

Above: Birds such as the Andean condor (Vultur gryphus) *can remain airborne with minimum expenditure of energy, by gliding rather than flying.*

Wing shape and beat

The shape of the wing is important for a bird's flying ability. Birds that remain airborne for much of their lives, such as albatrosses, have relatively long wings that allow them to glide with relatively little effort. The wandering albatross (*Diomedea exulans*) has the largest wingspan of any bird, measuring about 3.4m (11ft) from one wing tip to the other. Large, heavy birds such as Andean condors (*Vultur gryphus*) may have difficulty in flying early in the day, before the land has warmed up. This is because at this stage, there is insufficient heat coming up from the ground to create the thermal air currents that help to keep them airborne. In common with other large birds of prey, Andean condors seek out these rising columns of air, which provide uplift, and then circle around in them.

The number of wing beats varies dramatically between different species. Hummingbirds, for example, beat their wings more frequently than any other bird as they hover in front of flowers to harvest their nectar. Their wings move so fast – sometimes at over 200 beats per minute – that they appear as a blur to our eyes. At the other extreme, heavy birds such as swans fly with slow, deliberate wing beats.

Lightening the load

It is not just the lightness of the bird's skeleton that helps it to fly. There have been evolutionary changes in the body organs too, most noticeably in the urinary system. Unlike mammals, birds do not have a bladder that fills with urine. Instead, their urine is greatly concentrated, in the form of uric acid, and passes out of the body with their faeces, appearing as a creamy-white, semi-solid component.

1. When resting, a bird typically has a relatively upright stance.

2. As it leans forwards for take-off, it raises its wings and starts to lift its legs.

3. Leaving its perch, the bird pushes off into the air, and opens its wings.

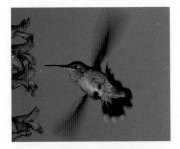

Above: Hummingbirds such as this broadtail (Selasphorus platycercus) have unparalleled aerial manoeuvrability, thanks to their rapid wing movements.

Below: The black-browed albatross (Diomedea melanophris) and its relatives often skim just above the waves.

The aerofoil principle

Once in flight, the shape of the wing is crucial in keeping the bird airborne. Viewed in cross-section from the side, a bird's wing resembles an aeroplane's wing, called an aerofoil, and in fact aeroplanes use the same technique as birds to fly.

The wing is curved across the top, so the movement of air is faster over this part of the wing compared with the lower surface. This produces reduced air pressure on top of the wing, which provides lift and makes it easier for the bird to stay in the air.

The long flight feathers at the rear edge of the wings help to provide the thrust and lift for flight. The tail feathers, too, can help the bird remain airborne. The kestrel (*Falco tinnunculus*), for example, having spotted prey on the ground, spreads its tail feathers to help it remain aloft while it hovers to target its prey.

A bird's wings move in a regular figure-of-eight movement while it is in flight. During the downstroke, the flight feathers join together to push powerfully against the air. The primary flight feathers bend backwards, which propels the bird forwards. As the wing moves upwards, the longer primary flight feathers move apart, which reduces air resistance. The secondary feathers further along the wing provide some slight propulsion. After that the cycle repeats itself.

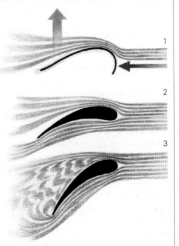

Above: The flow of air over a bird's wing varies according to the wing's position.
1. When the wing is stretched out horizontally, an area of low pressure is created above the wing, causing lift.
2. As the wing is tilted downwards, the flow of the air is disrupted, causing turbulence and loss of lift.
3. When the wing is angled downwards, lift slows, which results in stalling. The bird's speed slows as a consequence.

Flight patterns and formations

Different species of birds have various ways of flying, which can actually aid the birdwatcher in helping to identify them. For example, small birds such as tits (Paridae) and finches (Fringillidae) alternately flap their wings and fold them at their sides, adopting a streamlined shape, which helps to save energy. This produces a characteristic dipping flight. Large birds such as ducks and geese maintain a straighter course at an even height.

In some cases, it is not just the individual flying skills of a bird that can help it to stay airborne, but those of its fellows nearby. Birds flying in formation create a slipstream, which makes flying less effort for all the birds behind the leader. This is why birds often fly in formation, especially when covering large distances on migration.

4. Powerful upward and downward sweeps of the wings propel the bird forwards.

5. When coming in to land, a bird lowers its legs and slows its wing movements.

6. Braking is achieved by a vertical landing posture, with the tail feathers spread.

LOCOMOTION

For most birds, flight is the main means of locomotion. However, the ability to move on the ground or in water can be vital, particularly when it comes to obtaining food. Some birds have even lost the ability to fly, relying instead on their swimming or running skills to escape predators and find food.

Not all birds possess the ability to fly, but this does not mean they are handicapped in their natural environment. Penguins may appear to be rather clumsy shuffling around on land, but they are extremely well adapted to life in the water. Like other primarily aquatic birds, their webbed feet enable them to swim very effectively. Webbing is a common feature seen in aquatic birds. The skin folds linking the toes turn the foot into an effective paddle, allowing the bird to maximize its propulsive forward thrust by pushing against the water. On land, however, webbed feet do impose certain restrictions, because being linked together in this way means that the individual toes are not as flexible.

Aquatic locomotion

When penguins dive, their sleek, torpedo-shaped bodies allow them to swim fast underwater, reaching speeds equivalent to 40km/h (25mph). Their flippers, which evolved from wings,

Below: A group of king penguins (Aptenodytes patagonicus) *leap in and out of the water as they swim along, in a form of movement known as porpoising.*

help them to steer very effectively as they pursue fish, which form the basis of their diet. Like flying birds, penguins need effective wing muscles to control their movements, so their skeletal structure bears a close similarity to that of flying birds.

Flightless ducks and other aquatic birds, such as the Galapagos Island cormorant (*Nannopterum harrisi*), use a different method of locomotion: they rely entirely on their feet rather than their wings for propulsive power. Their skeletons differ from those of flying birds in that they lack the prominent keel on the sternum for the attachment of flight muscles.

Flightless land birds

A number of land birds have lost the ability to fly. Typically, they are birds that inhabit islands where, until the arrival of cats and rats brought by ships from Europe, they faced few if any predators. The arrival of predators has left them vulnerable, and many have since become extinct, including the dodo (*Raphus cucullatus*), a large, flightless pigeon from the island of Mauritius in the Indian Ocean. A high percentage of flightless birds evolved

Above: Penguins such as the chinstrap (Pygoscelis antarctica) *are less agile on land than they are in the sea, where their body shape lessens water resistance.*

on the islands of New Zealand, but many have since vanished, including all species of moa (*Dinornis* and related forms). Moas represent the most diverse group of flightless birds ever recorded. The last examples probably died out about the time of European settlement of these islands in the 19th century.

The giant moa (*Dinornis maximus*) was the largest member of the group and, indeed, the tallest bird ever to have existed. It would have dwarfed today's ostriches, standing up to 3.5m (11.5ft) high. There may have been as many as a dozen or more different types of moa, which filled the same sort of niche as grazing mammals, which were absent from New Zealand.

In the absence of predatory mammals, the moas faced no significant threats to their survival until the first human settlers reached New Zealand and started to hunt them. Their large size made them conspicuous, and, having evolved in an environment where they had been safe from persecution, they had lost their ability to fly. Moas were not even able to run fast, in contrast to modern flightless birds such as ostriches. These defenceless giants were soon driven to extinction.

Circulation

The circulatory system is vital in supporting the activities of both flighted and flightless birds, ensuring that their muscles are well supplied with oxygen. The heart acts as the pump, driving the blood around the body. The basic design of the heart is similar to that of a mammal, with the left side being highly developed because it does more work. Overall, the heart rate of birds is much more rapid than mammals of similar size, having been measured at 1,000 beats per minute in the case of canaries at rest. The heart beat rises dramatically during flight, but soon returns to normal when the bird touches down.

The respiratory system

Birds have lungs, located close to the vertebral column, but these do not expand and contract in the same way as those of mammals. Instead, birds rely on a series of air sacs that act rather like bellows, to suck

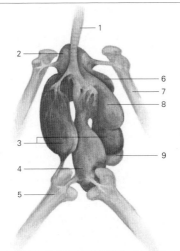

air through their respiratory system. In some cases, these link with the hollow limb bones, and thus help to meet the bird's high requirement for oxygen when flying. A bird's respiratory rate is a reflection of its body size, as well as its level of activity and lifestyle. Common starlings (*Sturnus vulgaris*), for example, typically breathe about 85 times every minute, whereas domestic chickens, which are more sedentary, have an equivalent respiratory rate of only about 20 breaths per minute.

1 Trachea
2 Interclavicular air sac
3 Lungs
4 Abdominal air sac
5 Femur (leg bone)
6 Cervical air sac
7 Humerus (wing bone)
8 Anterior thoracic air sac
9 Posterior thoracic air sac

Above: The razor-sharp inner claw of the cassowary (Casuarius unappendiculatus) is able to disembowel a person, making these birds very dangerous.

Ratites

Not all flightless birds are helpless in the face of danger, however. The large, flightless birds known as ratites, including cassowaries, ostriches, emus and rheas, are particularly well able to defend themselves. Their strong legs are quite capable of inflicting lethal blows, especially in the case of the cassowaries (Casuariidae), found in parts of northern Australia, New Guinea and neighbouring islands. These birds have an elongated and deadly sharp claw on their innermost toe. If the cassowary is cornered and unable to run away, it lashes out with its legs and is quite capable of disembowelling a person with its sharp

claws. The bird also has a hard, bony crest called a casque, which protects the top of its head.

The large ratites all share a similar body shape, having bulky bodies, long legs and long, slender necks. Like all flightless birds, they do possess wings, which assist them in keeping their balance and may also be used for display purposes. Most birds have four toes on each foot, but ratites have no more than three toes, and less in some cases. Ostriches have just two toes on each foot. The fastest birds on land, they can run at speeds equivalent to 50km/h (31mph). The reduction in the number of toes may help these birds to run faster.

Emus (*Dromaius novaehollandiae*) have the most rudimentary wings of all ratites, which are not even used for display purposes. The rheas (Rheidae) of South America have the most prominent wings of the ratites. They cover the rump, but they do not enable these birds to fly, even when they are young.

Kiwis (Apterygidae) are also ratites, but they are much smaller birds with shorter legs. Unlike other ratites, they are not fast runners, but rely on camouflage and their nocturnal habits to conceal their presence from predators, rather than speed to escape.

Running in flighted birds

Some birds that are able to fly still prefer to use their running abilities to obtain food and escape danger. They include the roadrunners (*Geococcyx californianus*) of North America. With their short wings, these birds can fly clumsily, but prefer to use their strong legs to overtake and pounce on prey. In general, flying uses considerable energy compared to running or hopping. Many birds will elect to move swiftly over the ground to pounce on a food item or avoid an enemy if they judge that the situation does not warrant flight.

Above: The height and keen eyesight of ostriches (Struthio camelus) means that they are hard to ambush in open country. Their pace allows them to escape from danger with little difficulty, while their long stride length when running enables them to cover large amounts of ground in a single step.

AVIAN SENSES

The keen senses of birds are vital to their survival, in particular helping them to find food, escape from enemies and find mates in the breeding season. Sight is the primary sense for most birds, but some species rely heavily on other senses to thrive in particular habitats.

All birds' senses are adapted to their environment, and the shape of their bodies can help to reflect which senses are most significant to them.

Sight and lifestyle

Most birds rely on their sense of sight to avoid danger, hunt for food and locate familiar surroundings. The importance of this sense is reflected by the size of their eyes, with those of

Field of vision

The positioning of a bird's eyes on its head affects its field of vision. The eyes of owls are positioned to face forwards, producing an overlapping image of the area in front known as binocular vision. This allows the owl to pinpoint its prey exactly, so that it can strike. In contrast, the eyes of birds that are likely to be preyed upon, such as woodcocks, are positioned on the sides of the head. This eye position gives a greatly reduced area of binocular vision, but it does give these birds practically all-round vision, enabling them to spot danger from all sides.

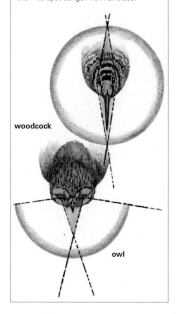

woodcock

owl

starlings (*Sturnus vulgaris*), for example, making up 15 per cent of the total head weight. The enlargement of the eyeballs and associated structures, notably the eye sockets in the skull, has altered the shape of the brain. In addition, the optic lobes in the brain, which are concerned with vision, are also enlarged, whereas the olfactory counterparts, responsible for smell, are poorly developed.

The structure of the eye also reveals much about a bird's habits. Birds of prey have large eyes in proportion to their head, and have correspondingly keen eyesight. Species that regularly hunt for prey underwater, such as penguins, can see well in the water. They have a muscle in each eye that reduces the diameter of the lens and increases its thickness on entering water, so that their eyes can adjust easily to seeing underwater. In addition, certain diving birds such as little auks (*Alle alle*) use a lens that forms part of the nictitating membrane, or third eyelid, which is normally hidden from sight. Underwater, when this membrane covers the eye, its convex shape serves as a lens, helping the bird to see in these surroundings.

Eye position

The positioning of the eyes on the head gives important clues to a bird's lifestyle. Most birds' eyes are set on the sides of their heads. Owls, however, have flattened faces and forward-facing eyes that are critical to their hunting abilities. These features allow owls to target their prey.

There are disadvantages, though – owls' eyes do not give a rounded view of the world, so they must turn their heads to see about them. It is not just the positioning of owls' eyes that is unusual. They are also able to hunt effectively in almost complete darkness. This is made possible in two

Above: Kiwis (Apteryx australis) *rely much more heavily on their sense of smell than other birds, as is reflected by the fact that their eyes are smaller.*

ways. First, their pupils are large, which maximizes the amount of light passing through to the retina behind the lens, where the image is formed. Second, the cells here consist mainly of rods rather than cones. While cones give good colour vision, rods function to create images when background illumination is low.

The positioning of the eyes of game birds such as woodcocks (*Scolopax rusticola*) allows them to spot danger from almost any angle. It is even possible for them to see a predator sneaking up from behind. Their only blind spot is just behind the head.

Smell

Very few birds have a sense of smell, but kiwis (Apterygidae) and vultures (forming part of the order Falciformes) are notable exceptions. Birds' nostrils are normally located above the bill, opening directly into the skull, but kiwis' nostrils are positioned right at the end of the long bill. They probably help these birds to locate earthworms

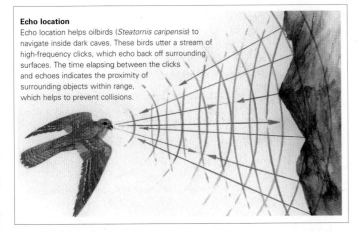

Echo location

Echo location helps oilbirds (*Steatornis caripensis*) to navigate inside dark caves. These birds utter a stream of high-frequency clicks, which echo back off surrounding surfaces. The time elapsing between the clicks and echoes indicates the proximity of surrounding objects within range, which helps to prevent collisions.

in the soil. Vultures have very keen eyesight, which helps them to spot dead animals on the ground from the air, but they also have a strong sense of smell, which helps when homing in on a distant carcass.

Taste

The senses of smell and taste are linked, and most birds also have correspondingly few taste buds in their mouths. The number of taste buds varies, with significant differences between groups of birds. Pigeons may have as few as 50 taste buds in their mouths, parrots as many as 400.

Birds' taste buds are located all around the mouth, rather than just on the tongue, as in mammals. The close

Below: Birds have good colour vision. It is this sense that encourages hummingbirds, such as this long-billed starthroat (Heliomaster longirostris), to home in on red flowers.

links between smell and taste can lead vultures, which feed only on fresh carcasses, to reject decomposing meat. They may start to eat it, but then spit it out once it is in their mouths, probably because of a combination of bad odour and taste.

Hearing

Birds generally do not have a highly developed sense of hearing. They lack any external ear flaps that would help to pinpoint sources of sound. The openings to their hearing system are located on the sides of the head, back from the eyes.

Hearing is of particular significance for nocturnal species, such as owls, which find their food in darkness. These birds are highly attuned to the calls made by rodents. The broad shape of their skull has the additional advantage of spacing the ear openings more widely, which helps them to localize the source of the sounds with greater accuracy.

Hearing is also important to birds during the breeding season. Birds show particular sensitivity to sounds falling within the vocal range of their chicks, which helps them to locate their offspring easily in the critical early days after fledging.

The oilbird (*Steatornis caripensis*), which inhabits parts of northern South America, uses echo location to find its way around in the dark, rather like bats do. Unlike the sounds bats make,

however, the clicking sounds of the oilbird's calls – up to 20 a second in darkness – are clearly audible to humans. The bird interprets the echoes of its call to avoid colliding with objects in its path, although it also uses its eyesight when flying. Cave swiftlets (*Aerodramus* species) from Asia, which also inhabit a dark environment, use echo location in a similar way to fly.

Touch

The sense of touch is more developed in some birds than others. Those such as snipe (*Gallinago* species), which have long bills for seeking food, have sensitive nerve endings called corpuscles in their bills that pick up tiny vibrations caused by their prey. Vibrations that could suggest approaching danger can also register via other corpuscles located particularly in the legs, so that the bird has a sensory awareness even when it is resting on a branch.

Wind-borne sensing

Tubenoses such as albatrosses and petrels (Procellariiformes) have a valve in each nostril that fills with air as the bird flies. These are affected by both the bird's speed and the wind strength. The valves almost certainly act as a type of wind gauge, allowing these birds to detect changes in wind strength and patterns. This information helps to keep them airborne, as they skim over the waves with minimal effort.

Below: A combination of senses, especially touch, helps oystercatchers (Haematopus ostralegus) to detect their prey, which is normally hidden from view.

PLANT-EATERS

All over the world, many birds depend on plant matter as part of their diet, with seeds and nuts in particular providing nourishment. A close relationship between plants and birds exists in many cases. Birds fertilize flowers when feeding on nectar, and help to spread their seeds when eating fruit.

Many different types of birds are primarily plant-eaters, whether feeding on flowers, fruit, nuts and seeds, or other plant matter. Plant-eating species have to eat a large volume of food compared to meat-eating species, because of the low nutritional value of plants compared with that of prey such as invertebrates.

In the last century or so, many species have benefited from the spread of agriculture, which now provides them with large acreages of suitable crop plants to feed on. These birds' feeding habits bring them into conflict with farmers when they breed rapidly in response to a swift expansion in their food supply. For example, populations of bare-eyed corellas (*Cacatua sanguinea*) have increased quickly in Australia thanks to the spread of arable agriculture there, and

Below: Birds such as the cactus wren (Campylorhynchus brunneicapillus) have a close association with particular plants. This wren not only feeds on the plants after which it is named, but also takes advantage of their protective thorns when nesting.

the associated provision of reservoirs for irrigation purposes. These birds have bred up to form huge flocks comprising many thousands of individuals, which inflict massive damage on crops as they ripen. They are now labelled as pests in some areas.

Adapting to changing seasons

Birds from temperate areas exist on a varied diet that is related to the seasons. Bullfinches (*Pyrrhula pyrrhula*), for example, eat the buds in apple orchards in spring – when they can become a pest – while later in the year, they consume seeds and fruit. Their bills, like those of most other members of the finch family, are stout and relatively conical, which helps them to crack seeds effectively.

Some birds store plant food when it is plentiful, to sustain them through the winter. Nutcrackers (*Nucifraga* species) collect hazel nuts, which they feed on in winter until the following year. Acorn woodpeckers (*Melanerpes formicivorus*) drill holes in trees that they fill with acorns, creating an easily accessible larder for the winter, when snow may cover the ground.

Flowers

A number of birds rely on flowers rather than the whole plant as a source of food. Pollen is a valuable source of protein, while nectar provides sugars. Not surprisingly, flower-feeders tend to be confined to mainly tropical areas, where flowers are in bloom throughout the year. Hummingbirds (Trochilidae), for instance, use their narrow bills to probe into flowers to obtain nectar. Some hummingbirds have developed especially curved or elongated bills, which allow them to feed on particular flowers. These birds help to pollinate the plants on which they feed by transferring pollen from flower to flower on their bills or even on plumage.

The digestive system

Birds lack teeth, so their food must be swallowed whole. Birds have a storage organ known as the crop, which is located at the base of the neck. From here, food passes down into the proventriculus, where the digestive process starts, before entering the gizzard, which is equivalent to the mammalian stomach. Nutrients are then absorbed through the wall of the small intestine.

The digestive system of plant-eaters differs in various respects from that of predatory species. Vegetable matter is less nourishing than meat, so plant-eaters generally need longer digestive tracts to process the large quantities of food they must consume in order to obtain enough nourishment. In addition, digesting plant matter poses certain difficulties. The gizzards of seed-eating species such as many finches (Fringillidae) have especially thick muscular walls, which serve to grind up the seeds.

1 Oesophagus	6 Large intestine
2 Crop	7 Liver
3 Proventriculus	8 Spleen
4 Pancreas	9 Small intestine
5 Gizzard	

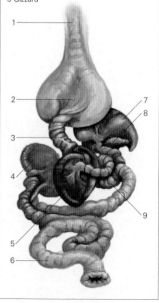

Above: Feeding on plants comes at a price, as many contain potentially harmful chemicals. Various parrots, such as these macaws (Ara species), make daily visits to cliffs to eat clay, which is believed to have a detoxifying effect on their digestive systems.

Sunbirds (Nectariniidae) found in Africa and Asia fill a similar evolutionary niche to hummingbirds, which they resemble in their small size and bright, often iridescent plumage. Unlike hummingbirds, however, they are not sufficiently agile to feed in flight, but have to perch within reach of the flower. Various members of the parrot family also feed on flowers, notably lories and lorikeets. Their tongues are equipped with tiny, bristle-like projections called papillae, which enable them to collect pollen easily.

Fruit

Exclusively frugivorous (fruit-eating) birds such as fruit doves (*Ptilinopus*) are found only in the tropics, where fruit is available throughout the year. These species usually dwell in tropical rainforests, where they have a valuable role to play in protecting the biodiversity of the forest. The seeds of the fruits they eat pass right through their digestive tracts unharmed, to be deposited far from the parent plant, which helps the plants to spread.

Plant matter

Relatively few birds feed almost entirely on herbage, although the bizarre hoatzin (*Opisthocomus hoazin*) from the rainforest of South America is one example. Equally unusual are the touracos (Musophagidae) of Africa, which also feed mainly on leaves, which they pluck along with fruits. Some parrots such as the eclectus (*Eclectus roratus*) are also believed to feed largely on plant matter rather than seeds or fruit.

The breakdown of vegetation presents considerable difficulty, since birds do not possess the necessary enzymes to digest the cellulose in plants. Birds such as grouse (Tetraoninae), which feed regularly on plant matter, have evolved long, blind-ending tubes known as caeca. These contain beneficial microbes that can break down cellulose.

Nuts and seeds

These dry foods are a valuable resource to many different types of birds, ranging from parrots to finches. However, cracking the tough outer shell or husk can be a problem. Finches such as grosbeaks have evolved a particularly strong bill for this purpose. Hawfinches (*Coccothraustes coccothraustes*) are able to crack cherry stones (pits) to extract the kernel.

Above: Red-billed queleas, or weavers (Quelea quelea), are the most numerous birds in the world. Massive flocks of these birds will wipe out crops of ripening millets in parts of Africa, to the extent that they are sometimes called "feathered locusts".

The most bizarre example of bill adaption for eating seeds is seen in the crossbills (*Loxia*) of northern coniferous forests. These birds have literally twisted upper and lower mandibles, which help them to crack open the seeds inside the larch cones, which they eat. Some cockatoos such as the Moluccan (*Cacatua moluccensis*) have bills that are even strong enough to open coconuts.

Below: Pink-footed geese (Anser brachyrhynchus) can be a problem in agricultural areas, since they will sometimes descend in large numbers to graze on young cereal crops.

PREDATORS AND SCAVENGERS

Just as with other vertebrates, there is a food chain within the avian kingdom. Some species hunt only other birds, while others seek a more varied range of prey, including, commonly, invertebrates. Even birds that feed mainly on seeds catch protein-rich insects to feed their chicks in the nest.

Some birds are active predators, seeking and killing their own food, while others prefer to scavenge on carcasses. Many predatory birds are opportunistic feeders, hunting when food is plentiful but scavenging when food becomes scarce. Both hunters and scavengers have evolved to live in a wide range of environments, and display correspondingly diverse hunting skills to obtain their food.

Birds of prey have sharp bills that enable them to tear the flesh of their prey into strips small enough to swallow. Eating whole animals can potentially cause digestive problems for these birds because of the bones, skin, feathers and other relatively indigestible body parts. Owls overcome this problem by regurgitating pellets composed of the indigestible remains of their prey. Kingfishers produce similar pellets of fish bones and scales. These are of value to zoologists studying the feeding habits of such birds.

Below: Peregrine falcons (Falco peregrinus) are adept aerial hunters, with pigeons – including homing pigeons – featuring prominently in their diet. These birds of prey display not just speed, but also superb manoeuvrability in flight, when pursuing their quarry.

Above: Vision is the main sense that allows most birds of prey, such as golden eagles (Aquila chrysaetos), to target their victims. These eagles have keen sight.

Birds of prey

Some avian predators feed mainly on other birds, such as the sparrowhawk (*Accipiter nisus*) – which is so-called because of its preference for hunting house sparrows (*Passer domesticus*). Another avian hunter, the peregrine falcon (*Falco peregrinus*), is among the most agile of all hunting birds. Strength is a feature of some species that prey on mammals, such as the golden eagle (*Aquila chrysaetos*), which can lift young lambs in its powerful talons, but often feeds on carrion. Yet other birds of prey target different groups of vertebrates, including fish and reptiles, while a great many species hunt insects and other invertebrates.

Hunting techniques

Many predatory birds hunt during the day, but not all, with most owls preferring to seek their prey at night. Mice and other creatures that are caught by owls are killed and eaten immediately. In contrast, shrikes (Laniidae) have a grisly reputation because they kill more prey than they can eat immediately. They store the surplus as a so-called larder. They impale invertebrates such as grasshoppers, and even sometimes small vertebrates, on to sharp vegetation, and return to feed on them later. Caching, as this behaviour is known, is especially common during the breeding period, and presumably developed as a way of ensuring that the shrikes have sufficient food to rear their young.

Some birds have evolved particular ways of overcoming prey in certain localities. In parts of Egypt, for example, eagles have learnt to prey on

Above: Like other cormorants, the white-necked cormorant (Phalacrocorax carbo) *brings fish that it catches underwater up to the surface before swallowing them.*

Cormorants (Phalacrocoracidae) dive down after fish, and can remain submerged for some time. Kingfishers (*Alcedo atthis*) have sharp eyesight. Having detected the presence of a fish from the air, they dive into the water, seizing their quarry in their pointed bill and then re-emerging immediately. They then kill the fish by battering it against their perch. The speed at which the kingfisher dives provides the momentum to break through the surface, and it closes its wings once submerged to reduce resistance.

Aquatic predators always try to swallow their prey such as fish head-first. That way, gills and scales do not get stuck in their throat. On land, predatory birds that hunt victims such as rodents employ a similar technique so they do not choke on fur and tails.

Scavengers

Vultures are the best-known of all scavengers. They can home in on carcasses from a great distance away, and so have become regarded as harbingers of death. Lammergeiers (*Gypaetus barbatus*) have developed a technique that allows them to feed on bones that their relatives cannot break open. They smash the bones into pieces by dropping them from a great height. It is a skill that they learn to perfect by choosing the right terrain on which to drop the bones.

The small Egyptian vulture (*Neophron percnopterus*) survives by using its small size, which is no match

Above: Precise judgement allows a kingfisher (Alcedo atthis) *to strike with deadly accuracy from a perch. These birds frequent stretches of clear water for this reason.*

at the site of a kill, to advantage: it can become airborne soon after dawn – before the thermal air currents needed by its larger relatives have been created – and seek out overnight casualities. In some parts of Africa, these vultures smash tough ostrich eggs by repeatedly throwing stones at them.

Birds other than vultures also scavenge on occasion rather than hunting. Road kills of birds and other animals offer rich pickings for a host of such species, ranging from corvids such as crows and magpies to road-runners (*Geococcyx californianus*).

Below: Griffon vultures (Gyps fulvus) *and similar scavengers usually have bald heads, because any plumage here would quickly become matted with blood.*

tortoises by seizing the unfortunate reptiles in their talons, and then dropping them on to rocky ground from the air to split open their shells.

Not all birds of prey are aerial predators. Species such as secretary birds (*Sagittarius serpentarius*), which range widely across Africa in grassland areas, prefer to seek their victims on the ground. Secretary birds have developed long, strong legs and yet have surprisingly small feet. Snakes feature prominently in the diet of these birds, which raise their wings when confronting one of the reptiles. This has the effect of breaking up the bird's outline, making it harder for the snake to strike. Meanwhile the bird uses its feet to stun the reptile by jumping up and down on it, before killing it with a stab of its sharp bill.

Aquatic predators

The osprey (*Pandion haliaetus*) is an unusual bird of prey that literally scoops up large fish swimming close to the water's surface while in flight. Other birds actually enter the water in search of their prey. They may not have sharp talons, but many have powerful bills that enable them to grab slippery fish without difficulty.

Pelicans are equipped with a large, capacious pouch beneath the lower part of their bill, which they use like a net to trawl the water for fish.

DISPLAY AND PAIRING

Birds' breeding habits vary greatly. Some birds pair up only fleetingly, while others do so for the whole breeding season, and some species pair for life. For many young cock birds, the priority is to gain a territory as the first step in attracting a partner. Birds use both plumage and their songs to attract a mate.

A number of factors trigger the onset of the breeding period. In temperate areas, as the days start to lengthen in spring, the increase in daylight is detected by the pineal gland in the bird's brain, which starts a complex series of hormonal changes in the body. Most birds form a bond with a single partner during the breeding season, which is often preceded by an elaborate display by the cock bird.

Bird song

Many cock birds announce their presence by their song, which both attracts would-be mates and establishes a claim to a territory. Once pairing has occurred, the male may cease singing, but in some cases he starts to perform a duet with the hen, with each bird singing in turn.

Singing obviously serves to keep members of the pair in touch with each other. In species such as Central and

Above: A male ruff (Philomachus pugnax) at a lek, where males compete with each other in displays to attract female partners. Ruffs do not form lasting pair bonds, so the hens nest on their own after mating has occurred.

South American wood quails (*Odontophorus*), the pair co-ordinate their songs so precisely that although the cock bird may sing the first few notes, and then the hen, it sounds as if the song is being sung by just one bird. Other birds may sing in unison. In African gonoleks (*Laniarius*), it may even be possible to tell the length of time that the pair have been together by the degree of harmony in their particular songs.

Studies have revealed that young males birds start warbling quite quietly, and then sing more loudly as they mature. Finally, when their song pattern becomes fixed, it remains constant throughout the bird's life.

It is obviously possible to identify different species by differences in their song patterns. However, there are sometimes marked variations between the songs of individuals of the same species that live in different places. Local dialects have been identified in various parts of a species' distribution, as in the case in grey parrots (*Psittacus erithacus*) from different parts of Africa. In addition, as far as some songbirds are concerned, recent studies

Below: A cock Wilson's bird of paradise (Didyllodes respublica) displaying. Bright plumage is often a feature of members of this family, but cock birds gain their breeding finery only slowly by progressive moults over several years. They move up through the display hierarchy until they can obtain a mate.

Below: Male masked weavers (Ploceus) build nests as part of their displays to attract the females. The techniques involved in nest-building are extremely complex and can be mastered only with practice. Hens are likely to choose older males as partners because they have superior nest-building skills.

Above: Mute swans (Cygnus olor) are one of the species that pair for life. They become highly territorial when breeding, but outside the nesting period they often form flocks on large stretches of water. In spite of their common name, they can vocalize to a limited extent, by hissing and even grunting.

have shown that over the course of several generations, the pattern of song can alter markedly.

Birds produce their sounds – even those species capable of mimicking human speech – without the benefit of a larynx and vocal cords like humans. The song is created in a voice organ called the syrinx, which is located in the bird's throat, at the bottom of the windpipe, or trachea.

The structure of the syrinx is very variable, being at its most highly developed in the case of songbirds, which possess as many as nine pairs of separate muscles to control the vocal output. As in the human larynx, it is the movement of air through the syrinx that enables the membranes here to vibrate, creating sound. An organ called the interclavicular air sac also plays an important role in sound production, and birds cannot sing without it. The distance over which bird calls can travel is remarkable – up to 5km (3 miles) in the case of some species, such as bellbirds (*Procnias*) and the bittern (*Botaurus stellaris*), which has a particularly deep, penetrating song.

Breeding behaviour

Many birds rely on their breeding finery to attract their mates. Some groups assemble in communal display areas known as leks, where hens witness the males' displays and select a mate. A number of different species, ranging from cocks of the rock (*Rupicola*) to birds of paradise (Paradisaeidae), establish leks.

In other species, such as the satin bowerbird (*Ptilonorhynchus violaceus*), the male constructs elaborate bowers of grass, twigs and similar vegetation that he decorates with items of a particular colour, such as blue, varying from flowers to pieces of glass. Male bowerbirds are often polygamous,

meaning that they mate with more than one female. Weaver birds, such as the orange bishop (*Euplectes orix*), demonstrate the same behaviour. The males moult to display brightly coloured plumage at the onset of the breeding season, and construct nests that are inspected by the females. Hens are often drawn to the older cocks, whose nest-building abilities are likely to be more sophisticated.

Pair bonding

Many male and female birds form no lasting relationship, although the pair bond may be strong during the nesting period. It is usually only in potentially long-lived species, such as the larger parrots and macaws, or waterfowl such as swans, that a life-long pair bond is formed.

Pair bonding in long-lived species has certain advantages. The young of such birds are slow to mature, and are often unlikely to nest for five years or more. By remaining for a time in a family group, the adults can improve the long-term survival prospects of their young.

Below: The dance of Japanese cranes (Grus japonensis) is one of the most spectacular sights in the avian world, reinforcing the life-long pair bond in this species. Dancing starts with the trumpeting calls of the birds as they stand side-by-side. Both sexes then start to leap into the air and display, raising their wings and tail feathers. Sometimes the birds even pick up sticks and toss them into the air.

NESTING AND EGG-LAYING

All birds reproduce by laying eggs, which are covered with a hard, calcareous shell. The number of eggs laid at a time – known as the clutch size – varies significantly between species, as does egg coloration. Nesting habits also vary, with some birds constructing very elaborate nests.

The coloration and markings of a bird's eggs are directly linked to the nesting site. Birds that usually breed in hollow trees produce white eggs, because these are normally hidden from predators and so do not need to be camouflaged. The pale coloration may also help the adult birds to locate the eggs as they return to the nest, thus lessening the chances of damaging them. Birds that build open, cup-shaped nests tend to lay coloured and often mottled eggs that are camouflaged and so less obvious to potential nest thieves.

Nesting holes

Many birds use tree holes for nesting. Woodpeckers (Picidae) are particularly well equipped to create nesting chambers, using their powerful bills to enlarge holes in dead trees. The diameter of the entry hole thus created

Above: A northern flicker (Colaptes auratus) – a member of the woodpecker family – returns to its nest hole. Tree holes offer relatively safe nesting retreats, although predators such as snakes may sometimes be able to reach them.

Below: Ostriches lay the largest eggs in the world, which can weigh up to 1.5kg (3.3lb). In comparison, a chicken's egg, shown in front of the ostrich egg, looks tiny. The egg nearest to the viewer is a hummingbird egg. These tiny birds lay the smallest eggs in the avian world, weighing only about 0.35g (0.01oz).

is just wide enough to allow the birds to enter easily, which helps to prevent the nest being robbed. Hornbills (Bucorvidae) go one stage further – the cock bird walls the hen up inside the nest. He plasters the hole over with mud, leaving just a small gap through which he can feed the female. The barrier helps to protect the nest from attacks by snakes and lizards. The female remains entombed inside until her young are well grown. At this stage she breaks out and then helps her mate to rear the chicks, having walled them back up again.

Nest-building

Some birds return to the same nest site each year, but many birds simply abandon their old nest and build another. This may seem a waste of effort, but it actually helps to protect the birds from parasites such as blood-sucking mites, which can otherwise multiply in the confines of the nest. Most birds construct their nests from vegetation, depending on which

The reproductive systems

The cock bird has two testes located within his body. Spermatozoa pass down the vas deferens, into the cloaca and then out of the body. Insemination occurs when the vent areas of the male and female bird are in direct contact during mating. Cock birds do not have a penis for penetration, although certain groups, such as waterfowl, may have a primitive organ that is used to assist in the transference of semen in a similar way.

Normally only the left ovary and oviduct of the hen bird are functional. Eggs pass down through the reproductive tract from the ovary. Spermatozoa swim up the hen's reproductive tract, and fertilize the ova at an early stage in the process. Generally, only one mating is required to fertilize a clutch of eggs. Spermatozoa may sometimes remain viable in the hen's body for up to three weeks following mating.

1 Testes	7 Magnum
2 Kidneys	8 Isthmus
3 Vas deferens	9 Egg with shell
4 Cloaca	contained in
	the hen's
5 Ova	reproductive tract
6 Infundibulum	10 Cloaca

Male   **Female**

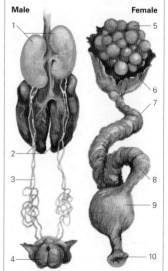

materials are locally available. In coastal areas, some seabirds use pieces of seaweed to build theirs. Artificial materials such as plastic wrappers or polystyrene may be used by some birds.

Nest styles

Different types of birds build nests of various shapes and sizes, which are characteristic of their species. Groups such as finches build nests in the form of an open cup, often concealed in vegetation. Most pigeons and doves construct a loose platform of twigs. Swallows are among the birds that use mud to construct their nests. They scoop muddy water up from the surface of a pond or puddle, mould it into shape on a suitable wall, and then allow it to dry and harden like cement.

The simplest nests are composed of little more than a pad of material, resting in the fork of a tree or on a building. The effort entailed in nest construction may reflect how often the birds are likely to nest. The platforms of pigeons and doves can disintegrate quite easily, resulting in the loss of eggs or chicks. However, if disaster does befall the nest, the pair will often breed again within a few weeks. At the other end of the scale, albatrosses expend considerable effort on nesting, because if failure occurs, the pair may not breed again for two years or so.

Cup-shaped nests are more elaborate than platform nests, being usually made by weaving grasses and twigs together. The inside is often lined with soft feathers. The raised sides of the cup nest lessen the likelihood of losing eggs and chicks, and also offer greater security to the adults during incubation. The hollow in the nest's centre is created by the birds compressing the material here before egg-laying begins.

Suspended nests enclosed by a domed roof offer even greater security. They are less accessible to predators because of their design and also their position, often hanging from slender branches. Some waxbills (*Estrilda*) build a particularly elaborate nest, comprising two chambers. There is an obvious upper opening, which is

Above: The piping plover (Charadrius melodus) from North America breeds in the open and so must also rely on camouflage to hide its presence when sitting on the nest.

always empty, suggesting to would-be predators that the nest is unoccupied. The birds occupy the chamber beneath, which has a separate opening.

Nest protection

Some birds rely on the safety of numbers to deter would-be predators, building vast communal nests that are occupied by successive generations and added to regularly. Monk parakeets (*Myiopsitta monarchus*) from South America breed in this way. Their nests may weigh over 200kg (4cwt) or more.

Other birds have evolved more sophisticated methods not only of protecting their nests, but also of minimizing the time that they spend incubating their eggs. Various parrots, such as the red-faced lovebird (*Agapornis pullaria*) from Africa, lay their eggs in termite mounds. The insects tolerate this intrusion, while the heat of the mound keeps the eggs warm. Mallee fowl (*Leipoa ocellata*) from Australia create a natural incubator for their eggs by burying them in a mound where the natural warmth and heat from decaying vegetation means that the chicks eventually hatch on their own and dig themselves out.

Other birds, such as the cowbirds (*Molothrus*) of North America, simply lay and abandon their eggs in the nests of other species. The foster parents-to-be do not seem able to detect the difference between their own eggs and that of the intruder, so they do not reject the cowbird egg. They incubate it along with their own brood, and feed the foster chick when it hatches out.

Birds that nest on the ground, such as the stone curlew (*Burhinus oedicnemus*), are especially vulnerable to predators and rely heavily on their fairly drab plumage as camouflage. Skylarks (*Alauda arvensis*) have another means of protecting their nest site – they hold one wing down and pretend to be injured to draw a predator away.

Below: Most eggs have a generally rounded shape, but seabirds such as guillemots (Uria aalge) breeding on rocky outcrops lay eggs that are more pointed. This shape helps to prevent the eggs from rolling over the cliff.

HATCHING AND REARING CHICKS

Birds are vulnerable to predators when breeding, especially when they have young in the nest. The chicks must be fed frequently, necessitating regular trips to and from the nest, which makes it conspicuous. The calls of the young birds represent a further danger, so the breeding period is often short.

Most birds incubate their eggs to keep them sufficiently warm for the chicks to develop inside. Larger eggs are less prone to chilling during incubation than small eggs, because of their bigger volume. In the early stages of the incubation period, when the nest may be left uncovered while the adult birds are foraging for food, eggs can withstand a lower temperature. Temperature differences also account for the fact that, at similar altitudes, incubation periods tend to be slightly longer in temperate areas than in tropical regions.

The eggshell may appear to be a solid barrier but in fact contains many pores, which are vital to the chick's wellbeing. These tiny holes allow water vapour and carbon dioxide to escape from the egg, and oxygen to enter it to reach the embryo.

Incubation

The incubation period often does not start until more than one egg has been laid, and sometimes not until the entire clutch has been completed. The interval between the laying of one egg and the next varies – finches lay every

Above: Breeding in one of the coldest places on Earth means that emperor penguins (Aptenodytes forsteri) can lay only a single egg, which they incubate on top of their feet, where special blood vessels help to warm it. After hatching, the chick is carried here too.

day, whereas gannets may lay only one egg every six days. If incubation does not start until egg-laying has finished, the chicks will all be of a similar size when they hatch, which increases their overall chances of survival.

The cock and hen may share incubation duties, as in the case of most pigeons and doves, or just one member of the pair may incubate. This is usually the hen, but there are exceptions. For example, in ostriches (*Struthio camelus*) and most other large flightless birds, it is the male who incubates the eggs and cares for the resulting chicks. Anis (*Crotophaga*) breed communally, and all members of the group share the task of incubation.

Below: A fertile chicken's egg, showing the development of the embryo through to hatching. 1. The fertilized egg cell divides to form a ball of cells that gradually develops into an embryo. 2. The embryo develops, nourished by the yolk sac. 3. The air space at the rounded end of the egg enlarges as water evaporates. 4. The chick is almost fully developed and ready to hatch. 5. The chick cuts its way out, and its feathers dry off.

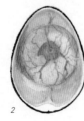

1   *2*   *3*   *4*   *5*

Nest parasites

Nest parasitism is common in many species of cuckoo, such as the European cuckoo (*Cuculus canorus*). The males do not establish breeding territories, but mate with females at random. The females lay a single egg in the nests of host species such as reed warblers (*Acrocephalus scirpaceus*). The rapid development of the cuckoo's egg is vital so that the chick hatches first, and can then throw the other eggs or chicks out of the nest. In this way, it monopolizes the food supply brought by its foster parents. Any other chicks that do survive this initial stage die later, as they lose out in competition for food with their gigantic nest mate.

Below: Foster parents such as this reed warbler continue to feed the young cuckoo even when the imposter dwarfs them in size.

Hatching

Incubation periods vary among bird species, ranging from as few as 11 days in the case of cowbirds (*Molothrus*), to over 80 days in some albatrosses (Diomedeidae). Before hatching, the chick uses the egg tooth on the tip of its upper bill to cut through the inner membrane into the air space at the blunt end of the shell, which forms as water evaporates from the egg. The chick starts to breathe atmospheric air for the first time. About 48 hours later, it breaks through the shell to emerge from the egg.

Chicks hatch out at various stages of development, and are accordingly able to leave the nest sooner or later.

Species that remain in the nest for some time after hatching, including parrots (Psittaciformes) and finches (Fringillidae), hatch in a blind and helpless state and are entirely dependent on their parents at first. Birds in this group are known as nidicolous. If not closely brooded, they are likely to become fatally chilled. In contrast, species that leave the nest soon after hatching, known as nidifugous, emerge from the egg and are able to move around on their own at this stage. They can also see and feed themselves almost immediately. The offspring of many game birds such as pheasants as well as waterfowl and waders are nidifugous, which gives them a better chance of survival, as they can run to escape from predators. Young waterfowl cannot take safely to the water at first, however, because they lack the oil from the preen gland above the base of the tail to waterproof their feathers.

Rearing and fledging

Many adult birds offer food to their offspring, even some nidifugous species. This can be a particularly demanding period, especially for small birds that have relatively large broods. Great tits (*Parus major*), for example, must supply their offspring with huge quantities of insects. They typically feed their chicks up to 60 times an hour, as well as keeping the nest clean.

Young birds usually leave the nest from about 12 to 30 days after hatching. However, some species develop much more slowly. Albatross chicks are particularly slow developers, spending up to eight and a half months in the nest.

When they first leave the nest, many young birds are unable to fly, simply because their flight feathers are not fully functional. If these feathers are not fully unfurled from the protective sheaths in which they emerged, they cannot function effectively. The strength of the wing muscles also needs to be built up, so it is not uncommon for young birds to rest on the sides of the nest, flapping their wings occasionally, before finally taking to the air for the first time. Chicks that

Above: Blue tits (Parus caeruleus) are typical of many birds that leave the nest before they are able to fly effectively. The young remain hidden in vegetation and are fed by their parents in these critical early days after leaving the nest.

are unable to fly immediately on fledging remain reliant on the adults, especially the cock, for food until they become fully independent.

For some young seabirds, fledging is a particularly hazardous process. From their cliff-ledge nests, they may simply flop down on to the water, where they are at risk from drowning until they master swimming skills. If they get swept out to sea, they may be caught by predators such as killer whales.

Below: The broad and often colourful gape of chicks allows parent birds such as this blackcap warbler (Sylvia atricapilla) to feed their offspring quickly and efficiently. Weak chicks that are unable to raise their heads and gape at the approach of a parent will quickly die from starvation.

SURVIVAL

The numbers of a particular species of bird can vary significantly over time, affected by factors such as the availability of food, climate, disease and hunting. When the reproductive rate of a species falls below its annual mortality rate, it is in decline, but this does not mean it will inevitably become extinct.

For many birds, life is short and hazardous. Quite apart from the risk of predation, birds can face a whole range of other dangers, from starvation and disease through to either deliberate or inadvertent human persecution. The reproductive rate is higher and age of maturity is lower in species that have particularly hazardous lifestyles, such as blue tits (*Parus caeruleus*). Such species often breed twice or more each year in rapid succession.

Rising and falling numbers

Some birds have a reproductive cycle that is geared to allow them to increase their numbers rapidly under favourable conditions. In Australia, for example, budgerigars (*Melopsittacus undulatus*) multiply rapidly when the rains come. Rainfall ensures not just the rapid germination of the grasses that form the basis of their diet, but also fills the waterholes in the arid interior of the continent where these parakeets are found. During periods of drought, however, when food and water become

Below: Galah cockatoos (Eolophus roseicapillus) have not just benefited from increased availability of food and water in their natural habitat thanks to agriculture, but they have also adapted to other changes in the environment too, such as roosting together on this aerial.

Above: Many birds watch over their offspring when they hatch, but are ill-equipped to defend them from predators, as in the case of this male Carolina wood duck (Aix sponsa).

much harder for these nomadic birds to find, the population plummets. But it can grow again rapidly when conditions become more favourable.

Regular fall-offs in populations can occur on a cyclical basis, as shown by the case of snowy owls (*Nyctea scandiaca*) in North America. As the numbers of lemmings, which form the major item in their diet, rise, so too does the snowy owl population. This is the result of more chicks per nest being reared successfully, rather than dying of starvation. When numbers of lemmings then fall rapidly, thanks to a shortage of their food, owls are forced to spread out over a much wider area

than normal in search of food, and their breeding success plummets accordingly. Later they gradually increase again over successive years, as the lemming population recovers.

Group living

Birds that live in flocks find mates more easily than other birds, and group life also offers several other advantages, including the safety of numbers. An aerial predator such as a hawk will find it harder to recognize and target individuals in a flying mass of birds, although stragglers are still likely to be picked off.

Coloration can also increase the safety of birds in flocks. In Florida, USA, there used to be feral budgerigar flocks made up of multicoloured individuals. The different colours reflected the diversity of colour varieties that were developed through domestication. Today, however, green is by far the predominant colour in such flocks, as it is in genuine wild flocks, simply because predators found it much easier to pick off individuals of other colours. Greater numbers of the

Cryptic coloration

Camouflage, also known as cryptic coloration, enables a bird to hide in its natural surroundings. It offers distinct survival benefits in concealing the bird from would-be predators. Cryptic coloration has the effect of breaking up the bird's outline, allowing it to blend in with the background in its habitat. Posture and, in particular, keeping still can also help, as movement often attracts the attention of would-be predators.

Below: Blending into the background can be useful for predators too, as in the case of this scops owl (Otus senegalensis), which often hunts insects in flight, as they fly within reach.

always the case. The expansion of agriculture in countries such as Australia has resulted in the greater availability of water in what was formerly arid countryside. This, in turn, has enabled birds such as galahs (*Eolophus roseicapillus*), a type of cockatoo, to spread over a much wider area and reproduce so rapidly that they have reached plague proportions. Shooting has helped to control numbers of these birds, but, overall, galah populations have expanded in recent years because of changes brought by humans.

Other birds have benefited more directly from human intervention, as is the case with the common starling (*Sturnus vulgaris*). These birds have spread across North America, following their introduction from Europe in the late 1800s.

Similarly, the common pheasant (*Phasianus colchicus*) is now native across most of Europe, thanks to human interest in these game birds, which are bred in large numbers for sport shooting. Many more survive than would otherwise be the case, thanks to the attention of gamekeepers who not only provide food, but also help to curb possible predators in areas where the birds are released.

Slow breeders

Birds that reproduce slowly, such as albatrosses (Diomedeidae) and sandhill cranes (*Grus canadensis*), are likely to be highly vulnerable to any changes in

Above: Snowy owls (Nyctea scandiaca) are often seen near coasts outside the breeding season. They are opportunistic hunters, even catching fish on occasion.

their surroundings, whether caused by human interference, climate change, disease, or other factors. Great concern has recently been focused on albatross numbers, which are declining wordwide. Many of these birds have been caught and drowned in fishing nets in recent years. Albatrosses are normally very long-lived and breed very slowly. Any sudden decline in their population is therefore likely to have devastating consequences that cannot easily be reversed.

Below: Sandhill crane (Grus canadensis) with chick. Long-lived, slow-breeding birds such as cranes are the least adaptable when faced with rapid environmental changes of any kind.

green budgies survived to breed and pass on their genes to their descendants, and so green became the dominant colour in the feral flocks.

Group living also means that when the flock is feeding and at its most vulnerable, there are extra eyes to watch out for predators and other threats. Within parrot flocks, birds take it in turns to act as sentinels, and screech loudly at any hint of danger.

Effects of humans

It is generally assumed that human interference in the landscape is likely to have harmful effects on avian populations. However, this is not

MIGRATION

Some birds live in a particular place all year round, but many are only temporary visitors. Typically, species fly north into temperate latitudes in spring, and return south at the end of summer. They have a wide distribution, but are seen only in specific parts of their range at certain times of the year.

Many species of birds regularly take long seasonal journeys. The birds that regularly undertake such seasonal movements on specific routes are known as migrants, and the journeys themselves are known as migrations. Migrations are different from so-called irruptions, when flocks of certain types of birds suddenly move to an area where conditions are more favourable. Birds migrate to seek shelter from the elements, to find safe areas to rear their young and, in particular, to seek places where food is plentiful. Birds such as waxwings (Bombycillidae) irrupt to a new location to find food when supplies become scarce in their habitat, but such journeys are less frequent and are irregular. The instinct to migrate dates back millions of years,

Right: This diagram illustrates the main migratory routes in the Americas, where birds fly either down the Central American isthmus, or across the Caribbean via the local islands. In following these traditional routes over or close to land, the birds avoid long and potentially hazardous sea crossings.

Below: The routes taken by birds migrating back and forth to Africa from parts of Europe and western Asia are shown here. Again, crossings are not always made by the most direct route, if this would entail a long and possibly dangerous sea journey.

to a period when the seasons were often much more extreme, which meant that it was difficult to obtain food in a locality throughout the year. This forced birds to move in search of food. Even today, the majority of migratory species live within the world's temperate zones, particularly in the Northern Hemisphere, where seasonal changes remain pronounced.

Migratory routes

The routes that the birds follow on their journeys are often well defined. Land birds try to avoid flying over large stretches of water, preferring instead to follow coastal routes and crossing the sea at the shortest point. For instance, many birds migrating from Europe to Africa prefer to fly over the Straits of Gibraltar. Frequently

---

Banding birds

Much of what we know about migration and the lifespan of birds comes from banding studies carried out by ornithologists. Bands placed on the birds' legs allow experts to track their movements when the ringed birds are recovered again. The rings are made of lightweight aluminium, and have details of the banding organization and when banding was carried out. Unfortunately, only a very small proportion of ringed birds are ever recovered, so the data gathered is incomplete, but now other methods of tracking, such as radar, are also used to follow the routes taken by flocks of birds, which supplements the information from banding studies.

Below: A mute swan (Cygnus olor) *wearing a band. Coloured bands can help to identify individual birds from some distance away.*

---

birds fly at much greater altitudes when migrating. Cranes (Gruidae) have been recorded flying at 5,000m (16,400ft) when crossing the mountainous areas in France, and geese (*Anser*) have been observed crossing the Himalayas at altitudes of more than 9,000m (29,500ft). Even if the migratory routes are known, it is often difficult to spot migrating birds because they fly so high.

Speed and distance

Migrating birds also fly at greater speeds than usual, which helps to make their journey time as short as possible. The difference can be significant – migrating swallows (*Hirundo rustica*) travel at speeds between 3 and 14km/h (1.8–8.7mph) faster than usual, and are helped no doubt by the greater altitude, where the air is thinner and resistance is less.

Some birds travel huge distances on migration. Arctic terns (*Sterna paradisea*), for example, cover distances of more than 15,000km (9,300 miles) in total, as they shuttle between the Arctic and Antarctic. They fly an average distance of 160km (100 miles) every day. Size does not preclude birds from migrating long distances, either. The tiny ruby-throated hummingbird (*Archilochus colubris*) flies over the Gulf of Mexico from the eastern USA every year, a distance of more than 800km (500 miles).

Preparing for migration

The migratory habits of birds have long been the subject of scientific curiosity. As late as the 1800s, it was thought that swallows hibernated in the bottom of ponds because they were seen skimming over the pond surface in groups before disappearing until the following spring. Now we know that they were probably feeding on insects to build up energy supplies for their long journey ahead.

Even today, the precise mechanisms involved in migratory behaviour are not fully understood. We do know that birds feed up before setting out on migration, and that various hormonal changes enable them to store more fat

Above: Many birds, including this bluethroat (Luscinta suecica), *set out on migration after moulting. Damaged plumage can make the task of flying harder.*

in their bodies to sustain them on their journey. Feeding opportunities are likely to be more limited than usual when birds are migrating, while their energy requirements are, of course, higher. In addition, birds usually moult just before migrating, so that their plumage is in the best condition to withstand the inevitable buffeting that lies ahead.

Navigation

Birds use both learned and visual cues to orientate themselves when migrating. Young birds of many species, such as swans, learn the route by flying in the company of their elders. However, some young birds set out on their own and reach their destinations successfully without the benefit of experienced companions, navigating by instinct alone. Birds such as swifts (Apopidae) fly mainly during daytime, whereas others, including ducks (Anatidae), migrate at night. Many birds fly direct to their destination, but some may detour and break their journey to obtain food and water before setting out again.

Experiments have shown that birds orientate themselves using the position of the sun and stars, as well as by following familiar landmarks. They also use the Earth's magnetic field to find their position, and thus do not get lost in cloudy or foggy weather, when the sky is obscured. The way in which these various factors come together has, however, yet to be fully understood.

BEHAVIOUR

Bird behaviour, or avian ethology as it is known, is a very broad field. Some patterns of behaviour are common to all birds, whereas other actions are very specific, just to a single species or even to an individual population. Interpreting behaviour is easier in some cases than in others.

All bird behaviour essentially relates to various aspects of survival, such as avoiding predators, obtaining food, finding a mate and breeding successfully. Some behaviour patterns are instinctive, while others develop in certain populations of birds in response to particular conditions. Thus the way in which birds behave is partly influenced by their environment as well as being largely instinctual.

Age, too, plays a part in determining behaviour, since young birds often behave in a very different

Aggression

Birds can be surprisingly aggressive towards each other, even to the point of sometimes inflicting fatal injuries. Usually, however, only a few feathers are shed before the weaker individual backs away, without sustaining serious injury. Conflicts of this type can break out over feeding sites or territorial disputes. The risk of aggressive outbreaks is greatest at the start of the breeding season, when the territorial instincts of cock birds are most aroused. Size is no indicator of the potential level of aggression, since some of the smallest birds, such as hummingbirds (Trochilidae) can be ferociously aggressive.

Below: A dispute breaks out between a pair of European nutcrackers (Nucifraga caryocatactes). Birds often fight with their wings outstretched, as they seek to batter their opponent into submission.

way to the adults. Some forms of bird behaviour are relatively easy to interpret, while others are a great deal more difficult to explain.

Garden birds

One of the first studies documenting birds' ability to adapt their behaviour in response to changes in their environment involved blue tits (*Parus caeruleus*) in Britain. The study showed that certain individuals learned to use their bills to tap through the shiny metallic foil covers on milk bottles to reach the milk. Other blue tits followed their example, and in certain areas householders with milk deliveries had to protect their bottle tops from the birds.

The way in which birds have learned to use various types of garden feeders also demonstrates their ability to modify their existing behaviour in response to new conditions when it benefits them. A number of new feeders on the market designed to thwart squirrels from stealing the food

Above: The posture a bird adopts while sunbathing can appear to indicate distress, as is the case with this Eurasian blackbird (Turdus merula), which is resting with its bill open and wings outstretched.

exploit birds' ability to adapt in this way. The birds have to squeeze through a small gap to reach the food, just as they might enter the nest. Once one bird has been bold enough to enter in this fashion, others observe and soon follow suit.

Preening

Although preening serves a variety of functions, the most important aspect is keeping the feathers in good condition. It helps to dislodge parasites and removes loose feathers, particularly during moulting. It also ensures that the plumage is kept waterproof by spreading oil from the preen gland at the base of the tail.

Preening can be a social activity too. It may be carried out by pairs of males and females during the breeding season, or among a family group.

This behaviour is seen in a variety of birds, ranging from parrots to finches. Some parrots perform mutual preening throughout the year, which reinforces the pair bond. In some species of psittaculid parakeets, however, such as the Alexandrine (*Psittacula eupatria*), the dominant hen allows her mate to preen her only when she is in breeding condition, in which case preening may be seen as a prelude to mating.

Bathing

Preening is not the only way in which birds keep their plumage in good condition. Birds often bathe to remove dirt and debris from their plumage. Small birds wet their feathers by lying on a damp leaf during a shower of rain, in an activity known as leaf-bathing. Other birds immerse themselves in a pool of water, splashing around and ruffling their feathers.

Some birds, especially those found in drier areas of the world, prefer to dust-bathe, lying down in a dusty hollow known as a scrape and using fine earth thrown up by their wings to absorb excess oil from their plumage. Then, by shaking themselves thoroughly, followed by a period of preening, the excess oil is removed.

Sunbathing

Sunbathing may be important in allowing birds to synthesize Vitamin D3 from the ultraviolet rays in sunlight, which is vital for a healthy skeleton. This process can be achieved only by light falling on the bird's skin, which explains why birds ruffle their plumage at this time. Some birds habitually stretch out while sunbathing, while others, such as many pigeons, prefer to rest with one wing

Right: The natural waterproofing present on the plumage ensures that birds do not become saturated when swimming or caught in a shower of rain. This would destroy the warm layer of air surrounding the body created by the down feathering, and leave them vulnerable to hypothermia. Nevertheless birds do need to dry their plumage, which is what this American anhinga (Anhinga anhinga) *is doing, with its wings outstretched.*

raised, leaning over at a strange angle on the perch. Vasa parrots (*Coracopsis*), found on the island of Madagascar, frequently behave in this fashion, although sunbathing is generally not common in this group of birds.

Maintaining health

Some people believe that when birds are ill, they eat particular plants that have medicinal properties, but this theory is very difficult to prove. One form of behaviour that does confer health benefits has been documented, however: it involves the use of ants. Instead of eating these insects, some birds occasionally rub them in among their feathers. This causes the ants to release formic acid, which acts as a potent insecticide, killing off lurking parasites such as mites and lice. Jays (*Garrulus glandarius*) and also starlings (Sturmidae) and Eurasian blackbirds (*Turdus merula*) are among the species that have been observed using insects in this way. Members of the crow family have also been seen perching on smoking chimney pots or above bonfires, ruffling their feathers and allowing the smoke to penetrate their plumage. The smoke is thought to kill off parasites in a process that confers the same benefits as anting.

Above: Birds such as the African yellow-billed oxpecker (Buphagus africanus) *form unusual associations with large mammals. These members of the starling clan frequently hitch a ride on the backs of animals such as buffaloes and rhinoceroses, where not only are they relatively safe from predators, but they also feed on the animal's resident colony of ticks.*

Below: The Eurasian green woodpecker (Picus viridis) *is hunting here for invertebrates on the ground.*

BIRDWATCHING

Thanks to their widespread distribution, birds can be seen in virtually any locality, even in the centre of cities. You don't need any special equipment to watch birds, but a pair of binoculars will help you to gain a better insight into avian behaviour, by allowing you to study birds at close range.

Birdwatching can be carried out almost anywhere around the world. Many people enjoy simply watching the birds that visit their garden. A greater variety of species can be seen if the birdwatcher ventures further afield, to local parks, woods or wetlands for example. Birdwatching holidays and sponsored birdwatching competitions offer opportunities to see an even greater variety of birds in different localities. Seasonal changes in bird populations mean that even if you visit the same area through the year, you will see new species at different times.

Above: At many major reserves where birds congregate, special permanent birdwatching hides have been set up to give visitors a good view without disturbing the birds themselves.

Drawing birds for reference

1. Sketching birds is relatively straight-forward if you follow this procedure. Start by drawing an egg shape for the body, with a smaller egg above, which will become the head, and another to form the rump. A centre line through the head circle will form the basis for the bill. Now add circles and lines to indicate the position of the wings and tail. Add lines for the legs and then sketch in the feet and claws.

2. Use an indelible fine-line felt-tip pen to ink in the shape of the bird that you have drawn previously in pencil, avoiding the unwanted construction lines.

3. Coloured pencils will allow you to add more detail after you have rubbed out any unwanted pencil markings.

4. If you take a number of prepared head shapes with you into the field, you can fill in the detail quickly and easily, enabling you to identify birds later.

Getting a good view

Binoculars can be purchased from camera stores and similar outlets, but it is important to test them before deciding which model to buy, particularly as they vary quite significantly in price. When purchasing binoculars, you will need to consider not only the power of magnification, but also how closely the binoculars can be focused, particularly if you going to use them at home, where the bird table is likely to be relatively close.

Binoculars vary according to their power of magnification and the length of the objective lens in millimetres, with the lens modifying the image. The lens' length and magnification are given in the specifications: binoculars described as 8x45 multiply the image by 8 compared with how it would appear to the naked eye and have an objective lens of 45mm, which is important in determining the focus.

Two important considerations stem from the power of magnification. First, the depth of field is important, since it affects the area of the image that is in focus. The greater the magnification, the shallower the depth of field. A deep depth of field can be helpful, since it ensures that a larger proportion of the birds on view are in focus, which avoids the need to refocus constantly. If the depth of field is shallow, only the birds in the centre will be in focus. Second, the degree of magnification also affects the field of vision – the area that you can see through the binoculars. A wide field of vision will help you to locate birds more easily.

Buying binoculars

A number of other factors may be considered when buying binoculars.
• Weight is important. Consider buying a lightweight pair if you intend using binoculars for long periods. They should also feel balanced in the hands.
• For people with large hands, small binoculars may be hard to adjust and not very comfortable to hold. Pay attention to the focusing mechanism – it needs to be easy to operate.
• Try the eyecups of the binoculars to see how comfortable they feel. If you wear spectacles, it is important that the cups give you a full field of vision. Binoculars with adjustable eyecups are more suited for spectacle-wearers.
• Is the design of good quality? It could be worthwhile paying extra for waterproofing. The better-quality

Below: A view of a hide. External camouflage, easy access and good viewing positions are essential features in the design of such units. Even so, it may take birds some time to accept the presence of a hide.

Above: A garden bird table will attract many species to feed, and if it is carefully sited, you should be able to see the birds easily, even from inside your home.

Right: Hanging cages are a compact type of food dispenser. They should be filled with special peanuts that are safe for birds. They may attract a wide variety of birds, including various tits, finches and even more unusual species, such as this great spotted woodpecker (Dendrocopus major).

designs have their chambers filled with nitrogen gas to prevent any condensation developing.
• The design should be robust, with a solid protective casing.

Fieldscopes

Apart from binoculars, dedicated bird-watchers often use birding telescopes, called fieldscopes. These are ideal for use in hides as they can be mounted in various ways, using either a bench clamp fitting or a tripod. Fieldscopes are equipped with lenses similar to those in binoculars, but are more suited to long-term use, when you are watching a nest for example, as you do not have to keep holding the scope while waiting for a bird to return. Instead, attach the scope to a branch or bench and train it on the nest, then simply be patient until you see the bird return.

Making notes

When observing birds either in the garden or further afield, it is always useful to have a notebook handy to write down details and make sketches.

When sketching, proceed from a few quick pencil lines to a more finished portrait as time allows. Water-soluble pencils are helpful for colouring sketches, as the colours can be spread using water and a small paintbrush. If you spot a bird you cannot identify, jot down the details quickly in your notebook. Note the bird's colours and markings. Notice the length of the neck and legs, and the shape of the bill. Assess the bird's size in relation to familiar species, and try to decide which family you think it belongs to. Your notes can then be compared with a field guide or other sources of information to identify the bird.

FIELDCRAFT

If you are seriously interested in birdwatching, you will need to develop fieldcraft skills. There is a significant difference between watching birds casually in a garden and tracking down particular species in remote areas, where preparation is important. Don't neglect your own safety in the wild.

Left: Hand-held binoculars or a viewing scope attached to a tripod can help you to study both common and rare species. Taking notes is useful, especially if you intend to write up details of your observations.

Research and careful preparation are vital to the success of any field trip. You should also select clothing and equipment suited to the particular place where you intend to study birds.

Clothing and equipment

Suitable clothing is vital to keep you warm and dry when birdwatching. Waterproof footwear will be needed when visiting wetlands, or after rain. Dull-coloured clothing will allow you to blend in with the landscape so you can approach the birds more closely. A camping mat can be useful if you intend spending time on the ground.

In addition to packing your binoculars, camera equipment and perhaps a viewing scope, you may also want to take a notebook or sketchpad. A field guide will help to identify birds, while a waterproof rucksack will protect all your belongings.

Preparation

It always helps to do your homework before setting out. Investigating the habits of the birds you hope to see will help you to decide on the best place to go, and the time of day when they are

most likely to be seen. It may be useful to draw up a checklist highlighting key features of the species concerned in advance. You can then refer to these in the field. Studying a local map prior to your visit will help you to orientate yourself in new surroundings. Good preparation is especially important in areas where you are likely to be unfamiliar with the birds concerned.

Photography

In the past, birdwatchers relied on 35mm SLR cameras and telephoto lenses to record their sightings. Today, however, birders are increasingly using digital cameras. These work very well when combined via a connector to a viewing scope that magnifies the image, like a telephoto lens. Digital cameras have the further advantage that they do not require film, but store images in their memory. Unwanted pictures can simply be deleted, while the best images can be transferred to a computer and printed out. Although you will not run out of film, digital cameras do use a surprising amount of power, so remember to take spare

Below: Plumage details, such as the handsome markings of this nutcracker (Nucifraga caryocatactes), may be captured using a conventional camera with a telephoto lens, or using a digital camera or camcorder linked to a viewing scope.

batteries with you on field trips. Digital camcorders can also be linked with viewing scopes, and are more flexible than cameras. Not only does a camcorder enable you to record the bird's song – which can be significant, especially if there is any doubt about identification – but you can also obtain a sequence of still images, especially if you can see the bird from different angles. Flight patterns can be recorded in this way, which again can help with identification. Even in relatively dark surroundings, some camcorders will function well.

Using hides and cover

On recognized reserves, there are likely to be hides in the best localities for birdwatching. Hides allow you to observe birds at relatively close quarters, and also offer excellent opportunities to photograph or film birds in their natural habitat. Even so, patience is likely to be needed for successful birding, as there will be no guarantees that you will see the species you hope to spot.

In areas where no hide is available, take cover behind shrubs, tree trunks or raised banks, or even in a parked car. Birds are highly attuned to the

slightest hint of danger, such as humans approaching. In areas where no cover is available, stand, kneel or lie in a comfortable position and try to move as little as possible. When approaching birds, make sure your position is downwind, so the sounds of your approach don't frighten them away.

Seeking rarities

Birdwatching magazines can be useful in identifying sites where rarities have been spotted. For up-to-the-minute news, you will need to seek out either a regularly updated website or an information phone line giving details of the latest sightings. Birders with access to email can also receive

Above: In some areas, there may not be any natural cover or hides available. To get close to birds, you will need to dress inconspicuously so you blend into the background, and try to keep as still as you possibly can. Birdwatching requires plenty of patience.

bulletins listing where particular rarities have cropped up. These are most likely to be recorded after bad weather such as fierce storms which can blow migrant birds off-course.

Bear in mind that many people will be drawn to a place where an unusual species has been sighted, and it is important not to create a disturbance or to trespass on private land. Similarly, it is a criminal offence in some areas to disturb breeding birds. Always act in a responsible manner when birdwatching.

Getting the best results

• Plan well beforehand, including checking tide times if relevant. Tidal areas can be particularly hazardous where there is quicksand.
• Remember that bird populations may vary according to the time of year.
• Never neglect your own safety. Let someone else know where you are going, and when you intend to return.
• Check the weather forecast first, and take a mobile phone in case you get into difficulties.
• Take a local map and also a compass to guide you if you get lost. Allow enough time to locate and then observe the birds.

Below: There are now many organized trips taking keen birders to far-flung parts of the world, offering unique opportunities to see new birds in exotic localities.

ZONES AND HABITATS

Birds have been exceedingly successful in colonizing the planet. Their warm-blooded nature and ability to fly have helped them to reach and then adapt to life in some of the world's most inaccessible places. They are found naturally on all continents, even successfully inhabiting Antarctica.

Zoologists divide the world into broad geographical zones, within which there are many different habitats. This approach reflects the movements of the Earth's landmasses through geological time, and so helps to show relationships between species occurring in various parts of the world today.

The Americas

In the distant past, North America was separated from its southern neighbour, and they had different origins. North America was originally attached to what is now Europe and later drifted westwards, while South America was once joined to a huge southern landmass that geologists call Gondwana, which included what is now the Indian subcontinent, Australia, Africa and Antarctica. South America split off at an earlier stage in

geological history than did North America – more than 100 million years ago – at a time when dinosaurs were in the ascendancy and the skies were occupied by flying reptiles called pterosaurs, rather than birds.

When birds began to evolve on this southern continent, they did so in isolation from the rest of the world. For this reason, the bird life that occurs today in this southern zone is known as neotropical, to distinguish it from that found in North America, which is known as nearctic. Later the avian populations of the Nearctic and Neotropical zones mingled somewhat by way of the Central American land bridge that was created when these two vast landmasses joined. However, unique forms still exist that are found only in South America, reflecting their isolated development in prehistory.

Above: This map shows how the different continents are believed to have formed and divided, giving rise to the familiar continents that we know today (see map below). These continental movements in turn have had direct effects on the distribution of avian populations.

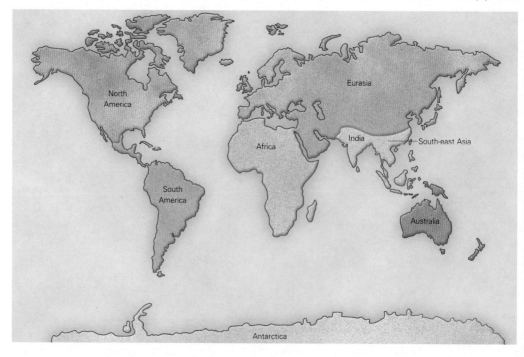

Above: The Indian subspecies of the ring-necked parakeet (Psittacula krameri) has succeeded in adapting to a free-living existence in suburban areas around European cities, including London and Amsterdam. Here the birds survive the winter mainly on bird-table offerings of seed put out for native birds.

The Palaearctic

Europe has been separated from North America by the Atlantic Ocean for more than 50 million years, but the bird species of these now separate areas still show some evidence of their common past. In prehistory, Europe formed, and still forms, part of a much broader area known as the Palaearctic realm, which extends right across the northern continent from Iceland eastwards to Japan. Fossilized remains suggest that this region was the cradle of avian evolution, where the first members of the group probably originated more than 80 million years ago. Most zoologists believe that the oldest known bird, *Archaeopteryx,* was not in fact the first of the avian line, but as yet its immediate ancestors have not been discovered.

The distribution of avian species in the Northern Hemisphere has been affected in the more recent geological past by the spread and subsequent retreat of the ice sheets from the far north. Today, Europe and Asia experience a climate similar to that of the corresponding area of North America, ranging from arctic to subtropical according to latitude. The two regions even have some birds in common, especially in the far north, where certain species have a circum-polar distribution – they are found right around the polar region.

Africa, southern Asia and Australasia

As part of the great southern continent of Gondwana, Africa used to be attached to South America, but subsequently remained in contact with what is now the Indian subcontinent during the critical early phase in avian evolution approximately 60 million years ago. This distant history is reflected even today by the large number of avian species found south of what has become the Sahara Desert. This zone is now described as the Ethiopian realm, although it covers virtually all of Africa.

The Indian subcontinent became a separate landmass when Gondwana broke up. It ultimately drifted north, colliding and eventually joining with what is now the Asian landmass, and creating the Himalayan Mountains in the process. As in Africa, the broadly tropical climate and the landscape have altered little since then, which has meant that a number of the species that evolved here are found nowhere else in the world.

East and south of India lie the islands that comprise the Australasian realm, which includes Australia, New Guinea and New Zealand. These islands once formed part of the vast landmass of Gondwana, but later broke away and have been isolated from the rest of the world for millions of years. A diversity of bird species found nowhere else in the world can be seen here as a result.

Present distribution

Birds' current distribution throughout the world is affected by a number of different factors, as well as the history of their evolution. The ability to fly has allowed birds to become very widely distributed, as has their warm-blooded nature, which has meant that they are far less vulnerable to climatic factors than cold-blooded creatures. Lifestyle, and particularly the range of foods that are available, also play a part. When birdwatching, there are certain groups of birds that you are most likely to encounter in specific types of habitat as a result of all these factors. The major avian habitats of the world are as listed on the pages that follow.

Below: Common, or European, starlings (Sturnus vulgaris) are now well established outside their natural range. This picture was taken in the USA, where the species was introduced in the 1800s. It has since spread widely across North America, and can also be seen in other localities, including Australia.

THE SEA

The world's oceans provide a very rich source of food for all birds able to exploit it. Fish and invertebrates such as squid and krill form the basis of the diet of seabirds, some of which range extensively across the world's oceans and are frequently sighted long distances from land.

The huge expanse of the oceans, and the difficulty of observing seabirds, means that relatively little is known about many species. This lack of knowledge was confirmed by the case of the Bermuda petrel (*Pterodroma cahow*). This species was believed to have become extinct during the 1600s, but, remarkably, a surviving population was rediscovered in 1951 after more than three hundred years. Seabirds survive out at sea with the help of special salt-excreting glands in

Above: Birds have come to recognize trawlers as sources of fish, swooping down to feed on whatever is thrown overboard, and haunting shipping lanes. Fulmars (Fulmarus glacialis) and gannets (Morus bassanus) can be seen here in the wake of a trawler off the Shetland Islands of Scotland.

Below: Not all seabirds feed on fish. This white-vented storm petrel (Oceanites gracilis) is feeding on planktonic debris, while paddling with its feet on the surface of sea.

the nasal area (just above their bills) that allow them to drink seawater without getting dehydrated.

Breeding habits

Many seabirds are social by nature, forming huge breeding colonies on rocky outcrops by the sea. Indeed, one of the main factors restricting seabird populations can be the lack of nesting sites. By congregating in large numbers the birds can maximize their reproductive success while reducing the effects of predators on their numbers. Nest-raiders such as black-backed gulls (*Larus marinus*) may be unable to inflict major damage on a breeding colony if the birds are so densely packed that the raiders cannot land.

Feeding

The feeding habits of seabirds have a significant impact on their lifestyle. Albatrosses (Diomedeidae), for example, spend most of their lives flying above the oceans. Their large wingspan allows them to glide almost effortlessly for long periods, swooping down to take food from the surface or even catching flying fish above the waves, rather than entering the water. Other species, such as gannets (Sulidae), dive beneath the surface to feed.

Right: The sea can be a hostile environment, with rough weather sometimes making feeding conditions difficult. High winds can batter birds and blow them off course, while oil spillages have presented a new threat in recent times. Ultimately, all seabirds are forced on to land to reproduce. Many species seek out remote oceanic islands to do so. There they can breed without being harassed by people or encountering introduced predators such as domestic cats.

Birdwatching tips
• Seabirds such as albatrosses are attracted to passing ships because of the food that is thrown overboard. This means they are relatively easy to locate in certain areas – for example near shipping lanes.
• Ornithologists can often take trips on local boats to view seabird colonies. These and other sea crossings may present a good opportunity to watch birds feeding out at sea.
• If you are prone to seasickness, don't forget to take medication beforehand if you think you may feel ill on a trip.
• Binoculars can easily be lost overboard from a small boat in choppy seas. Always sling them (and any camera equipment) around your neck, rather than simply holding them in your hands.

Typical sightings in seas and oceans, depending to some extent on location:
• Auks
• Gannets
• Albatrosses
• Petrels

Below: For most ornithologists, organized charter boat trips present the only way to reach seabird colonies.

1 Greater black-backed gull
2 Sea eagle
3 Black-headed gull
4 Cormorant
5 Puffin
6 Razorbill
7 Little auk
8 Peregrine falcon

SEASHORE AND ESTUARY

Tidal rhythms have a significant impact on the habits of birds found on seashores and estuaries. These birds usually group together to feed on mudflats and sandbars that are uncovered at low tide. As the incoming tide encroaches, the birds are forced to retreat to the shoreline.

Gulls typify the image of the seashore more than any other group of birds, being a familiar sight on coasts the world over. These adaptable birds also venture well inland, especially to locations where food is available, such as public parks with ponds and even the less salubrious surroundings of refuse dumps.

Above: Sanderlings (Calidris alba) demonstrate the features of a typical wader. The daily lives of such birds are directly influenced by the movements of the tide.

Below: Black-headed gulls (Larus ridibundus) are a species that differ significantly in appearance in winter. At this time their black head plumage is restricted to a crescent-shaped area on each side of the head.

Lifestyle and feeding

Wading birds that frequent seashores typically have relatively long legs compared with perching birds, which enable them to walk through shallow water. Their narrow bills allow them to probe for invertebrates concealed in the mud. Some waders have evolved more specialized feeding habits, which are reflected in the shape of their bills. The oystercatcher (*Haematopus ostralegus*), for example, has a chisel-like tip to its bill that allows it to split open mollusc shells.

Shorebirds feed on a range of creatures, and can therefore be sighted further inland, even if only seeking sanctuary from storms. Some shorebirds are migratory, spending summer as far north as the Arctic Circle before heading south for winter again.

Breeding habits

Many birds that live close to the shoreline have to breed in the open. The eggs and chicks of such species,

Birdwatching tips
• Always find out tide times before setting out to watch shorebirds. Birdwatching opportunities are usually greatest when the tide is going out, but be careful not to be trapped by the incoming tide.
• Watch out for quicksand.
• Natural cover on seashores is minimal, so try to blend into the landscape as far as possible. Choose a good vantage point and then stay put.
• Be aware of birds' breeding grounds and take care not to disturb them.
• Beware in tropical areas, especially if wading through water. Many dangers lurk in the shallows, including poisonous jellyfish, sea snakes and even crocodiles.

Typical sightings on estuaries and sea shores, depending on location:
• Plovers
• Ibises
• Gulls
• Terns

which include curlews (*Numenius arquata*) have markings that conceal them well among the sand or pebbles. Even the coloring of the adult birds often helps to conceal their presence, with typical shades of grey, brown and white plumage merging into the background of the shoreline.

Within the tropics, a number of shorebirds have adapted to living in coastal mangrove forests, the roots of which are submerged by the incoming tide. They include some of the most spectacular members of the group, such as the scarlet ibis (*Eudocimus ruber*). These birds use the mangroves for roosting and breeding because they can nest off the ground here.

Right: The day-to-day distribution of seashore and estuarine birds is likely to be influenced by the weather. If conditions are stormy, birds often retreat to estuaries and coastal lagoons; in icy winter weather, a variety of unexpected species may be seen at estuaries, since these stretches of water do not freeze over, unlike surrounding areas of freshwater such as lakes.

1 Peregrine falcon
2 Snipe
3 Barnacle goose
4 Mediterranean gull
5 Sooty albatross
6 Gannet
7 Arctic skua
8 Storm petrel
9 Whimbrel
10 Oystercatcher
11 Dunlin
12 Long-tailed duck
13 Black-headed gull
14 Common sandpiper

FRESHWATER LAKES, PONDS AND RIVERS

The speed of the water flow in freshwater habitats has a direct impact on the vegetation that grows there, which in turn influences the types of birds that may be seen. Some birds are drawn to lakes, ponds and rivers mainly for food, whereas others seek sanctuary from would-be predators there.

A wide variety of birds can be encountered by lakes, ponds and rivers, but not all are easy to observe. In areas of slow-flowing or still, shallow water where reed beds are well established, rails of various types (Rallidae) are often present, but these birds are shy by nature. Their mottled plumage provides camouflage, while their slim, tall body shape coupled with long, narrow toes allow them to move quietly through the vegetation.

Finding food

Many birds of prey hunt in freshwater habitats, swooping low over the water to seize fish by day and even at night. Fishing owls (*Scotopelia*) have sharp spines on the undersides of their feet that allow them to tighten their grip on fish hooked by their sharp talons. Other hunters rely on different strategies to catch food. Herons (Ardeidae) wait in the shallows and seize fish that swim in range of their sharp, powerful bills. Some fish-eating birds, notably some kingfishers (Alcedinidae), dive to seize their prey, which they may feed to their young in river bank nests.

Nesting

Some birds are drawn to lakes and rivers not so much by food but by nesting opportunities. Swallows (*Hirundo rustica*) collect damp mud from the

Above: A sharp bill, narrow head and powerful neck mean that birds such as the red-necked grebe (Podiceps grisegena) are well equipped to seize aquatic prey.

water's edge to make their nests, and may also catch midges flying above the water. Most birds that actually nest by ponds and rivers seek seclusion when breeding. They hide their nest away, or make it hard to reach by choosing a spot surrounded by water, while taking care to avoid sites that may flood. Mute swans (*Cygnus olor*) construct large nests, which restricts their choice of sites. Both sexes, but especially the cob (male), defend the nest ferociously. These largish birds are capable of inflicting painful, damaging blows with

their wings on would-be wild predators, dogs or even people who venture too close.

Birdwatching tips

• Patience is essential when watching freshwater birds, as many species are shy and easily frightened away.
• Certain localities, such as large lakes and gravel pits, are particularly good for spotting waterfowl in winter. Check local details in field guides or websites.
• Quietly paddling a canoe up a river can be a good way to spot birds, but plan carefully and be alert to possible dangers, such as strong currents, weirs or waterfalls on the route.
• Take great care near rivers when there is a risk of flooding, such as after heavy rain.

Typical sightings by lakes, ponds and rivers, depending on location:
• Ducks, geese and swans
• Rails
• Herons
• Birds of prey

Below: The keen eyesight and long legs of birds such as the great blue heron (Ardea herodias) help them to hunt effectively in freshwater habitats.

Below: An African jacana (Actophilornis africanus) on a hippopotamus. This bird's long toes support its weight when walking over lily pads, so it does not sink down.

Right: Reedbeds associated with freshwater habitats provide cover for many species of birds. The dense vegetation in such areas means that birdwatching can be difficult. The narrow body shape and agility of many freshwater birds allow them to move easily through dense vegetation, avoiding detection. Fortunately, birds swimming into open water will be much easier to spot.

1 Spoonbill
2 Grey heron
3 Mallard
4 Tufted duck
5 Glossy ibis
6 Ringed plover
7 Common coot
8 Eurasian kingfisher
9 Muscovy duck

TEMPERATE WOODLAND

The temperate woodlands of the Northern Hemisphere have altered significantly over time owing to climate change, receding in cold periods and expanding in warmer eras. Coniferous forests extend north to the treeless area known as the tundra, where it is too cold for even hardy trees to grow.

Bird life in coniferous forests is less varied than in deciduous, broad-leaved woodlands, largely because there are fewer feeding opportunities. Nonetheless some species manage to thrive in this cooler habitat.

Coniferous woodlands

Clark's nutcracker (*Nucifraga columbiana*) of North American forests is one such success. Their curving bills allow these specialized members of the crow family to extract the seeds from pine cones effectively.

The food supply in this habitat is not guaranteed, however. There are barren years when the trees do not produce as many cones as usual, forcing the birds to abandon their regular haunts and fly elsewhere. These unpredictable movements, known as irruptions, occur when birds suddenly appear in large numbers outside their normal range, searching for alternative sources of food. They later disappear

Below: Some predatory birds have adapted to life in temperate forests, especially owls such as this large-eared owl (Asio otis). These hunters depend largely on rodents for food.

Above: Ground birds such as the capercaillie (Tetrao urogallus) breed on the ground, concealing their presence as far as possible. Their chicks are able to move immediately after they hatch out.

just as suddenly as they arrived, and may not return again for years. In northerly areas the landscape is covered in snow for much of the winter. Some species, including various corvids and woodpeckers, prepare for the cold weather by burying stores of nuts or hiding them in trees.

Owls are frequently found in coniferous forests, preying on the rodents that can be quite plentiful there. However, owls may also be forced to hunt elsewhere if the numbers of their prey plummet, as occasionally happens when there is a shortage of pine cones.

Deciduous woodlands

A greater variety of feeding opportunities exists for birds in deciduous forests. Such woodland is more open, which means that there is a significant understorey of vegetation and insects are more plentiful. Migratory birds take advantage of the feeding opportunities in these forests in summer. Ground birds of various types, including wild turkeys (*Meleagris gallopavo*), are also found here. During the breeding season they congregate in forest clearings to display and mate. These birds eat a

Above: A pileated woodpecker (Dryocopus pileatus) male returns to the nest site. Trees provide relatively safe nesting havens, especially for birds such as woodpeckers that can create their own nesting holes.

variety of foods, ranging from seeds to berries and invertebrates, depending on the time of year.

Birdwatching tips

• Spring is a good time to spot birds in deciduous woodlands, before the trees are covered in leaves.
• Woodlands and particularly coniferous forests can be disorientating, so take a map and compass if you're going any distance in case you lose your bearings.
• In summer, woodland glades attract invertebrates, which in turn attract insectivorous birds in search of prey.
• Stand quietly in woodlands and listen – the song of woodland birds helps to reveal their presence.

Typical sightings in temperate woodlands, depending to some extent on location:
• Woodpeckers
• Finches
• Owls
• Warblers

Right: In many ways, temperate woodland is an ideal avian habitat during the warm months of the year, providing a wide range of food, excellent cover and a variety of nesting sites. During the winter months, however, life here can become much harsher. Once the leaves have fallen, the birds will be much more conspicuous, and food is likely to be scarcer. Survival will become even harder if snow blankets the ground.

1 Magpie
2 Black woodpecker
3 Sparrowhawk
4 Common pheasant
5 Wren
6 Blackcap warbler
7 Woodcock
8 European greenfinch

TROPICAL RAINFOREST

Over long periods, tropical rainforests have provided relatively stable environments compared with temperate forests, and are home to some spectacular species. Unfortunately, many tracts of forest are not easily accessible. Choose locations carefully to maximize your chance of seeing a wide range of birds.

Many of the birds inhabiting rainforest areas are brightly coloured, but their vibrant plumage is very effectively concealed in this dark, shadowy environment. Only flashes of colour may be seen as the plumage is lit by shafts of sunlight penetrating through the dense canopy of the forest.

Rainforest diversity

The stable environment of the rainforest has undoubtedly contributed to the diversity of bird life found there. Fruit is especially plentiful, and specialist fruit-eating birds, known as frugivores, are therefore numerous. Their presence is essential to the long-term wellbeing of the rainforest, as they help to distribute the seeds of fruits on which they feed. The seeds are excreted in their droppings, often some distance away from where the fruit was originally eaten. This method of seed dispersal helps to ensure the continued regeneration of the forest.

Birds of prey can also be observed in tropical rainforests, having adapted well to forest life, and there are even a

Below: A yellow-naped Amazon (Amazona ochrocephala) feeding. The unchanging climatic conditions in rainforests mean that food is readily available here through the year.

number of species that specialize in hunting other birds. These predators are relatively few in number, however, compared with the overall numbers of birds found in this habitat.

Many rainforest species have localized distributions. Toucans, for example, are confined just to the Americas, whereas the range of the spectacular birds of paradise is centred on the island of New Guinea in south-east Asia. Vast tracts of the world's rainforests are still so remote and inaccessible that even today, particularly in South America, new species of birds are still regularly being discovered by explorers each year.

Threatened habitat

It is well known that the world's rainforests are being felled alarmingly quickly. The fast rate of destruction means that it is possible that some species may become extinct before they have even been identified. Museum collections around the world contain various hummingbirds (Trochilidae) and tanagers (Thraupidae), for example, that are known only from single specimens. The birds' distributions are unrecorded and nothing more has been documented about them.

Above: Toucans are among the most distinctive of all birds found in tropical rainforests. Their large but lightweight bills assist them in reaching fruits that would otherwise be inaccessible.

Birdwatching tips

• Rainforests are potentially dangerous places, so go with an experienced guide or group, and don't be tempted to wander off into the forest on your own.
• You are often more likely to hear rather than see birds in this leafy environment.
• Pausing quietly for a time should allow you to spot bird life more easily.
• Photography is often difficult in the forest because of the low light.
• The high humidity, almost daily rainfall and biting insects in rainforests can create additional problems.

Typical sightings in tropical rainforests, depending to some extent on location:
• Parrots
• Barbets
• Cotingas
• Trogons

Right: The dense upper canopy of the rainforest provides both a screen and a vantage point for birds, depending on their lifestyle. Hunters may perch among the tallest trees or fly over the canopy, seeking signs of possible prey beneath, while nearer to the ground, nectar-eating birds seek flowers to feed from. Fruit is also abundant in these lush forests, so frugivorous species are commonly encountered here too.

1 Hawk-headed parrot
2 Motmot
3 Quetzal
4 Scarlet macaw
5 Purple honeycreeper
6 Harpy eagle
7 King vulture
8 Saffron toucanet
9 Mountain tanager

TUNDRA AND POLAR REGIONS

Birds have successfully colonized many harsh environments, including the treeless tundra and freezing Antarctic. A surprisingly wide range of birds may be sighted on the tundra, especially in summer, when many migratory birds arrive to breed.

The treeless lands of the far north are inhospitable in winter, so many birds visit only for the summer. Icy Antarctica is even harsher, yet birds such as penguins are year-round residents on coastlines.

Antarctic survivors

As the huge landmass of Antarctica drifted gradually southwards millions of years ago, so the seabirds there adapted their lifestyle to survive the harshest conditions on Earth. The freezing cold and biting winds combine to create a numbing wind-chill factor that few creatures could survive, but penguins have adapted to thrive in this habitat. The lack of nesting material and the threat of fatal chilling if the eggs or young are exposed to the elements for even a few seconds have affected their breeding habits. Emperor penguins (*Aptenodytes forsteri*) lay only a single egg, which is kept wedged between the top of their flippered feet

and their abdomen. Emperors have an increased number of blood vessels here, to convey heat to the developing embryo through the eggshell.

Penguins have reversed the general evolutionary path of birds to survive in this harsh environment. In the course of millions of years, most birds evolved increasingly lightweight bodies to facilitate flight, but the body weight of penguins increased because of a build-up of the subcutaneous fat that helps to insulate them against the bitter cold. The evolution of their wings into

Above: A rock ptarmigan (Lagopus mutus) hidden in the snow. This bird's white winter plumage provides excellent camouflage, and it becomes immobile at the hint of danger to complete its disguise.

flippers and their streamlined shape combine to make them highly effective marine predators.

The northern tundra

In the far north, the treeless tundra landscape is transformed during the brief summer months when the snow melts. The topsoil thaws too and the ground becomes boggy because the melt water cannot drain away through the permanently frozen layer beneath. Instead, water forms shallow pools at the surface, where mosquitoes and other insects breed in large numbers. These invertebrates and other food attract a variety of birds as temporary visitors. The migrants nest and quickly rear their young before the weather turns cold and they head south again.

Birdwatching tips

• Wear pale or dull-coloured clothing to conceal your presence in these cold, treeless areas where there is little natural cover. Of course, all clothing must be warm as well.

• Take mosquito repellent when visiting the tundra during the summer.

• Allow for the bright light when photographing in snowy landscapes. Glare reflecting off the snow may distort your camera's light readings, so you may need to compensate.

• An increasing number of ornithological trips to the Antarctic allow you to visit this part of the world accompanied by experienced guides.

Typical sightings in tundra or polar landscapes, depending on your location in the Northern or Southern Hemisphere:

• Waterfowl
• Snowy owls
• Waders
• Penguins

Below: Antarctic seabirds such as the cape petrel (Daption capense) benefit from the rich food supply in the southern oceans. These birds fly north to escape the worst winter weather, and only return to the shores of Antarctica during the brief summer to nest.

Right: Many birds found in areas where snow often blankets the ground and there is little natural cover have mainly white plumage. This is true of both predators such as snowy owls (Nyctea scandiaca) and also prey. Other adaptions that assist survival in cold habitats include extra feathering over the body extending to the feet, and greater reserves of body fat.

1 Snow goose
2 Gyr falcon
3 Pintado
4 Great shearwater
5 Snowy owl
6 Adele penguins
7 Storm petrel
8 Emperor penguin
9 Ptarmigan

GRASSLAND, STEPPE AND MOORLAND

Grasslands and moorlands offer relatively little cover to birds, and some are harsh places where both water and food may be scarce. A number of birds found in these areas are ground-dwellers, and they are often well camouflaged, which makes them hard to spot unless flushed from their hiding places.

Moors and grasslands are among the best habitats in which to spot predatory birds as they fly overhead seeking live quarry or carcasses to scavenge. Prey species are also present in numbers, but they are more difficult to spot because of their camouflage.

Above: A male greater prairie chicken (Tympanuchus cupido) shows off the barred plumage that is a feature of many birds found in moors and grasslands.

Spotting predatory birds

Large predators and scavengers such as condors (Cathartidae) fly high over grasslands, utilizing the warm air

currents known as thermals, which allow them to remain airborne with minimal effort. Smaller hunters such as hawks swoop down much lower over the open countryside as they search for the small mammals or birds that form the basis of their diet.

Flightless grassland birds

Perhaps surprisingly, one of the ways in which birds of open country avoid being attacked by predators is by being large and conspicuous. With the exception of the cassowaries (*Casuaris*) of New Guinea and Australia, which inhabit dense forest, all the world's other giant flightless birds – the rheas (Rheidae) of South America, the African ostrich (*Struthio camellus*) and the Australian emu (*Dromaius novaehollandiae*), inhabit grassland areas. Here their large size acts as a deterrent to potential predators, including mammals. If a hunter attacks, their ability to run fast allows

Left: Not all kingfishers live in forested areas. The kookaburra (Dacelo novaeguineae) occurs in open country in Australia.

them to escape from danger. If neither of these strategies works and the birds are trapped, they can lash out and inflict a potentially fatal kick with their powerful feet.

Moorland camouflage

On moorlands and steppes the weather can become cold and snowy in winter. Some of the birds found in this terrain undergo a seasonal moult at the onset of winter, from which they emerge transformed by lighter-coloured plumage to help conceal their presence.

Birdwatching tips

- Seek a good vantage point to increase your chances of spotting and following birds of prey.
- You will need a pair of powerful binoculars in grassland environments, as you will be combing relatively large and distant expanses of sky and land in search of birds.
- Use whatever natural cover is available to conceal your presence, such as tall vegetation and outcropping rocks.
- Horse riding can be a good way to cover long distances in grasslands and yet have a reasonable chance of spotting bird life, because birds are often less fearful of people on horseback.

Typical sightings in grassland habitats, depending to some extent on location:
- Eagles
- Vultures
- Grouse
- Hawks

Right: Avoiding predators is difficult in open countryside – especially hunters flying overhead. For prey species, the best strategy is to blend into the background and avoid being seen. While a relatively large number of mainly terrestrial birds are found in grasslands, therefore, these birds are often almost impossible to spot unless they take fright and fly up as you walk across the landscape. On the other hand, grasslands offer one of the best environments for observing birds of prey, since these birds are forced to spend relatively long periods on the wing searching for food.

1 Golden eagle
2 Brent goose
3 Red kite
4 Red grouse
5 Raven
6 Merlin
7 Wheatear
8 Skylark
9 Grey partridge

URBAN LIFE

Some birds display a remarkable ability to adapt to modern life, occurring right in the centre of cities.
They use buildings for nesting and, in the case of birds of prey, as vantage points for hunting, just as they
would use trees or rocky crags in the wild. City parks, in particular, have become major refuges for birds.

Cities tend to be slightly warmer than the surrounding countryside, and this warm microclimate offers a number of advantages for birds. Drinking water is less likely to freeze in cold weather, and in spring, insects are more abundant at an earlier time, as plants bud and grow more quickly because of the warmth.

Residents and visitors

Some birds live permanently in cities, taking advantage of parks, whereas

Above: Buildings can represent safe localities for nest-building. White storks (Ciconia ciconia) such as these have nested on town roofs for centuries in some parts of their range.

Above: Out of all birds, the feral pigeon (Columba livia) has adapted best to urban life, to the extent that it is now a common sight in cities around the world.

Below: Some birds of prey, such as this black kite (Milvus migrans), photographed flying over Bombay in India, have adapted to hunt in cities. Urban environments also offer many opportunities for scavenging – for example, from streetside refuse bins or city dumps.

others are more casual visitors, flying in to roost at night from outlying areas, or pausing here on migration. Deserted buildings offer a snug and relatively safe retreat for birds that roost in flocks, whereas birds of prey seek the inaccessible ledges of high-rise buildings. The abundance of feral pigeons (*Columba livia*) in built-up areas attracts peregrine falcons (*Falco peregrinus*), proving that they are just as adaptable as their prey. The falcons may keep pigeon populations in check, but if not, their numbers can be also curbed by feeding them with corn, which acts as a contraceptive.

A life above the bustle of city streets generally offers predatory species a fairly safe existence, compared with more rural areas where they risk being shot illegally. There are still dangers lurking on the city streets, however. High-rise office blocks with large expanses of glass can lure birds to a fatal collision.

Migrating birds still pass through cities on occasions, notably huge flocks of common starlings (*Sturnus vulgaris*). These congregate not just in city parks, but also roost on buildings and tree-lined streets when breaking their journey, creating a noisy chatter and plenty of mess.

Birdwatching tips

• City parks offer the best chances of spotting the largest number of species in urban environments, particularly if there is a sizeable pond or lake.
• Early morning is a good time to spot birds at close quarters in cities, before many people are on the streets.
• Don't forget about the dangers of traffic in your enthusiasm to spot particular birds.
• Join the local ornithological society to gain insight into the more unusual species found in local towns and cities.

Typical sightings in urban environments, depending to some extent on location:
• Falcons
• Owls
• Pigeons and doves
• Gulls

Right: The spread of cities inevitably influences the local avian populations, by altering the neighbouring habitat. When new development encroaches on surrounding land, for example, it becomes increasingly hard for birds that have fairly specialist feeding requirements, such as white storks, to obtain enough food for themselves and their young. Only opportunists such as pigeons are likely to thrive in crowded city centres, but a wider variety of birds use the oases of city parks.

1 White stork
2 Collared dove
3 Jackdaw
4 Kestrel
5 Swallows
6 House martins
7 Feral pigeon
8 Black redstart
9 House sparrow

GARDENS

An amazingly wide variety of birds have been recorded as regular garden visitors. It is possible to observe as many as 40 species regularly visiting bird tables in north-western Europe and North America. Feeding stations undoubtedly help to draw birds to gardens, but birds also visit as part of their natural behaviour.

Tidy, immaculately manicured gardens generally support less bird life than well-established gardens with plenty of mature shrubs that can be used for roosting and nesting. If there are stands of trees nearby, or even just lining the road outside, the range of birds visiting the garden will increase, and larger species will become more common. Artificial nesting sites, such as nest boxes of various types and sizes, can also help to increase the variety and numbers of birds that visit gardens regularly.

Birds face a major danger in gardens in the guise of the domestic cat. Huge numbers of individuals fall victim to these pets annually. The majority of the casualties are young fledglings, which lack the awareness and caution of adult birds. In areas where the cat population is especially high, there

Above: Bird tables and feeders help to attract birds into gardens by providing them with additional food sources. These are especially valuable during cold winter weather.

may be local declines in bird numbers. However, studies suggest that bird populations do not seem to be adversely affected by cats overall.

Helpers and pests

Birds are often regarded as gardeners' friends because they help to control the number of invertebrate pests in gardens. For example, tits (*Parus*) eat aphids on rose bushes, and thrushes (*Turdus*) hunt snails. At certain times of year, however, some birds can themselves become pests. Pigeons (*Columba*), in particular, often dig up newly planted seeds and eat them before they can germinate, unless the seeds are protected in some way. Later in the year, some species eat ripening berries.

Residents and migrants

Some birds are resident in garden settings throughout the year. Others are temporary visitors, migrating to warmer climes for the winter period. Hummingbirds (Trochilidae), for example, are resident in northern parts of North America for only part of the year, and head south for the winter. Meanwhile, winter migrants from further north may descend on gardens

at this time, as in the case of the fieldfare (*Turdus pilaris*) in Europe. Studies provide clear evidence that actual shifts in the behaviour and distribution of birds are currently occurring because of the availability of garden habitat and the provision of food there. The Eurasian blackbird (*Turdus merula*) has become a common sight in gardens, while in North America, the American robin (*Turdus migratorius*) has moved from its traditional woodland haunts into this type of environment too.

Above: A wide choice of bird food is currently available, along with various types of feeder to dispense it. These American goldfinches (Carduelis tristis) have been photographed eating sunflower seeds.

Right: In many respects, gardens offer an ideal habitat for birds. Food is readily available in these surroundings, as well as trees and shrubs, which provide good opportunities for roosting and nesting. Unfortunately, gardens can often be dangerous places for birds to visit, thanks to the popularity of cats as pets. Nor are cats the only danger in this type of habitat. Predatory birds, notably magpies (Pica pica), will raid the nests of smaller birds, taking both eggs and chicks.

Birdwatching tips

• You can encourage invertebrate-eating birds to visit your garden by creating a wild area or by establishing a compost heap where invertebrates can multiply.

• Positioning a bird table near a window will allow you to watch birds from inside the house, but take care to site it well away from cover where cats could lurk and ambush the birds.

• Keep a pair of binoculars handy indoors so you can get a better view of the bird table and any unexpected visitors to it, plus a notepad to record descriptions of any unusual birds you see.

• Try to avoid using insecticides on your garden, as these reduce the food that will be available for birds.

• Ordinary slug pellets will poison slug-eaters such as thrushes feeding in your garden. Use pellets that are described as safe for birds instead.

Typical sightings in gardens, depending to some extent on location:

• Tits
• Thrushes
• Starlings
• Hummingbirds

1 Ruby-throated hummingbird
2 Great tit
3 Virginian cardinal
4 Magpie
5 Cactus wren
6 Ring-necked parakeet
7 Collared dove
8 Eurasian blackbird
9 Common starlings
10 Nuthatch

ENDANGERED SPECIES AND CONSERVATION

It has been estimated that three-quarters of the world's birds may come under threat in the 21st century. Habitat destruction poses the most serious danger, so conservationists are striving to preserve bird habitats worldwide. Direct intervention of various kinds is also used to ensure the survival of particular species.

Around the world, threats to birds are varied and complex, but most are linked to human interference in the ecosystem, and will thus continue to grow as human populations increase.

Habitat destruction
Habitat destruction includes the deforestation of the world's tropical rainforests, which host a wide variety of birds, and also the conversion of many grassland areas into crop fields or livestock pasture. The first casualties of habitat destruction are often species with specialized feeding or nesting requirements, which cannot easily adapt to change.

In recent years, there have been a number of instances of opportunistic species adapting and thriving in altered habitats. One example is the common mynah (*Acridotheres tristis*), whose natural distribution is centred on India but has been introduced to many other localities worldwide, often to control locust numbers. Such success stories are the exception rather than the rule,

Below: The kagu (Rhynochetus jubatus) of the rainforests of New Caledonia, in the Pacific Ocean, is in danger of dying out completely because of the destruction of its habitat.

Above: The northern spotted owl (Strix occidentalis caurina) is currently threatened by the rapid felling of the ancient forests on the west coast of California.

however. Generally, the diversity of bird life in an area declines drastically when the land is modified or cleared.

Hunting and pollution
Unregulated hunting of adult birds, eggs or young threatens a variety of species worldwide. The birds may be killed for their meat or feathers, or captured live and sold through the pet trade. In many countries, laws are now in place to protect rare species, but hunting and trading still go on illegally.

Overfishing is a related hazard facing seabirds, especially now that trawling methods have become so efficient. Global shortages of fish stocks are forcing fishermen to target fish that had previously been of little commercial value, but that are an important part of seabirds' diets.

In agricultural areas, pesticides and herbicides sprayed on farmers' fields decimate bird populations by eliminating their plant or animal food supplies. Deliberate or accidental contamination of the soil, air or water

by industrial chemicals is another hazard, while in the oceans, seabirds are killed by dumped toxins and oil spills. Disease is another major threat that may increase.

Climate change
In the near future, global warming caused by increased emissions of carbon dioxide and other gases is likely to impact on many bird habitats, and will almost certainly adversely affect birds' food supplies. If plants or other foods become unavailable in an area, birds must adapt their feeding habits or face extinction. As temperatures rise, the melting of the polar ice caps will threaten seabird populations by destroying their traditional nesting areas. Rising sea levels will also threaten low-lying wetlands favoured by wading birds.

Theats to island birds
Some of the world's most distinctive birds have evolved in relative isolation on islands. Unfortunately, these species are also extremely vulnerable to changes in their environment, partly because their populations are small. One of the greatest threats comes from

Above: This guillemot (Uria aalge) killed in Scottish waters is just one of the countless avian victims claimed by oil spillages each year. Large spills of oil can have devastating effects on whole populations.

introduced predators, particularly domestic cats. Cats have been responsible for wiping out a host of island species, including the flightless Stephen Island wren (*Xenicus lyalli*) of New Zealand waters, which became extinct in 1894, thanks to the lighthouse-keeper's cat.

Cats are not the only introduced predators that can cause serious harm to avian populations. Grazing animals such as goats, introduced to islands by passing ships to provide future crews with fresh meat, have frequently destroyed the native vegetation, so reducing the birds' food supply.

Today, control of harmful introduced species is helping to save surviving populations of endangered birds on islands such as the Galapagos Islands off Ecuador, home to the flightless cormorant (*Phalacrocorax harrisi*) and other rare birds.

Conservation and captive-breeding

Preserving habitat is the best and most cost-effective way to ensure the survival of all the birds that frequent a particular ecosystem. A worldwide network of national parks and reserves now helps to protect at least part of many birds' habitats. In addition,

conservationists may take a variety of direct measures to safeguard the future of particular species, such as launching a captive-breeding programme. This approach has proven effective in increasing numbers of various critically endangered species, from the Californian condor (*Gymnogyps californianus*) of the USA, to the echo parakeet (*Psittacula echo*) of Mauritius. In some cases, the technique of artificial insemination has been used to fertilize the eggs.

Artificially or naturally fertilized eggs can be transferred to incubators to be hatched, effectively doubling the number of chicks that can be reared. This is because removing the eggs often stimulates the hen to lay again more quickly than usual. Hand-rearing chicks on formulated diets helps to ensure the survival of the young once hatched. When hand-reared chicks are later released into the wild, it is vital that they bond with their own species and retain their natural fear of people, so glove puppets shaped like the parent birds are often used to feed the chicks.

Reintroduction programmes

Breeding endangered species is relatively easy compared with the difficulties of reintroducing a species to an area of its former habitat. The cost of such reintroduction programmes is

Above: Glove puppets resembling the parent bird's head are often used when hand-rearing chicks such as this peregrine falcon (Falco peregrinus), to encourage the birds to bond with their own kind when eventually released.

often very high. Staff are needed not only to look after the aviary stock and rear the chicks, but also to carry out habitat studies. These assess the dangers that the birds will face after release and pinpoint release sites. The released birds must then be monitored, which may include fitting them with radio transmitters.

Ecotourism

Working with local people and winning their support is often essential to the long-term success of conservation programmes. This approach has been used successfully on some of the Caribbean islands, such as St Vincent, home to various indigenous Amazon parrots (*Amazona*). Increasing clearance of the islands' forests, a growing human population and hunting all threatened these birds.

Effective publicity about these rare parrots, including portrayals of them on currency and postage stamps, helped to raise local people's awareness of the birds as part of their islands' heritage. A publicity campaign brought the parrots' plight to international attention and attracted visitors to the region, which brought in much-needed foreign currency. Thus so-called "ecotourism" both helped the local economy and enlisted the islanders' support to conserve the parrots.

Left: The rapid destruction of the world's rainforests, seen here in Costa Rica, is the single most important threat facing tropical birds.

BIRDS OF THE WORLD

Identifying birds in many cases is not easy, particularly if you have only a relatively brief sighting. This part of the book has therefore been designed to simplify the task of identification as much as possible, by allowing you to link your sightings with the environment in which you spotted the bird. The section is divided into three main geographical regions, which are further split into particular habitats where birds are most likely to be spotted. It should be pointed out that this system is not infallible, as some birds are highly adaptable and range widely through different environments, but it is a useful starting point. Distribution maps accompanying all the illustrated entries provide a visual guide as to exactly where bird species are to be found within these regions, while the text provides information on the time of year and localities where the birds are most likely to be seen, in the case of migratory species.

The associated descriptions will help to clarify whether you have seen a cock bird or a hen, since there are often plumage differences between the sexes. Other information in these fact boxes about habitat, feeding and breeding habits should provide further help when it comes to identifying a particular bird. A bird's general shape, and the characteristic way in which it moves and behaves, all add up to what bird-watchers call its "jizz", which can help to identify birds even from a tiny speck in the sky or a dark shape scuttling behind a hedge.

Not every species in the world is covered, but the representative sample featured through the following pages means that you should at least be able to identify the type of bird you spotted. Browsing through these pages also affords an opportunity to learn more about the varying lifestyles of the world's birds, ranging from parrots living in the Amazon rainforests to the penguins of Antarctica, and the various members of the pigeon family that inhabit our city centres.

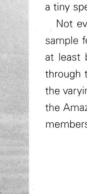

Left: Flamingos (Phoenicopteridae) *are one of the avian families that are represented both in the Americas and the Old World, often inhabiting quite harsh environnments.*

BIRDS OF
THE AMERICAS

There is a significant divide between the avifauna of South and North America, with the Central American isthmus acting as a cross-over zone. This divide is partly a reflection of the birds' feeding habits. Many fruit-eating species found in the Amazonian region, for example, are restricted to this area, where they are guaranteed a constant supply of food in the rainforest throughout the year. Some of the most unique birds in the world – such as toucans, with their bizarre and often colourful bills – are found in this part of the world. Hummingbird species, which include the smallest bird in the world, do range across both continents and through the Caribbean, although they reach their greatest diversity in South America. The localized distribution of some birds in parts of South America, combined with the often inaccessible terrain, means that new species are still being discovered here quite regularly.

Above from left: Roadrunner (Geococcyx californianus), *Virginian cardinal* (Cardinalis cardinalis), *toco toucan* (Ramphastos toco).

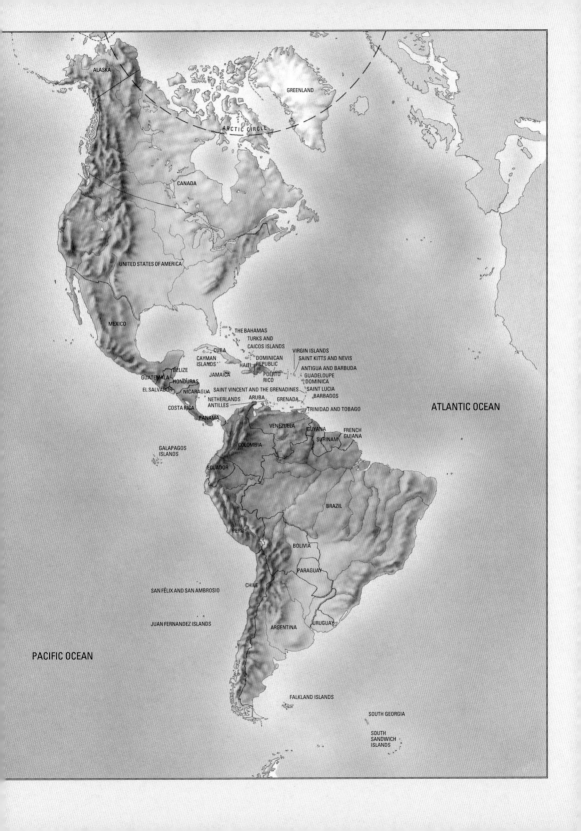

ALASKA

GREENLAND

ARCTIC CIRCLE

CANADA

UNITED STATES OF AMERICA

MEXICO

THE BAHAMAS
TURKS AND
CAICOS ISLANDS
CUBA
CAYMAN
ISLANDS
DOMINICAN
REPUBLIC
HAITI
JAMAICA
VIRGIN ISLANDS
SAINT KITTS AND NEVIS
ANTIGUA AND BARBUDA
GUADELOUPE
DOMINICA
SAINT LUCIA
BARBADOS
GRENADA
TRINIDAD AND TOBAGO

BELIZE
GUATEMALA
HONDURAS
EL SALVADOR
NICARAGUA
COSTA RICA
PANAMA

PUERTO
RICO
SAINT VINCENT AND THE GRENADINES
NETHERLANDS
ANTILLES
ARUBA

ATLANTIC OCEAN

VENEZUELA
GUYANA
SURINAM
FRENCH
GUIANA

GALAPAGOS
ISLANDS

COLOMBIA

ECUADOR

BRAZIL

PERU

BOLIVIA

PARAGUAY

SAN FÉLIX AND SAN AMBROSIO

CHILE

JUAN FERNANDEZ ISLANDS

ARGENTINA

URUGUAY

PACIFIC OCEAN

FALKLAND ISLANDS

SOUTH GEORGIA

SOUTH
SANDWICH
ISLANDS

OCEAN WANDERERS

These birds often have a wide distribution, roaming far out from the shore over the oceans. They may return to land only in order to nest, often choosing remote islands for this purpose, so they are not likely to be seen by the casual observer. However, they may be attracted to passing ships in search of offerings of food.

Long-tailed jaeger

Stercorarius longicaudus

The long tail feathers of this jaeger account for as much as 23cm (9in) of its overall length, and it is actually still the smallest member of this group of seabirds. Long-tailed jaegers breed in the Arctic region of North America, spending the winter at sea. Only on rare occasions are they observed on freshwater lakes.

Jaegers can be considered the pirates of the skies, menacing gulls and terns and harrying them to drop fish or other quarry, which they quickly swoop down on and seize before the prey falls into the water. The long-tailed jaeger is especially agile in flight, as reflected by its long, pointed wings, while its hooked bill is a formidable weapon. On occasion, long-tailed jaegers may resort to attacking other nesting seabirds, taking both their eggs and the chicks.

Identification:
Characteristic long, narrow tail feathers. Underparts are whitish, with a greyer tone on the flanks and around the vent. Head is blackish and the wings are dark. Sexes are alike.

Distribution: Occurring throughout the far north of North America and Greenland during the breeding period in the summer. Then flies south to spend the winter around the coast of South America and the western side of South Africa extending down into sub-Antarctic areas.
Size: 58cm (23in).
Habitat: Mainly open sea.
Nest: Depression on the ground.
Eggs: 1–2, olive with dark spots.
Food: Fish and other animal matter.

Fork-tailed storm petrel

Grey storm petrel *Oceanodroma furcata*

The bluish coloration of the fork-tailed petrel sets it apart from all other related species. These birds are most likely to be seen over open sea, swooping down to break the surface of the water occasionally with their legs. They feed both on the wing and on the sea surface. Like other storm petrels, they come ashore to breed, often on islands, seeking the security of underground burrows at this time. Breeding colonies can be savaged by introduced mammals, notably cats and rats. The nostrils of fork-tailed petrels are located in a tube above the bill, and serve to excrete excess salt from the body, ingested as a result of the bird's environment and diet.

Identification: Distinctive bluish-grey plumage is lighter on the throat and the undertail coverts. The tail is forked and the wings are a duskier shade of blue. Both the bill and the legs are black. The plumage around the eyes is mainly black. Sexes are alike.

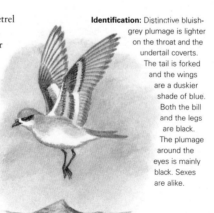

Distribution: North American west coast south to California. Also present on the Aleutians and neighbouring islands.
Size: 23cm (9in).
Habitat: Open sea.
Nest: Underground burrow.
Eggs: 1, white.
Food: Fish, invertebrates and plankton.

Black storm petrel (*Oceanodroma melania*): 23cm (9in)
Extends along the Californian coastline and offshore islands. This is the most common and largest of the black-coloured petrels, with a pale wing bar and a relatively slow flight pattern. Calls at night from underground burrows. Sexes alike.

Black-footed albatross (*Diomedea nigripes*): 91cm (36in)
Found in the northern Pacific Ocean extending from western North America to the Asiatic coast. Lives on the open seas. Predominantly brownish grey with a white face and undertail coverts, although occasionally paler. Feet are black. Sexes alike.

Waved albatross (*Diomedea irrorata*): 93cm (37in)
Occurs off the north-west coast of South America, west to the Galapagos Islands. Easily recognized by the combination of a whitish head and neck with a yellow suffusion, plus brown plumage elsewhere on the body. May be observed feeding at night, when squid are nearer the surface. Sexes alike.

White-tailed tropic bird (*Phaethon lepturus*): 81cm (32in)
Virtually pantropical distribution, but absent from the eastern Pacific. Smallest of the tropic birds. Slender shape, mainly white, occasionally a very pale rosy or peach colour, with distinctive black bars in an almost V-shaped formation across the back. Another black area is evident towards the end of each wing. Young birds lack the long tail (which accounts for half the total length of the adult) and have extensive barring on their upperparts.

Laysan albatross

Diomedea immutabilis

The Laysan is the most common albatross of the northern Pacific region. According to reports of sightings, especially from the larger islands, these birds now appear to be venturing closer to the shoreline of the Hawaiian islands. Unlike many albatrosses, the Laysan rarely follows ships, and comes to land only during the breeding season. It is thought that pairs remain together for life, and albatrosses rank among the longest-lived of all birds, having a life expectancy often exceeding half a century. They face few natural enemies, but sadly more are dying prematurely after seizing baited hooks intended for fish left on long lines by fishing boats. Albatrosses usually scoop up prey from the ocean surface while in flight.

Distribution: Extends from the northern Pacific Ocean to the western coast of North America. Especially common on Midway and Laysan islands, Hawaii.
Size: 91cm (36in).
Habitat: Open sea.
Nest: Area of ground.
Eggs: 1, white, may be blotched.
Food: Fish and other aquatic creatures.

Identification:
Relatively small. Predominantly white with a sooty-brown back, upper wings and tail and dark feathering around the eyes. In flight, the largish, pinkish feet extend beyond the tail. Yellow curved bill has a black tip. Sexes alike.

Hawaiian petrel

Dark-rumped petrel *Pterodroma phaeopygia* (E)

The alternative name of dark-rumped petrel is not a clear guide to identification, since various petrels display this feature. The Hawaiian petrel appears to be quite rare compared to other species and is thought to be declining in numbers. It spends its time at sea, coming on to land to breed. The largest colony is found around the Haleakala Crater on Maui. These petrels nest in underground burrows, remaining there during the day and emerging to search for food at night. Outside the breeding period, Hawaiian petrels are most likely to be sighted to the south-east of the Hawaiian islands.

Identification: Black upperparts, with white plumage just above the bill and extending right across the underparts. The underside of the wings are also mainly white, with a black area evident on each of the leading edges when seen from below. There is usually a white, V-shaped marking present at the base of the uppertail coverts, above the tail. Sexes are alike.

Distribution: Pacific Ocean, Hawaiian and Galapagos Islands.
Size: 43cm (17in).
Habitat: Open sea.
Nest: Underground burrow.
Eggs: 1, white.
Food: Fish and other aquatic creatures.

SEABIRDS

Although they feed mainly on fish, these birds have evolved quite different feeding strategies, ranging from the pelican's sieve-like bill that acts like a trawl, to the targeted diving and underwater swimming of the cormorants. Another group, typified by the frigatebirds, rely on others to do the hard work of catching fish, and resort to mugging them to seize their catches as they fly back to land.

Man o'war bird

Magnificent frigatebird *Fregata magnificens*

Distribution: Throughout the eastern Pacific Ocean, Gulf of Mexico and tropical parts of the Atlantic Ocean.
Size: 101cm (40in).
Habitat: Oceanic coastlines.
Nest: Platform of sticks.
Eggs: 1, white.
Food: Fish and invertebrates, including jellyfish. Also preys on baby turtles and seabird chicks.

These birds can glide for long periods, relying on their huge 229cm (7.5ft) wingspan to help keep them airborne on the air currents. The male's throat patch, prominent at close quarters, is far less visible when in the air. Pairs nest on the coast in areas where there are other smaller, fish-eating seabirds that can be harried for their catches, so that the frigatebirds do not have to obtain their own food. If necessary, however, they often catch flying fish, as well as other creatures found near the surface, including baby turtles. It is believed that although cock birds may breed annually if the opportunity is there, most hens nest only every second year.

Identification: Jet black, with a bare, bright red throat patch that can be inflated for display purposes. Hens are similar, but can be easily distinguished by white feathering on the breast. In immature birds, the plumage on the head is also white.

American white pelican

Rough-billed pelican *Pelecanus erythrorhynchos*

These pelicans are found mainly on stretches of fresh water, sometimes hunting in groups for fish and other creatures such as crayfish. Occasionally, they may fly long distances to obtain food if the waters that they inhabit have a low fish population. On migration, American white pelicans fly over land rather than the sea, although populations in the southern part of their range will remain in the same region throughout the year. These birds breed communally, usually on quite inaccessible islands. Their chicks associate together in groups, known as pods, before they are fully fledged.

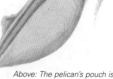

Above: The pelican's pouch is used to trawl for food.

Identification: Predominantly white plumage with contrasting black primary flight feathers. The large yellow bill develops a distinctive raised area on the ridge towards the tip from late winter through the breeding season. Sexes alike, but female is smaller.

Distribution: Western and central areas of North America, extending as far south as Guatemala and Costa Rica during the winter.
Size: 178cm (70in).
Habitat: Both freshwater and saltwater areas, not ranging far out to sea.
Nest: On the ground.
Eggs: 2–3, whitish with darker markings.
Food: Fish and other aquatic creatures.

Double-crested cormorant

Phalacrocorax auritus

These cormorants are found mainly in coastal waters, sometimes using unorthodox sites such as wrecked ships as perches. They also venture to inland areas, where they are found on suitable stretches of water. They can form large flocks, often hunting together for fish, which form the bulk of their diet. In the past, double-crested cormorant numbers have plummeted in some parts of their range because of DDT entering the food chain. This pesticide has had a harmful effect on eggshell thickness, and, as a result, has significantly reduced the number of chicks that hatch. The ban on DDT has seen their numbers rise again. These cormorants have also benefited from the increasing number of fresh-water reservoirs in various parts of their range, providing them with additional areas of habitat.

Identification: Adults are entirely black. Immatures show a whitish hue to their underparts. A double crest of feathers is evident on the back of the head during the breeding period, with a variable amount of white coloration. Has bare yellowish-orange skin around the face, with a powerful hooked bill. Females are smaller in size. Several different races are recognized through their range, differing in the extent of the white feathering forming the crest as well as in the depth of coloration.

Distribution: Much of the USA, south to parts of Central America in the winter. Also in parts of the Caribbean, from Florida to Cuba.
Size: 91cm (36in).
Habitat: Areas of fresh water and sea water.
Nest: Built of sticks and often seaweed.
Eggs: 3–4, pale blue.
Food: Fish and other aquatic creatures.

Brown pelican (*Pelecanus occidentalis*): 137cm (54in)
Coastal areas from southern USA south into South America. Dark brown in colour, with an area of white feathering on the head and neck. The bill is normally held flat against the neck on land, and used for trawling for fish in the water. Hens slightly smaller in size.

Blue-eyed cormorant (Imperial shag, *Phalacrocorax atriceps*): 76cm (30in)
Southern South America, from Chile to Argentina and Uruguay, and the Falkland Islands. Loose black crest with black plumage extending from above the upper bill over the head, back and wings to the tail. White on the sides of the head down over the underparts, with white patches on the wings. Blue skin encircling the eyes. Sexes alike.

Rock cormorant (Magellan shag, *Phalacrocorax magellanicus*): 71cm (28in)
Extends from the Pacific around to the Atlantic coast of South America; also present on the Falkland Islands. Distinctive patch of white feathering on the cheeks, with reddish skin encircling the eyes. Otherwise mainly black, with white chest and underparts. Sexes alike.

Pink-footed shearwater (*Puffinus creatopus*): 48cm (19in)
Occurs in the eastern Pacific, extending off the coast of the Americas. Also on Hawaii. Greyish-brown, and paler underparts with a variable amount of mottled brown coloration. Flesh-pink bill with dark tip. Sexes and young birds alike.

Rhinoceros auklet

Cerorhinca monocerata

These auklets congregate in areas where they can come ashore and excavate their nests in relative safety. They breed communally, with nesting densities of approximately 7 birds per square metre (square yard) having been recorded on Forrester Island, Alaska. Rhinoceros auklets dig long underground tunnels, using their bills and feet to excavate these burrows during the night. It will typically take a pair about 14 nights to construct an average tunnel about 213cm (7ft) long. The hen lays a single egg in a chamber at the end.

Identification: Sooty black upperparts. Underparts from the chin down to the chest and flanks are whitish, with a brownish-grey tone especially evident on the breast. White streaks on the face, creating a moustached effect, plus white crests extending from the eyes back to the nape of the neck that are less distinctive outside the breeding season. Orangish bill with characteristic horn-like swelling at the base of the upper bill, which largely disappears during the winter. Sexes alike.

Distribution: Western coast of North America, extending to the Aleutian islands across the Bering Sea.
Size: 38cm (15in).
Habitat: Coastal areas.
Nest: Underground chamber, may be lined with vegetation.
Eggs: 1, white spotted.
Food: Fish, such as anchovies, sand launce and herrings.

PENGUINS, BOOBIES AND SEA DUCKS

Bright plumage is not generally a feature associated with seabirds, where more subdued hues of black, brown or white predominate. There are exceptions, however, most notably in the case of some ducks that have spread to the marine environment from the freshwater haunts more usually occupied by these waterfowl. These birds are also more predatory by nature.

Galapagos penguin

Spheniscus mendiculus

These penguins have colonized the volcanic outcrops of the Galapagos Islands, seeking out fish such as sardines that feature prominently in their diet in coastal waters. Galapagos penguins usually fish together in pairs but hunt in larger groups sometimes too. When there is a change in the pattern of the ocean currents owing to El Niño, and fish then become scarce, penguin numbers may plummet. This decline occurred most dramatically in the early 1980s, when just a few hundred Galapagos penguins survived. Their numbers have since undergone a good recovery, aided by the fact that they can breed throughout the year.

Above: Penguins may not be able to fly, but their wings make powerful flippers underwater.

Distribution: Confined to the Galapagos Islands.
Size: 53cm (21in).
Habitat: Coastal regions.
Nest: In caves or crevices.
Eggs: 2, whitish.
Food: Fish.

Identification: A relatively small penguin, especially when compared with related species. A very thin white stripe extends from the eye around the throat, and the sides of the face are dark. White area under the lower bill and over much of the underparts, apart from an uneven, mainly black circle of feathers. Bill is pinkish at the base. Sexes alike, and patterning is less clearly defined in young birds.

Blue-faced booby

Masked booby *Sula dactylatra*

The blue-faced is the largest of the boobies, and preys upon correspondingly larger fish, swallowing those of up to 41cm (16in) without difficulty. Although these birds often dive quite deeply in search of fish, they may also catch flying fish at the surface. They sometimes lose their catch to frigatebirds that harry them as they fly back to land. Blue-faced boobies live in colonies, and prefer to nest on cliff faces. On remote islands in the absence of major predators, however, pairs may breed on the ground. While the hen is likely to lay two eggs, only one chick is normally reared, and the weaker chick loses out to its stronger sibling in the competition for food. Blue-faced boobies are long-lived, and young birds may not breed until their third year. Sadly, the number of these birds is declining in some areas because increased development is disturbing their habitat. A large population can be found around the Galapagos Islands off the western coast of South America.

Distribution: Pan-global around the Equator. Occurs both on the Pacific and Atlantic sides of the Americas, and in the Caribbean.
Size: 91cm (36in).
Habitat: Tropical oceans.
Nest: Accumulated droppings.
Eggs: 2, pale blue.
Food: Mainly fish.

Identification: Predominantly white but with black on the wings and a distinctive black tail. Has dark feathering on the face around the eyes, with a bluish tinge extending on to the yellowish bill. In hens, the bill is significantly duller.

Gentoo penguin (*Pygoscelis papua*): 81cm (32in)
Northerly distribution extends to Uruguay on the Atlantic coast of South America, ranging south to the Antarctic Peninsula. No lines on the face, and the upperparts are blackish apart from a distinctive white area above each eye. Underparts are white. Bill is mainly pinkish. Sexes alike.

Humbolt penguin (*Spheniscus humboldti*): 70cm (28in)
Occurs in the vicinity of the Humbolt Current along the shores of Chile and Peru. Distinctive pink fleshy edges at the base of the bill. Otherwise black and white, with a prominent white area on the throat. Sexes alike.

Surf scoter (*Melanitta perspicillata*): 55cm (22in)
Coastal waters of North America, extending on the western seaboard south from western Alaska. Breeds in fresh water and overwinters at sea. White patch on forehead and on the nape; rest of the plumage is blackish, with a brightly coloured bill. Hen is brown overall, with whitish areas on the sides of the face and more blackish on the top of the head. Bill is greyish.

Peruvian booby (*Sula variegata*): 76cm (30in)
Usually ranges down from south Peru to Chile; sometimes found as far north as southern Colombia. White plumage on the head down across the underparts. Wings and back are brown with white mottling. Brown tail and flight feathers. Bill is purplish grey. Sexes alike.

King eider

Somateria spectabilis

Like most birds from the far north, the king eider has a circumpolar distribution that reaches right around the top of the globe. Seasonal movements of these sea ducks tend to be more widespread than in other eiders, and they are remarkably common, with the North American population being estimated at as many as two million individuals. Huge groups of up to 100,000 birds will congregate together during the moulting period, although the groups split up during the breeding season when pairs nest individually across the Arctic tundra. King eiders are powerful swimmers and generally dive to obtain their food.

Distribution: Largely within the Arctic Circle.
Size: 63cm (25in).
Habitat: Tundra and open sea.
Nest: Hollow lined with down feathers.
Eggs: 4–7, olive buff.
Food: Predominantly crustaceans and marine invertebrates.

Identification: Orange area edged with black above the reddish bill in breeding condition. Light-grey plumage extends down the neck. Chest is pale pinkish white, with black wings and underparts. Ducks are mainly a speckled shade of brown, and the pale underside of their wings is visible in flight. In eclipse plumage, drakes are a darker shade of brown, with an orangish-yellow bill and white plumage on the back.

Oldsquaw

Long-tailed duck *Clangula hyemalis*

These sea ducks often congregate in large numbers, although in winter females and young birds tend to migrate further south in flocks than do adult drakes. They spend most of their time on the water, and obtain food by diving under the waves. They come ashore on to the tundra to nest, and ducks lay their eggs on the ground. The drakes soon return to the sea, where they start to moult. When migrating, they generally fly quite low in lines, rather than in any other organized formation.

Identification: Black head, neck and chest, with white around the eyes and white underparts. Head becomes white across the top outside the breeding season, with patches of black evident on the sides. Grey rather than brown predominates on the wings. Long tail plumes present throughout the year. The smaller ducks undergo a similar transformation, and the sides of the face become white rather than blackish.

Distribution: Northern coasts, with circumpolar range. Winters further south.
Size: 47cm (19in).
Habitat: Coastal waters and bays.
Nest: Hidden in vegetation or under a rock.
Eggs: 5–7, olive buff.
Food: Mainly crustaceans and marine invertebrates.

FLAMINGOS AND OTHER LARGER WATERBIRDS

A number of relatively large birds, ranging from flamingos to cranes and storks, have evolved to live in wetland areas, where their height can be an advantage in detecting food and wading through the water. Unfortunately, some have become so specialized in their habits that changes in their environment can have serious consequences for them, as in the case of flamingos.

American flamingo

Phoenicopterus ruber

The distinctive coloration of these birds comes from their diet of algae or small creatures that have eaten the microscopic plants. They feed in a unique fashion by walking along with their heads submerged, their long necks allowing them to filter relatively large quantities of water by sweeping their unusually shaped bills from side to side. As a result of their highly specific feeding requirements, American flamingos are vulnerable to habitat loss or pollution of the shallow coastal lagoons that they inhabit. Young are reared on nests of mud raised above the water level, and are covered in a whitish-grey down at first. At a month old, they moult into a brownish down. Their bills are short and straight at this stage. American flamingos are known to live for more than 30 years in the wild.

Identification: Bright, almost reddish plumage on the neck, with a paler pink body. Bill also has a pink hue behind the black tip. Outstretched wings in flight show black areas. Sexes alike.

Distribution: Islands in the Caribbean, Mexico, the north coast of South America and the Galapagos Islands. Other races found in parts of southern Europe, Africa and Madagascar, extending through the Red Sea into Asia.
Size: 145cm (57in) tall.
Habitat: Shallow saline lagoons.
Nest: Mud.
Eggs: 1, white.
Food: Small molluscs, crustaceans and plant matter.

Chilean flamingo

Phoenicopterus chilensis

Distribution: Ranges from highlands of Peru to Tierra del Fuego at the tip of the continent.
Size: Up to 105cm (41in) tall. Hens shorter and smaller.
Habitat: Highland salt lakes.
Nest: Mud.
Eggs: 1, white.
Food: Algae and invertebrates.

This is the most widely distributed South American flamingo, with a population extending more than 4,000km (2,500 miles). In the altiplano region of the Andes, they are usually observed at altitudes of 3,500–4,500m (11,500–15,000ft), but in parts of Argentina, east of the Andes, they occur at lower levels. In suitable areas, Chilean flamingos will congregate in large numbers, and as many as 100,000 have been counted on Lake Poopo in Bolivia. Lake Titicaca, found on the Bolivian border with Peru, is home to even greater numbers. Their calls are similar to the honking notes of geese.

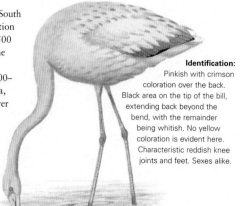

Identification: Pinkish with crimson coloration over the back. Black area on the tip of the bill, extending back beyond the bend, with the remainder being whitish. No yellow coloration is evident here. Characteristic reddish knee joints and feet. Sexes alike.

Wood stork

Wood ibis *Mycteria americana*

Although usually it is most likely to be encountered in freshwater areas, the wood stork may be seen in mangrove swamps where food is abundant. These birds are opportunistic predators, and are equipped with a powerful bill to seize creatures ranging from fish to young turtles and alligators. These large birds breed colonially, often on nesting sites surrounded by water. Up to 50 pairs or more may be found in the same area where conditions are favourable. Pairs accomplish nest-building quite quickly, in about three days, and the hen lays the eggs on a nest lining of leaves. These storks are long-lived, and their young are therefore slow to mature, often not breeding until they are five years old.

Identification: Bare, dark and unfeathered head is offset against the white plumage. The black feathering is confined to the wings and tail. Long bill, powerful at its base. White plumage in young birds tends to appear slightly soiled.

Distribution: Southern parts of the USA south as far as north-west Argentina.
Size: 119cm (47in).
Habitat: Marshland and lakes.
Nest: Made of sticks.
Eggs: 2–5, creamy white.
Food: Fish, amphibians and crustaceans.

Andean flamingo (*Phoenicoparrus andinus*): 160cm (63in)
In spite of its name, this flamingo has a much more restricted distribution than the Chilean, being found only in Chile and north-west Argentina. Purplish-red plumage on the head and neck. Yellow legs. Sexes alike.

American anhinga (snakebird, *Anhinga anhinga*): 91cm (36in)
From eastern coastal areas of the USA south through Central America and east of the Andes as far south as northern Argentina. Black with silvery grey markings on the wings and tail. Hens are brown on the head and neck, with no crest. The powerful bill is used to spear prey underwater, including snakes.

Black-necked stilt (black-winged stilt, *Himantopus himantopus*): 38cm (15in)
Widely distributed from southern USA south through South America. Also present in the Caribbean, Galapagos Islands and Hawaii. Predominantly white body, black wings and bill, with black on the head and neck. Pinkish legs. Hens have brownish-black backs.

Hudsonian godwit (*Limosa haemastica*): 38cm (15in)
Far north of North America, wintering in south-eastern South America. In the USA it is most commonly sighted on land adjoining the Gulf of Texas each April, during its migration north. Greyish head and neck, and chestnut feathering on underparts. Speckled white plumage on wings, and distinctive black underwing feathering. Long bill is reddish at the base. Hens larger, with whiter underparts.

Whooping crane

Grus americana (E)

Distribution: Restricted areas of Canada and the USA.
Size: 142cm (56in).
Habitat: Peat bog and marshland.
Nest: Flat mound.
Eggs: 2, buff with darker blotches.
Food: Omnivorous.

Standing up to 229cm (7.5ft) in height, this is the tallest bird found on the North American continent, as well as one of the most critically endangered. Its breeding grounds are in Wood Buffalo Park adjoining the Great Slave Lake in Canada. The population moves south in autumn to the wintering grounds at the Arkansas Refuge in Texas. The cranes pause on the long flight to feed on lakes and other similar stretches of water. Their name comes from the distinctive whooping sound of their calls. The graceful dancing display of males is considered one of the most spectacular sights in the natural world. Pairs form a lifelong bond. Nesting usually starts in May.

Identification: Red face and white plumage. The primaries are black although this may not be very evident when the wings are folded. Sexes alike. Young birds have a rusty hue, particularly on the head and neck.

RAILS, COOTS AND GALLINULES

Members of this family of waders are most likely to be encountered in relatively shallow stretches of fresh water, particularly where there is dense vegetative cover in the form of reeds. The narrow body shape of these waders helps them to move easily through such terrain, although they also swim quite well. Many species are shy by nature, which can make them difficult to observe.

King rail

Rallus elegans

Distribution: From southern Canada through eastern USA to parts of Mexico. Also present on Cuba and the neighbouring Isle of Pines.
Size: 48cm (19in).
Habitat: Freshwater and brackish marshes.
Nest: Cup-shaped.
Eggs: 10–12, creamy buff with purplish-brown spots.
Food: Both plant and animal matter.

Like many of the rails occurring in North America, king rails move south in winter to areas where the temperature is unlikely to drop significantly below freezing, as this would turn their feeding grounds to ice. Aquatic invertebrates feature prominently in their diet, but they are actually omnivorous, eating grass seeds and even fruit, such as blackberries, on occasion. They also prey on frogs and small water snakes. Sadly, in some parts of their range the numbers of king rail have fallen dramatically because of pesticides. Many are killed each year by passing traffic. They can also fall victim to a wide range of predators that may include alligators, raccoons and great horned owls.

Identification: Rusty brown, with darker scalloped patterning over the back and wings. Grey on the ear coverts behind the eyes. Cinnamon underparts with vertical black and white barring on the flanks. Long bill, brown at the tip and orangish further back. Sexes similar but hens are smaller in size.

Giant coot

Fulica gigantea

Occurring in the puna zone of the Andes at altitudes as high as 6,500m (21,320ft), these coots are reputedly not able to fly when adult, although young birds will fly quite readily, often moving down to lakes at lower altitudes for a time. They then return to their traditional haunts for breeding, and have specific nesting requirements. Giant coots construct huge platforms of water weed, often 3m (10ft) or more in length, in the shallows for nesting. The hen lays her eggs in a relatively small, raised cup area, and the same nest site is used and maintained over a number of years. The rim of the nest helps to conceal the chicks once they hatch and protects them from cold winds.

Identification: Predominantly dark slate grey, blacker on the head, neck, and undertail coverts. Bill is red, white and yellow, with the latter two colours on the flattened area called the shield, which extends over the top of the head. Sexes alike.

Distribution: Central Peru to Bolivia, Chile and north-west Argentina.
Size: 59cm (23in).
Habitat: Shallow lakes and smaller areas of water.
Nest: Large platform built on dense patches of water weed.
Eggs: 3–7, creamy grey with reddish-brown spots.
Food: Aquatic vegetation.

Clapper rail (*Rallus longirostris*):
41cm (16in)
Mainly coastal areas extending through Mexico and parts of the Caribbean to northern Peru and southern Brazil. Greyish sides to the face, speckled brown back, white throat with brown and white barring on the flanks and white undertail coverts. Hens are much smaller in size. Both brown and olive forms are recognized.

Yellow rail (*Coturnicops noveboracensis*):
17cm (7in)
Marshland areas of central and south-eastern parts of Canada to north-eastern USA, wintering further south in the USA, in Louisiana and Texas. Brown on top of the head, with a buff stripe above the eyes, and a brown stripe running across the eye. Sexes alike, but males may be slightly larger.

Sora (Carolina rail, *Porzana carolina*): 25cm (10in)
Freshwater marshland from south-eastern Alaska across much of the USA, sometimes also in brackish marshes when migrating to South America. Black area at base of bill, extending to the forehead, white spot behind the eyes with greyish coloration on the sides of the face, merging with barring on the flanks. Upperparts show dark streaking. Sexes alike.

Grey-necked wood rail (Cayenne wood rail, *Aramides cajanea*): 42cm (17in)
Mexico south to parts of Peru, Bolivia, northern Argentina and Uruguay. Grey area extending from the head to the upper breast with orangish-chestnut coloration on the lower breast. Black belly and undertail coverts. Upper wing coverts are greenish olive. Hens are smaller in size.

American coot

Fulica americana

Although there are no striking plumage differences between the cock and hen, they can easily be distinguished by a marked difference in their calls. Unlike some related species, American coots have proved to be highly adaptable, to the extent that their numbers appear to have increased overall in recent years. They rapidly colonize new areas of suitable habitat, although populations can be adversely affected by very cold springtime weather, which makes food hard to find. American coots often migrate south in large numbers to avoid the worst of the winter.

Identification: Predominantly slate grey, more blackish on the head. White undertail coverts. Bill is whitish, with red near the tip enlarging into a broad shield with red at the top. Sexes alike, although hens are often significantly smaller. Young birds predominantly brown, with duller bills.

Distribution: From Alaska southwards across much of North America through Central America and the Caribbean into parts of Colombia.
Size: 43cm (17in).
Habitat: Permanent areas of wetland.
Nest: Floating heap of dead aquatic vegetation.
Eggs: 3–12, buff with dense, fine blackish spotting.
Food: Aquatic vegetation.

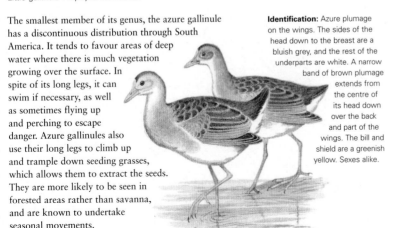

Azure gallinule

Little gallinule *Porphyrio flavirostris*

The smallest member of its genus, the azure gallinule has a discontinuous distribution through South America. It tends to favour areas of deep water where there is much vegetation growing over the surface. In spite of its long legs, it can swim if necessary, as well as sometimes flying up and perching to escape danger. Azure gallinules also use their long legs to climb up and trample down seeding grasses, which allows them to extract the seeds. They are more likely to be seen in forested areas rather than savanna, and are known to undertake seasonal movements.

Identification: Azure plumage on the wings. The sides of the head down to the breast are a bluish grey, and the rest of the underparts are white. A narrow band of brown plumage extends from the centre of its head down over the back and part of the wings. The bill and shield are a greenish yellow. Sexes alike.

Distribution: From Colombia eastwards to the Guianas and south through Peru to Bolivia, southern Brazil and into northern Argentina.
Size: 25cm (10in).
Habitat: Marshland with good cover.
Nest: Open cup of vegetation.
Eggs: 4–5, creamy with reddish-brown spots.
Food: Grass seeds and invertebrates.

LARGER WADERS

Colourful in some cases and highly adapted to their environments, some larger waders use their bills as sensory devices, probing for aquatic prey that may be concealed in mud or under loose stones. The group includes the spoonbills, which have among the most distinctively shaped bills of all birds. Many are quite tall, which enables them to spot potential prey over a wide area.

Scarlet ibis

Eudocimus ruber

The beautiful appearance of these ibises is derived in part from their diet, which helps to provide the pigment that gives them their characteristic coloration. They live in groups and comb the mudflats for crabs and other food with their stout but pointed bills. The scarlet ibis prefers to nest on islands, building a loose nest of sticks off the ground, often in mangrove swamps above the waterline. This can bring dangers, however, from crocodiles that lie in wait, hoping to seize chicks that have just left the nest and fall into the water.

Identification: Unmistakable, brilliant scarlet plumage, apart from blackish ends to the four longest primary flight feathers. Bill is black in breeding condition; reddish the rest of the year. Sexes alike. Young birds are much duller, with brownish and white areas of plumage.

Distribution: Concentrated in northern South America, from parts of Colombia and Ecuador through Venezuela and the Guianas along the coast of Brazil to the Amazon Delta. Has reappeared in the vicinity of São Paulo at Santos Bay, Brazil.
Size: 69cm (27in).
Habitat: Mangroves, mudflats and estuaries.
Nest: Sticks and similar material.
Eggs: 2, pale blue or greenish with brown blotches.
Food: Crustaceans, small fish and amphibians.

Whistling heron

Syrigma sibilatrix

Unlike most herons, the whistling heron is often encountered in areas of wet grassland rather than in standing water, although it may be observed in flooded fields and similar localities. In suitable areas where food can be found in abundance, these herons may congregate in groups of more than 100 birds, although they are more likely to be observed individually or in pairs. Their name is derived from their whistling calls, which have been likened to the sound of a flute.

Identification: Rigid black plumes at the rear of the head. The face is mainly black, with a white area under the chin and a large area of blue skin encircling the eyes. The neck and breast are a buff colour, becoming paler on the underparts. The back is greyish with black edging to the brownish feathers on each wing. The legs are fairly dark. The reddish bill becomes dark at the tip. Sexes alike. Young birds have streaking on the neck.

Distribution: Two distinct populations in South America: one in eastern Colombia and Venezuela; one further south, extending from Bolivia as far as south-east Brazil and north-east Argentina.
Size: 61cm (24in).
Habitat: Mainly wet grassland.
Nest: Platform of sticks.
Eggs: 3–4, pale blue with speckles.
Food: Invertebrates, also amphibians and reptiles.

Green ibis (*Mesembrinibis cayennensis*):
58cm (23in)
Occurs from eastern Costa Rica and Panama across much of the South American continent east of the Andes mountain range. Very dark overall with greenish suffusion on the wings and loose greenish plumage at the back of the head. The young lack the gloss on their plumage. Sexes are alike.

Whispering ibis (*Phimosus infuscatus*):
54cm (21in)
Two separate populations: one extends across northern South America from north-east Colombia and eastern Ecuador eastwards; the other occurs south of the Amazon in Brazil, Bolivia, Paraguay, Argentina and Uruguay. Blackish overall, with a bare area of reddish skin on the face. Bill is yellowish, legs are reddish. Sexes alike.

Buff-necked ibis (*Theristicus caudatus*):
76cm (30in)
Found in Colombia, Venezuela and French Guiana south to northern Argentina and Uruguay. Buff neck, darker on the crown. Mainly grey wings, with a characteristic white area. Buff on the chest, with black underparts. Sexes alike.

Black-crowned night heron (*Nycticorax nycticorax*): 64cm (25in)
Central North America through much of South America to Tierra del Fuego. Black back and crown, offset against a whitish face. Wings and tail are grey, and the underparts are white. Short legs. Hens are smaller in size, with shorter head plumes. Young birds are brown.

Sun bittern

Eurypyga helias

The sun bittern has no close relatives and resembles a rail in some respects. It has a relatively long tail and there is no webbing apparent between its toes. This bird has a fiery, brilliant coloration on the flight feathers and uses these to stunning effect during its mating display. Relatively little is known about the habits of these rather shy birds, which are most likely to be encountered on their own, or sometimes as pairs in damp areas of tropical forest. They use their bills to probe for food in wet areas, but rarely enter the water itself, and they do not fly far.

Identification: Black head with prominent white stripes above and below the eyes, and another white area on the throat. Neck and upperparts are brownish, broken with variable markings ranging from chestnut through grey to black. Orange areas on the wings are most apparent in flight. Dark markings also on the brownish breast, which becomes paler, almost whitish, on the underparts. Bill is straight and yellowish on the upper part. Legs are orangish yellow. Sexes alike.

Distribution: From southern Mexico south to western Ecuador and east to northern Argentina and Uruguay. Occasionally in Chile.
Size: 48cm (19in).
Habitat: Near streams in wooded areas.
Nest: Globular in shape, made of vegetation and mud.
Eggs: 2, buff with dark spots at the larger end.
Food: Invertebrates.

Roseate spoonbill

Ajaia ajaja

The distinctively enlarged and flattened tips on the spoonbill's beak are very sensitive. They act like a pair of hands, allowing these birds both to detect and grab crabs and similar creatures underwater without difficulty. Roseate spoonbills sometimes immerse their entire head when feeding, although they are more usually observed sweeping their heads from side to side in a characteristic way. These birds are often seen in small flocks on marshland and similar land near coasts. They nest off the ground, building loose piles of sticks.

Identification:
Predominantly pink in colour, variable in hue, with a more prominent scarlet patch on the shoulders. Has the characteristic spoon-shaped bill and bare greenish skin on the face. Sexes are alike. Young birds are much paler, with whiter areas on head, neck and breast.

Distribution: From southern USA into northern and eastern parts of South America as far south as Argentina. Also occurs in the Caribbean.
Size: 81cm (32in).
Habitat: Wetland areas, typically coastal areas including mangrove swamps.
Nest: Made of sticks.
Eggs: 3, white, brown spots.
Food: Small fish, amphibians and other aquatic creatures.

DUCKS, GEESE AND SWANS

Ducks are a group of waterfowl characterized by their relatively small size compared to swans and geese. They often inhabit stretches of open water, although they are typically quite secretive when nesting. Drakes usually moult before the onset of the breeding season into much more colourful plumage. For the remainder of the year they have duller, so-called "eclipse" plumage and more closely resemble hens.

Carolina wood duck

American wood duck *Aix sponsa*

Distribution: Occurs widely over much of North America and south to Mexico, being present in western, central and south-eastern parts of the continent, as well as on western Cuba.
Size: 51cm (20in).
Habitat: Wooded stretches of fresh water.
Nest: In tree holes.
Eggs: 5–9, buff.
Food: Mainly vegetable matter, from acorns to aquatic plants.

Although these ducks have been seen as far north as Alaska, they move south to warmer climes for the winter months. In some areas their numbers have benefited from the provision of artificial nesting boxes, so that today they rank among the most common water-fowl in the United States. Carolina wood ducks are likely to be seen dabbling for food in open stretches of water, dipping their heads under the surface, but they also come ashore to nibble at vegetation. Although vagrants sometimes crop up in the Caribbean, Carolina wood ducks observed in other parts of the world will be descendants of escapees from waterfowl collections.

Identification: Crest with glossy green and purple tones in breeding plumage. The lower neck and breast are chestnut with white speckling, while the abdomen is buff with barring on the flanks. Cock resembles the hen in eclipse plumage, but with a more brightly coloured bill. The hen is duller in overall coloration, with dark brown underparts.

Muscovy duck

Cairina moschata

These dull-coloured waterfowl are far removed in appearance from their more brightly coloured domesticated counterparts. They prefer freshwater areas but sometimes move into saltwater lagoons during the dry season. Muscovies live in groups and are arboreal by nature, with powerful claws that help them to climb trees and roost easily on branches. They generally prefer to nest off the ground, but in areas where they are not commonly hunted, hens may lay eggs on the ground in spots that are well camouflaged by surrounding vegetation. The young develop the white wing patches at one year of age.

Identification: Mainly black but with white patches on the wings and glossy greenish suffusion on the surrounding plumage. Has a prominent, dull reddish-purple bill knob. Hens are smaller and lack the knob on the bill. Young birds can be distinguished by their lack of white plumage.

Distribution: From Mexico south to parts of Argentina and Uruguay.
Size: 84cm (33in).
Habitat: Forested lakes and marshes.
Nest: Usually in a tree hollow.
Eggs: 8–15, white with greenish suffusion.
Food: Omnivorous.

Hooded merganser

Lophodytes cucullatus

These ducks occur only in small groups of often less than a dozen individuals. They can be difficult to observe, either when resting alongside the water or even when swimming and darting under the surface in search of food. In the far north, hooded mergansers fly south when their freshwater habitat starts to freeze at the onset of winter, often moving to coastal estuaries. They breed off the ground and sometimes nest as high as 25m (80ft) up in suitable trees. They can fly well, displaying great manoeuvrability at low levels.

Identification: Drakes have a white fan, edged with black, at the rear of the head. The face is black. The chest is white with black-and-white striping behind. The flanks are chestnut and the back is black. Ducks are mainly brown with a bushy crest. Cocks in eclipse plumage resemble hens but have yellowish rather than brown irises, and darker bills.

Distribution: Two distinct populations, one ranging south from Alaska on the western side of North America. The other extends widely over the east of the continent.
Size: 50cm (19in).
Habitat: Lakes and slow-flowing areas of water near woodland.
Nest: In tree hollows.
Eggs: 6–12, white.
Food: Mainly fish.

Barrow's goldeneye (*Bucephala islandica*): 53cm (21in)
Separate populations in western and eastern North America, also present on Greenland and Iceland. Dark green glossy head, with a white patch in front of each eye, and mainly white underparts. Cocks in eclipse plumage have black bills and retain the black-and-white barring on the sides of the wings. Hens are darker and duller, with a distinctive golden eye.

Ruddy duck (*Oxyura jamaicensis*): 43cm (17in)
Occurs across much of North America and down the west side of South America. Broad bill and upright tail feathers. Chestnut-brown coloration (replaced by brown in eclipse plumage), with black and usually white plumage on the head. Some regional variations in appearance. Hens are predominantly brown.

Whistling swan (tundra swan, *Cygnus columbianus*): 150cm (58in)
Breeds in the Arctic, with wintering populations in western and eastern USA. White, with small yellow patch sometimes evident on blackish bill. Sexes alike, but males may be larger. Young birds are greyer, with more reddish-orange bills.

Ross's goose (*Anser rossii*) 66cm (26in)
Breeds in the far north of central Canada, near the Perry River, wintering in south-west USA and along the Mexican border. Occurs in both snow (white) and blue phases, like its relative, the snow goose (*A. caerulescens*), retaining the white plumage on the head in its blue phase. Sexes alike, but males are often larger.

American wigeon

Anas americana

These wigeon are sometimes seen well outside their normal range, with reports of sightings in locations as far apart as Hawaii, the Komandorskiye Islands off Siberia and Europe. Almost every year a few vagrant American wigeon are recorded by birdwatchers in the British Isles. The ability of these ducks to cross the Atlantic Ocean is all the more surprising because they are essentially vegetarian in their feeding habits, browsing on plants in and out of the water. A number of American wigeon also migrate south each year to South America, and are observed here in larger numbers outside the breeding season.

Distribution: Much of North America, including the far north. Often moves southwards in winter.
Size: 56cm (22in).
Habitat: Freshwater marshland.
Nest: In a hollow often hidden in grass, lined with down feathers.
Eggs: 6–12, creamy white.
Food: Aquatic vegetation, small aquatic invertebrates.

Identification: In breeding condition, a prominent white stripe extends back over the top of the head, with a broad dark green area incorporating the eyes, and speckling beneath. The remainder of the plumage is brownish with a white belly and broader white area on the lower body close to the tail. Ducks have completely speckled heads and lack the drake's white forewing, which is retained in the eclipse plumage. The duck has paler chestnut coloration than the drake in eclipse plumage.

COTINGAS

The cotingas include some of the most colourful of all tropical birds, although their name comes from an Amazonian native American word meaning "washed white", which is used locally to describe the white bellbird. Their diet consists mainly of fruits and berries, and this group of birds is important in the dispersal of plants – undigested seeds from their food are passed on to the ground.

Scarlet cock-of-the-rock

Andean cock-of-the-rock *Rupicola peruviana*

With their spectacular bright red plumage, males frequently congregate together at traditional displays sites called leks, often deep in the forest. Here they seek to entice hens to mate with them. Their display calls have been likened to the squealing of pigs, although these cotingas are not noisy by nature. Their brilliant plumage blends into the dark background in the forest, making them hard to observe. The hen constructs her nest using damp mud.

Distribution: Colombia and Venezuela to parts of Ecuador, Peru and Bolivia.
Size: 32cm (12.5in).
Habitat: Humid, rocky areas of forest, often in ravines close to water.
Nest: Cup made of mud, located in a secluded rocky outcrop or cave.
Eggs: 2, buff with darker spotting.
Food: Mainly berries and other fruit.

Identification: Brilliant red dominates in the plumage, with crest feathers extending down over the bill, contrasting with black on the back and wings. Hens are significantly duller in colour, and are generally reddish brown with a smaller crest.

Fiery-throated fruiteater

Pipreola chlorolepidota

This is the smallest of the Andean fruiteaters. It is found at a lower altitude than related species, typically less than 1,000m (3,280ft) above sea level, in the foothills of the Andes. These members of the cotinga clan are most likely to be observed singly or in pairs. They may breed throughout the year, building a moss nest lined with small roots, usually close to the ground and often disguised in a creeper. The fiery-throated fruiteater is unusual in that it does venture up into the canopy of the forest, although it is also commonly seen in the lower levels, often seeking food in the company of other birds.

Identification: The underparts are dark green, with a yellowish-orange throat area; remainder of the plumage is also green. Bill is reddish. Hens closely resemble female scarlet-breasted fruiteater (*P. frontalis*), being predominantly green, with yellow barring extending from the throat over the entire underparts.

Distribution: Eastern areas of Ecuador and Peru.
Size: 11cm (4in).
Habitat: Humid tropical forest.
Nest: Cup-shaped.
Eggs: Probably 2, creamy and spotted.
Food: Mainly berries and other fruit, also invertebrates.

Orange cock-of-the-rock (Guianan cock-of-the-rock, *Rupicola rupicola*): 32cm (12.5in)
·Found in the Guianas west to Colombia, also in northern Brazil. Unmistakable shade of brilliant orange. The hen is mainly olive brown with an orange suffusion on the rump.

Pompadour cotinga (*Xipholena punicea*): 20cm (8in)
Extends from Colombia, eastwards to the Guianas and south to north-west Brazil. Wine-red plumage with white areas on the wings. Hens are grey, with white edging to some wing feathers. The eyes are whitish.

Plum-throated cotinga (*Cotinga maynana*): 19cm (7.5in)
Ranges from south-eastern Colombia to northern Bolivia and Amazonian Brazil. Turquoise with a small plum-coloured throat patch. Hens are brown with pale edges to the feathers. They have cinnamon plumage on the lower abdomen.

Barred fruiteater (*Pipreola arcuata*): 22cm (8.5in)
Found in Andean region of western South America at altitudes of 3,200m (10,500ft) in cloud forest. Blackish head, with barring confined to the chest and underparts, which are green in hens.

Red-crested cotinga (*Ampelion rubrocristatus*): 23cm (9in)
Found in the Andean region of Colombia and western Venezuela south to northern Bolivia. Greyish brown, with a blacker tone on the head, back and wings. Reddish crest at the back of the head is often kept flat. Undertail coverts are streaked with white. White areas on the underside of the tail. Bill is white with a black tip. Iris is red. Sexes alike.

Long-wattled umbrellabird

Cephalopterus penduliger

As the name suggests, the male of this species has a bizarre black-feathered wattle extending down from his chest that measures approximately 30cm (12in) long. It is inflated as part of his display, but shortened during flight and held close to the chest. The flight pattern of umbrellabirds is not dissimilar to that of woodpeckers, low and strong over the trees. Quiet by nature, solitary and rarely observed, males are most likely to be seen displaying on bare branches, when their booming calls are uttered. These calls are heard with increasing frequency during the nesting season, although it appears that the hen alone is responsible for rearing the offspring.

Identification:
Predominantly black in colour. Very long wattle, which is greatly reduced in females. Both have relatively small crests. Brown eyes help to distinguish these cotingas from related umbrellabirds.

Distribution: Western Colombia and north-western Ecuador.
Size: 51cm (20in) cock; 46cm (18in) hen.
Habitat: Lowland tropical forest.
Nest: Platform of twigs.
Eggs: 1, khaki coloured.
Food: Mainly palm fruits and insects.

Purple-breasted cotinga

Cotinga cotinga

One of the most striking features of these cotingas is their small yet broad bills, which allow them to pluck and swallow quite large fruits whole. They belong to the group often known as the blue cotingas, so-called because of the predominant colour of the cock bird. Individuals are most likely to be seen perching on dead treetops, although they fly with a strange rattling noise, which is thought to be caused by the modified shape of their flight feathers. Little is known about their breeding habits, but it is believed that hens incubate and rear their chicks on their own.

Identification:
Silhouette is like that of a dove. Distinctive reddish-purple feathering from the throat down to the middle of the belly; the remainder of the body is violet blue, apart from the black wings and tail. Small yet broad bill. Hens are dark brown, with white edging to the feathers, creating a scaly appearance over the whole body.

Distribution: Eastern Colombia to the Guianas and Brazil.
Size: 19cm (7.5in).
Habitat: Lowland tropical forest.
Nest: Small, flimsy and cup-shaped.
Eggs: Probably 1–2, bluish with rusty-brown markings.
Food: Primarily fruit.

QUETZALS, TROGONS AND JACAMARS

Quetzals have a special mythical significance in ancient New World culture and feature prominently in Mayan legend and symbolism. Trogons as a group have a much wider distribution overall, with relatives in the Old World. Jacamars are mainly found in South rather than Central America, and are characterized by their slim body shape, long tails and narrow bills.

Crested quetzal

Pharomachrus antisianus

Distribution: Colombia and western Venezuela to Brazil in the east and southwards as far as Bolivia.
Size: 33cm (13in).
Habitat: Humid forest. Typically occurs in cloud forest in the Andean region up to an altitude of about 3,000m (9,840ft).
Nest: Tree holes or termite nests.
Eggs: 2, light blue.
Food: Berries, other fruit and also invertebrates.

Quetzals have a distinctive, upright stance when perching, when they rest so quietly that they are easily overlooked. They are most likely to be seen close to fruiting trees on which they feed. These quetzals have an undulating flight pattern, and their calls are a loud sequence of rolling notes. The plumage of crested quetzals, like that of related species, is brightly coloured but fades quite rapidly after death, so museum specimens rarely display the vibrancy of living birds. Another unusual feature is their very thin skin.

Identification: Distinguished from other quetzals by the white undersides to the tail feathers; hens have barred feathering here. The hen can also be distinguished from the cock by her brown rather than green head, and a reduced area of red on the underparts. Young birds resemble the female.

White-tailed trogon

Trogon viridis

Like other trogons, the white-tailed may be sedentary for long periods, but is sufficiently agile to feed on fruit in flight, as well as to catch invertebrates on the wing. These trogons will also swoop on small vertebrate prey, such as lizards. The bill is short, but has a wide gape to facilitate swallowing. Their perching grip is unusual too, with two toes being directed in front of and behind the perch, rather than the more usual 3:1 perching configuration. In common with other trogons, they do not build a nest, but the hens simply lay their eggs in a suitable chamber. They have even been known to use a termite nest, and the presence of termites deters would-be predators. Here the nesting chamber is a hollow, constructed at the end of a tunnel that usually leads in an upwardly diagonal direction.

Identification: Glossy violet feathering from the head to the chest. Yellow underparts and a dark green back, with a distinctive, mainly white underside to the tail. Blue eye rings. Bill is bluish white. The hen is duller in appearance, slaty in colour with orangish-yellow underparts and a dusky upper bill.

Distribution: Costa Rica and Panama south to Colombia, Ecuador, Peru and Brazil. Also on Trinidad.
Size: 28cm (11in).
Habitat: Humid forest.
Nest: Usually in a tree hole.
Eggs: 2, light blue.
Food: Berries, other fruit and some invertebrates.

Pavonine quetzal (*Pharomachrus pavoninus*): 33cm (13in)
This is the only quetzal found east of the Andes mountains, ranging south to northern Bolivia. Distinctive red bill and red lower underparts, otherwise the plumage is a metallic shade of emerald green. The hen is less colourful and has a black underside to the tail.

Black-throated trogon (*Trogon rufus*): 25cm (10in)
Ranges from south-eastern Honduras down to Paraguay and north-eastern Argentina. Distinctive green-and-yellow coloration, separated on the chest by a thin white band. The hen is distinguished from the cock by her brown and yellow feathering.

White-eared jacamar (*Galbalcyrhynchus leucotis*): 20cm (8in)
Restricted to the northern part of the Upper Amazonian region. Recognizable by its large, pinkish bill and white areas of plumage behind the eyes. Reddish-chestnut overall with dark wings. Sexes alike.

Striped manakin (*Machaeropterus regulus*): 9cm (3.5in)
Extends from north-western South America, from Colombia and Venezuela south to Peru, Bolivia and Brazil, occurring in the Andes at altitudes of up to 1,500m (4,900ft). Brilliant red cap, with reddish streaking on the undersides of the body. The hen is a dull shade of green overall, and is paler and yellower on the underparts, with a white underside to the tail feathers. There are also darker streaks on the sides of the body, with a rufous hue on the flanks.

Paradise jacamar

Galbula dea

The jacamars form a group closely related to woodpeckers, and are members of the avian order Piciformes (which includes woodpeckers and trogons). Like trogons, they have a zygodactyl perching grip, with two toes directed forward over the perch and two behind. In common with related species, the paradise jacamar has a long, thin bill. It hunts insects on the wing, using its bill to grab prey in flight. These are not especially shy birds, and are most likely to be seen either in pairs or small parties in forest clearings or sometimes when swooping out across water. Their call note is a distinctive "pip" sound that is repeated frequently. These jacamars, unlike other species, often remain in the tree canopy, where they are difficult to observe thanks in part to their coloration. Paradise jacamars will often accompany groups of other birds, seizing any invertebrates that are disturbed as a result of the other birds' movements.

Identification: Distinctive dark body and a long tail that tapers along its length. White feathering under the throat and dark, glossy green wings. Bill is long and black. Sexes alike. The colour of the crown may be either pale grey or dark brown, depending on the race.

Distribution: Northern South America to parts of Brazil, Peru and Bolivia.
Size: 30cm (12in).
Habitat: Occurs in forest and more open country.
Nest: May excavate into the mounds of arboreal termites or a suitable bank.
Eggs: 2–4, glossy white.
Food: Invertebrates.

Golden-winged manakin

Masius chrysopterus

These small birds are most likely to be spotted flying through the understorey in forests, sometimes heading up into the canopy in search of fruit. Golden-winged manakins normally seek out berries, which they can pluck on the wing, as well as invertebrates, which figure more prominently in their diet during the breeding period when there are chicks in the nest. Little is known of their habits, but they appear to be relatively solitary by nature. Males use their bright wing coloration for display purposes.

Identification: Distinctive golden-yellow edging to the wings and a yellow crest on the forehead, with this colour extending on to the throat and back over the head, where it becomes orangish. The remainder of the plumage is glossy black. Hen is greenish, but with prominent yellow feathering in the vicinity of the chin and belly.

Distribution: In the Andean region of Colombia to Venezuela, Ecuador and Peru.
Size: 11cm (4in).
Habitat: Cloud forest and woodland.
Nest: Suspended cup-shape, made of moss and rootlets.
Eggs: 2, cream with brown spots.
Food: Berries and some invertebrates.

TOUCANS, ARACARIS AND TOUCANETS

Members of the toucan clan are virtually unmistakable, although not all of them have large, brightly coloured bills. Active and restless by nature, they often congregate in large numbers in fruiting trees, hopping from branch to branch. When roosting and breeding in tree holes where their bills could be an encumbrance, they pull their tail feathers up vertically and tuck their bills over their backs.

Crimson-rumped toucanet

Aulacorhynchus haematopygus

The term "toucanet" is applied to smaller members of this family, with green predominating in the plumage of all six *Aulacorhynchus* species. These toucanets are active and quite noisy birds, hopping from branch to branch in search of food. Eating is a two-stage process. Fruit is plucked and then skilfully tossed up into the air and swallowed whole. Stones (pits) are regurgitated later. Larger items can be held against the perch with the foot, allowing chunks to be torn off and then eaten in a similar way. The zygodactyl arrangement of these birds' toes, with two toes directed forwards and two behind the perch, helps them to hold their food securely.

Identification: Predominantly green, darker on the wings with distinctive red plumage over the rump. Dark, reddish-brown bill, with white at the base and prominent dull reddish skin encircling the eyes. Sexes alike.

Distribution: Colombia, Venezuela and Ecuador.
Size: 41cm (16in).
Habitat: Humid forest and secondary woodland.
Nest: Tree hollow.
Eggs: 3–4, white.
Food: Fruit, small vertebrates and invertebrates. May also steal eggs and chicks.

Toco toucan

Ramphastos toco

Distribution: The Guianas south to Brazil, Paraguay, Bolivia and northern Argentina.
Size: 53cm (21in).
Habitat: Unusual in ranging from forest to savanna. On rare occasions, large flocks have moved into towns where ripening fruit is plentiful nearby.
Nest: Hollow in tree, sometimes previously occupied by woodpeckers.
Eggs: 2, white.
Food: Berries other fruit and invertebrates. Also raids nests of other birds.

Just why toucans have such large, brightly coloured bills is something of a mystery. These lightweight, honeycombed structures contain a long, fringed tongue. Its function is unknown, but it probably helps these toucans to swallow food. It is thought that the bill may enable these birds to pluck fruits that would otherwise be out of their reach at the end of thin branches. The bright colours set against their subdued plumage may also be a useful defensive aid, and certainly, the serrated edges of the bill can inflict a painful wound. Toco toucans are less social by nature than other members of the family, although they may congregate in large groups in areas where food is plentiful. They have a call that has been likened to the sound of deep snoring.

Identification: Largest of the toucans. Glossy black plumage with prominent white bib on the throat and red around the vent. Bare area of bright blue skin around the eyes, with small area of surrounding yellow feathering. Large, broad bill displaying shades of yellow and yellowish-orange coloration, black at the base, with a prominent black tip to the upper bill. Sexes alike.

Lettered aracari

Pteroglossus inscriptus

These aracaris get their name from the traces on their upper bills, which look like lettering. Aracaris are social by nature, and are most likely to be observed in groups. It is thought that in some cases, the young of the previous year may remain with their parents and assist in the rearing of the following year's young. The chicks hatch with heel pads that help them to keep their balance, although their bills at this time are relatively small. These pads fall off once the young birds have left the nest. Aracaris and other toucans rely on an adequate number of tree holes for breeding purposes because, unlike woodpeckers, their bills are not strong enough to allow them to bore effectively into trees.

Identification: The lack of banding across the yellow feathering of the chest is distinctive. Upperparts are greenish. Traces similar to letters on the upper bill, whereas lower bill is mainly black. Sexes alike.

Distribution: Eastern Colombia to central and southern Brazil, and into northern Bolivia.
Size: 37cm (14.5in).
Habitat: Forested areas and more open woodland.
Nest: Tree holes.
Eggs: 2–3, white.
Food: Berries, other fruit, invertebrates and small vertebrates.

Red-billed toucan (*Ramphastos tucanus*): 61cm (24in)
Occurs in Venezuela and the Guianas into parts of Brazil and eastern Bolivia. Dark reddish sides to the bill, yellow on top, with a white chest and red band beneath. Predominantly black plumage elsewhere, although the vent area is red. Sexes alike.

Sulphur-breasted toucan (keel-billed toucan, *Ramphastos sulfuratus*): 48cm (19in)
Found in Central America, from southern Mexico to northern Colombia and Venezuela. Bill is pea-green with orange stripe on upper part. Brilliant yellow plumage on the chest, predominantly black elsewhere. Sexes alike.

Golden-collared toucanet (*Selenidera reinwardtii*): 33cm (13in)
Found in southern parts of Colombia, extending to parts of Ecuador, Peru and Brazil. Bill is a deep shade of red with a black tip. Plumage is mainly black and green, with a yellow collar and ear flashes. Hen has rufuous coloration, not black.

Spot-billed toucanet (*Selenidera maculirostris*): 33cm (13in)
Confined to Brazil. Predominantly ivory bill with black markings. Mainly black head and chest, whereas the hen has reddish-brown plumage here. Lower underparts are yellowish.

Many-banded aracari (*Pteroglossus pluricinctus*): 43cm (17in)
From Colombia and Venezuela south to northern Peru and Brazil. Black apart from ivory area down the sides of the upper bill. Two broad bands run across the underparts, which are pale yellow with reddish markings. Upperparts are dark. Blue skin around the eyes. Rump is red. Sexes alike.

Plate-billed mountain toucan

Andigena laminirostris

The four species of mountain toucan are all found at relatively high altitudes, and can be distinguished from the *Ramphastos* genus by their smaller bills. The plate-billed mountain toucan is so-called because of the presence of raised yellowish patches on each side of the beak. The function of these is unclear. Blue features prominently in the coloration of all mountain toucans, and the plumage is soft and quite loose. The wings of these toucans have the typical rounded shape associated with other members of the family, which means that they do not fly especially powerfully.

Distribution: Colombia and western parts of Ecuador.
Size: 51cm (20in).
Habitat: Humid and wet mountain forests.
Nest: Tree hollow.
Eggs: 2–3, white.
Food: Berries, other fruit, invertebrates and small vertebrates.

Identification: Characteristic yellow plate on each side of the upper bill, with black elsewhere and dull reddish base. Dark, sky-blue plumage on the underparts, with black cap on the head extending down the neck. Wings are olive brown. Sexes alike.

Left: Toucans roost and nest in tree holes.

BARBETS, BELLBIRDS, FRUITCROWS AND PUFFBIRDS

These birds are typical inhabitants of tropical forest. Barbets are also well represented in the Old World, whereas bellbirds and fruitcrows are confined to the Americas. Like other fruit-eating species, they have an important role in helping to spread the seeds of the plants on which they feed. Puffbirds, in contrast, feed on invertebrates and even on small vertebrates. They, too, occur only in the New World.

Toucan barbet

Semnornis ramphastinus

Distribution: Western parts of Colombia and Ecuador. Typically between 1,000 and 2,400m (3,280 and 7,870ft).
Size: 20cm (8in).
Habitat: Humid mountain forests.
Nest: Tree hollow.
Eggs: 2, white.
Food: Berries, other fruit and invertebrates.

The coloration of these barbets is not dissimilar to that of mountain toucans, which is how they got their name. Their bills, in contrast, are both stocky and powerful, enabling them to bore into wood to create or enlarge a nest in a tree hollow. Their tails are flexible, and can be carried either down or raised into a more vertical position. The toucan barbet's range is relatively restricted, and they tend not to be common, with just odd birds or pairs being sighted rather than groups. Like many barbets, they can call loudly, with members of a pair taking part in a duet of loud honking notes with each other. Calling of this type is most common during the nesting season.

Identification: Prominent bluish-grey area on the sides of the face and chest. Orangish-red underparts, becoming more yellowish towards the vent, with an olive-brown back and yellowish rump. Wings and tail are bluish-grey. Bill is tipped with black. Sexes alike.

Five-coloured barbet

Capito quinticolor

These barbets are not perhaps as colourful as their name might suggest. They have a localized distribution on the western (Pacific) side of the Andes, and they are not especially easy to observe, often occurring just as individuals hopping through the vegetation, or in pairs. They sometimes associate with other birds, possibly hoping to snatch invertebrates that may be disturbed as the flock moves from tree to tree. Five-coloured barbets do not range up into the mountains, but are found in lowland areas, at altitudes of 100m (330ft) or below.

Identification: Distinctive yellow V-shape at the top of the mainly black wings. The chest is predominantly white. Underparts are yellowish orange, with black spotting on the flanks and olive thighs. Hens have streaked upperparts and spotted underparts, and lack the crimson crown and nape seen in cocks.

Distribution: Restricted to western parts of Colombia, extending from Quibdó, Tadó and Chocó southwards along the Pacific coast as far down as western Nariño.
Size: 18cm (7in).
Habitat: Forested areas of the coastal lowlands.
Nest: Cavity in a tree.
Eggs: 3, white.
Food: Berries, other fruit and invertebrates.

Red-headed barbet (*Eubucco bourcierii*):
17cm (6.5in)
Ranges from Costa Rica and Panama south to
Colombia and Ecuador. Only cocks have red heads –
those of hens are greyish. Rest of the plumage is
greenish and striped on the underparts.

Prong-billed barbet (*Semnornis frantzii*):
18cm (7in)
Confined to western Panama and Costa Rica, where
this barbet is more common. Olive-green upperparts
with buff coloration on the upper breast. Crown is
a dull, golden-brown shade, with a raised crest
of glossy black feathers at the back of the head.
Lower bill is divided, with the tip of the upper bill
lying in the notch created where the two halves
join. Hens are easily distinguished from cocks by
the lack of black feathering.

White-necked puffbird (*Notharchus
macrorhynchus*): 25cm (10in)
The five recognized races of these puffbirds have
a wide distribution, ranging from Mexico south to
parts of Paraguay and north-eastern Argentina. This
species also occurs in Brazil and the Guianas. White
on the forehead, chest and abdomen. Black
elsewhere, in a band across the chest, around the
eyes and on the wings. Barred on the sides of
the body. Sexes alike.

Spotted puffbird (*Bucco tamatia*): 18cm (7in)
Northern South America, from Colombia, Venezuela
and the Guianas south through Ecuador to Peru and
east into Brazil. Cinnamon plumage across the
throat, black-and-white barring beneath, with a black
bar on the lower cheeks. Sexes alike.

Bare-throated bellbird

Procnias nudicollis

Bellbirds are named
because of the
sounds of the cock
bird's call, which
ranks among the
loudest and most
distinctive in the
avian world. The
hens, in contrast,
remain quiet.
When calling, the
cock bird chooses
a tall branch
in the tree
canopy, often
in quite a conspicuous
position, and subsequently
drops down to another
favoured branch lower in the
canopy. It is here that mating
may take place. The cock often uses
these two perches to carry out a
jumping display, dropping down on to
the lower branch to land in a crouched
position with his tail feathers spread.
Studies on this species have revealed
that bare-throated bellbirds move
seasonally, descending to lower altitudes
outside the breeding season.

Distribution: Southern Brazil,
north-eastern Argentina
and Paraguay.
Size: 24cm (9.5in).
Habitat: Montane forest.
Nest: Light and bowl-shaped,
often in a tree fork.
Eggs: 1, light tan with
brown mottling.
Food: Almost exclusively
frugivorous, feeding on
berries and other fruit.

Identification: Snowy-white
feathering, with blackish bill and
feet, plus a bare bluish-green
area under the throat extending
just around the eyes. Contrasting
dark irises, bill and legs. The
cock's calls are made by the
syrinx, located in the throat.
Hens are strikingly different, with
a dark head, green wings and
yellow-streaked underparts,
which become yellower on the
lower abdomen. Young birds
develop their bare throats by the
time they are one year old.

Purple-throated fruitcrow

Querula purpurata

Like bellbirds, these are cotingas, not corvids as their
common name might suggest. Purple-throated
fruitcrows are not active birds by nature, which means
they can be easily overlooked in forested areas. They are
most conspicuous either when in flight or feeding,
especially when they dart out quickly to seize berries or
feed in the company of other frugivorous birds such as
trogons. These fruitcrows live in groups of three or four
individuals, and although only the female incubates, all
members of the group provide
food for the young bird.
When displaying,
males inflate their
purple gorget of
feathers, which then
resembles a shield.

*Left: The fruitcrow's nest may be
at least 22m (70ft) off the ground.*

Distribution: Costa Rica and
Panama south to Amazonian
region of Brazil and
northern Bolivia.
Size: 28cm (11in).
Habitat: Tropical forest.
Nest: Cup-shaped, relatively
high off the ground.
Eggs: 1, blackish.
Food: Berries, other fruits
and invertebrates.

Identification: Predominantly black, with a distinctive area of purplish
plumage under the throat. Hens are entirely black in colour, as are
young birds of both sexes. The tail is quite short, with rounded wings.

CRACIDS, TINAMOUS AND GROUND BIRDS

There are a number of relatively large birds represented in the New World. The curassows, guans and chachalacas together form the family Cracidae. They tend to be more arboreal than the tinamous, which form a separate group. Antpittas and trumpeters are primarily ground-dwelling birds from this region, and they live and feed mainly on the forest floor.

Great tinamou

Tinamus major

Approximately 40 different species of tinamou occur from Mexico to the tip of South America. Like others of its kind, the great tinamou is difficult to observe, in spite of its size. These birds rarely fly unless there is danger close by, and they move quite quietly through the forest, where their coloration helps them to merge into the background. Their call consists of whistling notes, sometimes heard after dark. The nest is always well concealed in thick, inaccessible vegetation. The cock bird is believed to be largely responsible for incubating the eggs. The eggs themselves can vary quite widely in colour, even being violet in some cases. The chicks are able to move readily within a day of hatching. Their flight feathers grow rapidly, so that the young birds can fly when they are little bigger than a robin.

Identification: Large, plump appearance. Greyish-brown underparts, with a more olive hue across the back. White areas on throat, with chestnut feathering on the crown in many cases. Sexes alike but hens may be larger. Young birds are darker in colour than adults.

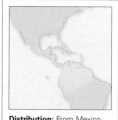

Distribution: From Mexico south to parts of Ecuador, Peru and Brazil, with approximately a dozen different subspecies being found throughout the area up to about 1,000m (3,280ft).
Size: 46cm (18in).
Habitat: Generally lowland areas in humid forests.
Nest: Leaf-lined scraping on the ground, often disguised in buttress roots.
Eggs: 6–7, glossy turquoise ranging to violet.
Food: Berries, seeds and invertebrates.

Andean guan

Penelope montagnii

These large birds are primarily arboreal by nature, living in groups of three to six individuals outside the breeding season. They tend to be encountered at higher altitudes than other guans, certainly in Colombia where they have been observed up to 3,500m (10,500ft). They sometimes leave the cover of dense forest in search of fruit, venturing into isolated trees where such food is plentiful. They usually forage in the branches, however, rather than on the ground. Andean guans have a loud honking call, which is heard more frequently during the breeding period. These birds have been heavily hunted, like related species, are shy, and avoid areas near human settlements.

Identification: Brownish overall, with greyish markings on the plumage extending from the head down to the breast. A small area of bare red skin forms the dewlap, which is often hard to observe from a distance, and the throat is more feathered than in other guans. Legs are reddish. Sexes alike.

Distribution: In the Andean region of Colombia, north-west Venezuela, Ecuador, Peru and Bolivia. This species may extend as far south as north-western parts of Argentina, although it is doubtful.
Size: 61cm (24in).
Habitat: Forested areas at relatively high altitudes.
Nest: Platform of leaves and twigs.
Eggs: 1–3, white.
Food: Berries, other fruit and seeds.

Grey-winged trumpeter

Common trumpeter *Psophia crepitans*

Distribution: North-western South America eastwards through the Guianas.
Size: 61cm (24in).
Habitat: Rainforest.
Nest: Leaf-lined tree cavity.
Eggs: 6, white.
Food: Fruits, plant matter and invertebrates.

Trumpeters are a common sight around native American settlements, and are easily tamed if obtained young. They make useful watchdogs, uttering loud grunts as warning calls. They are also valued for their snake-killing abilities, and these reptiles may feature as part of their natural diet. The plumage on the head and neck is short and has a velvety texture. Their overall appearance resembles that of miniature rheas, although trumpeters retain four toes on each foot. Their legs are powerful, allowing them not just to run but also swim effectively. Trumpeters spend most of their time on the ground, although they prefer to roost in trees when not active after dark.

Identification: Plumage predominantly black, with purplish feathering at the base of the neck. The plumage on the head is very short and has a plush texture. Grey coloration is apparent on the wings. Upright stance. Sexes alike.

Great curassow

Crax rubra

Distribution: Mexico southwards to Colombia and Ecuador.
Size: 91cm (36in).
Habitat: Lowland forest.
Nest: Platform off the ground.
Eggs: 2, rough-shelled, white.
Food: Plant matter.

The curassows tend to be more terrestrial than other cracids, although they invariably roost off the ground. Pairs also nest off the ground, sometimes at heights of up to 30m (100ft) in a suitable tree. Great curassows are most likely to be encountered individually or in pairs, rather than in larger groups. Cocks of this species have a deep, booming call and also utter high-pitched whistling notes. Their range has contracted in some areas, such as along the Pacific coast of Colombia, because of the combined effect of overhunting and deforestation. In areas where great curassows are not persecuted, these large birds are quite conspicuous.

Identification: Mainly black, with a white abdomen and undertail coverts. Striking yellow knob on the upper bill, which is absent in hens and immatures. Hens are mainly chestnut, but with black-and-white barring on the head and neck. Those from Central America may be darker and display more barring.

Above: There is a distinctive difference in appearance between the sexes.

Plain chachalaca (*Ortalis vetula*):
64cm (25in)
Southern Texas in the USA south to Mexico and Nicaragua, as well as the Honduran island of Utila. Predominantly brownish, with bare, blue skin on the face and flesh-coloured throat. Relatively noisy and quite adaptable by nature, in the face of primary deforestation. Sexes alike.

Band-tailed guan (*Penelope argyrotis*):
66cm (26in)
Found in parts of Venezuela and Colombia. Large red dewlap under the throat and frosty white plumage on the sides of the head. Has a distinctive pale tail band not seen in other guans, and also has a stocky appearance compared with related guans. Predominantly brown with white streaking on the breast and mantle. Sexes alike.

Wattled curassow (*Crax globulosa*):
89cm (35in)
South-eastern Colombia south to northern Bolivia and the western upper Amazonian region of Brazil. Predominantly black with a curly crest. Two distinctive red wattles at the base of the lower mandible, with a similar knob on the top of the bill at its base. These swellings are sometimes yellowish. Sometimes a marbled plumage patterning is evident over the wings. Hens have no wattles or knob, and have a white rather than chestnut belly and undertail coverts.

Giant antpitta (*Grallaria gigantea*):
27cm (10.5in)
Occurs in parts of Colombia and Ecuador, and lives on the forest floor. Reddish brown with black barring on the underparts. Olive-brown upperparts and greyish suffusion on the head. Sexes alike.

MACAWS

*The macaws include the largest and most spectacular members of the entire parrot family. All
17 species are characterized by their long tails and the prominent, largely unfeathered areas of skin on
their faces. Their distribution ranges from Central America
through to the southern parts of South America.*

Blue and gold macaw

Blue and yellow macaw *Ara ararauna*

Distribution: Eastern Panama
and Colombia south through
Amazonia to south-eastern
Brazil, Bolivia and Paraguay.
Size: 75–83cm (30–33in).
Habitat: Forested areas
near water.
Nest: Tall hollow tree.
Eggs: 2, white.
Food: Nuts, fruits and seeds.

Wooded areas are the normal habitat of these colourful macaws,
which usually feed in the treetops. Their presence there is
revealed by their loud, raucous calls, which are also uttered
when the birds are in flight. Although normally observed in
pairs or small family groups, blue and gold macaws do form
larger flocks, consisting of up to 25 individuals on occasion.
They are most likely to be observed during the morning and
again at dusk, as they fly back and forth between their roosting and feeding
sites. One of the main factors restricting the distribution of these macaws is
the availability of suitable palms as nesting sites. They are quite adaptable
in their feeding habits, eating a wide variety of plant matter and even
sometimes seeking nectar from flowers.

Identification: Predominantly blue upperparts, with contrasting golden-yellow underparts.
Greenish area on the forehead above the bill. Bare, unfeathered white skin on the sides of
the face, with small tracts of black feathers here and a black band beneath the throat.
Sexes alike. The rare Bolivian blue-throated macaw (*A. glaucogularis*) is similar in
its overall coloration, but can be distinguished by its prominent blue cheek patches.

Red and green macaw

Green-winged macaw *Ara chloroptera*

As in related species, these large macaws display isolated
feather tracts across the bare areas of skin on each
side of their face. Rather like fingerprints, this
feature is sufficiently distinctive to enable
individuals to be identified at close quarters.
Young birds display odd maroon rather
than crimson feathers here, and also have
dark eyes. Adult pairs remain together
throughout the year, although they may
not breed annually. They can live for
more than 50 years. Red and green
macaws usually feed in the canopy,
and are sometimes seen there in the
company of blue and gold macaws.
These parrots are able to use their feet like
hands to grasp their food. Pairs frequently
engage in mutual preening when resting in
trees during the hottest part of the day.

Identification: Rich crimson feathering
predominates, with both bluish and distinctive
green feathering evident on the lower part of the
wings. Sexes alike.

Distribution: Eastern
Panama in Central America
south across the Amazon
Basin to Bolivia, Brazil and
northern Argentina. Now very
rare in Panama and also at
the southern tip of its range
in Argentina, where there
never appears to have been
an established population.
Size: 73–95cm (29–37in).
Habitat: Forested areas.
Nest: Large hollow trees,
sometimes on cliff faces.
Eggs: 2, white.
Food: Fruits, seeds and nuts.

Spix macaw (Little blue macaw, *Cyanopsitta spixii*, E): 56cm (22in)
The last known survivor of this species in the wild disappeared towards the end of 2000, so the future of the species now depends on captive breeding of approximately 60 individuals surviving in collections around the world. These small macaws have only ever been sighted iin northern Bahia, north-eastern Brazil. Bluish plumage with a dark, greyish area of bare skin on the face. Sexes alike.

Great green macaw (Buffon's macaw, *Ara ambigua*, E): 77–85cm (30–33in)
There are several widely separated populations throughout its wide range, which extends from eastern Honduras to western parts of Colombia Mainly green plumage with a prominent area of red plumage above the bill. Whitish facial skin. Blue flight feathers, and a long reddish tail with a blue tip. Sexes alike.

Illiger's macaw (Blue-winged macaw, *Ara maracana*, E): 39cm (15in)
Deforestation has led to the disappearance of these small macaws from Argentina. They occur in wooded parts of Brazil, south of the Amazon, and to the south in Paraguay. Mainly green, with white skin around the eyes and a red forehead and rump. Some red on the belly. Sexes alike.

Red-bellied macaw (*Ara manilata*): 46cm (18in)
Northern South America, including Trinidad, south to Bolivia, Peru and north-east Brazil. Mainly green, with a bluer head and flight feathers. Bare yellowish area of skin surrounding the eyes. Reddish belly. Sexes alike.

Red and gold macaw

Scarlet macaw *Ara macao*

(E: Central America)

There are two different populations, with birds of Central American origin being recognizable by the blue tips to the prominent yellow feathers on the wings. Red and gold macaws are sometimes encountered in certain areas with other related multicoloured macaws, such as red and green macaws, although they do not appear to hybridize in the wild. Such mixed groups are most commonly observed congregating to feed on the soil of mineral-rich cliffs in parts of Peru. The mud that the parrots consume here is believed to neutralize plant toxins that they absorb as part of their diet. It appears that, certainly within some parts of their distribution, these macaws move seasonally in search of more plentiful feeding opportunities. They eat a considerable variety of foods, feeding in trees, rather than on or near the ground, which enables them to range widely across Central and South America.

Identification: The plumage of these large macaws is scarlet-red rather than crimson, which helps to distinguish them from the red and green macaw. Bright yellow plumage on the wings provides a further simple means of recognition. Sexes alike.

Distribution: Southern Mexico to Panama; widely distributed across the Amazonian region to Bolivia.
Size: 80–96cm (31–38in).
Habitat: Forested areas and savanna.
Nest: Hollow chamber in a tall tree.
Eggs: 2, white.
Food: Fruits, seeds and nuts.

Hyacinthine macaw

Hyacinth macaw *Anodorhynchus hyacinthinus* (E)

These vividly coloured macaws are the biggest parrots in the world. They fly with slow wingbeats and are usually seen in pairs or small family groups. Young hyacinthine macaws are unlikely to breed until they are seven years or even older, but these are potentially long-lived birds, with a life expectancy that can be measured in decades. They face relatively few predators, although in spite of their size and very powerful bills, they can fall victim to harpy eagles. In some areas hyacinthine macaws can be seen flying after dark, when the moon is shining. They are often noisy by nature, uttering a wide range of calls.

Identification: Predominantly a distinctive, deep shade of glossy blue, with prominent areas of bare yellow skin encircling the eyes and also present on the sides of the lower bill. Sexes alike.

Distribution: North-eastern Brazil, extending south-westwards to parts of Bolivia and Paraguay.
Size: 90–100cm (35–39in).
Habitat: Areas where Mauritia and other palms are growing.
Nest: Either a hollow tree or among rocks on inaccessible cliff faces.
Eggs: 2, white.
Food: Palm nuts, fruits and even water snails.

CONURES

Conures are a group of parakeets whose distribution is confined to parts of Central and South America. Their unusual name comes from the old generic name Conurus. *They are quite social birds by nature and are often seen in noisy flocks, congregating in large numbers where food is plentiful, and even invading agricultural regions on occasion.*

Queen of Bavaria's conure

Golden conure *Guaruba guarouba* (E)

Ranking among the most colourful of all conures, this species is most commonly seen in small groups. It occurs in regions where the forest is not subject to seasonal flooding, and so is absent from areas immediately adjacent to the Amazon River. Females sometimes share the same nest hole, with chicks of widely different ages being reared inside. The nesting chamber can be surprising deep, extending down for at least 2m (6.5ft). Deforestation is having an adverse effect on the numbers of these beautiful parrots, since they are dependent on older, more mature trees for nesting sites. Small flocks will sometimes descend to feed in fields, taking crops such as ripening maize, but they more commonly eat a variety of rainforest fruits and flowers.

Identification: Heavy bill, bright yellow coloration with no orange hues. Sexes alike. Young are a darker coloration, with green streaks on their upperparts.

Distribution: Centred on the Amazonia region of Brazil, south of the Amazon, and may range further afield.
Size: 36cm (14in).
Habitat: Rainforest extending to the edge of cultivated areas.
Nest: Cavity within a tree, up to 30m (100ft) above the ground.
Eggs: 2–4, white.
Food: Fruit and seeds, occasionally making raids on maize fields.

Sun conure

Aratinga solstitalis

The fiery coloration of these conures explains their common name. They are very social by nature, but in spite of their bright plumage, they can be hard to spot when roosting quietly on branches. When in flight, however, their sharp, harsh calls are often heard, drawing attention to the flock as it passes overhead. The coloration of sun conures often differs slightly between individuals, with some being of a brighter shade than others. The pattern of coloration is quite variable too, so it is often possible to distinguish between individuals in a flock. Large numbers of these conures may feed together on trees, and they have also been observed eating the fruits of cacti on the ground. It is possible that they move through their range according to the season, splitting up into smaller groups for much of the year.

Identification: The orange hues on the yellow plumage, black bill and smaller size distinguish this conure from Queen of Bavaria's conure. Sexes alike. Young are much duller, being largely green.

Distribution: Occurs in north-eastern parts of South America, being found mainly in parts of Guyana, Surinam and northern areas of Brazil. May also occur in French Guiana to the east.
Size: 30cm (12in).
Habitat: Palm groves, savanna and dry forest.
Nest: In hollows in palms or other trees.
Eggs: 3–4, white.
Food: Berries, other fruits, seeds and similar items. Sometimes cacti fruits.

Blue-crowned conure (*Aratinga acuticaudata*): 36cm (14in)
Occurs in separate populations in north-east, east and central-southern parts of South America. Green with dull bluish coloration on the crown. Sexes alike.

Yellow-eared conure (*Ognorhynchus icterotis*, E): 42cm (16in)
Northern Andean region of Ecuador and Colombia. A relatively large, almost macaw-like conure. Green body, with yellow extending from the bill to the tops of the eyes and across the underside of the cheeks. Sexes alike.

Patagonian conure (*Cyanoliseus patagonus*): Up to 50cm (20in)
Southern South America. Another relatively macaw-like conure, with distinctive, brownish wings, a grey chest broken by a band of variable white feathering, and golden-yellow underparts. Orangish-red area between the legs. Nests colonially in cliff faces. Sexes alike.

Slender-billed conure (*Enicognathus leptorhynchus*): 42cm (16in)
Restricted to Chile. Predominantly green, with red areas extending from the bill to the eyes and also present on the belly. Elongated upper mandible used to dig up roots. Also eats seeds. Sexes alike.

Green conure (*Aratinga holochlora*): 32cm (13in)
Extends from the far south of Texas in the USA south through Central America, occurring in eastern and southern Mexico south to northern Nicaragua. Predominantly green with a prominent white eye ring of bare skin and a pale bill. May be traces of yellow on the edge of the wings. The southern subspecies, known as the red-throated conure (*A. h. rubritorquis*), is easily distinguishable by its reddish throat.

Red-fronted conure

Wagler's conure *Aratinga wagleri*

Most conures of the genus *Aratinga* are predominantly green in colour, with the brighter coloration on their heads serving to distinguish the individual species. Red-fronted conures are noisy by nature, and their call notes resemble the braying of a donkey. They often congregate in large flocks consisting of as many as 300 individuals. Cliffs are favoured both as roosting and breeding sites, and are an important factor in determining the precise distribution of these conures within their range. Flocks of red-fronted conures sometimes descend into agricultural areas, where they are capable of causing serious damage to cultivated crops.

Identification: Red plumage may extend over the top of the head to just behind the eyes, depending on the race. Scattered red feathering may also be present on the throat. Thighs are red. Sexes alike. Young birds have greatly reduced area of red on the head.

Distribution: Discontinuous distribution down the western side of South America in the Andes mountains, from Venezuela to Peru.
Size: 36cm (14in).
Habitat: Most often in forested areas with cliffs nearby.
Nest: Often located on cliff faces.
Eggs: 3–4, white.
Food: A variety of wild and cultivated seeds and fruits, including maize crops.

El Oro conure

Pyrrhura orcesi

The *Pyrrhura* conures are sometimes known as the scaly-breasted conures because of the characteristic barring across their chests. Most of the species have restricted areas of distribution, and the El Oro conure was not discovered until 1980. It is believed to have a very restricted range, which may be no more than 100km (60m) long and 10km (6m) wide. There has been relatively little deforestation in this area, and the population appears to be quite stable where the forest is undisturbed. These conures are most likely to be observed feeding in the forest canopy, or flying overhead calling. They are typically seen in groups numbering between four and 12 individuals.

Identification: Red on the crown and bend of the wing. Chest barring is relatively indistinct in this particular species. Pale bill. Sexes alike. Young birds display less red.

Distribution: Apparently centred on El Oro province, Ecuador.
Size: 22cm (9in).
Habitat: Cloud forest, at altitudes between 600 and 1,300m (2,000–4,260ft).
Nest: Probably tree hollows.
Eggs: Not recorded.
Food: Fruits and seeds.

AMAZONS AND OTHER PARROTS

Amazon parrots are widely distributed in the New World from the extreme south of the USA and Mexico south through Central America and the Caribbean to South America. They are sometimes described as green parrots because this colour predominates in the plumage of many species. Pionus parrots are smaller in size, while the bizarre hawk-head is the only member of its group.

Imperial Amazon

Dominican Amazon *Amazona imperialis* (E)

The largest of all 27 species of Amazons, these parrots are also unusually coloured because most Amazons are predominantly green. It is sometimes seen in the company of the red-necked Amazon, and both are most likely to be seen in the vicinity of Dominica's highest mountain, Morne Diablotin. Hurricanes and agricultural development pose serious threats to the survival of these Amazons. Imperial Amazons have a wide range of call notes, which are often loud. Their alarm call has been likened to the sound of a trumpet. Pairs nest in hollow trees, but research suggests that they may breed only every two years or so, rather than annually, and then produce only a single chick.

Distribution: The Caribbean island of Dominica in the Lesser Antilles.
Size: 45cm (18in).
Habitat: Mountainous forest.
Nest: Tree cavities.
Eggs: 2, white.
Food: Fruits, nuts, seeds and palm shoots.

Identification: Green back. Purple neck and underparts. They can be confused with birds of prey owing to their large size and flight pattern (wingbeats followed by gliding). Sexes alike. Young have green on the cheeks.

Black-billed Amazon

Amazona agilis

Distribution: Central and eastern parts of Jamaica.
Size: 25cm (10in).
Habitat: Wet limestone forests and agricultural areas.
Nest: Tree cavities at least 18m (59ft) off the ground.
Eggs: 2, white.
Food: Fruits, seeds and nuts.

Two distinctive species of Amazon parrot inhabit the Caribbean island of Jamaica and sometimes associate together in mixed flocks. As its name suggests, the black-billed can be easily distinguished from the yellow-billed (*A. collaria*) by its beak coloration. Breeding occurs between March and May. These Amazons are shy birds by nature, and rarely tolerate a close approach. Their green plumage helps to conceal them in forests, making them very hard to spot, especially because they will remain silent if disturbed. Sadly, deforestation in various parts of the island is thought to be having an adverse effect on their numbers.

Identification: Mainly dark green with a bluish hue on the top of the head, black ear coverts and black edging to the feathers on the back of the head. Black bill. Sexes alike although hens may have some green feathers on the edge of the wings. Young birds lack any trace of red feathering on the wing edges, and this area is entirely green.

Mealy Amazon (*Amazona farinosa*): 38cm (15in)
Range extends from Central America, home of the distinctive blue-crowned race (*A. f. guatemalae*) across much of northern South America to Brazil. A large, green Amazon with a particularly raucous call. Sexes alike.

Red-necked Amazon (*Amazona arausiaca*, E): 40cm (16in)
Restricted to the Caribbean island of Dominica. Distinguished from the Imperial Amazon by its predominantly green coloration and distinctive red area of plumage across the throat, often extending to the upper breast. Sexes alike.

Thick-billed parrot (*Rhynchopsitta pachyrhyncha*, E): 38cm (15in)
Used to range regularly from Mexico into the US states of New Mexico and Arizona, particularly to the Chiricahua Mountains, but has suffered greatly from the clearance of pine trees, the cones of which provide its major source of food. Mainly green, with scarlet areas on the head, wings and thighs. Powerful bill. Sexes alike.

Dusky pionus (*Pionus fuscus*): 24cm (9.5in)
Occurs in lowland forests from the Colombian–Venezuelan border east to north-eastern Brazil. Unusual pinkish, purple and bluish-brown tones in its plumage. Sexes alike.

Hawk-headed parrot

Red-fan parrot *Deroptyus accipitrinus*

Completely unique among parrots, the hawk-headed possesses a stunning ruff of blue-edged, claret-red feathers at the back of its neck, which it can raise like a fan as part of its display. These parrots may be seen in small groups outside the breeding season. They feed largely in the treetops rather than descending to the ground, and raise their young either in natural tree hollows or in old woodpecker nests. Hawk-heads are noisy parrots, possessing a wide array of call notes. They often call loudly and fan the ruff of feathers around the neck if alarmed.

Distribution: Northern South America, to the east of the Andes mountains.
Size: 31cm (12in).
Habitat: Lowland rainforest.
Nest: Tree hollows, sometimes occupying old woodpecker nests.
Eggs: 2–3, white.
Food: Fruit, seeds, nuts and leaves.

Identification: These parrots fly quite slowly, with their tail feathers spread slightly apart. They may be confused with small hawks, thanks to the rounded tips to the wings and tail. Green back, wings and tail. Sexes alike. Young have some green feathering on the crown.

Blue-headed pionus

Blue-hooded parrot *Pionus menstruus*

The most widely distributed of the seven members of the *Pionus* genus, and one of the commonest New World parrots, the blue-headed is often seen either singly or in pairs, rather than in flocks. They do congregate in larger numbers in certain mineral-rich areas, consuming the soil in the company of other parrots. The mineral-rich soil is thought to neutralize toxins absorbed from their food, which is usually gathered in the forest canopy, although they occasionally raid maize fields. Blue-headed pionus are sometimes observed flying quite high and fast in a loose formation, when they become more conspicuous than many parrots. They often call loudly when in flight.

Identification: Rich dark blue head with black ear coverts. Otherwise green plumage overall. Bill has reddish markings on the sides. Sexes alike. Young birds have mainly green heads.

Distribution: Two separate populations: from southern Costa Rica to northern South America; also present over a wide area of central South America east of the Andes.
Size: 28cm (11in).
Habitat: Lowland tropical forest, into agricultural areas.
Nest: Tree cavities, or nest sites created by other birds.
Eggs: 2–4, white.
Food: Seeds, fruit and nuts, and sometimes maize.

SMALLER PARROTS AND PARAKEETS

The parrots of South America display their greatest range in size, from large macaws down to the small parrotlets that are often not much larger than the width of a human hand. Small species are often the hardest to spot, especially in a rainforest setting, because their coloration as well as their size helps to conceal their presence in this habitat.

Vulturine parrot

Pionopsitta vulturina

One of the most unusual of all parrots in terms of appearance, the vulturine parrot is so called because of its essentially unfeathered head, which is covered with fine, bristle-like plumage. It has been suggested that this characteristic has developed to stop the feathering becoming matted by fruit juices when these parrots feed. Young birds, distinguishable by their fully feathered heads, are believed to congregate in flocks on their own until they pair off for breeding. The call of the vulturine parrot is also very different from that of other parrots, and has a watery tone. These parrots are found in areas of lowland forest, where their presence is easily overlooked since they are quiet by nature.

Identification: Bald, blackish face with adjacent yellow area of plumage around the neck. Sexes alike. Young birds have fully feathered greenish heads and less yellow on the neck. Like that of the adults, the base of the bill (cere) is unfeathered and prominent.

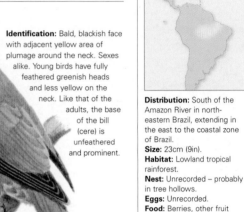

Distribution: South of the Amazon River in north-eastern Brazil, extending in the east to the coastal zone of Brazil.
Size: 23cm (9in).
Habitat: Lowland tropical rainforest.
Nest: Unrecorded – probably in tree hollows.
Eggs: Unrecorded.
Food: Berries, other fruit and seeds gathered in the forest canopy.

White-bellied caique

Pionites leucogaster

Most likely to be seen in small flocks, white-bellied caiques are quite bold by nature, and often tolerate a relatively close approach before flying off rapidly. Their wings make an unusual whirring sound as they become airborne, and are quite small relative to the birds' size. If disturbed, white-bellied caiques call out loudly. Their other call notes are more varied, and some have been likened to the sounds of tapirs. They sometimes associate in groups with blue-headed pionus, and can often be observed close to waterways, being less common in drier parts of their range in the south. Three distinct races of the white-bellied caique are recognized through the range of this species. In some cases the coloration of the tail feathers is yellow rather than green and the plumage on the thighs is also yellow.

Identification: White underparts and a yellow head distinguish this caique from other parrots in the region, notably the black-headed caique, which borders its northerly range. Sexes alike. Young birds have a brown crown and nape.

Distribution: Occurs in the area of central South America, south of the Amazon from Brazil to south-eastern Peru and northern Bolivia. Has also been reported in the eastern part of Ecuador, but its occurrence here is still to be verified.
Size: 23cm (9in).
Habitat: Lowland rainforest.
Nest: Usually high up in a tree cavity.
Eggs: 2–4, white.
Food: Berries, other fruit, seeds and nuts.

Red-winged parrotlet

Blue-fronted parrotlet *Touit dilectissima*

Distribution: Panama south into north-western South America where the species' precise range is still unclear. Extends south to near the Peruvian border.
Size: 15cm (6in).
Habitat: Wet forests, sometimes ranging up into cloud-forest areas.
Nest: Chamber located in arboreal termites' nests.
Eggs: Probably about 5, white.
Food: Berries, other fruit, blossoms and seeds.

The parrotlets can all be recognized by their small size and rather dumpy body shape, with short, squat tails. The red-winged, like related parrotlets, is quiet and easily overlooked in the forest canopy. Although three separate populations of these inconspicuous parrotlets have been identified, it is possible that these are not actually isolated, although this species is considered to be scarce in Central America. Red-winged parrotlets feed and roost in small groups, eating both seeds and fruit. They fly low over the trees, when their high-pitched calls are most likely to be heard. Their yellow underwing coverts are also conspicuous in flight.

Identification: Mainly green, with blue feathering on the front of the head. Pronounced areas of red feathering on the sides of the wings, reduced in hens. Young birds resemble hens, but their heads are predominantly green.

Spot-winged parrotlet (*Touit stictoptera*): 18cm (7in)
Scattered distribution in the eastern Andes, from Colombia to Peru, in mature, subtropical forests. Mainly green with blackish-brown area on the wings. Sexes similar except that cocks have white, spot-like edging to some of the wing feathers.

Golden-plumed conure (*Leptosittaca branickii*, E): 35cm (14in)
Andean region in forested areas. Recognizable by elongated, tufted band of yellow plumage under the eyes; rest of the plumage is green. Orangish suffusion on the breast. Sexes alike.

Rusty-faced parrot (*Hapalopsittaca amazonina*): 23cm (9in)
Occurs at relatively high altitudes in the Andean cloud forests of Colombia and Venezuela. Mainly green, with yellow streaking on the sides of the heads, lacking in young birds. Sexes alike.

Short-tailed parrot (*Graydidascalus brachyurus*): 23cm (9in)
Widely distributed along the Amazon and its tributaries, from Peru, Ecuador and Colombia in the west to French Guiana and Brazil. Predominantly green parrots with a plump appearance. Very noisy by nature. Often seen in large numbers on river islands. Sexes alike.

Cobalt-winged parakeet

Blue-winged parakeet *Brotogeris cyanoptera*

Distribution: Western area of the Amazon Basin, from Venezuela to Bolivia.
Size: 18cm (7in).
Habitat: Forests and open areas where trees are available nearby for roosting.
Nest: Probably tree holes but may use arboreal termite mounds.
Eggs: 5, white.
Food: Fruit and seeds.

Identification: Predominantly green, with cobalt blue flight feathers and an orange spot under the chin. Sexes alike. Young birds have greyer bills.

The seven species of the *Brotogeris* group are represented in both Central and South America. They are quite dumpy birds, all of similar size, with relatively narrow tail feathers. Green usually predominates in their plumage. They tend to be noisy, social birds by nature. Cobalt-winged parakeets are fast on the wing. Although they are sometimes seen flying across open areas and clearings, they tend to spend more time in the forest canopy than other members of the group, where their size and coloration make them relatively hard to observe. They are most likely to be encountered in lowland forests, sometimes in areas where seasonal flooding occurs.

WOODPECKERS

These birds are highly adapted to living in woodlands, and are able to hop up vertical trunks supported by their rigid, prong-like tail feathers and their powerful feet and claws. The largest member of the family, the ivory-billed woodpecker (Campephilus principalis), which measures 50cm (20in), is now believed to be extinct in the south-eastern USA, with just a tiny population surviving on Cuba.

Cream-coloured woodpecker

Celeus flavus

Distribution: Colombia and the Guianas south to Bolivia and Brazil.
Size: 28cm (11in).
Habitat: Wooded areas near water, ranging from mangrove to rainforest.
Nest: Tree hollow.
Eggs: 3, white.
Food: Invertebrates and possibly some vegetable matter.

In spite of their name, some of these woodpeckers are of a more yellowish shade than others, while buffish and cinnamon-white individuals are also known. Cream-coloured woodpeckers have a very distinctive call that sounds somewhat like a laugh. There is usually a close bond between members of a pair. These woodpeckers are likely to be encountered in a wide range of habitats, from mangrove swamps to savanna. They can also be found in agricultural areas, particularly coffee plantations, where they help to control insect pests.

Identification: Predominantly cream, although coloration can be quite variable, with an obvious crest. Crimson patches on the sides of the face. Wing coverts are brownish. Tail is black. Odd brown feathers may be apparent on the underparts. Hens lack the crimson plumage on the sides of the head.

Crimson-bellied woodpecker

Campephilus haematogaster

These large woodpeckers are not easy to spot, especially since they are more likely to be observed as individuals rather than as pairs or in larger groups. They are most commonly seen in the understorey, frequently quite low down on bigger trees in dense forest. They eat a variety of invertebrates, including the larvae of wood-boring beetles up to 15cm (6in) long, which they pull out from the bark using their strong, chisel-shaped bills. Crimson-bellied woodpeckers make a double rap when drumming, like related species, and have an alarm call that resembles a loud squeal. They tend to frequent relatively wet areas of montane habitat. The plumage of these woodpeckers typically appears less brightly coloured when it is worn, and the white barring on the undersides of the flight feathers can be seen only in flight.

Identification: Prominent area of red on the head. Two black stripes beneath, bordered by two yellowish-white stripes. The lower one is more extensive in hens, whose black feathering extends to the lower neck. Wings are black, rump is crimson. Underparts are crimson and black, and are blacker in the case of hens.

Distribution: Western Panama south to parts of Ecuador. Occurs in two apparently separate populations, with the nominate race ranging from eastern parts of Colombia south to Peru.
Size: 33cm (13in).
Habitat: Tropical forest.
Nest: Tree hollow.
Eggs: 2, white.
Food: Invertebrates.

Red-bellied woodpecker (*Melanerpes carolinus*): 23cm (9in)
South-eastern Canada and USA to southern Florida and the Gulf Coast. Red plumage from the bill over the head to the nape of the neck. This characteristic is usually absent in hens, or very greatly reduced. Black-and-white barred back and wings. Underparts are pinkish grey. These woodpeckers eat a wide variety of foods, ranging from fish to oranges, through the year.

Acorn woodpecker (*Melanerpes formicivorus*): 23cm (9in)
Western USA through Central America to Colombia. Black area encircling front of the face with a white band behind, encircling the eyes. Black streaking on the white breast, and the rest of the underparts are white. Scarlet area on the nape is absent in hens. Most likely to be found in oak woodland. Stores acorns as winter food.

Golden-naped woodpecker (*Melanerpes chrysauchen*): 19cm (7.5in)
Costa Rica to Panama and northern Colombia. Distinctive golden-yellow nape and red crown, with black plumage extending from the sides of the head to the back, where there is a broad white stripe. Hens are less colourful overall. Often drums on wood with its bill.

Powerful woodpecker (*Campephilus pollens*): 37cm (14.5in)
Andean region, from Colombia to Peru. Scarlet crest with white stripes extending from each side of the face over the wings, to create a V-shape here. White back and rump. Underparts barred. Hens lack the scarlet on the head, and have darker underparts.

Black-backed three-toed woodpecker

Picoides arcticus

Ranging over a huge area, these woodpeckers are most likely to be seen where there are numerous dead pine trees, especially if the surrounding area is flooded. They often occur in groups, breeding together in close proximity where conditions are favourable. In some years, flocks may move further south than usual, occasionally crossing into the US states of Nebraska, New Jersey and Ohio. This type of movement, known as an irruption, is usually the result of a shortage of food.

Distribution: Canada and northern USA, from Alaska east to Newfoundland in the north and south to New York State and California.
Size: 24cm (9.5in).
Habitat: Coniferous forest.
Nest: Tree hollow.
Eggs: 2–6, white.
Food: Mainly invertebrates, but also some vegetable matter, such as nuts.

Identification: Yellowish plumage on the head and crown, with two white stripes on each side of the face separated by an irregular, broad, black band. Wings and back are blackish, with some whitish feathering. The flanks of some birds are blacker than others, depending on the subspecies. The short inner hind toe, equivalent to the thumb, is missing, helping these birds to climb vertically. Hens are smaller and lack any yellow on the crown. Young birds are browner in colour, but with more white plumage on the wings. Markings on the underparts are not as clear as those of adults.

Red-headed woodpecker

Melanerpes erythrocephalus

These woodpeckers eat a wide range of plant and animal foods, and their diet is influenced by the season. They are unusual in that they hunt not only by clambering over the bark of trees, but also by hawking insects in flight. They will even swoop down on to the ground and hop along there seeking prey. Red-headed woodpeckers also raid the nests of other birds, seizing both eggs and chicks, as well as catching mice. In northern parts of their range, these woodpeckers often migrate southwards during the colder months of the year, seeking plentiful supplies of acorns and beech nuts when other foods are in short supply. They also lay down stores of food, concealing larger insects in cavities or hiding them under the bark, and returning to eat them later.

Distribution: Canada and the USA, ranging from Manitoba and southern Ontario in the north, southwards to Florida.
Size: 24cm (9.5in).
Habitat: Open woodland.
Nest: Tree hollow.
Eggs: 4–10, white.
Food: Plant and animal matter.

Identification: Scarlet plumage covering the head, bordered by a narrow band of black feathering. White underparts, bluish-black coloration on the back, part of the wings and the tail. Sexes alike. Young birds are much browner overall, including the head.

TANAGERS

The tanager group is comprised of approximately 240 different species, with representatives found throughout the Americas. The largest of the tanagers, up to 28cm (11in) long, is the magpie tanager (Cissopis leveriana), so-called because of its black and white plumage. Tanagers occur at a wide range of altitudes, from sea level up into the Andean region. Some North American species are migratory.

Paradise tanager

Tangara chilensis

These tanagers are rather shy by nature, and their coloration makes them hard to recognize against a dark woodland background. They are lively, restless birds with alert, curious natures. They occur in loose flocks, typically comprised of 10–15 individuals, and are sometimes seen in the company of related species. Paradise tanagers usually seek out food in the upper part of the canopy, hopping along the branches there and grabbing spiders and other invertebrates as well as seeking berries and fruit.

Distribution: Colombia east to the Guianas and Brazil. Also present in Peru and Ecuador. Although their scientific name suggests otherwise, these tanagers are not found as far south as Chile, reaching only as far as northern Bolivia.
Size: 13cm (5in).
Habitat: Lowland areas of woodland and forest.
Nest: Cup-shaped, made of vegetation.
Eggs: 2, whitish with purple-red speckling.
Food: Fruit and invertebrates.

Left: A paradise tanager on its nest. The Yuracares Native American tribe calls these birds "yeri yeri" because of the sound of their calls.

Identification: Essentially green on the sides of the face, violet-blue throat with vibrant sky-blue underparts. Rump red, with the back of the head and wings black. Sexes alike. There is some subspecific variation, and the rump colour is paler in immature birds.

Beryl-spangled tanager

Tangara nigroviridis

Social by nature, beryl-spangled tanagers are usually observed either in pairs or small flocks comprised of up to 15 individuals. They move fast, rarely resting for any time on a perch. These tanagers remain relatively close to the ground when foraging. They adopt a distinctive posture with their head down when seeking spiders and similar creatures, peering under branches and leaves. Their necks are surprisingly flexible, allowing these tanagers to pluck invertebrates from relatively inaccessible sites. There is some variation between races in their bluish-green plumage.

Identification: Black plumage around the bill, extending in a band around the eyes and over the back, is separated by bluish-green plumage, which is also present on the crown. Violet hues apparent over the wings. The rump is greenish blue, while the underparts are blackish with pronounced blue spangling. Sexes alike.

Distribution: Colombia and Venezuela south to parts of Ecuador, Peru and Bolivia.
Size: 12cm (5in).
Habitat: Relatively open areas of forest.
Nest: Cup-shaped, made of vegetation.
Eggs: 2, creamy white to pale green, with darker speckling.
Food: Berries, other fruit and invertebrates.

Blue-winged mountain tanager

Anisognathus flavinucha

These relatively large tanagers are the most common member of their genus in Colombia. They tend to be encountered throughout their range at lower levels than other related species, usually frequenting altitudes of 1,400–2,600m (4,600–8,500ft). They are most likely to be observed towards the tree-tops, in groups comprised of up to ten individuals. Blue-winged mountain tanagers are quiet by nature; their trilling calls are unlikely to betray their presence from any distance away. Their gape enables them to swallow some berries whole, while on other occasions they pull the skin off first.

Distribution: Colombia and Venezuela south into Bolivia.
Size: 19cm (7.5in).
Habitat: Forested areas in the Andean region.
Nest: Cup-shaped, made of vegetation.
Eggs: 2, greenish-white, speckled.
Food: Berries, other fruit and invertebrates.

Identification: Yellow stripe running over the crown, bordering black areas of plumage on the head. Underparts a matching shade of rich yellow. Back olive-yellow, with blue shoulder patches apparent on the wings. Colour of tail and rump varies, depending on subspecies. Sexes alike.

Green and gold tanager (*Tangara schrankii*): 12cm (4.5in)
Colombia and Venezuela to Ecuador, Peru, Bolivia and Brazil. Green plumage on the sides of the body and tail. The crown, underparts and rump are golden yellow. Forehead and area surrounding the eyes black. Hens and young birds have a green rump and black spotting on the crown.

Bay-headed tanager (*Tangara gyrola*): 12cm (4.5cm)
Costa Rica via Panama to Colombia, the Guianas, Brazil, Ecuador, Peru and Bolivia. Quite variable in coloration through its wide range, but generally brown plumage on the head. Wings greenish, while underparts may vary from green to blue.

Crested ant tanager (*Habia cristata*, E): 19cm (7.5in)
Confined to the western Andes of Colombia. Long, narrow, scarlet crest feathers, with scarlet throat. Upperparts reddish, with brown wings, underparts greyish. Young birds predominantly brown and have no crest. Feeds mainly on various insects, swooping down to snatch army ants on the march.

Grass-green tanager (*Chlorornis riefferii*): 20cm (8in)
Distribution extends through the Andean region, from Colombia via Peru to Bolivia. Brilliant grass-green coloration offset against chestnut-brown plumage on the sides of the face, and in the vent region. Bill and legs are red in adults. Bills of immatures are brown.

Purple honeycreeper

Cyanerpes caeruleus

Honeycreepers often move extensively through their range with their local distribution being affected by the whereabouts of flowering trees. Their narrow, curving bills enable these birds to probe flowers to obtain nectar, but their bill shape also allows them to feed on seed pots and to seize small invertebrates. Purple honeycreepers are sufficiently agile to catch insects in flight, although they cannot hover in front of flowers as hummingbirds do. They will, however, dive down to seize spiders that try to escape off branches by dropping down on gossamer threads.

Identification: A rich shade of purple, with a black bib under the throat and black on the wings. Legs are yellow. Hens are green, with yellowish striations on the underparts. Sky-blue patches extending back from the corners of the bill and on the top of the head.

Distribution: Panama south-east via Colombia to the Guianas, and south to Ecuador, Peru, Bolivia and Brazil.
Size: 10cm (4in).
Habitat: Flowering trees.
Nest: Cup-shaped nest made of vegetation.
Eggs: 2, white with reddish-chocolate blotches.
Food: Nectar, berries, other fruit and invertebrates.

NEW WORLD BLACKBIRDS
AND HUMMINGBIRDS

The bills of both these diverse groups of birds are very significant in terms of their lifestyles.
The New World blackbirds (quite unrelated to the European blackbird) use their bills rather like
knitting needles to weave intricate nests; the shape of the hummingbird's bill has a decided impact
on the type of flowers on which it feeds.

Crested oropendola

Psarocolius decumanus

During the breeding season, the remarkable call of the male crested oropendola is heard frequently. It has been likened to the noise made by a finger repeatedly plucking the teeth of a plastic comb. These oropendolas live in colonies comprised of several cock birds, one of whom is dominant, and as many as 30 hens. The crest is used as part of the male's display, which consists of elaborate posturing as well as distinctive singing. Ordinary call notes are much shorter and harsher in tone, and are uttered by both sexes. When foraging for food, crested oropendolas frequently associate with blue jays (*Cyanocorax* species).

Identification: Mainly black, with striking blue eyes and a slight crest. Large, relatively straight, pointed white bill, which is characteristic. Chestnut-brown rump, with yellow in the tail feathers and brown undertail coverts. Hens are similar but duller, and lack a crest.

Distribution: Western Panama south via Colombia to northern Argentina and south-east Brazil.
Size: 43cm (17in) cock; hen typically 33cm (13in).
Habitat: Typically lowland wooded areas.
Nest: Suspended nest built off tree branches.
Eggs: 1–2, pale green or greyish.
Food: Mainly invertebrates.

Left: The entrance to the nest of the crested oropendola is at the top, and isolated trees are favoured for nesting.

Troupial

Icterus icterus

These attractive icterids (blackbirds) are the national bird of Venezuela, and have been introduced to islands in the Caribbean, notably Bonaire, although they also occur naturally on the Netherlands Antilles. It can be difficult to distinguish young birds from the adults on the basis of their plumage, but the bare area of skin surrounding the eyes is a duller shade of blue with a greyish hue in immature specimens (as pictured). Unlike other icterids, troupials do not build their own nests. Instead, they take over those built by other birds, particularly rufous-fronted thornbirds (*Phacellodomus rufifrons*) and sometimes great kiskadees (*Pitangus sulphuratus*). Troupials then modify the nests with a new lining to meet their own needs.

Identification: Black head and bill, with black on the back and on the wings, where there is also white plumage. The plumage itself is quite rough in texture here. The remainder of the body is orangish yellow in colour, with a black tail. Bluish area of skin surrounds the eyes. Sexes alike.

Distribution: Northern South America from Colombia and Venezuela to the Caribbean.
Size: 23cm (9in).
Habitat: Relatively dry woodland.
Nest: Covered (roofed) nest.
Eggs: 3, white or pale pink with dark blotches.
Food: Mainly frugivorous, but also eats invertebrates, and may rob other nests for eggs.

Gorgeted woodstar (*Acestrura heliodon*):
6.5cm (2.5in)
Mountainous areas of eastern Panama south to
Venezuela and north-west Ecuador. The gorgeted
is the smallest of the woodstars. Stunning
pinkish gorget under the throat, lacking in hens,
with white feathering on the chest. Remainder of
the plumage is mainly green. The underparts of
hens are cinnamon.

Wedge-billed hummingbird (*Schistes
geoffroyi*): 8.5cm (3.5in)
Mountainous areas from Venezuela to Bolivia.
Bronzy-green upperparts. White stripe extends
downwards from each eye, with a blackish area
beneath. Short bill with a sharp point. Gorget is
brilliant green with purple plumage. White band
across upper chest. Hen has a duller gorget or
even a white throat, depending on subspecies.

Purple-crowned fairy hummingbird (*Heliothryx
barroti*): 11cm (4in)
South-eastern Mexico south to western Ecuador.
Distinctive, shiny violet-purple plumage on the
front of the crown, with a black stripe through
the eyes. Glossy green upperparts and pure
white underparts. Long tapering tail. Hen is
slightly larger, with a green crown.

Hoary puffleg (*Haplophaedia lugens*):
8.5cm (3.5in)
Uplands of south-west Colombia and the
neighbouring area of northern Ecuador. Green
upperparts with a coppery hue on head and
rump. Greyish-black underparts. Sexes alike.

White-tipped sicklebill hummingbird

Eutoxeres aquila

The highly distinctive, curved bill of these
hummingbirds enables them to draw nectar
from *Heliconia* flowers. They frequently
grasp on to the flower with their sharp
claws as they feed. Their relatively subdued
coloration and small size makes white-
tipped sicklebills hard to observe in
woodland, especially as they are solitary by
nature. They are also shy in contrast to
many hummingbirds, but are quite common
near their main food plant. They also hunt
for small invertebrates on bark. The nest of
these hummingbirds hangs down, often
suspended off a palm frond, with a
"tail" made of plant fibres beneath.

Distribution: Costa Rica
south to north-west Peru in
the Andean region.
Size: 11.5cm (4.5in).
Habitat: Lower areas of
forest and woodland.
Nest: Cup-shaped, made of
plant fibres.
Eggs: 2, white.
Food: Nectar, pollen and
small invertebrates.

Identification: Characteristic sickle-
shaped bill, with lower part
being yellow. Glossy deep-
green upperparts, and
heavy black-and-white
streaking on the
underparts. The
bronzy green tail
feathers have broad
white tips. Sexes
alike, but hens have
slightly shorter
wings compared
to cocks.

Long-tailed hermit

Phaethornis superciliosus

The body of these hummingbirds is tiny compared with the
length of their bill – which accounts for about a third of
their body length – and their long tail feathers. As is usual
behaviour with hummingbirds, males are highly territorial,
and each establishes a small area, singing there for long
periods and driving away potential rivals. The repetitive call
note may be repeated up to 100 times each minute in an
attempt to attract any female in the vicinity. After mating,
the hen will build the nest and incubate and rear the chicks
on her own. She keeps
her head up when
incubating, but the nest is
usually concealed beneath
a palm frond or similar
leafy vegetation.

Distribution: Mexico south
to northern Bolivia and the
Amazonian region of Brazil,
although distribution is not
continuous through this area.
Size: 13cm (5in).
Habitat: Lower levels in
forest and woodland.
Nest: Cone-shaped, made of
plant fibres.
Eggs: 2, white.
Food: Nectar, pollen and
small invertebrates.

*Left: The hen of the long-tailed
hermit always incubates the eggs
facing the vegetation that
conceals the nest.*

Identification: Dull
shade of brown with
bronzy green suffusion
over the back. Buff edging
to the rump. Greyish-buff
underparts, becoming buff on
the belly, with distinctive white
tips to the central tail feathers.
Sexes alike.

THE TURKEY, THE HOATZIN AND CURIOUS NOCTURNAL BIRDS

The Americas are home to one of the best-known and also some of the most bizarre birds in the world. The wild turkey is the original ancestor of all today's domestic strains, kept by farmers around the world. Grouse, too, are represented in this region. The New World is also home to a number of other distinctive and highly specialized birds, such as the hoatzin, oilbird and the potoos.

Wild turkey

Meleagris gallopavo

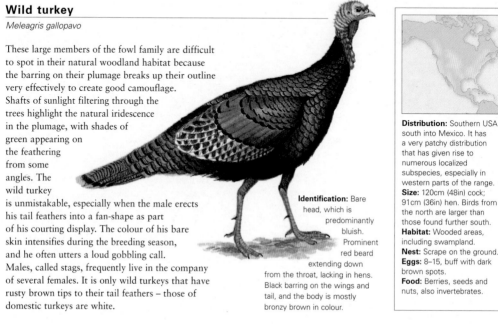

These large members of the fowl family are difficult to spot in their natural woodland habitat because the barring on their plumage breaks up their outline very effectively to create good camouflage. Shafts of sunlight filtering through the trees highlight the natural iridescence in the plumage, with shades of green appearing on the feathering from some angles. The wild turkey is unmistakable, especially when the male erects his tail feathers into a fan-shape as part of his courting display. The colour of his bare skin intensifies during the breeding season, and he often utters a loud gobbling call. Males, called stags, frequently live in the company of several females. It is only wild turkeys that have rusty brown tips to their tail feathers – those of domestic turkeys are white.

Identification: Bare head, which is predominantly bluish. Prominent red beard extending down from the throat, lacking in hens. Black barring on the wings and tail, and the body is mostly bronzy brown in colour.

Distribution: Southern USA south into Mexico. It has a very patchy distribution that has given rise to numerous localized subspecies, especially in western parts of the range.
Size: 120cm (48in) cock; 91cm (36in) hen. Birds from the north are larger than those found further south.
Habitat: Wooded areas, including swampland.
Nest: Scrape on the ground.
Eggs: 8–15, buff with dark brown spots.
Food: Berries, seeds and nuts, also invertebrates.

Oilbird

Steatornis caripensis

Distribution: Western Panama, Ecuador and Peru east to the Guianas.
Size: 48cm (19in).
Habitat: Caves and cliffs.
Nest: Made from regurgitated seed.
Eggs: 2–4, white with brown blotches.
Food: Fruit.

The oilbird is the only fruit-eating bird in the world that feeds at night. It spends its days roosting in the black interior of caves. Oilbirds have large eyes that glow red when a light is shone at them. They rely on a similar navigation system to bats, known as echolocation, to avoid collisions with objects when flying around in darkness. The system involves uttering a constant series of sharp calls while in flight, and listening to the echoes that bounce back to avoid flying into objects. Oilbirds will fly long distances – up to 25km (16 miles) – from their roosting caves in search of fruit each night.

Identification: Prominent hooked bill and very long wings. Rufous-brown upperparts with white spots edged with black running across the wings. Similar but smaller white-spotted patterning on the head and underparts, which are otherwise cinnamon-white. Long, tapering tail barred with black. Cock is greyer than the hen.

Great potoo

Nyctibius grandis

During the daytime the large eyes of the great potoo are dark, but they take on an eerie orange glow at night when these birds become active. They hunt large flying insects on the wing, swooping down to catch them. During the day giant potoos rest motionless on a tall branch in a hunched-up position, and their cryptic coloration helps to conceal their presence. They generally call only on moonlit nights, their vocalizations comprised of a series of guttural notes and louder, harsh, grating sounds. When breeding, the hen does not build a nest but simply lays her egg on a suitable area of a tree where it cannot roll away.

Identification: Large birds with variable coloration. Typically greyish-white to brown upperparts, and white underparts that are finely barred. Black spots on the breast. Tail feathers are barred with black borders. Sexes alike.

Distribution: Panama south to Peru and southern Brazil.
Size: 51cm (20in).
Habitat: Gallery forest, especially at the edges.
Nest: Knotholes or similar hollows in trees.
Eggs: 1, white with darker markings.
Food: Mainly insects.

Spruce grouse (*Dendragapus canadensis*): 41cm (16in)
From Alaska south to northern parts of the neighbouring USA. Prominent red area above the eye. Forehead down to the throat and upper breast are black with a white border. White barring on the flanks. Greyish upperparts. Hens are much duller, lacking the red and black areas, and are significantly smaller in size.

Ruffed grouse (*Bonasa umbellus*): 46cm (18in)
Alaska and north-west Canada to central USA. Distinguishable by the slight crest and ruff of black or reddish-brown feathering on the neck. There are two colour phases – the reddish-brown rather than grey phase predominates in south-west British Columbia in Canada. Hens have a shorter ruff and incomplete tail band.

Lyre-tailed nightjar (*Uropsalis lyra*): 76cm (30in) cock; 25cm (10in) hen
In highland areas of Colombia and Venezuela to Ecuador and Peru. Very distinctive ribbon-like tail, up to three times as long as the body. Brownish black with rufous barring and spots. Hens have shorter tails that lack the white tips.

Squirrel cuckoo (*Piaya cayana*): 43cm (17in)
Ranges from north-western Mexico south to Bolivia, Paraguay, Argentina and Uruguay, with 18 different races being recognized. Chestnut-brown head and wings, with greyish lower underparts. Long tail with pale tips to the feathers. Bare skin around the eyes is red in birds found east of the Andes mountains; greenish yellow elsewhere. Sexes alike.

Hoatzin

Opisthocomus hoazin

The hoatzin is often considered one of the most primitive birds on the planet, not just in terms of its appearance, but also because its chicks suggest a link back to reptile ancestors in the distant past. They hatch with claws on their wings, which enable them to grasp on to branches and climb back up if they slip off their fragile nest platform into water beneath. However, they can also swim well at this stage. The claws are lost once they are able to fly properly, although hoatzins are not powerful on the wing, preferring to glide short distances and hop from branch to branch. This is partly a reflection of their bulky, leaf-based diet, which means that their crop is voluminous in size and affects their balance.

Distribution: Northern Amazonian region of Brazil.
Size: 63.5cm (25in).
Habitat: Trees adjoining slow-flowing stretches of water.
Nest: Loose platform of sticks.
Eggs: 2–5, pinkish cream with pink, brown or blue spots.
Food: Leaves and shoots.

Identification: Long neck, loose crest and long tail with buff tipping. Plumage is bronzy olive with buff streaking on the upperparts. Throat and breast feathering are very pale buff. Lower underparts are chestnut. Sexes alike.

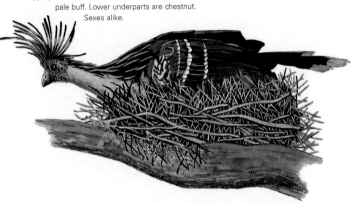

BIRDS OF PREY

These aerial predators often spend much of their time on the wing, gliding over the forest, and are thus most likely to be seen from vantage points that look down over the forest canopy. Whereas eagles and falcons seek their prey during the day, the role of night-time hunter is filled by owls.

Harpy eagle

Harpia harpyja

The immense power and strength of these eagles makes them fearsome predators, able to catch creatures ranging from birds such as large macaws to monkeys, sloths and even pigs. Reptiles such as iguanas and large snakes may also fall victim to these eagles. They are believed to use not just keen eyesight but also acute hearing to detect potential quarry in the forest canopy. However, they often prefer to hunt in clearings, or at areas where animals congregate, such as water sources. In the early morning, it is sometimes possible to see these magnificent eagles perched rather than flying overhead.

Identification: The female harpy eagle is much larger than the male, potentially weighing twice at much as her partner, up to 9kg (20lb). The head is greyish with a prominent, divided black crest. Upper chest is blackish, and underparts are white, aside from black-and-white barring on the tail feathers. There is fainter barring on the thighs. Wings are blackish. Young take at least five years to acquire full adult plumage. Their head and underparts are entirely white at first, changing gradually over successive moults.

Distribution: South Mexico through Central America, to Colombia and northern South America, ranging as far south as north-eastern Argentina, via eastern Bolivia and Brazil.
Size: Female 105cm (41in).
Habitat: Lowland tropical forest. They rarely soar over the forest, preferring instead to fly close to the canopy.
Nest: Platform of sticks.
Eggs: 2, whitish.
Food: Vertebrates.

Black and chestnut eagle

Oroaetus isidori

These eagles are most likely to be seen at altitudes of around 2,000m (6,600ft) but they have been observed from sea level up to 3,500m (11,500ft). Relatively little is known about their habits, and they are hard to observe since they hunt mainly in the canopy, preying on quite large creatures, including monkeys, which they seize in their powerful talons. Large trees are chosen to support the weight of their nest, which can measure up to 2m (6.5ft) in diameter. The cock bird is responsible for feeding the single chick, and appears to concentrate on hunting squirrels for it. The young eagle spends about four months in the nest, after which time its plumage darkens over successive moults until it assumes its adult coloration at four years old.

Identification: Head, including crest feathers, back, wings and top of the thighs are black. Lower chest and underparts are chestnut streaked with black. Tail is greyish with a black band at its tip. Iris is orange yellow. Feet are yellow. The female can be up to 20cm (8in) larger than the male.

Distribution: North-east Colombia and adjacent Venezuela south through Ecuador and Peru to Bolivia. Possibly no longer occurs in Argentina.
Size: Female 80cm (32in).
Habitat: Forested areas.
Nest: Platform of sticks.
Eggs: 1, whitish with brownish spots.
Food: Other vertebrates.

Sharp-shinned hawk (*Accipter striatus*): 34cm (13in)
Much of North America from Alaska and Canada south to the USA as far as Panama, with birds moving south in winter. Also on various Caribbean islands. Slate-blue upperparts and barred tail with variable white-and-chestnut areas on the underparts. Females are larger.

Boreal owl (Tengmalm's owl, *Aegolius funereus*): 29cm (11.5in)
Occurs in a broad band across North America from Alaska south to Oregon in the west and down to New Mexico. Distribution closely linked with coniferous forest. Brown wings with white spots. Underparts are chestnut with large whiter areas. Whitish facial disc with blackish edging. A separate race occurs in northern Europe and Asia. Females are larger.

Northern goshawk (*Accipter gentilis*): 68cm (26in)
North America to Mexico. A separate population is present through northern Europe and Asia. Variable depth of coloration. Wings are greyish. Underparts are white with greyish barring that extends right up around the neck. Darker area of plumage on the head and behind the eyes. Hens are larger.

Plumbeous forest falcon (*Micrastur plumbeus*): 37cm (15in)
South-west Colombia and northern Ecuador. Small, with dark greyish head and back. Barred underparts, with a characteristic single white band midway down the white-tipped tail feathers.

Great grey owl

Strix nebulosa

These owls move quite extensively through their large range, with North American individuals even having been sighted in the vicinity of New York on occasion. Much of this movement is triggered by the availability of food, especially voles, which these owls hunt almost exclusively during the breeding season. Pairs will often take over the abandoned nests of other birds of prey such as buzzards, although they sometimes nest on the ground. The number of eggs in the clutch is directly related to the availability of food, with breeding results therefore being closely correlated with fluctuations in vole populations.

Distribution: Circumpolar, from northern Canada and Alaska south to California, Idaho and Wyoming. A separate population extends across the far north of Europe and Asia.
Size: 69cm (27in).
Habitat: Coniferous forest.
Nest: Often a platform of sticks.
Eggs: 3–6, white.
Food: Small vertebrates, especially voles.

Identification: Plumage coloration consists mainly of grey streaking and barring on a white background. The dark markings on the so-called facial disc that surrounds the eyes form concentric rings. Yellowish bill, with a blackish patch beneath. Tail is relatively long. Hens are larger in size.

Great horned owl

Bubo virginianus

These owls are not found in areas of dense forest such as the Amazon. They prefer instead to hunt in semi-open terrain, where their keen eyesight enables them to swoop down on small mammals that form the basis of their diet. They are opportunistic hunters, however, and will take a much wider range of prey, from insects and amphibians to other birds, including smaller owls. Males are quite vocal, and sing loudly to attract a mate. Pairs split up at the end of the breeding season, but may reunite again later. They breed in a wide range of locations; an unpleasant stench may give away the location of the nest site because the male may stockpile food here for the offspring.

Identification: Variable through the species' wide range. Northerly populations generally have more brown in their plumage and on the facial disc. Populations further south have a more buff tone to the feathering. Bill is greyish black. Iris is yellow. Hens are larger than cocks.

Right: The name of these owls comes from the appearance of their so-called ear tufts.

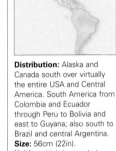

Distribution: Alaska and Canada south over virtually the entire USA and Central America. South America from Colombia and Ecuador through Peru to Bolivia and east to Guyana; also south to Brazil and central Argentina.
Size: 56cm (22in).
Habitat: Lightly wooded areas.
Nest: Abandoned nest or on the ground.
Eggs: 2–6, white.
Food: Small vertebrates.

GROUND BIRDS

The rhea is the largest bird found in the Americas today. The fossil record reveals that there used to be more gigantic birds, some of which were fearsome hunters, in this region before the southern landmass was invaded by predatory mammals from further north. A variety of other ground birds, especially quail, also now occur in this part of the world.

Greater rhea

Common rhea *Rhea americana*

The size of rheas prevents them from flying, but they are well equipped to defend themselves from most predators, and are able to run at speeds in excess of 60km/h (37mph). Their wings are larger than those of other flightless birds, with a claw on each so they can inflict serious injury at close quarters. Social by nature, rheas live in loose groups. When breeding, a number of hens are attracted to the male's nest and are persuaded to lay their eggs there. The eggs are golden yellow at first, changing to a whitish tone. The cock incubates the eggs and cares for the young chicks, which all hatch within a day or so of each other and start following him.

Identification: Tall and long-necked with greyish-brown plumage. Feathering only extends down the thighs, leaving the lower leg bare. Feet have three toes. Hens are lighter in colour and slightly smaller than cocks. Pure white albino individuals are surprisingly common, especially in the Argentinian race.

Below: Young rheas reach adult size at about four months, but they are unlikely to breed until at least two years old.

Distribution: Central and eastern South America, from parts of Brazil to Bolivia, Argentina and Uruguay.
Size: 140cm (55in).
Habitat: Open pampas to lightly wooded areas.
Nest: A scrape on the ground.
Eggs: Typically 13–30, golden yellow, then whitish.
Food: Omnivorous.

Common bobwhite

Northern bobwhite *Colinus virginianus*

Taxonomists have recognized at least 22 different races of these quail, and colour variation is quite marked in some cases. Differences in size are also apparent, with individuals found in southerly areas being smaller than those from northern regions. Common bobwhites live in groups, typically numbering around a dozen birds or so, and will invade agricultural areas, especially when crops are ripening. They generally prefer to seek cover on the ground, but will fly if threatened. Populations of these quails have also been introduced well outside their normal range, not only in other parts of the USA, including the north-west and Hawaii, but also further afield in New Zealand.

Identification: There is considerable variation through the birds' wide range. Most races have a black stripe running through the bill through the eyes, with a white stripe above and a broader white area on the throat. Chestnut underparts, usually speckled with white. Wings are brownish. Hens are duller, with buff rather than white patches on the head.

Distribution: North-eastern USA southwards through Mexico into western Guatemala.
Size: 25cm (10in).
Habitat: Woodland and farmland.
Nest: Scrape in the ground lined with vegetation.
Eggs: 10–15, dull white, often with blotches.
Food: Seeds and invertebrates.

Californian quail

Callipepla californica

These quail are highly adaptable through their range, and this characteristic has also led breeding populations of these popular game birds to be established in locations as far apart as Hawaii, Chile and King Island, Australia. Nesting on the ground makes Californian quail vulnerable to predators, and although the young are able to move freely as soon as they are hatched, relatively few are likely to survive long enough to breed the following year. Overgrazing by farm animals can adversely affect their numbers, presumably because of a reduction in the available food supply, although these quail also forage in crop-growing areas, and sometimes associate in groups of up to a thousand where food is plentiful.

Distribution: Western North America, from British Columbia, in Canada, southwards through California to Mexico.
Size: 27cm (11in).
Habitat: Semi-desert to woodland.
Nest: Grass-lined scraping on the ground.
Eggs: About 15, creamy white with brownish splodges.
Food: Seeds, vegetation and invertebrates.

Identification: Prominent, raised black crest that slopes forward over the bill. Top of the head is chestnut, with a white band beneath and another bordering the black area of the face. Chest is greyish, flanks are speckled. Hens lack the black and white areas, with greyish faces and smaller crests.

Crested bobwhite quail (*Colinus cristatus*): 22cm (9in)
Southern Central America, from Panama to Colombia, Venezuela, the Guianas and northern Brazil. Variable appearance. Distinctive crest, usually with a white stripe near the eyes. White speckling with thin, black borders on chestnut- or buff-coloured underparts. Hens are duller with a shorter crest, and lack the white eye stripe.

Scaled quail (Blue quail, *Callipepla squamata*): 29cm (11¹/₂in)
Southern USA south into Mexico. Blue-scaled plumage on the breast and neck down to the browner underparts. White-edged crest on the head. Wings are brownish. Hens have a smaller crest, with brown streaking on the head and throat.

Lesser prairie chicken (*Tympanuchus pallidicinctus*): 41cm (16in)
Restricted to the states of Colorado, Kansas, Oklahoma, Texas and New Mexico in the USA. Barred brownish and white plumage, with the tail having dark banding close to the tip. Buffish-yellow plumage above the eyes, with inflatable orange-red air sacs on the sides of the head. Sexes similar, but hens lack dark tail banding.

Sharp-tailed grouse (*Tympanuchus phasianellus*): 48cm (19in)
Northern North America from Alaska across much of Canada, south into the USA, where its distribution has shrunk recently. Distinguishable from other barred members of the grouse family by its pointed tail feathers. Pinkish inflatable air sacs on the head. Underparts are speckled. Cocks are significantly larger than hens.

Rock ptarmigan

Lagopus mutus

These grouse live in a region when natural cover is very scarce, and undergo a stunning transformation in appearance through the year. Their summer plumage is mottled brown, and their winter plumage is white, enabling them to merge into the snowy landscape. When snow is on the ground, they feed on buds and twigs of shrubs such as willow, which manage to grow in this treeless region. Pairs nest in the brief Arctic summer, often choosing a site protected by shrubs. The cock stays nearby while the hen incubates alone. The chicks are covered in down when they hatch and can move easily, but are not able to fly until their flight feathers have emerged fully, at about ten days old.

Distribution: Circumpolar, extending right across the far north of North America; also present on Greenland. A similar distribution occurs in Europe and Asia.
Size: 38cm (15in).
Habitat: Tundra.
Nest: Scrape on the ground lined with vegetation.
Eggs: 6–9, creamy buff, heavily blotched and spotted with blackish brown.
Food: Buds, leaves, berries and other plant matter.

Identification: Mottled, brownish head with red above the eyes. Similar patterning across the body in summer, becoming white in winter. Blackish stripes on the face, lacking in hens.

FINCHES, BUNTINGS AND BLACKBIRDS

Many of these medium-sized birds often feed on seeds for much of the year, but invertebrates become especially important in the diets of many during the breeding season. Such prey provides the essential protein that the nestlings need to grow and fledge rapidly. Most leave the nest when barely 14 days old, and the adult birds may nest again at this time.

Andean siskin

Carduelis spinescens

Distribution: The Andean region of Venezuela and Colombia to northern Ecuador.
Size: 10cm (4in).
Habitat: Scrub and relatively open countryside.
Nest: Made of plant fibres.
Eggs: 2, pale bluish white with darker markings.
Food: Seeds and invertebrates.

These siskins have a high-pitched and attractive song, often uttered in flight. They are most likely to be observed at altitudes from 1,500 to 4,100m (5,000 to 13,500ft). Here they are sometimes hard to spot in taller trees, although they also venture down to the ground in search of food. Andean siskins may be encountered in small flocks, and sometimes forage with other finches, seeking *Espletia* seeds – a particular favourite. It is not uncommon within the Ecuadorian population for some birds resembling mature cocks to actually be hens.

Identification: Black area extending from the bill to the top of the head. Plumage is greenish-yellow elsewhere and of a brighter hue on the underparts. Wings are black with distinct yellow markings across the flight feathers. Hen are duller in coloration, lacking the black cap, and with less yellow on the wings.

Hooded siskin (*Carduelis magellanica*): 14cm (5.5in)
Central-southern South America, in Bolivia, Peru, Paraguay, Argentina and Uruguay. Also a northern Andean population, from Colombia to Peru, and another in south-east Venezuela, Guyana and north-west Brazil. Black head and yellowish chest and upper abdomen, becoming whiter below, with a green back. Hens are less vividly coloured, with a greyish head and a greenish tone on the underparts.

Grassland sparrow (*Ammodramus humeralis*): 13cm (5in)
Colombia to the Guianas south to Bolivia, Uruguay and Argentina. Distinctive yellow plumage adjoining the bill, pronounced black streaking on the crown with chestnut edging, becoming browner on the wings. Underparts are pale brown, becoming whitish close to the vent. Sexes alike.

Dickcissel (*Spiza americana*): 18cm (7in)
Eastern North America, overwintering in Central and northern South America. Grey head, with yellow stripe above the eye leading back from the short, conical bill. Whitish area on the throat, with black beneath. Chest is yellowish, with white lower underparts. Back and wings are brownish, with darker striations. Hens are duller in coloration, lacking the prominent black area under the throat and with grey underparts.

Saffron finch

Sicalis flaveola

Distribution: Much of South America, from Colombia to Argentina; also on Trinidad.
Size: 14cm (5.5in).
Habitat: Lightly wooded areas.
Nest: Tree cavities.
Eggs: 4, pale blue with brownish spots.
Food: Seeds and invertebrates.

Although there are other finches with predominantly yellow plumage, the saffron finch is the most brightly coloured member of the group, and also has one of the widest distributions. It has been introduced to localities outside its natural range, and is consequently seen in parts of Panama and Jamaica. These attractive finches can frequently be observed on the ground foraging for food, often in small groups or individual pairs. They are usually quite tame by nature, particularly in parks and urban areas.

Identification: Bright yellow underparts, becoming more orange at the front of the crown. Olive-brown wings and tail. Short, pointed bill. Hens have brown, streaked upperparts with whitish underparts. Young birds are also streaked, with young cocks developing a yellowish neck collar and chest when they first moult into adult plumage.

Painted bunting

Passerina ciris

The cock painted bunting is popularly regarded as the most colourful of all North America's songbirds. Unfortunately, however, these relatively shy birds are not easily seen, often remaining concealed in vegetation, where their presence is more likely to be revealed by the cock's song. They have a warbling call as well as a short, harsh, warning note that is uttered at any hint of danger. The nest, too, is well hidden, and is constructed from a variety of vegetation. A pair may rear two broods in succession, and insects feature more prominently in their diet at this time. The hen builds the nest on her own and collects a variety of plant matter for this purpose, ranging from strips of bark and dead leaves to grass stems and rootlets. She chooses a well-concealed nest site, often in the fork of a tree.

Identification: Males are very colourful and unmistakable, with bluish-violet plumage on the head and rose-red throat and underparts. The wings and back are green, with darker tail and flight feathers. Hens are drab in comparison, with green upperparts, becoming more yellowish on the underside of the body, and no bars on the wing, unlike many other finches.

Distribution: Widely distributed across the southern USA and Mexico, with populations moving south in the winter as far as Panama. Also present on Cuba.
Size: 14cm (5.5in).
Habitat: Lightly wooded areas and brush.
Nest: Woven nest.
Eggs: 3–5, pale blue with darker spots.
Food: Mainly seeds, some invertebrates.

Red-winged blackbird

Agelaius phoeniceus

Unrelated to the European blackbird, the red-winged blackbird is a member of the icterid family. It frequents marshland areas when nesting, but is seen in a much wider range of habitats during winter. In North America, red-winged blackbirds move southwards over the winter period, typically travelling distances of about 700km (440 miles). Populations in Central American parts of their distribution tend to be sedentary throughout the year, however. There is quite marked variation in the appearance of these birds through their wide range, and it is also not uncommon for individuals to display pied markings. Both sexes sing, particularly at the start of the nesting period, and some of their call notes are different, so it is possible to tell them apart.

Identification: Only the mature male in breeding plumage displays the typical glossy black feathering and red shoulder patches with a paler buff border. Females have dark streaks running down their bodies, with more solid brownish coloration on the head, sides of the face and over the wings.

Distribution: Occurs over much of North America, breeding as far north as Alaska, and south into Central America.
Size: 24cm (9.5in).
Habitat: Relatively open country.
Nest: Cup-shaped.
Eggs: 3, pale greenish blue with dark spots.
Food: Seeds and invertebrates.

PIGEONS AND DOVES

The characteristic dumpy appearance of pigeons and doves, along with their relatively subdued coloration, means that they can be quite easily identified. There is actually no strict zoological distinction between these two groups, although the term "pigeon" is usually applied to larger species, particularly members of the Columba *genus.*

Mourning dove

Carolina dove *Zenaida macroura*

These doves are so-called because of the plaintive, mournful sound of their calls. They have benefited from the provision of bird tables, particularly in the northern part of their range, and often visit gardens for the food being offered. Their powerful wings and sleek shape help these doves to fly long distances on migration, and northerly populations overwinter in Central America. In southern US states, such as Florida, mourning doves are resident throughout the year. They prefer to seek food on the ground if not feeding on a bird table, and groups often wander across fields in search of seeds and other edible items. Mourning doves are now overwintering further north than they did in the past, partly as a result of more feeding opportunities from bird tables.

Identification: There is some variation in appearance through these doves' wide range, with cocks displaying pinkish-buff coloration on the face, extending down to the underparts, with a dark streak just above the neck. The upper surface of the wings and tail are brown, with several large dark spots evident on the wings. Hens are duller in coloration, being browner overall.

Distribution: Right across North America, from southern Canada southwards across the USA through Central America to Costa Rica and Panama, but distribution is affected by the season. Also occurs on the Greater Antilles in the Caribbean.
Size: 34cm (13in).
Habitat: Lightly wooded areas.
Nest: Loose pile of twigs.
Eggs: 2, white.
Food: Seeds and some invertebrates.

Black-winged dove

Metriopelia melanoptera

The male black-winged dove has a very distinctive, rather attractive chirruping call, unlike the more usual cooing calls associated with this group of birds. His call is heard more frequently during the breeding season, as he fans his tail and flicks his wings, making the white areas of plumage on these areas more visible. These doves are often sighted in association with the smaller bare-faced ground dove (*M. ceciliae*), and frequently occur in the vicinity of puyas shrubs, which provide both roosting and breeding sites. Pairs may also nest in buildings, however, and sometimes even on the ground among rocky outcrops that provide them with some protection from possible predators. The nest itself is a relatively loose structure, and usually sited quite close to the ground.

Identification: Compact body shape. Predominantly brown, aside from the black flight feathers and tail, with a white area at the shoulder that is usually hidden. There is a slight pinkish tinge on the head, and bare orangish-red skin around the eyes. Hens are duller in colour and a slightly paler shade of brown. This tends to increase in depth of colour during the breeding period.

Distribution: The western side of South America, from Colombia and Ecuador through Peru, Chile and Argentina to Tierra del Fuego at the southern tip of the continent.
Size: 23cm (9in).
Habitat: Upland arid areas.
Nest: Platform of twigs.
Eggs: 2, white.
Food: Seeds of grasses and other plants.

Inca dove (*Scardafella inca*): 22cm (8.5in)
Ranges from south-western USA south as far as
Costa Rica, up to altitudes of 3,000m (9,840ft).
Sometimes recorded as a vagrant as far north as
Ontario in Canada. Greyish olive brown, with black
scaly edging to the individual feathers over the entire
body, more bluish grey on the head, with pinkish
underparts. Underwing area seen in flight is brown.
Sexes alike.

Buckley's ground dove (Ecuadorian ground dove,
Columbina buckleyi): 18cm (7in)
North-western Ecuador to north-western Peru.
Greyish-brown upperparts and more pinkish
underparts, with greyish coloration most marked on
the head. Black underwing coverts. Hen is browner,
with less contrast in her plumage.

Eared dove (golden-necked dove, *Zenaida
auriculata*): 28cm (11in)
Occurs over most of South America, aside from the
Amazon region and the Andean uplands. Very
common, especially in north-eastern Brazil, where
migratory flocks, thought to be comprised of a
million birds, can occasionally be observed. Some
variation in colour through the range. Two black lines
behind and below the eyes, with a prominent green
iridescent area behind the eyes. Wings are brownish
with variable dark wing spots. Underparts are
pinkish. Hens are duller in appearance.

Spot-winged pigeon (American spotted pigeon,
Columba maculosa): 33cm (13in)
Two separate populations. One ranges from south-
west Peru into western Bolivia and Argentina,
distinguishable by the white edging to the grey
feathers on the wings. The other, with more
pronounced white areas creating the impression of
spots, extends southwards into south-western
Brazil, Paraguay and Uruguay. Head and underparts
have a pinkish-grey tone. Hens greyer overall.

Gold-billed ground dove

Croaking ground dove *Columbina cruziana*

These small doves are a relatively
common sight in gardens and
parks, and have adapted well to
changes in habitat throughout
their range. They may
sometimes be seen in large
numbers where food is
abundant, seeking seeds and
other plant matter on the
ground. The distinctive
croaking calls uttered by cock
birds are more likely to be heard
during the breeding period. In common
with many other pigeons and doves, the
hen lays on a relatively flimsy nest. The
young doves may leave the nest at just
ten days old, before they are able to fly
effectively, and hide in nearby vegetation.

*Above: Both members of the pair
incubate the eggs.*

Identification: Predominantly brownish with
pinker underparts and greyish head. Bluish-grey
wing coverts display variably positioned reddish-
brown spots across them and a magenta stripe
across the top. The bill is yellow at the base,
while the tip is black. Hens are similar, but are
a much more even shade of
brown overall. The tail is
relatively short.

Distribution: Coastal region
from Ecuador through Peru to
northern Chile.
Size: 15cm (6in).
Habitat: Open woodland
and scrub.
Nest: Loose platform of
twigs.
Eggs: 2, white.
Food: Seeds of grasses and
other plants.

Bare-faced ground dove

Bare-eyed ground dove *Metriopelia ceciliae*

These doves may range at altitudes up to 4,500m
(15,000ft). When breeding, they will, unusually, seek
out holes in cliffs or even the protection offered by
buildings, rather than nesting in a tree or shrub.
In the vicinity of human habitation,
they often nest on houses, and forage
for food in surrounding gardens.
Elsewhere, they may fly quite
long distances from their
roosting sites in search of food. These
doves are very quiet by nature, and are
unlikely to betray their presence by their
calls. They are also very adept at
running along the ground to escape
from danger.

Identification: Bright area of
bare, yellowish-orange skin
encircles the eyes. Back and
wings are brownish with much
paler, buff-coloured mottling
at the centres of individual
feathers. Chest is pinkish brown
with brownish
underparts.
Hens are
usually slightly
duller in coloration.

Distribution: Northern Peru
south into northern Chile,
western Bolivia and north-
west Argentina.
Size: 16cm (6in).
Habitat: Dry, upland country.
Nest: Loose platform.
Eggs: 2, white.
Food: Seeds of grasses and
other plants.

ANIS AND OTHER SMALLER HUNTERS

There are a number of smaller predatory birds that have evolved different hunting strategies. While hawks and falcons, with their high degree of aerial mobility, are well known, others such as the anis comprise a small group restricted to the Americas. They tend to feed on invertebrates, but they may also catch small vertebrates such as lizards as well.

Groove-billed ani

Crotophaga sulcirostris

These unusual members of the cuckoo clan have a relatively slim body shape and are highly social by nature, living in groups. They even sometimes associate with the slightly larger smooth-billed ani, although they can be distinguished in flight by their more languid flight pattern as they flap their wings and glide. Neither species is a powerful flier. Groove-billed anis have unusual breeding behaviour: a number of females will lay eggs in the same location, reflecting their highly social natures. Up to 18 eggs have therefore been recorded in a single nest. Although these birds sometimes take over open nests abandoned by other birds, they may also construct a suitably large receptacle for their eggs from sticks and other vegetation. Groove-billed anis typically feed on the ground in groups by walking along and seizing prey that comes within reach, which may include lizards.

Identification: Dull black in colour, with a distinctively shaped bill. The culmen (central ridge of the bill) is in the form of a smooth curve from the tip to the forehead. Grooves in the bill leading to the nostrils are apparent on the sides. Iris is blackish. Tail is long, with a rounded tip. Sexes similar, although hens may be slightly smaller in size.

Distribution: South-western USA south through Central America and Colombia, Venezuela and Guyana as far as northern Chile and Argentina; also present on Caribbean islands from Aruba to Trinidad.
Size: 30cm (12in).
Habitat: Scrub and pastureland.
Nest: Bowl-shaped, made of vegetation.
Eggs: 4, blue-green with chalky glaze.
Food: Mainly invertebrates.

Smooth-billed ani

Crotophaga ani

This species tends to occur in more humid areas than the groove-billed, although they are similar in their habits. They are a common sight, partly as a result of their size and the way in which they frequently perch in the open, even on fences. In cattle-ranching areas in Colombia, the anis' habit of following the herd has led to them being nicknamed *garrapateros*, and they are welcomed by ranchers for removing ticks from their animals. Smooth-billed anis breed communally, like their groove-billed cousins, with as many as 29 eggs being present in a single nest.

Identification: Dull, black plumage, with a decidedly rounded shape to the tail. Bill is black, with a distinctive smooth, raised area on the top of the upper bill closest to the eyes. Sexes similar but hens are smaller in size. Recently fledged young of this species lack the raised area on the bill, resembling groove-billed anis at this stage, although the sides of their bills are smooth.

Distribution: Southern Florida through Central America west to Ecuador and east into northern Argentina. Also present in the Caribbean.
Size: 33cm (13in).
Habitat: Brushland and open areas of country.
Nest: Large cup of vegetation.
Eggs: 4, bluish green, with chalk-like glaze.
Food: Invertebrates.

Burrowing owl

Athene cunicularia

These small owls will hunt during the day, but are most active at dusk. Their small size allows them to nest underground in burrows that may have been dug originally by prairie dogs or other rodents, or may be constructed by the birds themselves. These tunnels can extend over 3m (10ft) in length. Unusually, the owls decorate the entrance with dried cattle dung, whose odour is thought to deter potential mammalian predators from investigating inside. Burrowing owls invariably choose an open area for the entrance to their nest site, rather than concealing it in long grass.

Identification: Brownish edging on the facial disc on the sides of the eyes, with more distinctive brownish stripes beneath the yellowish bill and white eyebrows. Chest and wings are brownish, with generally whiter underparts in the case of the North and Central American race. Burrowing owls seen in Florida and the Caribbean are a darker shade of brown. Sexes alike. Young birds are buff in colour, with white underparts.

Distribution: North America from British Columbia east to Manitoba and south into Central America. Separate population in Florida and the Caribbean. Also occurs in South America, especially in the east from Brazil south to Tierra del Fuego.
Size: 26cm (10.5in).
Habitat: Lightly wooded country.
Nest: Underground burrow.
Eggs: 5–6, white.
Food: Mainly larger invertebrates.

Short-eared owl (*Asio flammeus*):
43cm (17in)
Most northerly population extends across northern North America from Alaska eastwards. Also present in north-west South America across the southern part of the continent and on the Galapagos Islands and Hawaii. Relatively small head, with slight tufts of plumage above the eyes. Variable coloration, brownish with white markings on the wings. Pale-streaked chest and black feathering encircling the eyes. Sexes alike.

Swainson's hawk (*Buteo swainsoni*):
56cm (22in)
From Alaska southwards, mainly in the central USA. Usually migrates south for the winter to southern Brazil, Argentina and Paraguay via Central America, although some may remain in the southern USA. White area from above the bill to the throat. Chest is brown and underparts are whitish with brown barring. Head and upperparts are dark. Tail is barred. Rarer reddish and black morphs occur, with these colours predominating on the underparts. Hens are larger.

Snail kite (*Rostrhamus sociabilis*):
45cm (18in)
Ranges from the Everglades of Florida south through Central America west of the Andes to Argentina. Also on Cuba. Dark grey with a white area under the tail. The bare skin from the black bill to around the eyes is reddish, becoming more colourful in the breeding season, but yellow in hens, which also have white striping under the throat. Red irises. Feeds mainly on aquatic snails.

Long-winged harrier

Circus buffoni

These harriers have powerful wings and are believed to fly over the Andes on occasion, and regularly travel long distances when migrating. They are occasionally seen well outside what is usually regarded as their normal range, with individuals having been sighted on the Falkland Islands as well as at Tierra del Fuego. Long-winged harriers are most likely to be encountered in relatively open countryside, often in marshland and similarly wet environments.

Identification: Normal colour form has a whitish area around the eyes and bill, with a further white necklace of markings beneath. Chest and wings are predominantly blackish, with white underparts. Greyish barring on the flight feathers and tail. There is also a melanistic form, in which the white plumage is replaced by black apart from on the rump. Female has brownish rather than black plumage and is significantly larger.

Distribution: South America, from south-west Colombia eastwards to the Guianas, through parts of Brazil to Argentina, eastern Bolivia and central Chile.
Size: 56cm (22in).
Habitat: Relatively open, lowland tropical areas.
Nest: Concealed on the ground in rushes.
Eggs: 2–4, whitish.
Food: Small vertebrates.

CONDORS AND OTHER BIRDS OF PREY

The birds featured here include the birds of prey most closely linked with the New World, in the guise of the two species of condor, as well as the bald eagle, symbol of the USA. The Californian condor ranks as one of the rarest birds in the world. There is also the roadrunner, which, thanks to its unusual habits, has become famous worldwide as a cartoon character.

Andean condor

Vultur gryphus

Andean condors are the only vultures from the New World to show clear sexual dimorphism. With a potential lifespan measured in decades, and a correspondingly slow breeding cycle, pairs are only likely to rear a chick in alternate years. In spite of their strong bills, which allow them to rip open carcasses without difficulty, Andean condors are not active hunters. In coastal areas they scour seal colonies, sometimes descending in large numbers to scavenge when food is readily available.

Identification: Massive, vulture-like appearance. The bare skin on the cock's head is red, and black in the larger hen. Cock birds also display a prominent comb on the head, as well as a wattle that is absent in hens. There is a ruff of white feathering below, encircling the neck. The rest of the plumage is predominantly black aside from the greyish-white areas on the wings.

Distribution: Andean region of South America, right down this mountain range from Venezuela to Tierra del Fuego in the far south.
Size: 130cm (51in).
Habitat: Open mountainous terrain, but sometimes near sea level, where these birds seek carcasses of marine animals. Prefers to be well away from human habitation.
Nest: Caves on cliffs.
Eggs: 1, white.
Food: Carrion.

Californian condor

Gymnogyps californianus (E)

These majestic birds used to soar effortlessly on the thermals, covering huge distances in search of large carcasses in true vulture fashion, but heavy persecution brought them to the very edge of extinction. Collisions with powerlines also reduced their numbers, until the species was virtually extinct. The last remaining wild Californian condors were caught in 1987 and integrated into a highly expensive captive-breeding programme, carried out at zoological collections at Los Angeles and San Diego. Five years later, the first birds bred in captivity were released back into the wild, and other releases have followed. It takes about eight years for these condors to attain sexual maturity.

Identification: Huge size, predominantly black with white areas on and under the wings. Bare, variable pinkish-orange skin on the head and neck. This entire area of bare skin is grey in young birds. Sexes alike.

Distribution: Area north of Los Angeles, California. Releases carried out around the San Joaquin Valley in California; birds are fitted with radio telemetry equipment to track movement.
Size: 134cm (53in).
Habitat: Lightly wooded terrain.
Nest: Usually in caves.
Eggs: 1, white.
Food: Carrion.

Roadrunner

Geococcyx californianus

These unusual members of the cuckoo clan are built for speed. Their common name derives from their habit of frequenting roads that attract lizards and other reptiles to bask on the heat of the tarmac early in the day to raise their body temperature. Roadrunners can run at speeds up to 37km/h (23mph), and although they can fly, they rarely take to the wing. They have a distinct zygodactyl foot structure, with two toes directed forwards and two behind, which may assist their balance, compared with the more usual 3:1 perching configuration. Their calls resemble the cooing of doves, and they also communicate by bill-chattering.

Distribution: South-western parts of the USA, across from California into Mexico.
Size: 61cm (24in).
Habitat: Open country, including desert areas.
Nest: Low platform of sticks.
Eggs: 4–10, white.
Food: Insects, lizards and small snakes.

Identification: Loose, ragged, dark crest spotted with white. Streaked upper chest becoming white on the underparts. Back and wings brown with buff and whitish edging to the feathers. Powerful, sharp-tipped bill. Grey rump and long tail. Strong legs. Sexes alike.

Crested caracara (common caracara, *Polyborus plancus*): 59cm (23in)
Occurs in southern USA south through Central America across South America to Tierra del Fuego and the Falkland Islands. Black cap and crest on the head, with whitish area beneath becoming barred on the back and chest. Wings and abdomen show more blackish coloration. Bare, reddish skin on the face. Hens are slightly larger.

Puna hawk (variable hawk, gurney's hawk, *Buteo poecilochrous*): 61cm (24in)
Occurs in the Andean region from southern Colombia south to Chile and Argentina. Exists in both light and dark morphs. Light-coloured cocks have whitish underparts and grey upperparts, and the flight feathers are blackish at their tips. The tail is white with dark speckling and a black bar. Hens have a chestnut area at the top of the wings. The entire body aside from the tail is dark slaty grey in the case of the dark morph. Hens are distinguishable from cocks by the chestnut feathering extending over the upper breast, with black-and-white barring on the lower underparts.

Turkey vulture (*Cathartes aura*): 81cm (32in)
Ranges across much of the USA south through Central America and across much of the southern continent. Also occurs on islands ranging from the Greater Antilles in Central America to the Falkland Islands off the coast of southern South America. North American population moves south in the winter. Can find carcasses by scent, and feeds mainly on mammals. Bare, reddish-pink head and brownish-black plumage with slight iridescence. Variation in size through its wide range. Sexes alike.

Bald eagle

Haliaeetus leucocephalus

Distribution: From the Aleutian Islands and Alaska east across Canada and south across the USA into northern Mexico.
Size: 96cm (38in).
Habitat: Areas where there are large stretches of water.
Nest: Often huge, located in a tree or sometimes on the ground.
Eggs: 1–3, white.
Food: Vertebrates and some carrion, especially in the winter when hunting is more difficult.

The national symbol of the USA, the bald eagle is a highly adaptable species, and is encountered as far north as the freezing tundra of Canada and south to the searing desert heat of Mexico. Feeding habits are diverse; these eagles tend to catch fish during the summer months, switching at other times of the year to birds as large as geese, which are seized in flight. They hunt both by sight and sound, and are drawn to areas where sea otters are feeding by recognizing their calls. The species remains far more common in the northern part of its range, where it has been subject to less habitat disturbance.

Identification: Distinctive white head and tail, yellow bill and talons. Remainder of the plumage is predominantly brown, with lighter edging to some of the feathers on the back and wings. Female is larger, and young birds have dark bills.

Above: Bald eagles may migrate more than 2,000km (1,250 miles).

HUMMINGBIRDS AND JAYS

One of the unique sights of the Americas is the presence of hummingbirds feeding in gardens, either from flowers or special feeders. These birds are a source of fascination as they hover in flight and feed, demonstrating their remarkable aerial agility. However, they may not always be resident throughout the year, with some species moving to warmer climes for the winter.

Ruby-throated hummingbird

Archilochus colubris

Distribution: Breeds in eastern North America, moving southwards to Florida and south-westwards to Texas through Central America to Panama for the winter. Sometimes seen in the adjoining region of the Caribbean.
Size: 9cm (3.5in).
Habitat: Lightly wooded areas with flowering plants.
Nest: Cup built in trees bound with spiders' silk.
Eggs: 2, white.
Food: Nectar, pollen, sap and invertebrates.

The small size of these hummingbirds is no barrier to flying long distances, which they do back and forth to their wintering grounds each year. Cock birds usually arrive back in their breeding areas about a week before the hens are seen in May. Staying in temperate areas would mean that these birds would have difficulty finding sufficient plant nectar to sustain them through the winter. In fact, ruby-throated hummingbirds are far less specialized in their feeding habits than some members of this family, and have been recorded feeding on more than 31 different types of plant, although they display a preference for red flowers. Hens build their nest alone, binding it with the silk threads of spiders' webs, and are responsible for rearing the chicks on their own. Tiny invertebrates feature prominently in their diet at this stage.

Identification: Metallic, greenish-bronze upperparts. Has a large glossy red area of plumage under the throat. The remainder of the underparts are whitish. Hens are similar in appearance, but they have a dusky white area on their throat instead of the glossy red patch of the cocks.

Anna's hummingbird

Calypte anna

These hummingbirds are sometimes seen feeding at the holes in tree bark drilled by sapsuckers (*Sphyrapicus* species), which results in the plant's sap oozing, providing an accessible source of nutrients. At the outset of the breeding season, males become very territorial. Soon afterwards, hens begin to seek out suitable nest sites, which can include human-made structures, such as electric wires. They gather small lengths of plant fibres and bind them together with silk from spiders' webs. Lichens are used to fill in gaps between the stems, and the cup is lined with feathers. The chicks leave the nest for the first time when only 18 days old.

Identification: Mostly rose-coloured head, with a bronzy-green area behind the eyes and a small white spot evident here as well. Upperparts are a shade of metallic, bronzy green, and underparts are green and whitish. Hens lack the rose-coloured plumage on the head, and have a brownish throat.

Distribution: Western USA, from California and offshore islands south-eastwards to Arizona; may move to southern Oregon during the winter. Sometimes even recorded in Alaska.
Size: 10cm (4in).
Habitat: Generally woodland areas with flowers.
Nest: Cup-shaped.
Eggs: 2, white.
Food: Nectar, pollen, sap and invertebrates.

Steller's jay

Cyanocitta stelleri

Ranging over a vast area, Steller's jay has proved to be a highly adaptable species. In some areas, such as at picnic sites in the Rocky Mountains in Colorado, these jays have become very tame, accepting food from people. Elsewhere, they are much shyer. They eat a varied diet; where food is likely to be hard to find because of snow in winter, they forage for acorns in the autumn, which are then stored for later use. Family groups may remain together over the winter in northern areas, and the young leave in the spring when the adult pair start to nest again. Mud is often used rather like cement to anchor the bulky nest of twigs together.

Identification: Dark, greyish-blue head and back, with blue underparts. Tail and wings are blue with black barring. North American variety have darker coloration and more prominent crests than those occurring further south, which have a much bluer appearance. Sexes alike.

Distribution: The largest distribution of all North American jays, extending from Alaska south through Central America to Nicaragua.
Size: 32cm (13in).
Habitat: Woodland and forest.
Nest: Mound of twigs.
Eggs: 2–6, greenish or bluish with brown spotting.
Food: Omnivorous.

Black-chinned hummingbird (purple-throated hummingbird, *Archilochus alexandri*): 10cm (4in) Breeding range extends from south-west British Columbia across southern USA into Mexico. Moves further south over the winter. Black area merging into broader purple area on the sides of the face and throat. Underparts are buffy brown, and upperparts are dull bronzy green. Hen is similar, also with a white stripe behind the eyes, and buffy on the sides of the face and throat.

Broad-tailed hummingbird (*Selasphorus platycercus*): 11cm (4.5in) Breeding range from California through Texas into southern Mexico and Guatemala. Winters entirely in Central America. Wide tail feathers. Metallic, deep reddish-purple throat and sides of the face, with buffy-brown underparts and metallic green upperparts. Hens are duller, with brown speckling on the buffy throat plumage.

Rivoli's hummingbird (magnificent hummingbird, *Eugenes fulgens*): 13cm (5in) Breeding range from southern Arizona and New Mexico in the USA, with these birds wintering in Mexico. A separate population in Central America ranges as far south as western Panama. Deep purple coloration on the head, becoming blackish with a white spot behind the eyes, and a brilliant green throat. Hens have lighter brown underparts. Light green upperparts in both sexes.

Blue jay (*Cyanocitta cristata*): 30cm (12in) Eastern North America down to Florida, with southerly populations being smaller. Blue crest, white area on the face, edged by black feathering. Wings are blue with distinctive white markings. Black barring extends from the flight feathers to the tail. Underparts are white. Sexes alike.

Green jay

Inca jay *Cyanocorax yncas*

These woodland birds are found in two distinct populations. Birds forming the northern population are better known as green jays, while the southerly and more social Andean races are usually described as Inca jays. One of the most unusual features of these jays is their habit of seeking out smoking areas of woodland, not only in search of small creatures that may be escaping the flames, but also to hold their wings out, allowing the smoke to permeate their plumage. This action is believed to kill off parasites such as lice that may be lurking on their bodies. Young green jays may remain with their parents and help to rear the new chicks before establishing their own territories.

Identification:
Green plumage is characteristic. The northern race has a combination of blue and black plumage on the head, being green elsewhere, and underparts including the underside of the tail are yellowish. Iris is black. South American race has a pronounced blue crest above the bill, and pale green plumage extending right over the forehead. Iris is yellow. Sexes alike.

Distribution: Northern population extends from Texas to Honduras, while the separate South American form ranges from Colombia to Ecuador.
Size: 27cm (10.5in).
Habitat: Woodland and forest.
Nest: Platform of twigs and similar material.
Eggs: 3–5, greyish lilac with dark speckling.
Food: Omnivorous.

TITS, WRENS AND MOCKINGBIRDS

Although none of these birds is brightly coloured, most have a lively song that draws attention to their presence. Some develop into regular bird-table visitors and can become quite tame as a result. They are generally lively and active by nature, irrespective of their size. A number of their species undertake seasonal movements, especially those found in the far north.

Tufted titmouse

Parus bicolor

Distribution: Eastern North America, from southern Ontario south to the Gulf of Mexico, although not present in southern Florida. Range appears to be expanding in some areas of Canada.
Size: 15cm (6in).
Habitat: Light, deciduous woodland.
Nest: Small tree holes and nest boxes.
Eggs: 3–8, creamy white with brown spots.
Food: Invertebrates in summer; seeds during winter.

This is the largest member of the tit family occurring in the New World. It is quite conspicuous through its range, thanks in part to its noisy nature. The vocal range of male tufted titmice is especially varied, and individuals are able to sing more than 15 different song patterns. Hens also sing, but not to the same extent and mainly during spring and early summer. The range of these titmice has increased northwards, largely because bird-table offerings guarantee them food throughout the year. In the south, they have been recorded as hybridizing with black-crested titmice (*P. atricristatus*) in central parts of Texas. The resulting offspring have greyish crests and a pale orange band above the bill. In spite of their small size, these titmice are determined visitors to bird tables, driving off much larger species. They can be equally fierce in defending their nests.

Identification: Characteristic black band immediately above the bill, with grey crest and crown. Cheeks and underparts are whitish, with pale reddish-orange flanks. Sexes alike. Young birds are duller overall, with less contrast in their plumage.

Above: The nest cup of this tit is lined with soft material.

Carolina chickadee

Parus carolinensis

This species is very closely related to the black-capped chickadee (*P. atricapillus*), which occurs further north, and it is not unknown for the birds to hybridize where they overlap. Studies of their song patterns have revealed that the Carolina chickadee has a four-note call, whereas the black-capped has a two-note whistle. Although pairs have their own territories during the summer, Carolina chickadees form larger groups in the winter months. During cold weather, they spend much longer periods of time roosting in tree hollows to conserve their body heat, sometimes remaining there for up to 15 hours per day. This is also the time of year when chickadees are most likely to be seen visiting bird tables in search of food.

Identification: Black area extends to the back of the head, with black under the bill, broadening across the throat. White on the sides of the face. Underparts are whitish with a slightly orange cast. Wings and tail are primarily greyish olive. Sexes alike.

Distribution: North-eastern USA south to Texas and northern Florida. Occasionally recorded in Ontario, Canada.
Size: 12cm (5in).
Habitat: Light, broad-leaved woodland.
Nest: In small holes in trees, also uses nest boxes.
Eggs: 3–9, white with reddish-brown spots.
Food: Invertebrates and seeds.

Bushtit (*Psaltriparus minimus*): 11cm (4½in)
Ranges from British Columbia in Canada south and eastwards through the USA to parts of Mexico and Guatemala in Central America. Three groupings are recognized. The northern common bushtit has brownish ear coverts, brown cap and grey upperparts, with paler, more whitish underparts. Hens have greyer throats. In the lead-coloured variety, grey coloration extends on to the cap. In the Central American black-eared form, cock birds have black areas on the sides of the face.

House wren (*Troglodytes aedon*): 13cm (5in)
Southern Canada through Central America as far as Argentina. Birds in northern parts of the range move south for the winter. Greyish upperparts, brown wings and tail with black barring. Lighter underparts. Pale ring around the eye and no striping on the head. Sexes alike.

Northern mockingbird (*Mimus polyglottos*): 28cm (11in)
Southern Canada through the USA to southern Mexico and the Caribbean. Relatively dull, with grey upperparts, paler on the underparts. Broad white area on the wings, most apparent in flight. Sexes alike.

Red-breasted nuthatch (*Sitta canadensis*): 11cm (4½in)
South-east Alaska and Canada into western and north-eastern USA. May move south in the winter. Black areas on the head, separated by a white line, with grey on the wings. Underparts are rusty orange. Hens similar but distinguished by their grey head coloration.

Cactus wren

Campylorhynchus brunneicapillus

This is a surprisingly large wren that is often seen in the vicinity of cacti, building its bulky nest of dried grass within the protective spines of these plants or thornbushes. The calls of the cactus wren have a decidedly monotonous tone, consisting simply of the sound "chut" repeated over and over again. The cactus wren does not raise its tail vertically in true wren fashion, but holds it horizontally. These birds prefer to remain near the ground, flying low and hunting for invertebrates here. Nests near the ground are concealed so they are less apparent to predators.

Identification: Brown area on the top of the head extending over the nape, with a white stripe passing through the eye, and white streaking on the back. Prominent black spotting on the breast, becoming more streaked on the pale underparts. Barring apparent on the wings and tail. Sexes alike.

Left: Cactus wrens inhabit arid areas.

Distribution: South-western USA from California southwards as far as central Mexico.
Size: 22cm (8.5in).
Habitat: Arid areas and desert.
Nest: Large structure made of vegetation.
Eggs: 4–7, creamy white with spots.
Food: Invertebrates.

Catbird

Dumetella carolinensis

The song of these relatives of the mockingbird incorporates a sound like a cat's miaowing, and is the reason for their common name. Catbirds also possess a harsher alarm call in their vocal repertoire. They can often be heard singing after dark, especially on moonlit nights. Catbirds are quite shy by nature, and their coloration also helps them to blend into the background. Their chestnut underparts are most conspicuous during the cock's courting display, when he chases the hen in the early stages of courtship. When on the move, the catbird flicks its long tail repeatedly. Insects are a vital part of catbirds' diet, especially when they are rearing chicks, as the insects provide valuable protein. Catbirds may catch their insect prey above water, and these birds are often observed in areas close to ponds and streams.

Identification: Slate grey in colour, with a distinctive black cap. Also has chestnut underparts, which may not be clearly visible. Sexes alike.

Distribution: Southern Canada south and eastwards across the USA to central Florida, moving south in the winter as far as Panama and Cuba.
Size: 23cm (9in).
Habitat: Scrubland, hedgerows and gardens.
Nest: Loosely constructed cup of vegetation.
Eggs: 4–6, glossy blue green.
Food: Fruit and insects.

SONGBIRDS

Many of these birds are a common sight, thanks to their adaptable natures. They often undertake seasonal movements southwards to warmer climes in search of more favourable feeding opportunities over the winter period. Their return is keenly anticipated, however, as an indicator of the arrival of spring. Pairs will then breed perhaps twice before returning south again.

Virginian cardinal

Northern cardinal *Cardinalis cardinalis*

The range of these cardinals continues to increase both in northern and western areas, especially since the first breeding record from Canada, which dates back to 1901. This expansion probably results from bird-table offerings. The stout, conical bill of these birds is adapted to crushing seeds, although Virginian cardinals will also hunt invertebrates, particularly when they have chicks in the nest.

Distribution: From southern Ontario, Canada south through the USA to the Gulf of Mexico, and southwards as far as Belize.
Size: 23cm (9in).
Habitat: Edges of woodland, parks and gardens.
Nest: Cup-shaped, made of vegetation.
Eggs: 3-4, whitish or greyish white, with darker spots and blotches.
Food: Seeds and invertebrates.

Identification: Predominantly red, with a pointed crest. A black mask surrounds the bill extending back to the eyes and down on to the throat. Wings, back and tail are of a slightly duller shade. Hen is predominantly brown, with a slight reddish suffusion over the wings and tail. The bill in adults of both sexes is bright red, whereas that of young birds is blackish, enabling them to be distinguished from adult hens.

Scarlet tanager

Piranga olivacea

These tanagers undertake long flights each year to and from their breeding grounds. Individuals sometimes venture further afield, and are observed in more northerly and westerly areas than usual, even reaching Alaska on rare occasions. A pair of scarlet tanagers rears only one brood during the summer before returning south. These birds catch invertebrates in the undergrowth and also in flight. More unusually, scarlet tanagers rub live ants on to their plumage. This behaviour, known as anting, results in formic acid being released by the ants among the feathers, which in turn drives out parasites, such as lice, from the plumage. The birds' bright coloration is linked in part to their diet.

Identification: Mainly yellowish olive, with underparts being more yellowish than upperparts. Cock distinguishable from the hen by having black rather than brownish wings and tail. In breeding plumage, the male has characteristic vivid scarlet plumage. Young cock birds in their first year have more orange rather than scarlet plumage.

Distribution: Migrates north to south-eastern Canada and eastern USA, overwintering in Central and South America, east of the Andes to Peru and Bolivia.
Size: 17cm (7in).
Habitat: Light forest and woodland.
Nest: Cup-shaped, made of stems and roots.
Eggs: 2-5, whitish to greenish blue with dark markings.
Food: Mainly invertebrates.

Blue grosbeak

Guiraca caerulea

In spite of the cock bird's distinctive plumage, the blue grosbeak is not as conspicuous as its coloration would suggest. Indeed, in poor light its feathering can appear so dark that, at a distance, it is sometimes confused with the male common cowbird (*Molothius ater*). The grosbeak's melodious song is most commonly heard early in the day, although the birds may start singing again at dusk. The song consists largely of short notes interspersed with longer trills. Cock birds usually return from their winter haunts a few days ahead of hens, frequently spending this time searching for food in groups on the ground before splitting up to nest. Pairs are likely to rear two broods of chicks over the summer period before migrating south again during September.

Identification: A dull shade of blue, with a large, greyish bill. The wings are darker, with two distinctive wing bars close to the shoulder. Hens are predominantly brownish, lighter on the underparts, and also display two buff-coloured wing bars. They have some bluish feathering on the rump. Young cock birds have more widespread blue feathering among their plumage.

Distribution: Occurs widely across the USA from California in the west through to New Jersey on the east coast, and south to Costa Rica. Northern populations overwinter in Central America, ranging from Mexico to Panama.
Size: 19cm (7.5in).
Habitat: Brush, often near water.
Nest: Cup-shaped.
Eggs: 3–4, pale blue.
Food: Seeds and invertebrates.

---American robin (*Turdus migratorius*): 28cm (11in)
Ranges from Alaska and Canada in summer south across much of the USA and through Central America to southern Mexico. Chestnut-reddish plumage on the breast and upper abdomen, with white below. Upperparts are predominantly greyish. White area around the eye and striping under the throat. Hens are significantly paler and browner in appearance.

Eastern bluebird (*Sialia sialis*): 18cm (7in)
Ranges from southern Canada to the Gulf states and Arizona, extending as far south as Nicaragua. Migrates south from northern areas for the winter, staying no farther north at this stage than southern parts of New England and southern Michigan. Blue head, wings and tail are offset against rusty red breast feathering, which becomes whiter on the abdomen. Hens are duller, with more greyish-blue upperparts. Young birds are brown and speckled, with areas of whitish and some blue plumage.

Cedar waxwing (*Bombycilla cedrorum*): 18cm (7in)
South-east Alaska and Canada to southern-central parts of the USA. Ranges further south into Panama over the winter. Brown, pointed crest with black stripe from the sides of the bill through the eyes to the back of the head. Small white area back from the base of the lower bill. Remainder of the plumage is mainly olive green with yellower underparts. Tail is grey with yellow tips. Distinctive red, wax-like colouring on the secondary flight feathers (which is why these birds are known as waxwings) but no white is evident here. Sexes alike.

American goldfinch

Carduelis tristis

These attractive songbirds are common throughout their range, although those in northern areas move south to warmer areas for the winter. They are often seen in larger flocks at this time, frequently in the company of related birds such as redpolls (*Acanthis* species). Their diet varies through the year, and is influenced by the availability of food. Invertebrates, which provide protein, are important for rearing chicks in the nest. Seeds are consumed through much of the year, while shoots and buds of trees such as spruce and willow will be eaten when other foods are in short supply.

Distribution: Canada southwards through much of the USA to northern Mexico.
Size: 14cm (5.5in).
Habitat: Wooded or lightly wooded areas.
Nest: Cup-shaped.
Eggs: 2–7, pale blue.
Food: Seeds, other plant matter and invertebrates.

Identification: Brightly coloured yellow plumage, with a black cap and black wings and tail, and white bars on the wings. Duller in winter plumage, being a more olive shade, and the black cap is far less distinct. Hens can be recognized by their olive-yellow upperparts and more yellowish underparts, becoming brownish during winter, especially on the upperparts. The white wing barring is still apparent, enabling hens to be distinguished easily from juveniles.

BIRDS OF EUROPE
AND AFRICA

The distribution of birds occurring in this part of the world, especially those found in Europe, often extends eastwards into Asia as well. Many northerly species also undergo regular seasonal movements in response to the climate, overwintering in more southerly latitudes, with some even flying as far as southern Africa. Those groups of birds most commonly associated with tropical areas – such as parrots, for example – are poorly represented in this region of the world, partly because of the absence of suitable feeding opportunities in Europe. Urban development in this part of the world has also had a marked impact on the distribution of a number of species, and some have adapted to urban environments better than others. Human involvement has also seen the introduction of avian species into Europe from outside their natural range, often for sporting purposes, as in the case of various species of pheasants and partridges.

Above from left: Kestrel (Falco tinnunculus), ostrich (Struthio camelus), bee-eater (Merops apiaster).

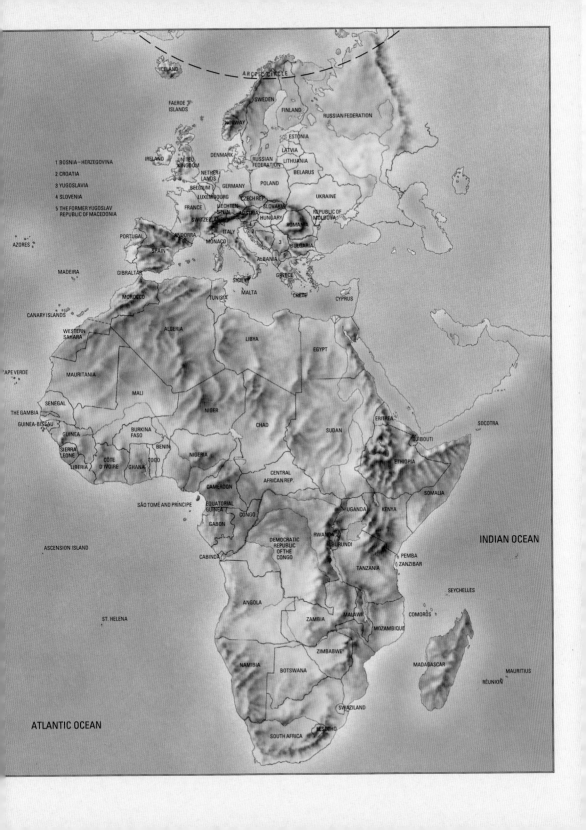

SEABIRDS

Some seabirds have evolved to live largely on the wing. Others, such as the little auk, have adapted to a more aquatic lifestyle. The auks have sometimes been described as "penguins of the north", but they are not closely related to penguins, which are confined to the southern oceans, although their coloration is similar.

Gannet

Northern gannet *Sula bassana*

Distribution: Along the eastern seaboard of North America extending across the Atlantic via southern Greenland and Iceland beyond Norway, southwards through the Mediterranean down to the west coast of North Africa.
Size: 88–100cm (35–39in).
Habitat: Sea.
Nest: Usually on cliffs, built from seaweed and other marine debris held together by droppings.
Eggs: 1, whitish.
Food: Fish.

This species is the largest of all gannets and can weigh up to 3.6kg (8lb). It is the only member of this group found around the North Atlantic. These gannets are powerful in the air. Their keen eyesight allows them to detect shoals of fish such as herring and mackerel in the ocean below. When feeding, gannets dive down into a shoal, often from a considerable height, seizing fish from under the water. Their streamlined shape also enables them to swim. Breeding occurs in the spring when the birds form large colonies in which there is often a lot of squabbling. The young mature slowly, and are unlikely to breed until they are at least four years old.

Identification: Mainly white, aside from pale creamy yellow plumage on the head extending down the neck, and black flight feathers. Tail feathers are white, and the feet are dark grey. Sexes alike. Young birds are dark brown in colour.

Great skua

Catharacta skua

These large, powerfully built birds can sometimes look rather like buzzards in flight, soaring above the ocean. When landing on the sea, great skuas glide down and hover in an unusual way before actually touching down on the water. They are highly opportunistic feeders, catching fish themselves and also robbing other seabirds of their catches. These birds also eat carrion, and their diet tends to be most variable during the breeding period, when they spend time on land. At this time they may even be observed eating berries or catching small rodents.

Identification: Predominantly dull brown with lighter streaking and barring. Distinctive white wing flashes visible when in flight. Strong, powerful hooked bill and relatively short tail. Sexes similar but hens may have more yellowish-brown markings on the neck. Young birds have brown underparts.

Distribution: Ranges widely throughout the Atlantic Ocean.
Size: 50–58cm (20–23in).
Habitat: Sea and coast.
Nest: Depression on the ground.
Eggs: 2, olive grey to reddish brown with darker markings.
Food: Typically fish and carrion.

Manx shearwater (*Puffinus puffinus*): 35cm (14in)
Widely distributed through the North Atlantic, as far as the coast of Iceland and south through the North Sea to the eastern coast of Spain. Also ranges further south off the north-western coast of Africa, and the southern tip of the continent. Sooty black upperparts, white beneath, including the undertail coverts. Sexes alike.

Parasitic jaeger (Arctic skua, *Stercorarius parasiticus*): 44cm (17in)
Present in the Atlantic Ocean extending up to the Arctic, but usually wintering south of the Equator. Sleek, gull-like appearance with long, narrow tail extensions averaging nearly 9cm (3.5in) in the summer. Dark crown with greyish wings and tail and white underparts at this time. Also occurs as a dark morph, lacking white plumage. Young birds have a barred appearance. Sexes are alike.

Guillemot (*Uria aalge*): 46cm (18in)
Ranges from off the western coast of Iceland and Ireland south to Spain and east through the North Sea as far as Scandinavia. Rather penguin-like appearance when standing vertically, but unlike penguins, can fly. Black head, chest and back, with white underparts and some streaking on the flanks. Thin white band over each wing, just above the flight feathers. Narrow, pointed black bill. Sexes alike.

Razorbill (*Alca torda*): 43cm (17in)
Similar distribution to the guillemot, with which it may associate, but also extends further south to North Africa and the western Mediterranean. Rather similar in coloration to the guillemot, too, but easily discernible by the broad, flat bill that has a white horizontal stripe on it, and its longer tail. A white stripe also extends to the eyes. Sexes alike.

Puffin

Fratercula arctica

These auks have unmistakable bills, said to resemble those of parrots. Young puffins have much narrower and less brightly coloured bills than the adults. Puffins come ashore to nest in colonies on cliffs and coastal areas where they can breed largely hidden from predators. Sand eels figure prominently in their diet at this time, and adult birds often fly quite long distances to obtain food. When underwater, puffins use their wings like flippers, enabling them to swim faster. Adult birds fly back to their young with eels arranged in a row, hanging down each side of their bills. They can carry as many as ten fish at a time in this way.

Left: The appearance of the puffin's bill varies depending on the bird's age and the time of year.

Right: Puffins excavate nesting tunnels underground or use existing holes.

Distribution: Throughout the northern Atlantic, including Spitzbergen.
Size: 32cm (13in).
Habitat: Sea and coastal areas.
Nest: Underground burrows.
Eggs: 1, white.
Food: Fish.

Identification: Whitish sides to the face, with black extending back over the crown. Black neck, back and wings; underparts white, with a grey area on the flanks. Broad, flattened bill with red area running down its length and across the tip. Greyish base with yellow area intervening. Bill less brightly coloured and sides of the face greyish during the winter. Sexes alike.

Little auk

Alle alle

In spite of its relatively restricted distribution, the little auk is considered to be possibly the most numerous seabird in the world. It forms huge nesting colonies in the Arctic region during the brief summer, before heading south at the approach of winter as the sea starts to freeze. Little auks are often more likely to be spotted at this time of year, frequently flying very low over the waves or even through them on occasion. Sometimes, however, fierce storms make feeding virtually impossible, and in a weakened state, little auks are driven into coastal areas. This phenomenon is often described as a "wreck".

Identification: In summer plumage, the head and upper part of the chest are black. The back, wings and upper surface of the tail feathers are also black, aside from white streaks apparent over the wings. During the winter, the black on the face is broken by white, leaving a black band across the throat. The bill is small and black. Sexes alike.

Distribution: Icelandic coast to northern Scandinavia, across the North Sea to the coast of eastern England.
Size: 20cm (8in).
Habitat: Sea and coastal areas.
Nest: Cliffs or crevices.
Eggs: 1, pale blue.
Food: Microscopic plankton.

GULLS

Gulls are linked in many people's minds with the seaside, but some species have proved very adept at adjusting to living alongside people and generally profiting from this association. A number of different gulls have now spread to various inland localities. Shades of white and grey generally predominate in the plumage of these birds, making them quite easy to recognize.

Herring gull

Larus argentatus

These large gulls are often seen on fishing jetties and around harbours, searching for scraps. They have also moved inland and can be seen in areas such as rubbish dumps, where they scavenge for food, often in quite large groups. Herring gulls are noisy by nature, especially when breeding. They now frequently nest on rooftops in coastal towns and cities, a trend that began as recently as the 1940s in Britain. Pairs can become very aggressive at breeding time, swooping menacingly on people who venture close to the nest site or even to the chicks once they fledge.

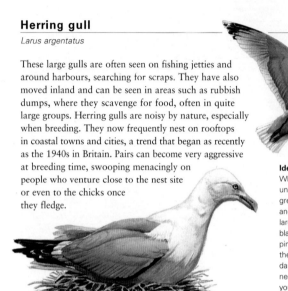

Left: The herring gull's pink legs are a distinctive feature.

Identification: White head and underparts, with grey on the back and wings. Prominent large, white spots on the black flight feathers. Distinctive pink feet. Reddish spot towards the tip of the lower bill. Some dark streaking on the head and neck in winter. Sexes alike. The young birds are mainly brown, with prominent barring on their wings and dark bills.

Distribution: Atlantic, north of Iceland and south to northern coast of Spain, through the North Sea and Baltic areas, north of Scandinavia.
Size: 60cm (24in)
Habitat: Coastal and inland areas.
Nest: Small pile of vegetation.
Eggs: 2–3, pale blue to brown with darker markings.
Food: Fish and carrion.

Black-headed gull

Larus ridibundus

These gulls are a common sight not only in coastal areas but also in town parks with lakes. They move inland during the winter. They are also often seen following tractors ploughing at this time of year, seeking worms and grubs in the soil. Black-headed gulls nest close to water in what can be quite large colonies. Like many gulls, they are noisy birds, even calling at night. On warm, summer evenings, they can sometimes be seen hawking flying ants and similar insects in flight, demonstrating their airborne agility.

Identification: These gulls have their distinctive black heads only during the summer, with a white collar beneath and white under-parts. Wings are grey, and the flight feathers mainly black. In the winter, the head is mainly white, aside from black ear coverts, and a black smudge above each eye. In the winter, the bill is red at the base and dark at the tip.

Above: The black feathering on the head is a transient characteristic, appearing only in the summer (above right).

Distribution: Across most of Europe into Asia. Also present on the North African side of the Mediterranean.
Size: 39cm (15in).
Habitat: Coastal areas.
Nest: Scrape lined with plant matter.
Eggs: 2–3, pale blue to brown with darker markings.
Food: Typically molluscs, crustaceans and small fish.

Great black-backed gull

Larus marinus

These large gulls can be extremely disruptive when close to nesting seabird colonies. Not only will they harry returning birds for their catches of fish, but they also take eggs and chicks on occasion too. In winter, great black-backed gulls move inland to scavenge on rubbish tips, although they are generally wary of people and are unlikely to be seen in urban areas. Banding studies have revealed that many of those that overwinter in Britain are actually birds of Norwegian origin, which return to Scandinavia to breed the following spring. Pairs are often quite solitary at this time, especially when nesting near people, but they are more likely to nest in colonies on uninhabited islands.

Identification:
Has a white head and underparts with black on the back and wings. Is a large size. Has a white-spotted black tail and a large area of white is apparent at the wing tips in flight. The bill is yellow with red tip to the lower bill. Has pale pinkish legs. Sexes alike.

Distribution: From northern Spain north to Iceland and eastwards through the North Sea and Baltic to Scandinavia. Also present on the eastern side of North America.
Size: 74cm (29in).
Habitat: Coastal areas.
Nest: Pile of vegetation.
Eggs: 2–3, brownish with dark markings.
Food: Fish and carrion.

Lesser black-backed gull (*Larus fuscus*): 56cm (22in)
Breeds around the shores of the extreme north of Europe, moving as far south as parts of North Africa in the winter. Similar to the great black-backed but smaller and lacks the prominent white seen on the flight feathers when the wings are closed. Legs are yellow rather than dull pink. Much smaller area of white on the outstretched upper surface of the wings in flight. Sexes alike.

Kittiwake (*Larus tridactyla*): 42cm (17in)
Occurs widely around the shores of northern Europe, down to the western Mediterranean. White head and underparts, with grey on the back and wings. Yellow bill, dark feet and black flight feathers. In winter plumage, grey extends to the back of the head, with blackish, crescent-shaped marking behind the eyes. Sexes alike. Young birds have more black on the wings and a black collar.

Glaucous gull (*Larus hyperboreus*): 68cm (27in)
Coastal areas of northern Europe, including Iceland. Very pale bluish-grey wings with white edges. Head and underparts white in summer, developing grey streaks in winter. Sexes alike. As in other species, young birds are more mottled overall.

Yellow-legged gull (*Larus cachinnans*): 58cm (23in)
Found in coastal areas of southern England and mainland Europe to North Africa, and also around the Black and Caspian seas. Has a white head and underparts, grey back and wings and small white spots on the black flight feathers. The wings have large black areas towards the tips. The bill and legs are yellow and there is a red spot on the lower bill. Grey suffusion on the head in winter. Sexes alike. Was recognized as a form of the herring gull (*L. argentatus*) but now considered a separate species.

Common gull

Larus canus

The common gulls often ranges over considerable distances inland, seeking earthworms and other invertebrates to feed on. In sandy coastal areas they will search for shellfish as well. There is a distinct seasonal variation in the range of these gulls. They leave their breeding grounds in Scandinavia and Russia at the end of the summer, heading further south in Europe to France and various locations in the Mediterranean. They overwinter here before migrating north again in the spring. In spite of its rather meek appearance, this species will bully smaller gulls such as the black-headed gull to take food from them. Common gulls and black-headed gulls are often found in the same type of environment inland and tend to show a preference for grassland and agricultural areas.

Distribution: Iceland, Great Britain and the Baltic region. Main breeding grounds are in Scandinavia and Russia. Extends across Asia to western North America.
Size: 46cm (18in).
Habitat: Coasts and inland areas close to water.
Nest: Raised nest of twigs and other debris.
Eggs: 2–3, pale blue to brownish olive with dark markings.
Food: Shellfish, small fish and invertebrates.

Identification: White head and underparts with yellow bill and yellowish-green legs. Wings are greyish with white markings at the tips, which are most visible in flight. Flight feathers are black with white spots. Tail is white. Dark eyes. Greyish streaking on the head in winter plumage. Sexes alike. Young birds have brown mottled plumage and it takes them more than two years to obtain adult coloration.

TERNS

Terns as a group can usually be distinguished quite easily, even from gulls, by their relatively elongated shape. Their long, pointed wings are an indication of their aerial ability, and some terns regularly fly longer distances than other migrants. Not surprisingly, their flight appears to be almost effortless. When breeding, terns tend to nest in colonies.

Common tern

Sterna hirundo

These terns are only likely to be encountered in northern parts of their range between April and October, after which they head south to warmer climes for the duration of the winter. Travelling long distances means that they are powerful in flight and yet are also agile. Their strongly forked tail helps them to hover effectively, adjusting their position before diving in search of fish. Their long bills provide another simple way of distinguishing them from gulls. This species is represented on all continents and is very versatile in its feeding habits. Common terns may hawk food on the wing or dive into the oceans to obtain their quarry.

Identification: Long body shape with black on the top of the head extending down the back of the neck. Rest of the face and underparts whitish grey. Back and wings greyish, with long flight feathers. Narrow white streamers on the tail. Bill red, aside from the dark tip, which becomes completely black in the winter. The plumage in front of the eyes becomes white during this time. Legs and feet red. Sexes alike.

Distribution: Great Britain and Scandinavia and much of Central Europe during the summer, migrating south to parts of western and southern Africa for the winter.
Size: 36cm (14in).
Habitat: Near water.
Nest: Scrape on the ground.
Eggs: 3, pale brown with dark spots.
Food: Mainly fish, but also eats crustaceans.

Sandwich tern

Cabot's tern *Sterna sandvicensis*

A summer visitor to northern Europe, this species is often sighted slightly earlier than the common tern and then leaves just before its relative. The sandwich tern is significantly larger, and also surprisingly noisy, with the sounds of its calls having been likened to those of a grating cartwheel. Although these terns may skim over the water surface seeking food, they also dive spectacularly from heights of as much as 10m (33ft). Sandwich terns usually breed in high-density colonies in the open on sand bars and similarly exposed coastal sites, although they may sometimes nest on islands in lakes.

Identification: Shaggy black crest evident at the back of the head. The entire top of the head is black during the summer, while a white forehead is characteristic of the winter plumage. The bill is long and black with a yellow tip. Rest of the head and underparts are white, and the wings are grey. Sexes alike.

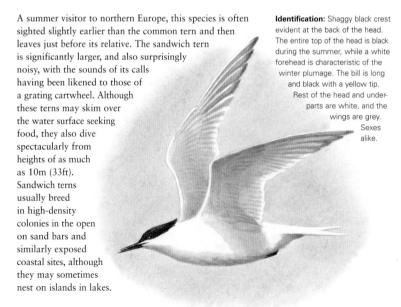

Distribution: Found around the shores of Great Britain and northern Europe, as well as the Caspian and Black seas, wintering further south in the Mediterranean region and Africa. Also occurs in parts of southern Asia, the Caribbean and South America.
Size: 43cm (17in).
Habitat: Coastal areas.
Nest: Scrape on the ground.
Eggs: 1–2, brownish white with darker markings.
Food: Fish, especially sand eels.

Roseate tern

Sterna dougallii

In northern parts of their range, these terns are brief summer visitors, only likely to be present from about the middle of May until the end of August. Their distribution is quite localized. They are most likely to be seen where the shore is shallow and sandy, providing them with better fishing opportunities. They dive into the water to catch their prey from heights of no more than 2m (7ft). They may also take fish from other terns, and their shorter wings and quicker wing beats make them more agile in flight. Unlike some other terns, roseate terns avoid open areas when nesting, preferring sites concealed among rocks or vegetation.

Identification: This tern gets its name from the slight pinkish suffusion on its whitish underparts. Compared to other terns, has relatively long tail streamers and quite short wings. The bill is primarily blackish with a red base in the summer. The entire top of the head is black in the summer, and the forehead becomes white in winter. Sexes alike. Subspecies differ in both wing and bill length.

Distribution: The British Isles south to Spain and North Africa. Winters in western Africa.
Size: 36cm (14in).
Habitat: Coastal areas.
Nest: Scrape on the ground.
Eggs: 1–2, cream or buff eggs with reddish-brown markings.
Food: Mainly fish.

Little tern (*Sterna albifrons*): 25cm (10in)
Found in coastal areas in northern Europe. Also breeds in central Europe. Overwinters in Africa. Has a white forehead with black edges. These form a black cap that extends down the nape of the neck. The bill is yellow with a black tip. The legs are orange-yellow. Has black edges to the primary feathers, while the remainder of the wings are grey. The chest and underparts are white. Sexes are alike.

Caspian tern (*Sterna caspia*): 55cm (22in)
Breeds mainly in the Baltic region, overwintering in western Africa. Is sometimes seen in the Mediterranean area. Has a black top to the head that becomes streaked in winter plumage. Has grey wings and a white chest and underparts. Large red bill with black tip. Sexes are alike.

Lesser crested tern (*Sterna bengalensis*): 40cm (16in)
Found along the North African coast and less commonly in the Gulf of Suez and the Red Sea. Occasionally seen in Europe. Black top to the head with a crest. Wings, rump and upper tail are grey. Remainder of the plumage is white. Has a slender yellow bill. The legs are black. In winter plumage, the area of black on the head is reduced. Sexes are alike.

Gull-billed tern (*Sterna nilotica*): 42cm (17in)
Ranges from the coast of northern mainland Europe south to the Mediterranean. Winters in Africa. Black cap on the head extends down to the nape of the neck. Frosty grey wings, back and tail feathers, which have white edges. Remainder of the plumage is white. In winter plumage, the black cap is replaced by blackish ear coverts. Bill relatively short and black. Sexes are alike.

Arctic tern

Sterna paradisaea

It can be very difficult to distinguish this species from the common tern, but the Arctic tern's bill is shorter and does not have a black tip in the summer. The tail, too, is longer, and the tail streamers are very evident in flight. Arctic terns undertake the most extensive migrations of any birds, flying almost from one end of the world to the other. Breeding in the vicinity of the Arctic Circle, these birds then head south, often beyond Africa to Antarctica, before repeating the journey the following year, although it appears that at least some young birds stay for their first full year in the Antarctic Ocean. Arctic terns will nest communally, often frequenting islands for breeding purposes. They react aggressively to a potential predator in their midst, with a number of individuals turning on and mobbing any intruder. Arctic terns may steal food from other birds – for example, from puffins in the Faeroe Islands.

Identification: Black area covering the entire top of the head, with white chest and underparts. Wings grey. Bill dark red, becoming black in the winter when the forehead is white. Sexes alike.

Distribution: Breeds in northern Europe and the Arctic, overwintering in southern Africa.
Size: 38cm (15in).
Habitat: Seas and fresh water.
Nest: Hollow on the ground, lined with vegetation.
Eggs: 2, brownish, bluish or greenish with dark markings.
Food: Fish and invertebrates.

WADERS

The description of 'wader' is given to birds that usually inhabit shallow waters, seeking their food as they walk along an uncovered beach or mudflat at low tide. Waders are often sighted in mixed groups, taking advantage of feeding opportunities as these become available. Seasonal movements of waders are quite common, with some breeding in the far north during the summer months

Eurasian oystercatcher

Haematopus ostralegus

The large size of these waders, coupled with their noisy nature, makes them quite conspicuous. The oystercatcher's powerful bill is a surprisingly adaptable tool, allowing these birds not only to force mussel shells apart, but also to hammer limpets off groynes and even prey on crabs. Inland, oystercatchers use their bills to catch earthworms in the soil without difficulty. Individuals will defend favoured feeding sites such as mussel beds from others of their own kind, although oystercatchers may sometimes form large flocks of thousands of individuals, especially in the winter.

Identification: The head, upper chest and wings are black. The underparts are white and there is a white stripe on the wings. Has a prominent, straight orangish-red bill, which may be shorter and thicker in cock birds. Legs are reddish. In winter plumage, adults have a white throat and collar and pale pink legs. Sexes are alike.

Distribution: Around the shores of Europe, especially Great Britain, extending to Asia. Also present in North Africa.
Size: 44cm (17in.)
Habitat: Tidal mudflats, sometimes in fields.
Nest: Scrape on the ground.
Eggs: 2–4, light buff with blackish-brown markings.
Food: Cockles, mussels and similar prey.

Avocet

Pied avocet *Recurvirostra avosetta*

The unique shape of the avocet's long, thin, upward-curving bill enables these birds to feed by sweeping the bill from side to side in the water, locating their prey predominantly by touch. Pairs may show very aggressive behaviour when breeding. They can be present in large numbers, nesting at high densities, in some areas. Although they most frequently move about by wading, avocets can also swim well and will place their heads under water when seeking food. When migrating, avocets tend to fly quite low in loose lines. Birds from western areas tend to be more sedentary compared with those occurring further east. These tend to overwinter in Africa as well as the Mediterranean region.

Identification: Slender, with long, pale blue legs. The black plumage on the top of the head extends down to the nape. Black stripes extend over the shoulder area and around the sides of the wings. Black flight feathers. Long, thin black bill curves upwards at the tip. Hens often have shorter bills and a brownish tinge to their black markings.

Distribution: North-western Europe, often close to the coast, and southern Europe and North Africa. Also extends into western Asia.
Size: 46cm (18in.)
Habitat: Lagoons and mudflats.
Nest: Scrape on the ground lined with vegetation.
Eggs: 4, pale brown with faint markings.
Food: Small crustaceans and other invertebrates.

Black-winged stilt (*Himantopus himantopus*): 36cm (14in)
Found in southern Europe. Overwinters in Africa. The top of the head to the nape is blackish. The ear coverts are black. The back and wings are jet black and the underparts are white. The bill is long and black. The legs are very long and red. Sexes are similar, except that hens lack the dark head markings and the plumage on the back is more brownish in colour.

Sanderling (*Calidris alba*): 20cm (8in)
Breeds in the Arctic. Can be seen on migration and during the winter on the shores of Europe. Has a rufous coloration and black speckling on the breast. The underparts are white. The back and wings are grey with black and buff markings. During the winter, rufous markings are less evident but a broad wing bar with black edging is seen in flight. Sexes are alike.

Knot (*Calidris canutus*): 25cm (10in)
Breeds in the Arctic and migrates south along northern and western European coasts as far as North Africa. Distinctive rufous underparts in summer, with black and rufous speckling on the wings offset against areas of grey plumage. Black legs and grey upperparts. In winter plumage has streaking on the head, chest and flanks, greyish-white underparts and grey-green legs. Sexes alike.

Dunlin (red-backed sandpiper, *Calidris alpina*): 20cm (8in)
Circumpolar. Greyish head and wings in winter plumage with streaking on the breast. Underparts are white. In summer, has a more distinctive black streaking, with brownish and black plumage on the wings. The abdomen is mainly black. Has white flanks. Sexes are alike.

Stone curlew

Thick knee *Burhinus oedicnemus*

The stone curlew is a wader that has adapted to a relatively dry environment, and its mottled plumage enables it to blend in well against a stony background. When frightened, it drops to the ground in an attempt to conceal its presence. These birds are also frequently active after dark, when they will be much harder to observe. Their loud call notes may be heard, however, sounding rather like "curlee" and audible over distances of 2.5km (1.5m) when the surroundings are quiet. On occasion, stone curlews living close to coastal areas fly to mudflats, feeding when the flats are exposed by the sea.

Distribution: Breeds at various localities in Europe, extending from southern England southwards. Ranges into southern Asia and south to parts of northern Africa.
Size: 45cm (18in).
Habitat: Open, relatively dry countryside.
Nest: Bare scrape on the ground.
Eggs: 2, pale buff with dark markings.
Food: Invertebrates, typically caught at night.

Identification: Streaked plumage on the neck, upper breast and wings, with prominent white stripes above and below the eyes. White wing bars edged with black are also apparent on the wings. Abdomen and throat are whitish. Long, thick yellowish legs. Bill is mainly blackish, but yellow at the base. Sexes alike. However, there is a little variation among races and some have a greyer tint to their feathers than others.

Ringed plover

Greater ringed plover *Charadrius hiaticula*

In spite of their relatively small size, these waders have strong migratory instincts. They breed mainly in the far north, and are most likely to be seen in Europe during May and again from the middle of August for about a month. After that time, they leave European shores on their way south to Africa for the winter. Ringed plovers typically breed on beaches and on the tundra. They can be seen in reasonably large flocks outside the nesting season, often seeking food in tidal areas.

Identification: Black mask extends over the forehead and down across the eyes. There is a white patch above the bill and just behind the eyes. A broad black band extends across the chest. The underparts are otherwise white. The wings are a greyish brown and the bill is orange with a black tip. In winter plumage, the black areas are reduced, apart from the bill which becomes entirely blackish. White areas extend from the forehead to above the eyes. Cheek patches are greyish brown and there is a similar band on the upper chest at this time. Sexes are alike.

Distribution: Western Europe and North America, wintering in Africa. Also recorded in parts of Asia.
Size: 19cm (7.5in).
Habitat: Coastal areas and tundra.
Nest: Bare scrape on the ground.
Eggs: 4, stone-buff with black markings.
Food: Freshwater and marine invertebrates.

WATERBIRDS

Although some waterbirds, such as herons, feed in a similar fashion to waders, their larger size allows
them to wander into deeper water, and thus affords them greater opportunity to feed, as well as enabling
them to take larger prey such as fish. Certain waterbirds such as divers will actually disappear under
the water in search of food, however, rather than hunting from above.

Grey heron

Ardea cinerea

These large, opportunistic hunters are often shy
on the ground and can be hard to spot. They are
usually seen in flight, with their long necks tucked back
on to their shoulders and their legs held out behind the
body. They fly with relatively slow, quite noisy wing beats.
When hunting, grey herons are patient predators. They stand
motionless, looking closely for any sign of movement in the
water around them, lunging quickly with their powerful bills
to grab any fish or frog that swims within reach. During the
winter, when their freshwater habitats are frozen, grey herons
often move to river estuaries in search of food. These birds
frequently nest in colonies, with some breeding sites being
used for centuries by successive generations.

Identification: Powerful yellow bill. White head with black area and longer
plumes off the back of the head. Long neck and chest are whitish with a
black stripe running down the centre. Wings are grey with black areas at
the shoulder. Underparts are lighter grey. Long yellowish legs. Sexes alike.

Distribution: Throughout
most of Europe into Asia,
apart from the far north. Also
occurs in North Africa and
ranges south around the
Sahara Desert.
Size: 100cm (39in).
Habitat: Areas of water
with reeds.
Nest: Platform of sticks built
off the ground.
Eggs: 3–5, chalky blue.
Food: Fish and other aquatic
vertebrates.

Eurasian spoonbill

Platalea leucorodia

Distribution: Breeds in
northern temperate parts of
Europe and Asia, as far east
as China. Winters further
south in tropical parts of
Africa and South-east Asia.
Indian birds are sedentary.
Size: 93cm (37in).
Habitat: Mudflats and
marshes.
Nest: Stick platforms off
the ground.
Eggs: 3–4, white with
brown markings.
Food: Fish, other aquatic
creatures and vegetation.

The enlarged surface area of these birds' bills enables
them to feed more easily as they move their heads from
side to side in the water. Young spoonbills, however, have
a narrower, light-coloured bill with no enlargement at its
tip. They can also be identified in flight by the black tips
to their outer flight feathers. It can take up to four years
for them to start nesting, and they may live for
nearly 30 years. Spoonbills can swim if
they need to, but they usually inhabit
calm, shallow stretches of water.
When resting, they may
perch on one leg and
tuck their bills over
their backs. In flight,
however, they will
extend their necks.

Identification: Highly distinctive
enlarged, yellow-edged, spoon-
like tip to the black bill. Has a
crest of feathers on the back
of the neck that is longer in the
male, and an orange patch of
plumage on the chest at breeding
time. The rest of the feathering
is white. The legs are black.

White stork

Ciconia ciconia

Distribution: Summer visitor to much of mainland Europe. Winters in western and eastern parts of North Africa, depending on the flight path. Also occurs in Asia.
Size: 110cm (43in).
Habitat: Wetland areas.
Nest: Large platform of sticks, located off the ground.
Eggs: 3–5, chalky white.
Food: Amphibians, fish, small mammals and invertebrates.

Identification: Large, tall, mainly white bird with prominent black areas on the back and wings. Has a long red bill and legs. Sexes are alike. Young birds are smaller and have a dark tip to the bill.

Considered to be a harbinger of good fortune, these birds often return year after year to the same nest site on the top of a building, adding annually to their nest, which can develop into a bulky structure. The return of these storks in the spring from their wintering grounds in Africa helped to foster the widespread myth of the link between storks and babies. The migration of white storks on their two flight paths in April each year – over the Strait of Gibraltar and further east over the Bosphorus – is a spectacular sight. They fly with their long necks extended and their legs trailing behind their bodies. The journey back to Africa is repeated each August. The numbers of white storks have declined in some areas over recent years due to drainage of their wetland habitat.

Great crested grebe

Podiceps cristatus

Great crested grebes are primarily aquatic birds and their flying ability is restricted by their short wings. They can dive very effectively, however, and often disappear underwater if they feel threatened. Rarely observed on land, these grebes are relatively cumbersome because their legs are located well back on the body and this restricts their ability to move fast across open ground. Their toes are not fully webbed, unlike those of waterfowl, but they can swim quickly thanks to the streamlined shape of their body. They use the ruff-type facial feathers during their display.

Distribution: Europe east to China and southwards across much of Africa. Also Australia and New Zealand.
Size: 51cm (20in).
Habitat: Extensive reedy stretches of water.
Nest: Mound of reeds.
Eggs: 3–6, chalky white.
Food: Fish and invertebrates.

Identification: Black from top of the head down to the back. Brownish areas on sides of body in winter. During summer, there is an extensive black crest, with a chestnut ruff at rear of head edged with black. Bill reddish pink. Sexes are alike.

Great northern loon (common loon, *Gavia immer*): 88cm (35in)
Present on Icelandic and British coasts. Also occurs in North America and Greenland. Has a black head, with barring on the neck and throat. The back is patterned black and white and has white spots. The underparts are white. There is less contrast in the winter plumage, with white extending from the lower bill and throat down over the underparts. In winter, the eyes are dark rather than red. Sexes are alike.

Little grebe (*Tachybaptus ruficollis*): 29cm (11in)
Found in most of Europe on a line from southern Scotland southwards. Also present in North Africa and the Middle East. Black head, chestnut patches on the neck and a yellow gape at the corners of the bill. Dark feathering on the back and wings with brown flanks. In the winter, light buff plumage replaces darker areas. Sexes alike.

Little egret (*Egretta garzetta*): 65cm (26in)
Southern Europe, overwintering mainly in Africa and the Middle East. White plumage, with blue-grey area at the base of the bill. Long, white nuptial plumes at breeding time. Legs blackish, but with very unusual yellow toes. Sexes alike.

CRAKES

This group of birds may be observed in the open, but, if frightened, they usually dart back into cover along the edges of the stretches of water that they usually frequent. They can all be recognized by their relatively narrow body shape, which enables them to slip easily and quietly through reeds and similar vegetation.

Water rail

Rallus aquaticus

Being naturally highly adaptable, these rails have an extensive distribution, and have even been recorded foraging in tidal areas surrounded by seaweed in the Scilly Isles off south-west England. In some parts of their range, they migrate to warmer climes for the winter. Water rails survive in Iceland during the winter thanks to the hot thermal springs, which never freeze. Water rails are very territorial when breeding and, as in other related species, their chicks hatch in a precocial state.

Identification: Prominent, long, reddish bill with bluish-grey breast and sides to the head. Narrow, brownish line extending over the top of the head down the back and wings, which have black markings. Black-and-white barring on the flanks and underparts. Short tail with pale buff underparts. Sexes alike.

Distribution: Extensive, from Iceland throughout most of Europe, south to North Africa and east across Asia to Siberia, China and Japan.
Size: 26cm (10in).
Habitat: Reed beds and sedge.
Nest: Cup made of vegetation.
Eggs: 5–16, whitish with reddish-brown spotting.
Food: Mainly animal matter, but also some vegetation.

Coot

Eurasian coot *Fulica atra*

Open stretches of water are important to coots, enabling them to dive in search of food. During the winter, these birds may sometimes assemble in flocks on larger stretches of waters that are unlikely to freeze over at this time. These coots may find food on land or in the water, although they dive only briefly in relatively shallow water. When breeding, pairs are very territorial, attacking chicks of other coots that venture too close, and even their own chicks, which they grab by the neck. Such behaviour is often described as tousling. The young usually respond by feigning death and this results in them being left alone.

Identification: Has a sooty, grey, plump body with a black neck and head. The bill is white with a white frontal plate. This iris is a dark brownish colour. A white trailing edge on the wings is evident in flight. Long toes have no webbing. Sexes are alike.

Distribution: From Great Britain east throughout Europe, except the far north, south into North Africa and east to Asia, as well as Australia and New Zealand.
Size: 42cm (16.5in.)
Habitat: Still and slow-flowing stretches of water.
Nest: Pile of reeds at the water's edge.
Eggs: 1–14, buff to brown with dark markings.
Food: Plant and animal matter.

Spotted crake (*Porzana porzana*): 22cm (9in)
Found in western and central parts of Eurasia and as far east as southern Siberia and north-west China. Winters in North Africa and southwards from Ethiopia . Has a distinctive, heavily white-spotted breast, although the abdomen is streakier. Has prominent brown ear coverts, with a bluish-grey stripe above, and black markings on the wings. The undertail area is pale buff and whiter at the tip, but may show dark spots in some cases. The bill is yellow, although red at the base. Sexes are alike.

Little crake (*Porzana parva*): 19cm (7.5in)
Found in areas of Spain and Portugal. The range then extends eastwards through Europe to China. Overwinters in southern Asia and northern parts of Africa. Has a slaty-blue head and underparts. Black markings are found predominantly across the top of the wings. The remainder of the back is brown. Has a black-and-white speckled under-tail area. The bill is yellow with a red base. Adult hens are easily distinguished by their white chest area which turns buff on the underparts. Sexes are alike.

Baillon's crake (*Porzana pusilla*): 18cm (7in)
Has a sporadic distribution through Europe and overwinters in North Africa. Also occurs further south, in Africa and on Madagascar. Ranges through Asia to parts of Australia and New Zealand. Has a slaty-blue head and underparts, although the Baillon's crake can be distinguished from the little crake by far more extensive barring on the flanks and heavier white speckling on the wings. The bill is dull with no red area. Hens may have paler plumage on the throat.

Moorhen

Common moorhen *Gallinula chloropus*

Although usually found in areas of fresh water, moorhens are occasionally seen in brackish areas – for example, on the Namibian coast in south-western Africa. Their long toes enable them to walk over aquatic vegetation, and they also feed when swimming or browsing on land. Their diet varies according to the season, although seeds of various types make up the bulk of their food. If danger threatens, moorhens will either dive or swim underwater. They are adept divers, remaining submerged by grasping on to underwater vegetation with their bills. In public parks, moorhens can become quite tame, darting in to obtain food provided for ducks.

Distribution: Very wide, from Great Britain east throughout Europe except for the far north. Occurs through much of Africa, especially southern parts, and also through much of South-east Asia and parts of the Americas.
Size: 30cm (12in).
Habitat: Ponds and other areas of water edged by dense vegetation.
Nest: Domed structure hidden in reeds.
Eggs: 2–17, buff to light green with dark markings.
Food: Omnivorous.

Identification: Slate-grey head, back and underparts. Greyish-black wings. A prominent white line runs down the sides of the body. The area under the tail is white and has a black central stripe. Greenish-yellow legs have a small red area at the top. The bill is red apart from a yellow tip. Sexes are alike.

Purple swamp hen

Porphyrio porphyrio

The European population of the purple swamp hen has become much scarcer over recent years because of habitat changes, specifically drainage of the wetland areas. In some other localities, however, such as the Nile Valley of Egypt, the species has expanded its range thanks to the greater availability of suitable habitat created by irrigation schemes. Purple swamp hens are most likely to be observed late in the day, when they venture out in search of food. These birds are rather clumsy on short flights, literally running across the surface of the water to take off, and flying with their legs hanging down rather than being held against the body. They are unable to fly when moulting.

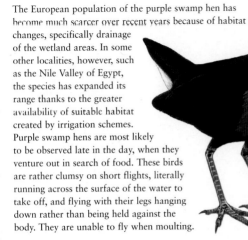

Identification: Relatively large, with vivid blue and purplish shades predominating in the plumage and prominent white undertail coverts. The wings especially may have a greenish hue in some cases. Bill is dull red with brighter frontal plate. Long legs are pinkish red. Sexes alike.

Distribution: Southern Europe, sporadic locations in North Africa and southern parts of that continent. Also present in Asia, Australia and New Zealand.
Size: 50cm (20in).
Habitat: Reedy lakes and marshes.
Nest: Platform of vegetation just above the water.
Eggs: 2–7, whitish to green with dark spots.
Food: Mostly vegetarian.

WETLAND BIRDS

These birds can be encountered in a range of habitats, typically close to coastal areas. In many cases, their plumage provides them with excellent camouflage, allowing them to blend in against the background. They have relatively long legs and an upright stance, as well as a bill that enables them to seek food in shallow water.

Curlew

Eurasian curlew *Numenius arquata*

The distinctive call note of the curlew, which gives it its name, is audible from some distance away. This wader's large size and its long, narrow bill also help to identify it. Its legs are so long that its toes protrude beyond the tip of the tail when in flight. Curlews are most likely to be observed in coastal areas outside the breeding season. They feed here by probing in the sand with their bills, although elsewhere they use their bills to pick berries and catch snails.

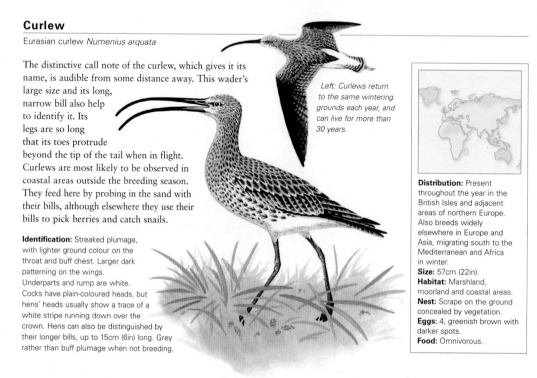

Left: Curlews return to the same wintering grounds each year, and can live for more than 30 years.

Identification: Streaked plumage, with lighter ground colour on the throat and buff chest. Larger dark patterning on the wings. Underparts and rump are white. Cocks have plain-coloured heads, but hens' heads usually show a trace of a white stripe running down over the crown. Hens can also be distinguished by their longer bills, up to 15cm (6in) long. Grey rather than buff plumage when not breeding.

Distribution: Present throughout the year in the British Isles and adjacent areas of northern Europe. Also breeds widely elsewhere in Europe and Asia, migrating south to the Mediterranean and Africa in winter.
Size: 57cm (22in).
Habitat: Marshland, moorland and coastal areas.
Nest: Scrape on the ground concealed by vegetation.
Eggs: 4, greenish brown with darker spots.
Food: Omnivorous.

Little ringed plover

Charadrius dubius

These plovers favour areas with exposed gravel for breeding purposes, and their coloration helps to camouflage them very effectively. Little ringed plovers migrate from their breeding grounds in Europe typically by the end of September, and return the following March. They are more likely to be seen in coastal regions outside the breeding period. They do not tend to associate in mixed flocks with other waders, choosing instead to form small groups on their own. These birds may also be seen near temporarily flooded areas on occasion, including farmland.

Identification: Broad black lines extend across the top of the forehead and from the bill back around the eye. A broader black band runs across the chest. The brown crown is surrounded by white, which also forms a collar around the neck. The entire underparts are white and the legs are pinkish brown. The bill is black. In winter plumage, the entire head is brownish, with a pale buff area above the bill extending above the eyes. Chest collar is a brownish grey rather than black. The sexes are alike.

Distribution: Ranges from southern Scandinavia south across much of Europe, wintering in Africa. Also present in Asia.
Size: 18cm (7in).
Habitat: Sandy areas near fresh water.
Nest: Scrape on the ground.
Eggs: 3, stone-buff with dark markings.
Food: Invertebrates.

Red-wattled lapwing (*Vanellus indicus*):
35cm (14in)
Found in south-eastern Turkey, the Middle East and southern Asia. Has black feathering on the head. White areas on the sides of the face extend down around the black breast and on to the underparts and rump. The back and wings are brown. The bill and an area around the eyes are red. The legs are yellow. The black flight feathers and a band across the tail are evident in flight. Sexes are alike.

Pacific golden plover (*Pluvialis fulva*):
25cm (10in)
Breeds in the far north of Europe, including Iceland, and may winter as far south as North Africa. Black area on the sides of the face extends down over the chest and underparts, which is bordered by white feathering and barring from above the bill down the sides of the body. Coarse, mottled pattern of brown, black and white plumage over the wings. Very upright stance on grey legs. In winter plumage underparts also become mottled with black-and-white feathering. Sexes alike.

Black-winged pratincole (*Glareola nordmanni*):
28cm (11in)
Ranges from the eastern Mediterranean north into Asia in summer and overwinters largely in southern Africa. Has a black area on the fore-head and lores extending down to form a stripe under the bill and there is a buff-coloured area under the throat. The remainder of the plumage is brownish grey with white underparts. The bill is dull with little red apparent, and becomes even blacker during the winter. The contrast in the plumage at this time is also reduced. Sexes alike.

Lapwing

Northern lapwing *Vanellus vanellus*

These birds are also known as peewits in some areas because of the sound of their calls. Flocks of lapwings are a common sight in farmland areas where they comb the ploughed soil for invertebrates. They are quite easily recognized from a distance because of their crests. Lapwings may breed in loose groups, and the scrape that is used by a pair is lined with what often becomes quite a substantial pile of vegetation. The lapwing may move long distances during prolonged spells of severe winter weather, sometimes congregating in huge flocks in estuaries when freshwater areas become frozen.

Distribution: Occurs from southern Scandinavia southwards to the Mediterranean, and migrates eastwards as far as Japan. Also occurs in North Africa and may also be seen further south.
Size: 30cm (12in).
Habitat: Marshland and farmland.
Nest: Scrape on the ground.
Eggs: 4, light brown with dark markings.
Food: Mainly invertebrates.

Identification: Long, narrow, black backward-curving crest, with black on the face, which is separated by a white streak in hens. Underparts are white, apart from chestnut undertail coverts. Wings are dark green, with a greyer-green area on the neck. The white cheek patches behind the eyes are broken by a black line. Outside the breeding period, the facial plumage is buff, and white areas are restricted to the chin and throat.

Snipe

Common snipe *Gallinago gallinago*

These waders are very shy by nature, and may even be nocturnal in their feeding habits, probing damp ground with jerky movements of their stocky bills. If surprised in the open, snipes sometimes freeze but often they take off almost vertically, powering away and flying in a zigzag fashion, before plunging back down into suitable cover. In some parts of their range, such as the British Isles, they remain sedentary. Those inhabiting more northerly latitudes, however, often migrate south to Africa to avoid severe winter weather, when frozen ground makes it difficult for them to find sufficient food.

Identification: Pale buff stripe running down the centre of the crown, with buff stripes above and below the eyes. Dark mottled plumage on the chest and wings. Underparts are white. White stripes run down the wing, with a white border to the rear of the wings. Long bill, which may be larger in hens. Sexes otherwise alike.

Distribution: Ranges from Iceland both west across North America and east through Europe and Asia. May migrate to southerly latitudes for the winter.
Size: 28cm (11in).
Habitat: Marshland and wet pasture.
Nest: Scrape on the ground.
Eggs: 3, greenish buff with dark markings.
Food: Invertebrates.

SWANS AND GEESE

These large, unmistakable birds regularly fly long distances to and from their breeding grounds, especially swans. They also rank among the longest-lived of all waterfowl, with a possible life expectancy of more than two decades. Young birds are unlikely to breed until they are three or four years old. When observing them, remember that both geese and swans can be aggressive on occasion.

Mute swan

Cygnus olor

These swans are seen in a wide range of habitats, and may even venture on to the sea occasionally, although they do not stray far from the shore. They prefer to feed on aquatic vegetation, but will sometimes graze on short grass. In town and city parks, mute swans often eat a greater variety of foods, such as grain and bread provided for them. They rarely dive, but use their long necks to dabble under the surface of the water to obtain food. Pairs are very territorial when breeding, and the male swan, called the cob, will actively try to drive away people who venture too close with fierce movements of its wings.

Identification: Mainly white, with a black area extending from the eyes to the base of the orange bill. A swollen knob protrudes over the upper part of the bill. The legs and feet are blackish. Hens are smaller with a less pronounced knob on the bill. Traces of staining are often evident on the head and neck. Young birds are browner.

Distribution: Resident in the British Isles and adjacent areas of western Europe, often living in a semi-domesticated state. Also occurs in parts of Asia. Localized introduced populations in South Africa, the eastern USA, Australia and New Zealand.
Size: 160cm (63in).
Habitat: Larger stretches of fresh water and estuaries.
Nest: Large pile of heaped-up aquatic vegetation.
Eggs: 5–7, pale green.
Food: Mainly vegetation.

Whooper swan

Cygnus cygnus

Although some Icelandic whooper swans are sedentary throughout the year, the majority of these birds undertake regular migrations, so they are likely to be observed in southern Europe only during the winter months. They often frequent areas around inland waterways at this time, such as the Black and Caspian seas. Pairs nest on their own, and the young chicks fly alongside their parents on the journey south. In the winter, whooper swans may sometimes invade agricultural areas, where they eat a wide range of foods varying from potatoes to acorns, although generally they prefer to feed on aquatic vegetation.

Identification: Body plumage is white, although it may sometimes be stained. The base of the bill is yellow, extending as far down as the nostrils, and the tip is black. Legs and feet are grey. Hens are a little smaller, while young birds have pinkish rather than yellow bases to their bills.

Above left: These swans fly in a V-shaped formation when migrating. Huge numbers may congregate together at their wintering grounds.

Distribution: Iceland and Scandinavia east to Siberia. Overwinters further south.
Size: 165cm (65in).
Habitat: Ponds and lakes, typically in wooded areas. Often overwinters close to the coast.
Nest: Mounds of plant matter, often moss.
Eggs: 3–7, pale green.
Food: Vegetation.

Berwick's swan (tundra swan, *Cygnus columbianus*): 127cm (50in)
Present on the Northern coast of the Americas and migrates south for the winter. Also present on the northern Russian coast to Siberia and winters in the British Isles and north-western Europe. Overwinters south of the Caspian Sea and at a similar latitude in eastern Asia. White, with yellow on the bill that never extends to the nostrils. Hen is smaller in size.

Pink-footed goose (*Anser brachyrhynchus*): 75cm (29.5in)
Found in eastern Greenland, Iceland and Spitzbergen. Overwinters in northern Britain and Denmark southwards. Has a brown head with white streaking on the neck and more prominent markings on the wings and underparts. Bill is pinkish but dark at its base. Legs and feet are pinkish. Sexes alike.

Barnacle goose (*Branta leucopsis*): 70cm (27.5in)
Found in eastern Greenland, Spitzbergen, Novaya Zemlya and Baltic areas. Winters in the British Isles and north-western Europe. Black line from the bill to the eyes. Facial area is mainly white. Neck and upper breast are black. Whitish underparts with grey barring. Wings are grey with black-and-white lines. Sexes alike.

Brent goose (*Branta bernicla*): 66cm (26in)
Ranges from the far north of the USA east to Greenland, Iceland and Siberia. Winters further south in Britain and adjacent parts of north-western Europe, as well as in eastern Asia and US coastline. Has a black head and neck, with a trace of white on the side of the neck. Wings are greyish-black. Barred underparts are dark with white markings. Abdomen is white. Sexes are alike.

Canada goose

Branta canadensis

There are a number of different races of Canada goose and these all differ a little in plumage and size. This species has proved to be highly adaptable. Its numbers have grown considerably in Europe, especially in farming areas, where these geese descend in flocks to feed on crops during the winter once other food has become more scarce. When migrating, flocks fly in a clear V-shaped formation. In common with many waterfowl, Canada geese are not able to fly when moulting, but they take readily to the water at this time and can dive if necessary to escape danger. The geese prefer to graze on land, returning to the relative safety of the water during the hours of darkness.

Identification: Distinctive black head and neck. A small area of white plumage runs in a stripe from behind the eyes to under the throat. A whitish area of feathering at the base of the neck merges into brown on the chest. The wings are dark brown and there is white on the abdomen. The legs and feet are blackish. Sexes are alike.

Distribution: Throughout the far north of the Americas, wintering in the southern USA. European population occurs in the British Isles and elsewhere in north-western Europe.
Size: 55–110cm (22–43in).
Habitat: Very variable, but usually near water.
Nest: Vegetation on the ground.
Eggs: 4–7, whitish.
Food: Vegetarian.

Snow goose

Anser caerulescens

Although considered a vagrant rather than a regular visitor to north-western parts of Europe, the snow goose is a relatively common sight in some areas during the winter months. They are especially attracted to farmland, where grazing opportunities are plentiful, and this appears to be helping these birds to extend their range. As with all waterfowl, however, there is always the possibility that sightings of snow geese could represent escapees from waterfowl collections, rather than wild individuals. The calls of snow geese have been likened to the barking of a dog.

Above: Blue snow geese are much less common than their white counterparts.

Identification: Blue-phase birds (above) are dark and blackish, with white heads and white borders to some wing feathers. Young birds of this colour phase have dark heads. White-phase birds (left) are almost entirely white, with dark primary wing feathers. Young of this colour phase have greyish markings on their heads. Sexes alike.

Distribution: Mainly far north of the Americas, Greenland and north-eastern Siberia, but frequently overwinters in Great Britain and nearby coastal areas of north-western Europe.
Size: 84cm (33in).
Habitat: Tundra and coastal lowland agricultural areas.
Nest: Depression lined with vegetation.
Eggs: 4–10, whitish.
Food: Vegetarian.

DUCKS

Waterfowl are generally conspicuous birds on water, but their appearance and distribution can differ markedly through the year. Drakes often resemble hens outside the breeding season, and their plumage is much plainer at this time. Some species are migratory, heading south to escape freezing conditions, although others may be found on stretches of water that could be covered in ice for some periods.

Mallard

Anas platyrhynchos

Distribution: Occurs throughout the Northern Hemisphere and resident through western Europe. Also occurs in North Africa.
Size: 60cm (24in).
Habitat: Open areas of water.
Nest: Scrape lined with down feathers.
Eggs: 7–16, buff to greyish green.
Food: Plant matter and some invertebrates.

These ducks are a common sight, even on stretches of water in towns and cities, such as rivers and canals. They may congregate in quite large flocks, especially outside the breeding season, but they are most evident in the spring, when groups of unpaired males chase potential mates. The nest is often constructed close to water and is frequently hidden under vegetation, especially in urban areas. These birds feed both on water, upending themselves or dabbling at the surface, and on land.

Identification: Metallic-green head with a white ring around the neck. Chest is brownish with grey underparts, and blackish area surrounds the vent. Bluish speculum in the wing, most evident in flight, bordered by black-and-white stripes. Hen is brownish buff overall with darker patterning, and displays same wing markings as drake. Hen's bill is orange, whereas that of male in eclipse plumage (outside the breeding season) is yellow, with a rufous tinge to the breast.

Ruddy shelduck

Tadorna ferruginea

Although these ducks are resident in some parts of their range throughout the year, they are more often migratory. Occasionally, they may be encountered well outside their natural range, and there have been verified sightings reported from countries as far apart as Iceland, Oman and Kenya. They are quite noisy birds by nature, and the calls of drakes are of a higher pitch than those of hens. These shelducks favour stretches of water surrounded by open countryside, allowing them to graze on the surrounding vegetation. Huge flocks may assemble in some areas where conditions are favourable for feeding after the breeding season.

Identification: Cinnamon shade to the head, with paler whitish area around the eyes. Black neck ring; remainder of the body is orange-brown. Greenish gloss to black feathering on the rump. Tail and flight feathers are black. Bill, legs and feet are black. White under the wings. Hens lack the neck collar, which is less apparent in drakes outside the breeding season.

Distribution: North-western Africa, south-western Europe and Asia. Overwinters in eastern Africa.
Size: 70cm (27.5in).
Habitat: Inland, can be some distance from water.
Nest: Down-lined under cover.
Eggs: 8–15, creamy white
Food: Aquatic creatures and plant matter.

Shoveler

Northern shoveler *Anas clypeata*

The broad bill of these waterfowl enables them to feed more easily in shallow water. They typically swim with their bill open, trailing it through the water to catch invertebrates, although they also forage both by upending and catching insects on reeds. Shovelers choose wet ground, often some distance from open water, as a nesting site, where the female retreats from the attention of other drakes. Like the young of other waterfowl, young shovelers take to the water soon after hatching.

Identification: Dark metallic-green head and orange eye. White chest and chestnut-brown flanks and belly, and a black area around the tail. Both back and wings are black and white. The remainder of the body is predominantly white. Broad blue wing stripe, which enables drakes to be recognized even in eclipse plumage, when they resemble hens. Very broad black bill. Hens are predominantly brownish, but with darker blotching. Yellowish edges on the bill and paler area of plumage on the sides of the tail feathers.

Distribution: Widely distributed throughout the Northern Hemisphere, overwintering as far south as central Africa.
Size: 52cm (20in).
Habitat: Shallow coastal and freshwater areas.
Nest: Down-lined scrape.
Eggs: 8–12, green to buff white.
Food: Aquatic invertebrates and plant matter.

Teal (green-winged teal, *Anas crecca*): 38cm (15in)
Found throughout Europe. Resident in the west, migrating south to parts of northern Africa. Also found in Asia and North America. Brown head with broad green stripes running across the eyes and yellow stripes above and below. Chest is pale yellow with black dots. Body and wings are greyish with a yellow area under the tail, and a white edge to the sides of the wings. Hens are mottled brown, with a pale whitish area beneath the tail and a green area on the wing. Bill is dark. Drakes in eclipse plumage resemble hens.

Garganey (*Anas querquedula*): 41cm (16in)
Ranges from England and France eastwards across Europe, overwintering south of the Sahara; present in Asia. Prominent white stripe from the eyes down along the neck. Remainder of the face and breast area are brown with black barring. Greyish area on the body. Wings are greyish black. Brown mottling over the hindquarters. Hens have mottled plumage with a distinctive buff-white area under the chin. Drakes in eclipse plumage resemble hens but with greyish areas on the wings.

Ferruginous duck (*Aythya nyroca*): 42cm (17in)
Occurs throughout much of eastern Europe into Asia, overwintering around the Mediterranean and further south in Africa, as well as in parts of southern Asia. Chestnut plumage, lighter on the flanks than the back, with white eyes. Very obvious white wing stripe. Whitish belly, underwing and undertail area. Greyish bill, black at the tip. Hens are similar but have a pale band across the bill and brown eyes (which distinguishes them from drakes in eclipse plumage).

Pintail (northern pintail, *Anas acuta*): 62cm (24in)
Throughout the Northern Hemisphere, migrating south for the winter to central Africa. Long, narrow black tail. Head is blackish, with white stripes on the neck down to the breast and underparts. Grey flanks. Wings are greyish with prominent wing stripes. Hens are brown, with darker patterning on the plumage and a long, pointed tail with a white edge to the wings in flight.

Pochard

Aythya ferina

These diving ducks are most likely to be seen in areas of open water, where they often dive for food. Stretches of water with islands are favoured, however, as these provide relatively secure nesting sites, particularly if there is overhanging vegetation. Pairs stay together during the nesting period. After that, pochards form larger flocks, sometimes moving away from lakes and similar stretches of still water to nearby rivers, especially when it is likely that ice will form on the water's surface.

Distribution: Resident in parts of western Europe, extending eastwards into Asia and overwintering as far south as Africa.
Size: 49cm (19in).
Habitat: Marshland and lakes.
Nest: Down-lined under cover.
Eggs: 6–14, greenish grey.
Food: Aquatic creatures and plant matter.

Identification: Chestnut-brown head and neck, with black chest and a broad grey band encircling the wings and body. Black feathering surrounds the hindquarters. Eyes are reddish. Black areas are replaced by greyish tone in eclipse plumage. Hens are significantly duller in coloration, with a brownish head with buff areas and notably a stripe extending back from the eyes. Brown also replaces the drake's black plumage.

OWLS

Although owls tend to be nocturnal by nature, the snowy owl, which inhabits the far north where there is almost constant daylight during the summer, hunts during the day. Owls are predatory birds, and it is possible to discover their diet by examining their pellets, which are made up of the indigestible remains of their prey regurgitated after a meal.

Tawny owl

Strix aluco

The distinctive double call notes of these owls reveal their presence, even when it may be hard to spot them because of their dark coloration. They prefer old woodland, where trees tend to be large enough to provide hollow nesting cavities, although tawny owls will adapt to using nest boxes, which has helped to increase their numbers in some areas. Nocturnal by nature, these owls may occasionally hunt during the daytime, especially when they have chicks in the nest. They usually sit quietly on a perch, waiting to swoop down on their quarry. Young tawny owls are unable to fly when they first leave the nest, and adults are very aggressive at this time to protect their offspring.

Identification: Tawny brown with white markings across the wings, and darker striations over the wings and body. Slight barring on the tail. Distinctive white stripes above the facial disc, which is almost plain brown. Some individuals have a greyer tone to their plumage, while others have a more rufous feathering. The bill is yellowish brown. Sexes are similar, although females are generally larger and heavier. Females can be distinguished by their song, which is a higher pitch.

Distribution: Across Europe (not Ireland) to Scandinavia and east to Asia. Also occurs in western North Africa.
Size: 43cm (17in).
Habitat: Ancient temperate woodland.
Nest: Tree holes.
Eggs: 2–9, white.
Food: Small mammals, birds and invertebrates.

Barn owl

Tyto alba

These owls will roost in dark environments, and have adapted to using buildings for this purpose in various parts of their range. They may be seen in open country, swooping over farmland, with some individuals choosing to pursue bats in areas where the mammals are common. Males in particular will often utter harsh screeches when in flight, which serve as territorial markers, while females make a distinctive snoring sound for food at the nest site. They pair for life, which can be more than 20 years. Barn owls have adapted to hunting alongside roadside verges, but here they risk being hit by vehicles.

Distribution: Worldwide. Throughout western Europe, Africa (apart from the Sahara) and the Middle East.
Size: 39cm (15in).
Habitat: Prefers relatively open countryside.
Nest: Hollow tree or inside a building.
Eggs: 4–7, white.
Food: Voles, amphibians and invertebrates.

Identification: Very pale in colour, with whitish, heart-shaped face and underparts, although in northern, central and eastern parts of Europe, the underparts have a decidedly yellowish-orange tone. Top of the head and wings are greyish with spots evident. Eyes are black. Male birds are often paler than females.

Little owl (*Athene noctua*): 27cm (11in)
Ranges across western Europe and Asia, and from northern Africa to the Middle East. Was successfully introduced to the British Isles in the late 1800s, and now occurs in England and Wales. Has a large, round, brown head with white eyebrows. Head and wings are spotted with white. Pale underparts are streaked with brown. Has a pale bill. The iris is yellow. Hens may be slightly bigger.

Great grey owl (*Strix nebulosa*): 68cm (27in)
Circumpolar, from Scandinavia east through Asia, and also across most of North America. Greyish overall with darker streaking on the wings and underparts. Fine circular patterning of grey lines on the face, with highly distinctive white half-circles extending around the inner side of the eyes, which are yellow. White line of patterning also apparent on the wings. Hens may be slightly bigger.

Long-eared owl (*Asio otus*): 37cm (14.5in)
Ranges from mainland Europe across Asia. Also found in western North Africa and North America. Characteristic tufts on the head are only raised when the owl is alert. The facial area is an orangish-yellow with a white central area extending between the orange eyes and around the bill. Underparts are pale yellow with black streaking. Hens have more rusty-buff faces, otherwise sexes are alike.

Eagle owl

Eurasian eagle owl *Bubo bubo*

The scientific name of the eagle owl – *Bubo bubo* – reflects the sound of its calls, which can be audible on still nights from quite a distance away. A pair will call alternately before mating, and the call notes of the female are higher in pitch. In spite of their large size, these owls fly quietly and may sometimes be seen soaring. Formidable hunters, they take large, potentially dangerous quarry, attacking buzzards and herons on occasion. Even so, eagle owls have adaptable feeding habits, and may resort to catching earthworms and fish as well as eating carrion when hunting opportunities are limited.

Distribution: Throughout southern Europe, north to Scandinavia and east across Asia. Small populations in parts of western Europe and western North Africa.
Size: 73cm (29in).
Habitat: Rocky areas, relatively open country.
Nest: Cliff ledges or occasionally on the ground.
Eggs: 1–4, white.
Food: Mammals and birds.

Identification: Brownish with dark markings on the wings. Underparts are buff brown with streaking most evident on the breast. Prominent ear tufts. Black bill. Orange iris. Hens are often slightly bigger. There may be great variation in appearance through their wide range, with at least 13 different varieties being recognized.

Snowy owl

Nyctea scandiaca

The plumage of these owls enables them to blend in well in the tundra region where they commonly occur. In this harsh environment, their numbers are closely related to the availability of their prey, and their population increases rapidly when lemmings are rife. Once the lemming population declines, however, so does that of the snowy owls, and breeding success is greatly reduced, so that pairs may not nest at all in some years. Adult birds are likely to be forced to abandon their usual territories at this time and have to fly south in search of other sources of food. Unusually, snowy owls are active during the daytime.

Distribution: Circumpolar in the Northern Hemisphere, moving further south in winter.
Size: 65cm (25.5in).
Habitat: Woodland, extending to the tundra.
Nest: Scrape on the ground.
Eggs: 3–11, white.
Food: Mainly lemmings but also birds, invertebrates and fish.

Identification: Cocks are white with yellow eyes and feathering down to the claws. Hens have brown barring all over their bodies apart from their faces, which are white. Young are similar to hens.

CUCKOOS AND WOODPECKERS

These groups of birds have adapted in different ways to survive in colder northern climates, where invertebrates are in short supply during the winter months. While members of the cuckoo clan migrate south to Africa for the winter, where they can find sufficient invertebrates, woodpeckers rely mainly on seeds and nuts for food during this period.

Cuckoo

Common cuckoo *Cuculus canorus*

The distinctive call of the common cuckoo has traditionally been regarded as one of the earliest signs of spring in Europe, when these birds return from their African wintering grounds. Typically, these cuckoos are resident in Europe only between April and September. Adult cuckoos have an unusual ability to feed on hairy caterpillars, which are often plentiful in woodland areas through much of the summer. Common cuckoos are parasitic in their breeding habits, with hens laying single eggs in the nests of other smaller birds such as hedge sparrows, wagtails and meadow pipits. The unsuspecting hosts hatch a monster in their midst, with the cuckoo chick throwing eggs or potential rivals out of the nest in order to monopolize the food supply.

Right: The young cuckoo lifts eggs on its back to eject them from the nest.

Identification: Grey head, upper chest, wings and tail, and black edging to the white feathers of the underparts. In hens this barring extends virtually up to the throat, offset against a more yellowish background. Some hens belong to a brown colour morph, with rufous feathering replacing grey, and black barring apparent on the upperparts.

Distribution: Across Europe and east to Asia. Also present in North Africa. Northern European birds overwinter in eastern and southern parts of Africa, while Asiatic birds range out to the Philippines.
Size: 36cm (14in).
Habitat: Wide range, thanks to host species.
Nest: Parasitizes that of host species.
Eggs: 1 per nest, resembles that of its host.
Food: Invertebrates, including caterpillars.

Nightjar

European nightjar *Caprimulgus europaeus*

The nightjar is a regular summertime visitor to Europe. Their nocturnal habits make these birds difficult to observe, but they have very distinctive calls that have been likened both to the croaking of a frog and the noise of a machine. The calls are uttered for long periods and carry over a distance of 1km (0.6m). Even during the daytime, the mottled plumage of these birds provides them with excellent camouflage, especially in woodland, particularly as they usually narrow their eyes to slits, which further conceals their presence. Nightjars spend much of their time resting on the ground during the daytime, but are sufficiently agile to catch moths and beetles in flight after dark. These birds may sometimes be seen hunting night-flying invertebrates. If food is plentiful, a pair may nest twice in succession before migrating south.

Identification: Fine bill. Long wings. Greyish-brown mottled appearance overall, with some black areas too, especially near the shoulder. White areas below the eyes and on the wings, although white spots on the wings are seen only in cock birds.

Distribution: Europe and North Africa, east to Asia. Northern European birds overwinter in central and southern parts of Africa, and those found in the south migrate to western Africa.
Size: 28cm (11in).
Habitat: Heathland and relatively open country.
Nest: Scrape on the ground.
Eggs: 2, buff with darker markings.
Food: Invertebrates.

Great spotted cuckoo

Clamator glandarius

These lively cuckoos will hunt for invertebrates in trees and on the ground, hopping along rather clumsily. Great spotted cuckoos are bold by nature, parasitizing the nests of magpies and similar corvids, as well as sometimes laying in the nests of starlings in Africa. The hen usually removes eggs already present in the host bird's nest before laying, but if any remain and hatch, the nestlings are reared alongside the young cuckoos. Their relatively large size and noisy nature make these cuckoos quite conspicuous, particularly after the breeding period, when they form flocks.

Identification: Silvery grey top to the head with slight crest. Darker grey neck, back and wings, with white spots over the wings. Pale yellow plumage under the throat extending to the upper breast. The remainder of the underparts are white. Sexes alike, although their song notes are different. Young birds are much darker in colour – black rather than grey with rusty brown flight feathers.

Distribution: Ranges throughout southern Europe from Spain to Iran in Asia. Migrates to north-eastern and southern Africa.
Size: 39cm (15in).
Habitat: Relatively open country.
Nest: Parasitizes that of host species.
Eggs: 1 per nest, resembles those of the host.
Food: Invertebrates.

Senegal coucal (*Centropus senegalensis*): 40cm (16in)
Ranges across Africa from Senegal to Sudan and Tanzania. Also present in Egypt and southern Africa. Strong bill, with black plumage extending over the head down the neck. Underparts are lemon. Back is dark brown. Wings are rusty brown and tail is long and black. Sexes alike.

Lesser spotted woodpecker (*Dendrocopos minor*): 16cm (6in)
Ranges across most of Europe, south to Algeria and Tunisia, east into Asia. Buff area above the bill. Males have a red area on the crown; hens have black. Black tail, white barring on wings. Barring on underparts with reddish area around the vent. Black stripes on the sides of the face.

Green woodpecker (European green woodpecker, *Picus viridis*): 36cm (14in)
Found throughout Europe (except Scotland and Ireland), east to Asia. Red plumage from above the bill down the nape. Black area around the eyes. Greyish area on the throat. Underparts are greyish green. Upperparts are more greenish with yellower tone on the rump. Cocks have red centres to the black streak below the lower bill.

Wryneck (Eurasian wryneck, *Jynx torquilla*): 18cm (7in)
Present across much of Europe and North Africa, migrating south for the winter. Has mottled grey plumage on the head and over the back and a barred tail. There is a brownish tone on the wings and a dark stripe running across and behind the eyes. Throat and upper breast are buff streaked with black. The underparts are whitish with dark barring. Sexes alike.

Great spotted woodpecker

Picoides major

Identification: A black area runs from the bill around the sides of the neck and links with a red area at the back. Wings and upper tail are predominantly black, although there is a white area on the wings and barring on the flight feathers. There is a deep red area around the vent and large white spots on the underside of the tail. Hens lack the red area on the hindcrown.

These woodpeckers are likely to be seen in both coniferous and deciduous woodland habitats, especially in areas where the trees are mature enough for the birds to excavate chambers for roosting and nesting. Their powerful bill enables them to extract grubs concealed under bark and to wrest the seeds from pine cones – the birds use so-called "anvils", which may be existing tree holes, as vices to hold the cones fast so as to gain more leverage for their bills.

Distribution: Most of Europe (except Ireland and the far north of Scandinavia). Also found in North Africa. Ranges east into Asia.
Size: 25cm (10in).
Habitat: Woodland.
Nest: Tree hollows.
Eggs: 5–7, white.
Food: Invertebrates, eggs and seeds.

CORVIDS

Studies suggest that corvids rank among the most intelligent avian species. Many of these birds display an instinctive desire to hoard food, such as acorns, to help sustain them through the winter months. Their plumage is often predominantly black, sometimes with grey and white areas. Corvids are generally noisy and quite aggressive by nature.

Magpie
Common magpie *Pica pica*

Bold and garrulous, magpies are a common sight throughout much of their range. They are often blamed for the decline of song-birds because of their habit of raiding the nests of other birds. They are usually seen in small groups, although pairs will nest on their own. If a predator such as a cat ventures close to the nest, there will be a considerable commotion, resulting in the nesting magpies being joined by others in the neighbourhood to harry the unfortunate feline. Magpies sometimes take an equally direct approach when seeking food, chasing other birds, gulls in particular, to make them drop their food. Magpies are quite agile when walking, holding their long tails up as they move.

Identification: Black head, upper breast, back, rump and tail, with a broad white patch around the abdomen. Broad white wing stripe and dark blue areas evident below on folded wings. Depending on the light, there may be a green gloss apparent on the black plumage. Sexes alike, but the cock may have a longer tail.

Distribution: Much of Europe and south to North Africa. Represented in parts of Asia and North America.
Size: 51cm (20in).
Habitat: Trees with surrounding open areas.
Nest: Dome-shaped stick pile.
Eggs: 2–8, bluish green with darker markings.
Food: Omnivorous.

Nutcracker (spotted nutcracker, *Nucifraga caryocatactes*): 35cm (14in)
Present in Scandinavia and southwards and eastwards into Asia. Dark brown crown, with white-speckled brown plumage over the body, apart from a white area around the vent and the brownish-black wings. Sexes are alike.

Jackdaw (western jackdaw, *Corvus monedula*): 34cm (13in)
Ranges throughout western Europe and North Africa. Present in southern Scandinavia and east into Asia. Dark grey, lighter on the neck. Eye is pale blue. Relatively short bill. Sexes are alike.

Carrion crow (*Corvus corone*): 51cm (20in)
Found in western and south-western parts of Europe. Has black plumage that sometimes appears slightly glossy. The broad, blunt bill is curved on its upper surface, with no bare skin at the base and feathering around the nostrils. Sexes are alike.

Red-billed chough (*Pyrrhocorax pyrrhocorax*): 80cm (31in)
Small populations are found on cliffs of south-western and western parts of Britain. Also found in Ireland and around the Mediterranean. Glossy black plumage with a distinctive, curved, narrow red bill. Legs and feet are pinkish. Sexes alike.

Jay
Eurasian jay *Garrulus glandarius*

Throughout their wide range, there is some local variation in the appearance of these jays, both in the depth of colour and the amount of black on the top of the head. However, their harsh call, which resembles a hoarse scream, coupled with a flash of colour, help identify them. Jays are shy by nature and rarely allow a close approach. They store acorns and other seeds in the autumn, and such caches help to sustain them through the winter when the ground may be covered in snow, restricting their opportunities to find other food. During the summer, these jays may raid the nests of other birds, taking both eggs and chicks.

Distribution: Throughout most of Europe (except Scotland and the extreme north of Scandinavia). Also present in North Africa and Asia.
Size: 35cm (14in).
Habitat: Woodland.
Nest: Platform of twigs.
Eggs: 3–7, bluish green with dense speckling.
Food: Omnivorous.

Identification: Pinkish brown with a greyer shade on the wings. Streaking on the head. Broad, black moustachial stripe with whitish throat. White rump and undertail area. Tail is dark. White stripe on the wings with black and blue markings on the sides of the wings. Sexes alike.

Rook

Corvus frugilegus

These highly social corvids nest in colonies, partly because they inhabit areas of open country-side where there are few trees available. There is, nevertheless, a strong bond between the members of a pair. The rookery serves as the group's centre, which makes them vulnerable to human persecution, but although they eat corn, they are valued for consuming invertebrates as well. The rook's bill is adapted to digging in the ground to extract invertebrates, especially cranefly ("daddy-long-legs") larvae. Outside the breeding season, it is not uncommon for rooks to associate with other corvids, such as jackdaws, crows and ravens, as an alternative to the rookery may be used as a roosting site at this time.

Distribution: Throughout Europe east to Asia. Some populations move south in the winter to the north Mediterranean.
Size: 49cm (19in).
Habitat: Close to farmland.
Nest: Made of sticks built in trees.
Eggs: 2–7, bluish green with dark markings.
Food: Omnivorous, but mainly invertebrates.

Identification: Entirely black plumage, with a pointed bill that has bare, pinkish skin at its base. The nostrils of adult rooks are unfeathered, distinguishing them from carrion crows. Rooks also have a flatter forehead and a peak to the crown. Sexes alike.

Raven

Common raven *Corvus corax*

Distribution: Mainly south-western Europe and North Africa north to Scandinavia and east throughout most of northern Asia. Also present in North America, Greenland, Iceland and the British Isles.
Size: 67cm (26in).
Habitat: Relatively open country.
Nest: Bulky, made of sticks.
Eggs: 3–7, bluish with darker spots.
Food: Carrion.

Identification: Very large in size with a powerful, curved bill. Entirely black plumage. Wedge-shaped tail in flight, when the flight feathers stand out, creating a fingered appearance at the tips. Males often larger than females.

The croaking calls of the raven are a foolproof way of identifying this bird, and its size is also a good identifier. Ravens are the largest members of the crow family occurring in the Northern Hemisphere. The impression of bulk conveyed by these birds is reinforced by their shaggy throat feathers, which do not lie sleekly. There is a recognized decline in size across their range, with ravens found in the far north larger than those occurring further south. Pairs occupy relatively large territories, and even outside the breeding season they tend not to associate in large flocks. When searching for food, ravens are able to fly quite effortlessly over long distances, flapping their wings slowly.

VULTURES AND EAGLES

As a result of their size, these large birds of prey are usually quite conspicuous in flight. Population densities are quite low, however, and these birds have often suffered great persecution by people because of fears that the birds will attack domestic stocks of fish and farm animals. They tend to be quite scarce, therefore, and today are observed mainly in more remote areas of countryside.

Griffon vulture

Eurasian vulture *Gyps fulvus*

These vultures are most likely to be seen in areas of relatively open countryside with surrounding cliffs and these are used for nesting and roosting. They glide over plains, using their keen eyesight to help them locate carcasses, although, these days groups of these birds may often be encountered scavenging at rubbish dumps within their range. Hot currents of air, known as thermals, enable these vultures to soar and remain airborne with little effort. Griffon vultures nest in colonies that have been known to consist of as many as 150 pairs. Chicks develop slowly, often not embarking on their first flight until they are nearly 20 weeks old. Young birds are unlikely to breed until they are at least four years old.

Identification: Dark brown area on the head around the eyes, with the top of the head and neck whitish. Light brown body, back and wings, darker flight feathers and tail. Relatively elongated horn-coloured bill that is curved on the upper tip. Legs and feet grey, and whitish on the inner thighs. Sexes are alike. Young birds have a darker brown back and a brown neck collar. Can be distinguished from the African white-backed vulture (*G. africanis*) by its larger size and paler plumage.

Distribution: The Iberian Peninsula and western North Africa, east into Asia and the Middle East. Young birds may migrate further south into western and eastern Africa.
Size: 110cm (43in).
Habitat: Mountain country.
Nest: Sticks on rocky crag.
Eggs: 1, white with reddish-brown markings.
Food: Carrion.

Osprey

Pandion haliaetus

The distribution of the osprey extends naturally to all inhabited continents, making it one of the most widely distributed of all birds. They have adapted to feeding on stretches of fresh water as well as on estuaries and even the open sea, swooping to grab fish from just below the water's surface using their powerful talons. Ospreys are capable of carrying fish typically weighing up to 300g (11oz) without difficulty. In many areas, especially in Europe, ospreys are migratory, and the birds head south to Africa for the duration of the northern winter. Those occurring in Scotland and Scandinavia fly south of the Sahara, rather than joining the resident osprey population in North Africa.

Left: Osprey feed only on fish, pouncing on those just below the surface.

Identification: Brown stripes running across the eyes down over the back and wings. Eyes are yellow. Top of the head and underparts are white, with brown striations across the breast, which are most marked in hens. Tall, upright stance, powerful grey legs and talons. Hens significantly heavier than cocks.

Distribution: Global, with European ospreys ranging from parts of Scandinavia west to the British Isles and south to the Iberian Peninsula and other areas in Europe. Widely distributed in the winter in Africa south of the Sahara.
Size: 58cm (23in).
Habitat: Close to stretches of water.
Nest: Platform of sticks in a tree.
Eggs: 3, white with darker markings.
Food: Fish.

Black vulture (Eurasian black vulture, *Aegypius monachus*): 107cm (42in)
Ranges from Spain and the Balearic Islands eastwards to the Balkans, and from Turkey across Asia. Some birds overwinter in north-eastern Africa. Pale bluish skin encircles the nostrils. Bald head with a brownish area around the eyes. Plumage is a dark sooty black. Sexes are alike.

Egyptian vulture (*Neophron percnopterus*): 70cm (27.5in)
Distributed around the Mediterranean into Asia, on to the Canary Islands and south of the Sahara and across Africa to Tanzania and Arabia. Pale-coloured, whitish plumage with brown markings is prominent over the wings and flight feathers. Has a bald bright yellow area of skin on the sides of the face and along the bill, which may have a dark tip. Sexes are alike.

Short-toed snake eagle (*Circaetus gallicus*): 67cm (26in)
Ranges across mainland Europe north to Finland and east to Asia. Also present in western North Africa. Birds from western Europe migrate south to the Sahel region in West Africa. Has a mottled brown head and wings and this extends to the breast. The underparts are white with brown barring. The flight feathers are a darker brown and the tail is barred. Sexes are alike.

Lesser spotted eagle (*Aquila pomarina*): 64cm (25in)
Ranges from eastern Europe to Turkey and around the Caspian Sea. Overwinters in eastern Africa. Chocolate brown. Feathering extends to the feet. Bill is yellow at base with a dark tip. Sexes alike.

Golden eagle

Aquila chrysaetos

These eagles generally inhabit remote areas away from people, where they are likely to be left undisturbed. When seen in flight, the golden eagle's head looks relatively small compared to its broad tail and large, square-ended wings. Although it has some yapping call notes not unlike those of a dog, its calls are generally quite shrill. Its hunting skills are well adapted to its environment. In some areas, for instance, the golden eagle takes tortoises, dropping the reptiles from a great height in order to smash their shells before eating them; in other areas, they may prey on cats. They prefer to capture their quarry on the ground, swooping down low, rather than catching birds in the air.

Distribution: Sporadic through the Mediterranean area into Asia. Present in Scotland, Scandinavia and eastwards into Asia. Also occurs in North Africa.
Size: 90cm (35in).
Habitat: Mountainous areas.
Nest: Massive cliff nest made of sticks.
Eggs: 2, white with dark markings.
Food: Mainly birds and mammals.

Identification: Brown overall, with yellowish-brown plumage restricted to the back of the head, extending down the nape of the neck. Eagles inhabiting desert areas, such as the Middle East, tend to be slightly paler overall. Bill is yellow with a dark tip. Feet are yellow with black talons. Hens are bigger than cocks.

Imperial eagle

Eastern imperial eagle *Aquila heliaca* (F)

The population of these eagles declined dramatically during the 20th century because of persecution by humans. Thanks to effective protection, however, there are now signs that their numbers are increasing again in areas such as Hungary. Here they can be seen in areas of open countryside, rather than retreating to the relative safety of mountain forests, away from persecution. Imperial eagles, like others of their kind, are potentially long-lived birds, having few natural enemies apart from people. Their longevity, which is measured in decades not years, is mirrored in their development. Young birds may not breed for the first time until they are six years old, when they are still likely to be in immature plumage.

Identification: Mainly dark brown, with a paler buff area at the back of the head extending down around the neck. Restricted patches of white appear in the shoulder area. The bill is yellow with a dark tip and the feet are yellow. Sexes alike. This species is now regarded as distinct from the Spanish imperial eagle (*A. adalberti*), which has small white shoulder patches.

Distribution: Eastern Europe into Turkey and east across much of Central Asia. Migrates south to eastern Africa and Arabia as well as to parts of Asia for the winter.
Size: 84cm (33in).
Habitat: Prefers open country.
Nest: Made of sticks and other vegetation.
Eggs: 2, white with dark markings.
Food: Small mammals, birds and carrion.

HAWKS AND HARRIERS

These predatory birds can be easily identified by their sharp, pointed bills and powerful talons. They prey on both other birds and mammals, with some resorting to carrion and invertebrates. There are recognized colour variants, known as morphs, which may cause the plumage of some individuals to be either lighter or darker than usual.

Red kite

Milvus milvus

Distribution: Wales, Iberian Peninsula and the adjacent area of North Africa. Extends north-east across Europe to southern Sweden and into the Caucasus.
Size: 66cm (26in).
Habitat: Lightly wooded areas.
Nest: Platform made of sticks in a tree.
Eggs: 1–4, white with reddish-brown markings.
Food: Small birds, mammals and carrion.

Although they are very agile hunters, red kites also seek out carrion such as dead sheep. This behaviour has resulted in their persecution in some areas because of misplaced fears that these birds actually kill lambs. When seeking prey, red kites will circle repeatedly over an area, relying on their keen eyesight to spot movement on the ground. They then drop and sweep low to home in on their target. Up until the 1700s, flocks of red kites were common scavengers on the streets of London where they were sufficiently tame to swoop down and steal food from children. It was their propensity to scavenge, however, that led to a dramatic reduction in their numbers as they were easily killed using carcasses laced with poison.

Identification: Predominantly reddish brown, with a greyish head streaked with darker markings. Darker mottling over the wings, with some variable streaking on the underparts as well. Feet are yellowish with black talons. White area under the wings and forked tail can be clearly seen in flight. Sexes alike.

Hen harrier

Northern harrier *Circus cyaneus*

Hen harriers have a very distinctive hunting pattern. They fly low over moorland, seeking not just small mammals but also birds such as grouse, which has led to their persecution by gamekeepers in various parts of their range. Over the winter period, however, these harriers may be forced to feed largely on carrion. Their range extends further north than that of related species, into tundra regions. However, they are not resident in far northern regions throughout the year, and head south before the start of winter in the Northern Hemisphere. Hen harriers are unusual in that they not only frequently roost but also breed on the ground. After the breeding season, they often congregate at communal sites, which are used for several generations.

Identification: Mainly chestnut streaked with white. Darker over the wings. Narrow white band around the eye, with a solid brown area beneath. Has a barred tail, a dark bill and yellow legs. Hens are larger.

Distribution: Throughout much of the Northern Hemisphere. Extends across most of Europe, including Scandinavia, east to Asia. Often moves south for the winter as far as North Africa.
Size: 52cm (20in).
Habitat: Moorland.
Nest: On the ground, hidden in vegetation.
Eggs: 3–5, whitish.
Food: Small mammals and birds.

Common buzzard

Eurasian buzzard *Buteo buteo*

With its rather stocky and broad appearance, the buzzard's silhouette in flight helps to confirm its identity. Buzzards are capable of soaring for long periods before suddenly swooping down to seize creatures such as rabbits, which are its traditional prey, particularly in many parts of Europe. At the other extreme, buzzards can also sometimes be observed hunting invertebrates, walking purposefully on the ground in search of their quarry. They may even be spotted on roads on occasion, feeding on road kill, and sometimes even placing themselves in danger from passing traffic. Buzzards remain one of the most common raptors in Europe, however, thanks in part to their adaptability.

Identification: Mainly dark brown, with a variable amount of white plumage around the bill and on the underparts. The tail is barred with paler plumage around the vent. The legs and feet are yellow and the bill is yellow with a dark tip. White plumage predominates in the pale morph. Hens are often larger.

Distribution: Resident in western Europe. Summer resident in parts of Scandinavia and east across Asia. European migratory birds overwinter in parts of southern and eastern Africa.
Size: 57cm (22in).
Habitat: Areas with trees.
Nest: Platform made of sticks, usually in a tree.
Eggs: 2–4, white.
Food: Small mammals and other prey.

Black kite (*Milvus migrans*): 60cm (24in)
Present on much of mainland Europe to Asia and Australia. Also occurs in North Africa and over-winters in Africa south of the Sahara. Mainly brown but darker on the wings. The underparts are decidedly rufous. Barring on the tail. Some grey markings on the head. Sexes are alike.

Common black-shouldered kite (*Elanus caeruleus*): 30cm (12in)
Present in North Africa and widely distributed in Africa south of the Sahara. Grey on the head, extending down the back over the wings. Whitish sides to the face and white underparts. Prominent black area on each wing extending down from the shoulders. Sexes alike.

Montagu's harrier (*Circus pygargus*): 50cm (20in)
Found in Europe and North Africa and then east to Asia. Overwinters in Central and eastern Africa south of the Sahara. Predominantly grey, with barring on the lower underparts. Has a narrow white rump. Hens are larger and brown areas replace the grey areas of plumage. In the dark morph, males are blackish and hens are a dark chocolate brown.

Goshawk (northern goshawk, *Accipiter gentilis*): 50–68cm (20–27in)
Widely distributed throughout the Northern Hemisphere. Extends across most of Europe into Asia, with a small population in north-western Africa. Also present in North America. Grey on the head, more silvery over the wings and tail. Rest of plumage is mainly white with grey barring. Hens are bigger than cocks. In the rare white morph, birds are much paler than normal.

Sparrowhawk

Eurasian sparrowhawk *Accipiter nisus*

These birds of prey tend to favour birds that feed on the ground, and males tend to take smaller quarry than females, reflecting the difference in their respective sizes. Even females rarely take birds much bigger than pigeons, however, although they will prey on thrushes. Pairs nest later in the year than many songbirds, so that they can prey on nestlings more easily to feed their own chicks. Their short wings mean that sparrowhawks are very agile in flight, able to manoeuvre easily in wooded areas. They approach quietly with the aim of catching their target unawares, and seize their prey using their powerful feet.

Identification: Grey head, back and wings with darker barring on the grey tail. The underparts are barred. Has bare yellow legs and feet with relatively long toes. Cock birds are smaller than hens and have pale rufous areas on the lower sides of the face that extend to the chest. In addition, the barring on their underparts is browner.

Left: Young male sparrow-hawks fledge several days before the heavier females.

Distribution: Resident throughout most of Europe, (apart from the far north of Scandinavia), North Africa and the Canary Islands. Migratory birds overwinter around the Red Sea. Distribution also extends east to Asia.
Size: 28cm (11in).
Habitat: Lightly wooded areas.
Nest: Made of sticks in a tree.
Eggs: 4–6, pale blue with reddish-brown markings.
Food: Mainly birds.

FALCONS

Agile, aerial predators, these birds of prey are opportunistic, relying on their strength and speed to overcome their prey, which frequently includes smaller birds. In the past, falcon populations have been adversely affected by organochlorine pesticides such as DDT, but today there has been a resurgence in numbers in many areas, with populations even moving into urban areas.

Kestrel

Common kestrel *Falco tinnunculus*

These birds of prey are often seen hovering over the sides of busy roads, which provide them with good hunting opportunities. They catch prey largely undisturbed on the roadside as traffic passes by. The keen eyesight of kestrels enables them to spot even small quarry such as grasshoppers on the ground, and in the winter, they may resort to hunting earthworms drawn to the surface by heavy rainfall. Kestrels will also venture into towns, hunting in parks.

Identification: Bluish-grey head, with a black stripe under the eyes and a whitish throat. Has dense black spotting on the pale brownish chest, extending to the abdomen. Wings are chestnut brown with black markings. Rump and tail feathers are grey with black tips. Hens are similar to cocks, but have browner heads and distinct barring across the tail feathers.

Distribution: Throughout western Europe to southern Asia and North Africa. Also breeds in Scandinavia.
Size: 37cm (14.5in).
Habitat: Open countryside.
Nest: Platform made of sticks in a tree or in farm buildings.
Eggs: 3–7, pale pink with dark brown markings.
Food: Invertebrates and small mammals.

Peregrine falcon

Falco peregrinus

The power of the peregrine falcon is such that it can swoop down on other birds at great speed. Indeed, it is thought that they can dive as quickly as 350km/h (217mph). Pigeons are a favourite prey although these falcons may also hunt waterfowl. The impact made by their feet when they strike in the air is so great that their quarry is frequently killed instantaneously. These falcons are highly adaptable and can very occasionally be sighted in cities, where apartment blocks replace the crags from which they would normally fly on hunting excursions.

Identification: Has dark grey upperparts. A broad blackish stripe extends down below the eyes and the surrounding white area extends right around the throat. The barring on the chest is lighter than on the abdomen. Darker markings are apparent on the grey feathers of the back and wings. The tail is barred with paler grey feathering at the base. The legs and feet are yellow. Has relatively narrow wings when seen in flight. Hens are much larger than male birds.

Distribution: Resident throughout most of western Europe and much of Africa, apart from the Sahara Desert and the central rainforest band. One of the most adaptable and widely distributed birds of prey, occurring on all continents.
Size: 38–51cm (15–20in).
Habitat: Usually near cliffs, sometimes open ground.
Nest: Usually on cliff ledges.
Eggs: 3–4, whitish with red-brown markings.
Food: Birds.

Red-footed falcon (*Falco vespertinus*): 34cm (13in)
Mainly found in eastern Europe and Asia but with a few recorded sightings in western Europe, including the British Isles. Predominantly bluish-grey overall with red on the lower abdomen and undertail coverts. The legs are a bright red. Hens are rufous-brown with a white area on the face below the eyes. Their wings are blue-grey with black barring and their legs are pinkish.

Hobby (Eurasian hobby, *Falco subbuteo*): 35cm (14in)
Ranges across most of mainland Europe, north to southern Scandinavia, east to Asia and south to North Africa. Over-winters in southern Africa. Long, pointed, dark bluish-grey wings. A white band extends around the sides of the face. White underparts with barring. Reddish area on the lower abdomen. Barred underside to the tail. Sexes are alike.

Lanner falcon (*Falco biarmicus*): 50cm (20in)
Extends throughout south-eastern Europe, Arabia and much of Africa apart from the central rainforest area. Slaty-grey or brownish-grey upperparts although those from North Africa are a more bluish shade. A dark stripe extends down below the eyes into a whitish area that extends across the cheeks on to the throat. Underparts are white with dark barring. Legs and feet are yellow. Sexes alike but hens are larger.

Saker falcon (*Falco cherrug*): 55cm (22in)
Occurs in central Europe, via Russia eastwards across southern latitudes in Asia, extending to China. Westerly populations may migrate around the eastern Mediterranean and North Africa for the winter. Also observed at this stage in Arabia and eastern Africa, Sudan, Ethiopia and northern parts of Kenya. Predominantly brown with a paler head. Underparts heavily streaked on the breast and darker areas on the flanks. Dark underwing coverts broken with some whitish markings. Sexes are alike. A rare grey morph is also seen occasionally.

Merlin

Pigeon hawk *Falco columbarius*

These highly adaptable hawks can be observed in a wide range of environments. They tend to breed in the far north where there is little cover, swooping low and fast above the ground in search of prey. Pairs may sometimes seek out and pursue their quarry together, increasing their chances of making a kill. Indeed, merlins have even been seen hunting in the company of other birds of prey. The merlin prefers to tackle birds in flight rather than seizing individual birds when they are perching.

Distribution: Present in the British Isles throughout the year. Occurs in Scandinavia, moving south in the winter down to North Africa. Occurs in Asia and the Americas also.
Size: 33cm (13in).
Habitat: Lightly wooded and open countryside.
Nest: In trees or sometimes on the ground.
Eggs: 3–6, buff with variable reddish speckling.
Food: Mostly birds.

Identification: Orange-brown underparts and collar with dark streaking. Crown and wings are bluish-grey with dark streaking. Streaking also on the whitish cheeks. A broad dark band on the tail with a white tip. Hens have brownish-grey upperparts with a series of four or five narrow light bands extending down the tail. Upperparts are whitish with brown markings. Males usually smaller than females.

Gyr falcon

Falco rusticolus

The largest member of its genus, the gyr falcon is well adapted to surviving in the far north, where its coloration helps to conceal its presence, even in areas where there is little tree cover. These falcons are often sighted in coastal regions, where they prey on seabirds. They tend to fly quite low when hunting in open countryside, taking grouse and similar birds as well as small rodents, and prefer to catch their quarry on the ground rather than in flight. When breeding, pairs may even adopt artificial sites, nesting in buildings associated with oil pipelines, for example.

Identification: Variable in colour, but typically bluish-grey with barring across the back and wings. Tail is barred. Sides of the face are dark. Underparts are whitish with dark barring. The white morph (*left*), has white underparts and occurs predominantly in Greenland. Two grey morphs exist: the lighter grey occurs in Iceland and the dark grey in parts of Scandinavia and northern Russia.

Distribution: Iceland and Scandinavia. Annual vagrant in the British Isles.
Size: 63cm (25in)
Habitat: Mainly taiga and tundra.
Nest: On cliff ledges.
Eggs: 3–4, buff with dense reddish speckling.
Food: Small birds and mammals.

AFRICAN PARROTS

*Africa is home to just 22 species of parrot – fewer than are found on any other continent where these birds naturally occur. The African population includes island residents such as the echo parakeet (*Psittacula echo*) from Mauritius, one of the rarest species in the world and a close relative of the ring-necked parakeet, as well as the bizarre, black-coloured vasa parrots found on Madagascar.*

Grey parrot

Psittacus erithacus

The highly distinctive coloration of these parrots enables them to be identified without difficulty, although they are not always easy to spot in their forest habitat. They are more conspicuous in the early morning and evening, when they fly above the trees in flocks, often calling loudly, to and from their feeding grounds. These parrots roost in mature trees, giving them a good view of the surrounding area. They are not easy to approach and often fly off at the first hint of danger. When feeding, at least one bird acts as a sentinel, calling loudly to warn the others of any approaching threat.

Identification: Mainly grey (a silvery shade in some cases) with bright red tail feathers. The timneh subspecies (*P. e. timneh*) from western Africa is not only smaller, but has a maroon tail and a horn-coloured, rather than black, upper bill. Sexes are alike.

Distribution: Across central Africa from the Gulf of Guinea east to Kenya and Tanzania. Occurs south to Angola.
Size: 33cm (13in)
Habitat: Woodland areas from rainforest to mangroves and savanna.
Nest: Tree hollow, often 10m (33ft) high or more.
Eggs: 2–3, white.
Food: Fruits, nuts and seeds, often sought in trees.

Senegal parrot

Yellow-bellied parrot *Poicephalus senegalus*

These parrots tend to be observed only in small groups, although much bigger flocks may congregate in areas where food is plentiful, raiding agricultural areas when crops are ripening. Groundnuts are a particular favourite of these parrots. In some areas, such as southern Mali, seasonal movements have been reported, with the parrots heading further south during the dry season, when areas of standing water become scarce. These birds are very shy by nature – they are difficult to observe when they are perched and fly off rapidly when disturbed. At such times their calls, which frequently consist of whistling notes, become more raucous.

Identification: Has a greyish head with a green back and wings. Has a distinctive V-shaped green area on the chest, with orangish-yellow plumage beneath. The distinctive western subspecies (*P. s. versteri*) has more reddish underparts and darker green plumage. Sexes are alike.

Distribution: Western central parts of Africa, extending from Senegal to northern parts of Cameroon and south-east of Chad.
Size: 23cm (9in).
Habitat: Open countryside and forest.
Nest: Tree hollow, typically 10m (33ft) off the ground.
Eggs: 2–4, white.
Food: Fruit, greenstuff, seeds and cultivated crops, especially groundnuts and millet.

Peach-faced lovebird

Rosy-faced lovebird *Agapornis roseicollis*

Living and breeding in flocks, these small parrots are encountered at altitudes from sea level up to 1,600m (5,250ft). They may be present in large numbers in agricultural areas when crops are ripening, a time when flocks will join together. When breeding, they may take over the abandoned nests of weaver birds, allowing them to nest in colonies. Peach-faced lovebirds have an unusual way of building their own nests: hens collect strips of nesting material and carry it back to the nest site folded and tucked into the plumage of the rump area. The nest may be sited in a wide range of localities, from cliff faces to the eaves of buildings.

Identification: Predominantly green although darker on the wings. Has a blue rump, a reddish forehead and rose-pink facial feathering that extends on to the upper breast. This rosy coloration is less pronounced in young birds, which may show traces of darker markings on their bill when fledging. Sexes alike, although pinkish coloration is reputedly paler in hens but not usually apparent. Angolan race (*A. r. catumbella*) is more lightly coloured overall.

Distribution: South-west Angola southwards to South Africa.
Size: 15cm (6in).
Habitat: Dry, wooded country.
Nest: Tree hollow or disused weaver-bird nest.
Eggs: 4–6, white.
Food: Mainly seeds, including cultivated crops such as millet and sunflower.

Masked lovebird (*Agapornis personata*): 14cm (5.5in)
Present in northern and central parts of Tanzania. The blackish head merges into a yellow collar and underparts. Wings and abdomen are green. Prominent white areas encircle the eyes. The bill is red. The legs and feet are greyish. Sexes alike.

Fischer's lovebird (*Agapornis fischeri*): 14cm (5.5in)
Found in eastern Africa – mainly in northern Tanzania. Has a reddish-orange head that becomes paler around the throat and the back of the neck, where there is a yellowish area. The underparts are light green, the wings are dark green and the rump is mauve. Has a prominent white eye ring of bare skin. The bill is red and the legs and foot are grey. Sexes are alike.

Jardine's parrot (*Poicephalus gulielmi*): 28cm (11in)
Present in central Africa from Liberia and northern Angola east to Uganda, Kenya and Tanzania. Predominantly green but with blackish feathering on the back and wings that is offset by green edging. There is a variable amount of orange plumage on the crown and the edges of the wings and thighs. The bill is greyish and the feet are pinkish. Sexes are similar, although cocks may have a more reddish-orange iris.

Vasa parrot (*Coracopsis vasa*): 50cm (20in)
Occurs on Madagascar and the Comoros, off the coast of south-eastern Africa. Predominantly brownish-black but with a greyer hue on the upperparts. Has grey undertail coverts. The bill varies seasonally from horn-coloured to grey. Sexes are alike, although cocks in breeding condition develop a prominent swelling in the region of the vent.

Ring-necked parakeet

Rose-ringed parakeet *Psittacula krameri*

Distribution: Found in a band across Africa from Senegal east to the Sudan and Uganda. Also occurs throughout Asia east to China.
Size: 40cm (16in).
Habitat: Light woodland of various types.
Nest: Tree cavity high off the ground; sometimes on a rocky ledge.
Eggs: 3–6, white.
Food: Cereals, fruit and seeds.

Identification: The African race (*P. k. krameri*) has more yellowish-green plumage, and black on the bill, than the Asiatic form (*right*), which is now established in various areas including parts of England, well outside its natural range. Hens and young birds of both sexes lack the distinctive neck collar seen in cocks, which is a combination of black and pink. Head is green.

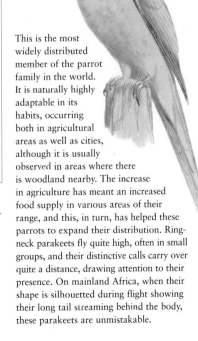

This is the most widely distributed member of the parrot family in the world. It is naturally highly adaptable in its habits, occurring both in agricultural areas as well as cities, although it is usually observed in areas where there is woodland nearby. The increase in agriculture has meant an increased food supply in various areas of their range, and this, in turn, has helped these parrots to expand their distribution. Ring-neck parakeets fly quite high, often in small groups, and their distinctive calls carry over quite a distance, drawing attention to their presence. On mainland Africa, when their shape is silhouetted during flight showing their long tail streaming behind the body, these parakeets are unmistakable.

BARBETS

The most obvious distinguishing feature of barbets is the narrow, hair-like feathers surrounding the bill, which resemble a beard (the name "barbet" is derived from the German word for "beard"). All barbets are somewhat dumpy, compact birds, and representatives of the group occur in both the Old and New Worlds.

Levaillant's barbet

Crested barbet *Trachyphonus vaillantii*

Distribution: Most of southern Africa from Angola and Tanzania southwards, except for the south-western part of the continent.
Size: 22cm (9in).
Habitat: Open country.
Nest: Hollow chamber.
Eggs: 3–5, white.
Food: Mainly invertebrates, although also eats fruit and berries.

Although there are slight variations in the patterning of these barbets, these do not distinguish between the sexes. Levaillant's barbets are quite conspicuous birds, and are sometimes observed perching in trees or searching for food on the ground, often near termite mounds. They sometimes seek the relative security of termite mounds for breeding, tunnelling into them to create a safe nesting chamber. Their intrusion is apparently not resisted by the insects, who would usually deter most potential predators. One advantage of nesting in a termite mound is that the heat generated by their surroundings will usually keep the eggs warm when the adult birds leave their nest.

Identification: Has a reddish-orange area on the top of the head and lores, with a long black crest behind. The wings are predominantly blackish with white markings. A black band with white spots extends across the chest. The underparts are yellowish with some reddish streaks, becoming paler with fewer markings on the abdomen. The rump is yellow and red at the base. The tail feathers have white tips. The bill is a pale greenish yellow. Sexes are alike.

Double-toothed barbet

Lybius bidentatus

The unusual coloration and shape of the bill of these barbets helps to identify them in the field. The notch on the bill, which looks like a tooth, may help the birds to grasp their food. Their diet may feature more fruit than that of barbets inhabiting more open areas of country, and double-toothed barbets have a reputation for attacking ripening bananas. They are most likely to be seen in pairs than in larger groups, and pairs may breed throughout much of the year in some parts of their range. They use their strong bills to excavate a nesting site in a suitable tree by hammering at the trunk. Even so, a dead tree or branch is usually preferred as it is softer and easier for tunnelling

Distribution: Western central Africa, from Guinea south to Angola and east to parts of Sudan, Ethiopia, Kenya and Tanzania.
Size: 23cm (9in).
Habitat: Woodland but not rainforest.
Nest: Tree hollow. Nesting chamber lined with wood chips for nesting material.
Eggs: 3–4, white.
Food: Invertebrates and fruit such as berries.

Identification: Predominantly black upperparts. Has a large red area on the underparts. The rump and an area on the side of the body are white. Has a blackish area around the eyes and a red wing bar. The prominent toothed bill is whitish. Sexes are alike.

Black-collared barbet (*Lybius torquatus*):
15cm (6in)
Widely distributed across southern Africa. Distinctive crimson plumage on the face extends across the throat to the breast, with yellow beneath. The crown, nape and chest band are all black. The wings are a greenish black with some yellow evident. Sexes are alike.

D'Arnaud's barbet (*Trachyphonus darnaudii*): 17cm (7in)
Ranges in eastern Africa from Sudan, Ethiopia and Somalia west across Uganda and Kenya to south-west Tanzania. Has a black crown that is often spotted with yellow, although yellow is usually more evident on the sides of the face. Variable black markings feature on the throat and breast. The underparts are mainly a pale yellow colour. The undertail coverts are red and the upperparts are brown with white spotting. Individuals differ from each other slightly in their pattern of markings. Sexes are alike.

Pied barbet (*Lybius leucomelas*): 16cm (6in)
Present in southern Africa where it can be found in Zimbabwe, Botswana and South Africa. Has a deep red forehead, with black behind, and adjacent white stripes with some yellow suffusion extend to the back of the neck. An irregularly-shaped black area runs from below the bill down on to the chest. The remainder of the underparts are white. The wings are black apart from white markings that have a sporadic yellow suffusion. Sexes are alike.

Red-faced barbet (*Lybius rubrifacies*): 15cm (6in)
Present in southern Uganda and north-western Tanzania. An area of red plumage above the pale greyish bill extends to the sides of the face but not on to the crown or throat. The remainder of the plumage is blackish and there is a yellow edging to the wings. Sexes are alike.

Yellow-fronted tinkerbird

Pogoniulus chrysoconus

These small, relatively slim members of the barbet family will sit for long periods during the day on a well-concealed branch, uttering their monotonous-sounding call. It can be surprisingly difficult to locate them from their sound alone, however. Their lively, agile nature becomes evident when they seek food. They hover and pick insects off branches, or hop up a trunk like woodpeckers seeking grubs. They eat fruit, too, especially the berries of mistletoe and similar plants. As a result, the yellow-fronted tinkerbird helps to distribute these plants around their environment, passing seeds out in their droppings.

Distribution: Broad band across much of central Africa from Senegal east to north-west Ethiopia and Uganda.
Size: 11cm (4in).
Habitat: Savanna.
Nest: Tree hole.
Eggs: 2–3, white.
Food: Invertebrates and fruit.

Identification: Prominent yellow plumage above the upper bill, appearing almost orange in some cases, with alternating black-and-white stripes on the sides of the head. A similar, although mottled, colour combination extends over the wings, with some yellow evident on the flight feathers. The rump is sulphur yellow. Underparts are whitish with a yellowish suffusion. Legs and the long, stout bill are black. Sexes alike.

Naked-faced barbet

Gymnobucco calvus

The lack of feathering on the face of these barbets may help to prevent their plumage from becoming stained and matted by fruit juices. Young birds leave the nest with their heads almost fully feathered, but this plumage is shed and not replaced as they grow older. Social and noisy by nature, naked-faced barbets are quite conspicuous birds, encountered predominantly in lowland areas. They nest in colonies, often seeking out dead trees, where it is easier to create nesting chambers. Using their powerful bills, they excavate chambers that typically extend 23cm (9in) below the entrance. As many as 30 pairs have been reported occupying a single tree.

Identification: Predominantly brown, with significantly darker upperparts and tail. Underparts are light brown. Large, powerful bill, with beard of longer brown feathers at its base. Has bare blackish-brown skin on the head. The bare ear holes at the back of the head are clearly evident. Sexes are alike.

Distribution: From Guinea in western Africa east and south around the coastline of Africa as far as northern Angola.
Size: 18cm (7in).
Habitat: Wooded areas.
Nest: Tree hollow.
Eggs: 3, white.
Food: Invertebrates and fruit.

BEE-EATERS, KINGFISHERS AND SHRIKES

This group of birds are hunters, preying mainly on invertebrates. Although some kingfishers feed mainly on fish, those found in forested areas tend to be more insectivorous. Shrikes have a reputation for caching food in the form of so-called "larders" – they spear their prey on the sharp spines of plants, returning to retrieve the bodies when they are hungry.

Bee-eater

European bee-eater *Merops apiaster*

In spite of their name, European bee-eaters hawk a much wider range of prey in the air than simply bees. More than 300 different invertebrates have been identified in their diet, ranging from dragonflies to butterflies. They have even been known to swoop on spiders, seizing the arachnids from their webs. Although individual birds hunt on their own, European bee-eaters nest in colonies of up to eight pairs. Sandy cliffs, where they can excavate their breeding tunnels with relative ease, are favoured nesting sites. Outside the breeding season, groups roost huddled together on branches.

Identification: Whitish band above the black bill, merging into blue above the eyes. Chestnut brown extends from the top of the head down over the back, and across the wings. Golden scapulars and rump. Black band extends from the bill across the eyes. Throat is yellow, with a black band separating this area from bluish underparts. Hens have more green on wings and scapulars.

Distribution: Much of southern Europe extending into adjacent parts of Asia and into North Africa. Overwinters in western and southern Africa.
Size: 25cm (10in).
Habitat: Open country.
Nest: Tunnel in bank or cliff.
Eggs: 4–10, white.
Food: Mainly flying invertebrates.

Hoopoe

Eurasian hoopoe *Upupa epops*

The unusual appearance of these birds usually helps to identify them easily, especially as they are most likely to be observed in open country. When in flight, the broad shape of their wings is clearly visible and the tall crest is held flat over the back of the head. A hoopoe often raises its crest on landing, however. The hoopoe uses its long bill to probe for worms in the ground, or to grab prey such as lizards scurrying through the grass. Hoopoes are not especially shy of people, and pairs sometimes nest in buildings. They may often be observed dust-bathing, which keeps their plumage in good condition. The "hoo, hoo" sound of their call gives them their common name.

Identification: Mainly pale buff, although more orange on the crown and with black edging to the feathers. Alternate bands of black-and-white coloration on the wings. Long, narrow, downward-curved bill. Sexes are alike.

Above: The wing barring of the hoopoe extends under the wings, shown to best effect when in flight.

Distribution: Throughout most of Europe, although usually absent from Scandinavia and the British Isles. Overwinters in Africa south of the Equator. Also occurs in parts of North Africa and much of central Africa.
Size: 29cm (11in).
Habitat: Relatively open country.
Nest: In secluded holes.
Eggs: 5–8, whitish to yellowish olive.
Food: Mainly invertebrates, especially worms.

Kingfisher

Common kingfisher *Alcedo atthis*

These birds are surprisingly hard to spot, as they perch motionless scanning the water beneath them for fish. When it has spotted its prey, the kingfisher appears as a flash of colour as it dives. A protective membrane covers its eyes as it enters the water. Its wings provide propulsion, and having seized the fish in its bill, the bird then darts out of the water and back on to its perch with its catch. This movement happens incredibly fast, with the whole process taking little more than a mere second. The kingfisher first stuns the fish by hitting it on the perch and then swallows it head first. It regurgitates the bones and indigestible parts of its meal later.

Left: Kingfishers dive at speed into the water, aiming to catch their intended quarry unawares.

Identification: Bluish-green colour that extends over the head and wings. Back is pale blue, and a blue flash is also present on the cheeks. An area under the throat and across the back of the neck is white. Cheek patches and underparts are orange. Bill is black. In hens, the bill is reddish at the base of the lower bill.

Distribution: Occurs across most of Europe, apart from much of Scandinavia. Also present in North Africa and ranges eastwards through southern Asia to the Solomon Islands.
Size: 18cm (7in).
Habitat: Near slow-flowing water.
Nest: Tunnel excavated in sandy bank.
Eggs: 6–10, white.
Food: Small fish. Also preys on aquatic insects, molluscs and crustaceans.

Roller (European roller, *Coracias garrulus*): 32cm (12.5in)
Ranges from southern Europe east to Asia. Overwinters in western and southern Africa. Has shades of blue coloration with a greenish hue on the underparts. Has a prominent area of reddish-brown feathering over the back and wings and blue wing coverts. Powerful blackish bill. Sexes alike.

Woodland kingfisher (*Halcyon senegalensis*): 23cm (9in)
Occurs in a broad band across much of Africa south of the Sahara. Migratory in some areas. Has a greyish head that merges into a pale blue colour over the nape. The wings are blue with black areas. The rump and tail are blue. The upper bill is red and the lower bill is black. Sexes are alike.

Woodchat shrike (*Lanius senator*): 19cm (7.5in)
European distribution centres on the Mediterranean. Also occurs in western North Africa. Overwinters south in a band extending across Africa south of the Sahara. Mainly black upperparts although a chestnut area extends from the back of the head down over the neck. The underparts are white. Has a prominent white wing bar. Hens are mainly brownish, with mottled plumage and white under the chin.

Fiscal shrike (common fiscal, *Lanius collaris*): 23cm (9in)
There are two distinct populations. One ranges from sub-Saharan western Africa eastwards, the other occupies much of southern Africa. Has black upperparts with a prominent white bar. The underparts are white. Hens have rufous flanks.

Red-backed shrike

Lanius collurio

In common with many insectivorous species, the red-backed shrike migrates south each autumn, spending the winter in savanna where food is more plentiful. In some parts of this shrike's breeding range, its nests are parasitized by the common cuckoo. Unlike many such host species, however, pairs learn to recognize cuckoo eggs laid alongside their own and discard them from the nest. Cock birds often impale their prey during the breeding season, and this behaviour ensures a more constant supply of food for the chicks, although there is always a risk that scavengers will steal it.

Identification: Light grey crown. Black stripe extends from the bill across the eyes. Pinkish underparts with reddish-brown back and wings. Hens have brownish area at the front of the crown, grey behind and dark brown wings. Underparts are white with darker edging to the feathers. Brown patches behind the eyes.

Distribution: Mainland Europe, except for most of the Iberian Peninsula and northern Scandinavia. Extends into Asia, and overwinters in Africa south of the Equator.
Size: 18cm (7in).
Habitat: Open country.
Nest: Cup-shaped in the fork of a bush or tree.
Eggs: 5–9, variable coloration.
Food: Invertebrates.

SWIFTS, SWALLOWS AND MARTINS

This group of birds spend most of their lives in flight. They undertake long journeys, with European populations migrating south at the approach of winter and heading to parts of Africa, and then returning to Europe to breed in the following spring. Pairs frequently return to the same nest site that they had occupied previously – a remarkable feat of navigation after a journey covering thousands of kilometres.

Swift

Common swift *Apus apus*

Distribution: Found virtually across the whole of Europe, also extending to North Africa and Asia. Overwinters in southern Africa.
Size: 16.5cm (6.5in).
Habitat: In the air.
Nest: Cup-shaped structure under cover.
Eggs: 2–3, white.
Food: Flying invertebrates, such as midges and moths.

Flocks of swifts are most likely to be spotted when they are uttering their distinctive screaming calls, flying low overhead in search of winged insects. At other times, they may be seen as little more than distant specks, wheeling at heights of more than 1,000m (3,300ft). Their flight pattern is quite distinctive, consisting of a series of rapid wingbeats followed by gliding into the wind. The structure of their feet does not allow them to perch, although they can cling to vertical surfaces. Swifts spend their lives in the air when they are not breeding, apparently they are able to sleep and mate in flight. If hunting conditions are unfavourable, such as a cool summer, nestling swifts respond by growing more slowly, while adults can undergo short periods of torpidity to avoid starvation.

Identification: Dark overall, with pointed wing tips and a forked tail. Pale whitish throat area. Sexes alike.

Swallow

Barn swallow *Hirundo rustica*

The return of swallows to their breeding grounds in Europe is one of the welcomed signs of spring. Although pairs return to the same nest each year, they do not migrate together. Cock birds arrive back before their partners and jealously guard the site from would-be rivals. Cocks fight with surprising ferocity if one of the birds does not back down. Although swallows sometimes use traditional nesting sites, such as caves or hollow trees, they now commonly build their nests inside buildings, such as barns, choosing a site close to the eaves. It can take as many as 1,000 trips to collect damp mud, carried back in the bill, to complete a new nest.

Identification: Chestnut forehead and throat, with dark blue head and back, and a narrow dark blue band across the chest. Wings are blackish. Underparts are white with long streamers on the tail feathers. Sexes alike.

Distribution: Throughout most of the Northern Hemisphere. European swallows overwinter in sub-Saharan Africa.
Size: 19cm (7.5in).
Habitat: Open country, close to water.
Nest: Made of mud built off the ground.
Eggs: 4–5, white with reddish and grey spotting.
Food: Flying invertebrates.

Alpine swift (*Apus melba*): 23cm (9in)
Found throughout southern Europe and North
Africa. Overwinters in southern Africa. Plain brown
upperparts with a black collar around the neck.
Throat, chest and upper abdomen are white. Lower
underparts are brown. Tail is short. Sexes alike.

Red-rumped swallow (*Hirundo daurica*):
17cm (7in)
Occurs in southern Europe, the Mediterranean
and North Africa. Overwinters in sub-Saharan
Africa. Dark bluish area on the head and back,
separated by a wide chestnut collar. Wings are
blackish. Pale chestnut rump with narrow
streaking, as on the underparts. Sexes alike.

Rock martin (pale crag martin, *Hirundo fuligula*):
13cm (5in)
Occurs in Africa, apart from the central region.
Also extends into south-western Asia. Brownish
upperparts. Rufous-brown underparts. Those in
northern areas are lighter and greyer. Sexes alike.

Plain sand martin (brown-throated sand martin,
Riparia paludicola): 12cm (5in)
Sporadic distribution in north-western and sub-
Saharan Africa. Also occurs on Madagascar.
Predominantly brown overall, with a greyish-
brown tinge to the throat and breast. Remainder
of the underparts are white. Sexes alike.

Congo sand martin (*Riparia congica*):
11cm (4.5in)
Confined to three regions of the Congo River,
hence its common name. Similar to the sand
martin but the brown breast band is less
defined. Sexes are alike.

House martin

Delichon urbica

The breeding habits of the house martin
have changed significantly thanks to the
spread of buildings in rural areas. They
traditionally nested on cliffs faces, but over
the past century these birds began building
on the walls of houses and farm structures,
as well as beneath bridges and even on
street lamps, where a ready supply of
nocturnal insects are attracted after dark.
The nest is usually spherical and normally
made of mud. The base is built first. This
is followed by the sides, and on average
the whole process takes up to two weeks to
complete. House martins are highly social
by nature, occasionally nesting in huge
colonies made up of thousands of
pairs where conditions
are suitable. Even
outside the breeding
period, they will
associate in large
flocks of hundreds
of individuals.

Identification: Dark
bluish head and back
with black wings. White
underwing coverts,
underparts and rump. Tail
feathers are dark blue.
Sexes alike.

Distribution: Throughout
Europe, overwintering in
Africa south of the Sahara
Desert. Also present across
much of Asia.
Size: 13cm (5in).
Habitat: Open country, close
to water.
Nest: Made of mud,
cup-shaped.
Eggs: 4–5, white.
Food: Flying invertebrates.

Sand martin

African sand martin; bank swallow *Riparia riparia*

In the summer months, sand martins are usually observed
relatively close to lakes and other stretches of water, often
swooping down to catch invertebrates over the surface.
They are likely to be nesting in colonies nearby, in tunnels
that they excavate on suitable sandy banks. These
can extend back for up to 1m (3ft), and the nesting
chamber is lined with grass, seaweed or similar
material. The eggs are laid on top of a softer
bed of feathers. When the young birds leave the
nest, they stay in groups with other chicks,
until their parents return to feed them,
typically bringing about 60 invertebrates back
on each visit. Parents recognize their
offspring by their distinctive calls. If
danger threatens, the repetitive alarm
calls of the adult sand martins cause the
young to rush back to the protection
of the nesting tunnels.

Identification: Predominantly
brown, with white plumage on
the throat, separated from the
white underparts by a brown
band across the breast. Long
flight feathers. Small black bill.
Sexes alike.
Immature
sand
martins
have
shorter
flight
feathers and
are browner
overall than
the adults.

Distribution: Ranges across
Europe and Asia to North
America, overwintering in
sub-Saharan Africa and
South America.
Size: 11cm (4in.)
Habitat: Open country, close
to water.
Nest: Holes in sandbanks.
Eggs: 3–4, white.
Food: Flying invertebrates.

PHEASANTS AND PARTRIDGES

A number of pheasants and partridges have been specially bred and released well outside their native ranges for sporting purposes, so that sightings far removed from their usual areas of distribution are not unusual. In Europe, these game birds are most likely to be observed during the winter, when there is less natural cover available and groups may be forced to forage more widely for food.

Common pheasant

Ring-necked pheasant *Phasianus colchicus*

There can be considerable variation in appearance between individuals of this species in Europe. This variation is due to hybridization between different races, resulting in the loss of distinguishing characteristics. Even odd black-feathered (melanistic) examples are not uncommon. This situation has arisen largely as a result of widespread breeding of these pheasants and their release into the wild for shooting. Their natural range is actually in Asia. They usually live in groups comprised of a cock bird with several hens. They forage for food on the ground, although they fly noisily and somewhat clumsily when disturbed and may also choose to roost off the ground.

Right: Its mottled plumage provides the common pheasant hen with good camouflage.

Identification: Prominent areas of bare red skin feature on each side of the face. They are surrounded by dark greenish, metallic plumage. Has a variable white area of plumage at the base of the neck. The remainder of the plumage is brown, with the underparts a more chestnut shade with dark blotching apparent. Hens are lighter brown overall, with darker mottling, especially on the back and wings.

Distribution: Now present throughout most of western Europe, apart from much of the Iberian Peninsula. Occurs in a band in central Asia as far east as Japan, and has also been introduced to the United States, Tasmania, Australia and New Zealand.
Size: Cock 89cm (35in); hen 62cm (24in).
Habitat: Lightly wooded areas.
Nest: Scrape on the ground.
Eggs: 7–15, olive brown.
Food: Plant matter, such as seeds, berries and young shoots, and invertebrates.

Red-legged partridge

Alectoris rufa

The adaptable nature of these partridges is reflected by the fact that the species is now breeding well outside its natural range, having first been brought to England as long ago as the late 1600s for sporting purposes. During the 20th century, however, the chukar partridge, which hybridizes with the red-legged variety, was introduced to the British Isles. Today it can be difficult to determine whether the partridges sighted are pure or cross-bred red-legged individuals, even in their natural range, thanks to their similarity in appearance to chukars. Red-legged partridges form individual pairs when breeding. The cock bird chooses, then prepares, the nest site.

Identification: The prominent black collar with similar streaking extending back around the neck helps to identify this species. Black stripe extends across the eye with narrow white band above and white area extending down around the throat. Bluish-grey area above the bill, and bluish-grey on the breast and barred flanks. Brownish abdomen. Hens smaller and lack tarsal spur on the legs.

Distribution: Found naturally in Europe from the Iberian Peninsula to Italy. Introduced to the rest of Europe.
Size: 38cm (15in).
Habitat: Open countryside.
Nest: Scrape on the ground.
Eggs: 9–12, pale yellowish brown with dark spotting.
Food: Plant matter and some invertebrates.

Rock partridge

Alectoris graeca

The name of these partridges stems from the fact that they are often observed on rocky slopes, ranging to altitudes as high as 2,700m (8,850ft) in Italy. They often move down to lower levels when snow collects on the slopes in the winter, and they avoid north-facing slopes. Throughout the year, rock partridges are rarely sighted far from water. They are most likely to be observed in flocks, although their coloration provides excellent camouflage when they are on the ground. When flushed, their flight is quite low and fast, and they will dip down into nearby cover again as soon as they are out of apparent danger. Rock partridges nest as individual pairs, and their chicks are fully grown by three months old.

Distribution: Central southern Europe, from France east to Italy, Greece and the former Yugoslavia. Also present on Sicily.
Size: 36cm (14in).
Habitat: Rocky alpine areas.
Nest: Scrape on the ground.
Eggs: 8–14, yellowish brown with some darker spotting.
Food: Plant matter and some invertebrates.

Identification: Grey crown with black stripe running from around the red bill across the eye and down on to the chest, which has bordering white feathering. Underparts are greyish-blue, becoming fawn on the underparts, with black-and-white barring on the flanks. Brownish suffusion over the back. Sexes are alike.

Helmeted guineafowl

Numida meleagris

There is considerable diversity in the appearance of these guineafowl through their wide range. In the past, taxonomists have recognized more than 30 different races, but this figure has been whittled down to approximately nine today. The shape of the casque and wattles, as well as the depth of the blue coloration on the sides of the head, help to distinguish the various subspecies. Helmeted guineafowl prey readily on invertebrates, even to the extent of picking off ticks from warthogs. When searching for seeds or other food on the ground, they scratch around using their powerful toes. The young are able to fly just 14 days after hatching, and family groups link up with the main flock again after a month or so.

Identification: Distinctive horn-coloured casque on the top of the head, often with adjoining area of red skin, and blue areas on the sides of the face extending down the neck. Traces of fine down feathering may be visible, but head is largely bare. Plumage is dark overall broken with variable white spots. Sexes similar but hens are smaller than cocks.

Distribution: Much of Africa south of the Sahara, apart from areas of central Africa. Introduced elsewhere, including Saudi Arabia and the Caribbean.
Size: 53–63cm (21–25in).
Habitat: Open country, especially savanna.
Nest: Scrape on the ground, often hidden in long grass.
Eggs: 6–12, creamy buff with brown-and-white speckling.
Food: Plant matter and invertebrates.

Chukar partridge (*Alectoris chukar*):
35cm (14in)
Found in southern Europe eastwards to Asia. Introduced to the British Isles and elsewhere. Very similar to the rock partridge but has a cream (rather than white) area on the sides of the face and chest, a broader white stripe above the eyes, and black is present only on the side of the lower mandible rather than the whole bill. Numerous races recognized through its wide range. Hens lack the tarsal swelling of cocks, and their head patterning is less colourful.

Grey partridge (*Perdix perdix*):
32cm (12.5in)
Occurs in a broad band across central Europe, from Ireland eastwards to Asia. Orange-brown face, with stripe extending further back on the sides of the head. Crown, neck and much of the underparts are greyish with dark edging to the plumage. The prominent dark brown feathering on the belly is absent or reduced in size in hens. The flanks are barred with brown. Wings are brown with black speckling. Tail is reddish brown.

Barbary partridge (*Alectoris barbara*):
35cm (14in)
Natural range is in North Africa. Introduced to southern Spain and also present on Sardinia. Dark stripe on the crow, with a greyish-white area beneath and a lighter fawn stripe extending across the eyes. The remainder of the head and throat area are greyish white. Has a reddish-brown border to the bib with black-and-white speckling behind. The chest is otherwise greyish and the abdomen is fawn. The back and wings are greyish with a fawn suffusion. Has brown and black markings on the flanks on a whitish background. Sexes are alike.

QUAILS AND BUSTARDS

This group of birds inhabit open areas of country, relying mainly on their often cryptic coloration to conceal their presence. The distribution of grouse extends to the frozen wastelands of the tundra zone in the far north. They are adapted to living on the ground here, and also have plumage that extends right down over the toes to restrict heat loss and guard against frostbite.

Common quail

Eurasian migratory quail *Coturnix coturnix*

Although these relatively small quails often inhabit agricultural areas, they are hard to spot thanks to their shy natures and the effective camouflage provided by their plumage. Common quails prefer to remain concealed, but take to the wing when necessary, when they are both agile and fast. Their wings appear relatively large when flying, reflecting the fact that these small birds may fly long distances each year. There is a distinction between the resident African population and migratory birds, with the latter being slightly larger in size and not as rufous in coloration. Throughout their range, these quails tend to occur in areas of grassland, as this vegetation provides them with natural cover.

Identification: A pale stripe runs above the eye and a thinner, narrower black stripe runs beneath. There is a small white area faintly bordered by black on the upper chest. The top of the head and back are dark brown. The remainder of the underparts are fawn, becoming paler on the abdomen. Hens lack the white patch, have mottled plumage and are duller in their overall colouration. Young common quail look very similar to the adult hens, but can be distinguished by the absence of stripes on the lower part of their cheeks and the absence of barring on their flanks.

Distribution: Occurs in Europe in summer, wintering in Africa south of the Sahara. Also resident in North Africa.
Size: 18cm (7in).
Habitat: Open country.
Nest: Grass-lined scrape on the ground.
Eggs: 5–13, buff with darker markings.
Food: Seeds and some invertebrates.

Great bustard

Otis tarda

These massive birds have declined greatly in number over recent years owing to the combination of hunting and habitat change. They still flourish in undisturbed areas, where they are seen in groups throughout the year. The display of the cock is an amazing sight as he bends forwards, raising his wings and inflating his throat sac. His head disappears from view, creating what has been likened to a foam bath. In spite of their size, great bustards are quiet birds by nature, uttering a short call resembling a bark only if alarmed. Although adults will hunt voles, invertebrates are favoured for rearing chicks, which is accomplished by the hen alone.

Identification: Grey head and neck, with a rufous area at the base. Black and chestnut markings on the wings, with prominent white areas. Underparts and tips of tail feathers are also white. Hens have more extensive but paler rufous coloration on the neck, and less white on the wings.

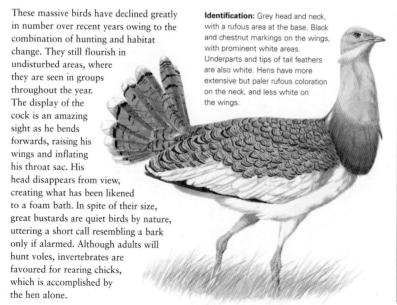

Distribution: Scattered throughout the Iberian Peninsula. Also present in parts of central Europe and ranges eastwards into Asia.
Size: Cock 105cm (41in); hen 75cm (29.5in).
Habitat: Open steppes and farmland.
Nest: Flattened area of vegetation.
Eggs: 2–4, greenish or olive brown.
Food: Plant matter, invertebrates and small mammals.

Willow grouse (red grouse, *Lagopus lagopus*):
35–43cm (14–17in)
Has a circumpolar distribution, which includes
northern areas of the British Isles (where the
race concerned is called red grouse) and
Scandinavia. Has a brownish head and
upperparts, and white underparts. Becomes
pure white during the winter. Hens are similar
but have much more speckled upperparts, but
also become pure white in winter.

Black grouse (Eurasian black grouse, *Tetrao
tetrix*): Cock 58cm (23in); hen 45cm (18cm)
Present in Scotland and northern England.
Extends from Belgium north to Scandinavia and
east across northern Asia. Also occurs in the
Alpine region. Predominantly jet black, with
scarlet combs above the eyes. Odd white areas
form a wing bar and undertail coverts and
create spotting in the shoulder area. The tail
feathers are decidedly curved. The hen is
predominantly brown speckled with black
barring, and has a narrow white wing bar.

Hazel grouse (*Bonasa bonasia*):
40cm (16in)
Occurs in north-eastern France, Belgium and
Germany north to Scandinavia and eastwards
across Asia. Has a distinctive-looking solid black
throat patch outlined in white and a tall crest.
The back, vent and legs are greyish. Darker
abdominal markings are highlighted on a white
background. Rufous patches appear the sides of
the chest. Hens have a speckled throat patch
and a smaller crest.

Caucasian black grouse (*Tetrao mlokosiewiczi*):
55cm (22in)
Present in parts of Turkey and the Caucasian
Mountains. Almost entirely black, apart from
a small white patch in the shoulder area of each
wing and a prominent red stripe above each eye.
Relatively long, slightly curved tail. Hens are
greyish brown overall, with relatively fine barring
over the body and dark ear coverts.

Capercaillie

Western capercaillie *Tetrao urogallus*

Cocks are similar in some respects to New
World turkeys, adopting a very similar
display pose with their tail feathers fanned
out in a circle. They display communally to
hens at sites known as leks. After mating
with her chosen partner, the hen nests and
rears the young by herself. The weather in
the critical post-hatching period has a major
impact on the survival rate of the chicks. In
wet springs, many become fatally chilled.
Hens are about a third of the weight of
cocks. Both sexes have strong, hooked bills,
which enable them to nip off
pieces of tough vegetation,
such as Scots pine shoots,
with relative ease, allowing
them to survive even when
there is snow covering
the ground.

Distribution: Scotland and
mountainous areas in
western Europe. Also ranges
through much of Scandinavia
and northern Asia.
Size: 80–115cm (31–45in).
Habitat: Areas with
coniferous and deciduous
trees.
Nest: Shallow scrape on
the ground.
Eggs: 6–10, yellow with light
brown blotches.
Food: Mainly buds
and shoots.

*Left: The male capercaillie uses
its tail feathers to form a fan
shape when displaying.*

Identification: Greyish-black head
with an obvious red stripe above each
eye. Green area on the chest, with
chestnut wings. Rump and tail are
blackish. Underparts are variable,
ranging from predominantly white to
black. Legs are covered with brown
feathers, toes are exposed. Hens have an
orangish patch on the sides of the face and chest,
brown mottled upperparts and whiter underparts.

LARKS, PIPITS, WAGTAILS AND FLYCATCHERS

Although the coloration of this group of birds tends to be relatively subdued, some members such as the skylark are well known for their song. They are dependent on invertebrates for a major part of their diet, so a number of the species occurring in Europe, especially flycatchers, migrate further south in the autumn each year to obtain a more dependable food supply during the winter.

Common skylark

Alauda arvensis

The coloration and patterning of the skylark help it to remain hidden on the ground, where it sometimes freezes to escape detection. If disturbed at close quarters, however, it takes off almost vertically. Skylarks are unusual in that they reveal their presence readily by singing. They engage in what are described as song flights – fluttering their wings, they rise slowly through the air to a height of typically 100m (330ft) or so. The distinctive rounded song of the skylark can be heard through most of the year, even in the depths of winter. During the breeding period in the spring and summer, a sitting hen may draw attention away from her nest site by feigning injury, dragging one wing along the ground and taking off only as a last resort.

Above: The skylark's nest is well concealed on the ground.

Identification: Greyish-brown plumage over the back and wings, with speckling becoming paler on the flanks. Underparts are mainly white. Whitish stripe extends back from the eyes, and ear coverts are greyish. Short crest on the crown, although it is not always visible. Hens are similar but lack the crest.

Distribution: Resident throughout much of western Europe from Denmark southwards. Also occurs in North Africa. Breeding range extends further north to Scandinavia and eastwards to Asia.
Size: 18cm (7in).
Habitat: Open countryside, especially farmland.
Nest: On the ground hidden in grass.
Eggs: 3–5, greyish, darkly spotted eggs.
Food: Plant matter and invertebrates.

Grey wagtail

Motacilla cinerea

Fast-flowing streams and similar stretches of water are areas where grey wagtails are most likely to be observed, as they dart fearlessly across rocks in search of invertebrates. They live in pairs and construct their cup-shaped nest in a well-concealed locality, usually close to water and sometimes in among the roots of a tree or an ivy-clad wall. These wagtails have benefited from some changes in their environment, taking advantage of millstreams and adjacent buildings to expand their area of distribution, but they can still be forced to leave their territory in search of food during severe winters, especially if the water freezes.

Identification: Grey head and wings, with a narrow white band with black beneath running across the eyes. White border to the black bib on the throat. Underparts are yellow, which is brightest on the chest and at the base of the tail. Sexes similar but hens have a grey or even greyish-white bib and much whiter underparts. Darker feathering disappears from the throat in winter.

Distribution: Resident throughout most of western Europe, except Scandinavia. Also present in North Africa and Asia, where the population tends to be more migratory.
Size: 20cm (8in).
Habitat: Near flowing water.
Nest: In rock crevices and similar sites.
Eggs: 4–6, buff with greyish, marbled markings.
Food: Invertebrates.

Pied wagtail

Motacilla alba

These lively birds have adapted to changes in their environment, moving from coastal areas and marshland into farmland. Today they can even often be observed hunting on and beside roads. Pied wagtails are not especially shy birds, and the movements of their tail feathers, which give them their common name, strike an unmistakable jaunty pose. The race that breeds in the British Isles is different from that observed elsewhere in Europe as cocks have black plumage on their backs during the summer. This area turns to grey for the rest of the year. The mainland European form is often described as the white wagtail as these birds have a greyish back for the whole year.

Identification: Variable through range. Prominent white area on the head with a black crown and nape. A black area extends from the throat down on to the chest. The rest of the underparts are white. The back is grey or black depending on where the wagtail is from. Hens have more ashy-grey backs, which form a smudged border with the black feathering above.

Distribution: Resident throughout western Europe and in western North Africa, with the winter distribution there more widespread. Seen in Scandinavia and Iceland only during the summer.
Size: 19cm (7.5in).
Habitat: Open areas.
Nest: Concealed, sometimes in walls.
Eggs: 5–6, whitish with grey markings.
Food: Invertebrates.

Greater short-toed lark (*Calandrella brachydactyla*): 16cm (6in)
Breeds mainly in southern Europe and North Africa although sometimes seen as far north as the British Isles. Overwinters in Africa and the Middle East. Has largely unmarked white underparts. A dark patch of feathering features on each side of the throat. Has a dark wing bar although wings are otherwise brownish and streaked. The eye stripes are white, and the ear coverts are a darker brownish colour. Sexes are alike.

Bar-tailed desert lark (*Ammomanes cincturus*): 14cm (5.5in)
Extends from north-western Africa into parts of the Middle East. Pale sandy-brown overall, with brownish wings, darker at the tips of the flight feathers. Has a black bar across the tail feathers, which is clearly visible in flight. Sexes are alike.

Meadow pipit (*Anthus pratensis*): 15cm (6in)
Resident in the British Isles and neighbouring parts of western Europe east to Denmark. Individuals from more northerly and easterly areas overwinter around the Mediterranean. Brownish head and wings with darker markings. Dark streaking on the breast and flanks, which are a darker shade of buff. Underparts become whiter in the summer. Sexes are alike.

Collared flycatcher (*Ficedula albicollis*): 13cm (5in)
Occurs as a summertime breeding visitor in central eastern parts of Europe, overwintering in Africa. Similar to the pied flycatcher, but cocks are usually identified by the presence of a white collar encircling the neck and a white area on the rump. Hens have a distinct white patch on the edge of the wings and greyer upperparts.

Pied flycatcher

Ficedula hypoleuca

These flycatchers hawk invertebrates in flight, as well as catching slower-moving prey such as caterpillars by plucking them off vegetation. They are frequently seen in oak woodlands in Europe during the summer, but may range north to the taiga, where mosquitoes hatching in pools of water during the brief summer provide an almost constant supply of food. Pied flycatchers are closely related to collared flycatchers and may sometimes hybridize with them. It is usually possible to identify the male offspring of these pairings by the narrow area of black plumage evident on the nape of the neck.

Distribution: Summer visitor to Europe, breeding as far north as Scandinavia. Overwinters in Africa.
Size: 13cm (5in).
Habitat: Areas in which insects are common.
Nest: Hole in a tree.
Eggs: 5–9, pale blue.
Food: Invertebrates.

Identification: Plumage in summer is a combination of black and white, with white patches above the bill and on the wings. Underparts are white and the remainder of the plumage is black. Hens also have whitish underparts, with a white area on the wing, while the upperparts are brownish. Cocks during winter resemble adult hens, but retain blackish wing and uppertail coverts.

PIGEONS AND DOVES

The columbiforms have adapted well to living in close association with people, although their presence is not always welcomed. Large flocks of feral pigeons can cause serious damage to buildings in urban areas, not just with their droppings but also by pecking at the mortar, which is a source of calcium. Their adaptable nature is further reflected by the fact that they will often breed throughout much of the year.

Rock dove

Columba livia

Although true rock doves have a localized range, their descendants – feral pigeons – are a very common sight even in large capital cities. In the past, monastic communities kept and bred rock doves, and the young doves, known as squabs, were highly valued as a source of meat. Inevitably, some birds escaped from their dovecotes, and the offspring of these birds, which reverted to the wild, gave rise to today's feral pigeons. Colour mutations have also occurred, and apart from the so-called "blue" form, there are now red and even mainly white individuals on city streets today, scavenging whatever they can from our leftovers.

Identification: Dark bluish-grey head, slight green iridescence on the neck, with light grey wings and two characteristic black bars across each wing. Feral pigeons often have longer wings than rock doves. Reddish-purple coloration on the sides of the upper chest. Remainder of the plumage is grey with a black band at the tip of the tail feathers. Sexes alike.

Above: The rock dove nests on loose twigs.

Distribution: Occurs naturally in northern areas of Scotland and nearby islands, and in western Ireland. Also found around the Mediterranean. Distribution of the feral pigeon extends throughout Europe and southern Africa, as well as to other continents.
Size: 35cm (14in).
Habitat: Originally cliffs and mountainous areas.
Nest: Loose pile of twigs or similar material.
Eggs: 2, white.
Food: Mainly seeds.

Wood pigeon

Columba palumbus

Distribution: Occurs throughout virtually all of western Europe, ranging eastwards into Asia and also present in north-western Africa.
Size: 43cm (17in).
Habitat: Areas with tall trees.
Nest: Platform of twigs.
Eggs: 2, white.
Food: Seeds, plant matter and invertebrates.

Identification: Grey head, with a reflective metallic-green area at the nape of the neck and characteristic white patches on the sides. Bill is reddish at the base, becoming yellow towards the top. Purplish breast becoming paler on the underparts. Tip of tail is black. White edging to the wings most evident in flight, forming a distinct band. Sexes alike.

These pigeons can be significant agricultural pests in areas of arable farming. Even in towns, they will frequent parks where there are established stands of trees, and descend into nearby gardens and allotments to raid growing crops. On occasion, however, they also eat potential crop pests such as snails. Pairs sometimes nest on buildings, but they prefer a suitable tree fork. Their calls are surprisingly loud and are often uttered soon after dawn. Outside the breeding season, these birds congregate in larger numbers. Their relatively large size means that they appear quite clumsy when taking off if danger threatens.

Collared dove

Streptopelia decaocto

The westerly spread of these doves during the second half of the 20th century was one of the most dramatic examples of the changing patterns of distribution among bird species. In this case, the triggers for the distribution change are unclear. Collared doves had been recorded in Hungary in the 1930s, and they moved rapidly over the next decade across Germany and Austria to France, and also headed north to Denmark and the Netherlands. The species was first sighted in eastern England during 1952, and a pair bred there three years later. The earliest Irish record was reported in 1959, and by the mid-1960s the collared dove had colonized almost all of the UK. No other bird species has spread naturally so far and so rapidly in recent times, to the extent that the collared dove's range now extends right across Europe and Asia.

Identification: Pale greyish-fawn with a narrow black half-collar around the back of the neck. Dark flight feathers with white edging along the leading edge of the wing. White tips to tail feathers visible when spread. Depth of individual coloration can vary. Sexes are alike.

Above: The collared dove is a frequent visitor to towns and will happily build its nest on the roof tops.

Distribution: Across Europe, apart from the far north of Scandinavia and the Alps, eastwards to Asia. More localized on the Iberian Peninsula and in North Africa particularly.
Size: 34cm (13in).
Habitat: Parks and gardens.
Nest: Platform of twigs.
Eggs: 2, white.
Food: Seeds and some plant matter.

Laughing dove

Streptopelia senegalensis

These highly adaptable doves are often seen in urban habitats, particularly in areas where they are expanding their range. In Australia, for example, bird-table offerings have afforded them a constant supply of suitable food, allowing them to become established here well away from their natural range. In North Africa, they are frequently encountered near oases, which has led to them becoming known as palm doves. Their fast breeding cycle, with chicks hatching and leaving the nest within a month of the eggs being laid, means that they can increase their numbers rapidly under favourable conditions. Pairs may attempt to breed throughout most of the year, rather than having a prescribed breeding period like many bird species, particularly those occurring outside the tropics.

Distribution: Widely distributed in Africa, both north and south of the Sahara Desert, although absent from western central parts. Also extends throughout the Middle East to Asia. Introduced to Western Australia.
Size: 26cm (10in).
Habitat: Acacia woodland, oases and open country.
Nest: Loose platform of twigs.
Eggs: 2, white.
Food: Mainly seeds and invertebrates.

Identification: Reddish brown, with brown and black speckled collar under the neck. Grey bar on the leading edge of the wing. Pale underparts. Has a long, relatively dark tail. Sexes are alike.

Stock pigeon (stock dove, *Columba oenas*): 32cm (12.5in)
Throughout Europe, but absent from much of Scotland, northern Scandinavia and most of the mountainous central region. Range does extend to north-western Africa and east to Asia. Grey head with green iridescence on the neck. Wings are dark grey with black markings and a black band across the tips of the tail feathers. Pale grey rump and lower underparts. The chest is pinkish grey.

European turtle dove (*Streptopelia turtur*): 27cm (10.5in)
Much of Europe but not common in Ireland, Scotland or Scandinavia. Present in North Africa. More brightly coloured on the wings than its East Asian cousin, having orange-brown feathers with darker centres. Black-and-white barring on the sides of the neck. Head is greyish. Underparts are pale with a slight pinkish hue. White edge to the tail feathers.

Cape dove (Namaqua dove, *Oena capensis*): 26cm (10in)
Found in Africa south of the Sahara, including Madagascar. Also present in southern Israel and Arabia. Black area from the forehead down on to the chest, with bluish grey behind. Long, narrow tail. Dark flight feathers and black markings on the wings, with rufous underwing areas. Upperparts are light grey, whiter on the underparts. Hens lack the black area on the face, displaying only a narrow stripe extending from the bill to the eye.

SPARROWS, WEAVERS AND WHYDAHS

Various members of this group of birds have benefited from the impact of human changes to the environment. These changes have led not only to a greater availability of food, but also to a corresponding increase in nesting sites in urban areas. These birds tend to live in flocks, and in some cases cock birds are transformed by a nuptial moult at the start of the breeding season.

House sparrow

Passer domesticus

A common sight on bird tables and in city parks, house sparrows have adapted to living closely alongside people, even to the extent of nesting under roofs in buildings. These sparrows form loose flocks, with larger numbers congregating where food is readily available. They spend much of their time on the ground, hopping along and ever watchful for passing predators such as cats. It is not uncommon for them to construct nests during the winter time, which serve as communal roosts rather than being used for breeding. The bills of cock birds turn black at the start of the nesting period in the spring. During this time, several males often court a single female in what has become known as a "sparrows' wedding". In more rural areas, these sparrows will sometimes nest in tree hollows, and even construct domed nests on occasion.

Identification: Rufous-brown head with a grey area on top. A black stripe runs across the eyes and a broad black bib runs down over the chest. Has a whitish area under the tail. The ear coverts and the entire underparts are greyish. Hens are a duller shade of brown with a pale stripe behind each eye and a fawn bar on each wing.

Distribution: Occurs throughout virtually all of Europe and eastwards into Asia. Also present in North and south-east Africa.
Size: 15cm (6in).
Habitat: Urban and more rural areas.
Nest: Buildings and tree hollows.
Eggs: 3–6, whitish with darker markings.
Food: Seeds and invertebrates, which are especially sought during the breeding season.

Orange weaver

Red bishop *Euplectes orix*

The stocky bills of these weavers not only assist them in cracking the seeds that form the basis of their diet, but also make highly effective needles, allowing them to weave their elaborate nests effectively. This is a learned skill, which improves with practice, and young cocks, with their clumsily constructed nests, are far less likely to attract mates than experienced males. Cocks are polygamous, with each mature male mating with several hens and providing each with a nesting site, although he will take no direct role in hatching the eggs or rearing the chicks.

Above: By weaving their nests, orange weavers can site them in areas where they are more likely to be out of reach of predators.

Distribution: South of the Sahara, extending eastwards to Ethiopia and south to southern Africa.
Size: 13cm (5in).
Habitat: Grasslands.
Nest: Woven from grasses.
Eggs: 3–4, pale blue.
Food: Seeds, vegetation and some invertebrates.

Identification: Cocks in breeding colour have a ruff of orangish red around the head, with a black face, lower breast and upper abdomen. Darker blackish-red area over the mantle, Lower back and abdomen are orangish-red. Flight feathers are brown. Hen and out-of-colour cock (left) have brownish-black streaking on the upperparts, with a pale yellowish stripe above each eye, buff underparts and light streaking on the sides of the breast.

Pintailed whydah

Vidua macroura

The finery and display of the cock bird attracts a harem of hens during the breeding period. After mating, however, the female pintailed whydah lays individual eggs in the nests of waxbills, rather than constructing her own. As many as 19 different species have been recorded as playing host to young whydahs, and this species ranks among the most adaptable of all birds displaying parasitic breeding behaviour. Unlike the common cuckoo, however, young whydahs do not kill their fellow nestlings but are reared alongside them, even mimicking their mouth markings on hatching. This fools the hosts into believing that the whydah is one of their own.

Identification: Breeding cocks have a black cap, and white collar, sides of the face and underparts. Remainder of the upperparts is black, apart from white wing bars and very long tail plumes. Hens and out-of-colour cocks have black stripes running from the sides of the bill up to the eyes, and a black area on the crown. Speckling is evident over the back and wings. Underparts are a lighter shade of fawn.

Distribution: Occurs widely across Africa south of the Sahara Desert.
Size: 11cm (4in) excluding male's tail plumes, which reach 25cm (10in).
Habitat: Open country.
Nest: Parasitizes those of other species, mainly waxbills.
Eggs: 3, whitish.
Food: Seeds and some invertebrates.

Tree sparrow (*Passer montanus*): 14cm (5.5in)
Present in all mainland Europe apart from northern Scandinavia, western England, northern Scotland and central Ireland. The top of the head is reddish-brown and there is a black bib beneath the eyes. A white area on the cheeks below the eyes extends back around the neck and is broken by central black patches. Grey chest. The wings are light brown and black, broken by a white wing bar edged by black. Sexes are alike.

Red-collared whydah (*Euplectes ardens*): 13cm (5in)
Ranges in eastern and central Africa. Breeding males are black, apart from a scarlet, crescent-shaped area on the upper breast. Long tail feathers add 15cm (6in) to their overall length. Hens and out-of-colour cocks have black and brown streaking on their upperparts and buff coloration on their underparts.

Indigo bird (*Vidua chalybeata*): 13cm (5in)
Ranges in western Africa from Mauritania to Chad and Nigeria. Crown has a pale streak with a darker border. Breeding cocks have bluish-black plumage, and reddish bill, legs and feet. Hens and out-of-colour cocks have dark and light brown streaking on the upperparts and buff-white underparts.

Napoleon weaver (Golden bishop, *Euplectes afer*): 13cm (5in)
Ranges in western Africa from Senegal to Chad, the Central African Republic and the Congo. Has a yellow crown and back with a blackish hue on the collar, a yellow breast and black abdomen. The wings and tail are brownish black. There is streaking on the upperparts. Buff underparts with darker streaking. Breeding cocks have a black mask and throat. Hens and out-of-colour cocks have a black head.

Red-billed weaver

Black-faced dioch; red-billed quelea *Quelea quelea*

This weaver is considered to be the most numerous bird in the world, with the total population estimated at ten billion individuals. It lives in large flocks that can inflict massive damage on ripening crops of millet and other seeds. To reflect this, red-billed weavers are often called feathered locusts. These birds breed communally. Nests are built closely together in thorn trees, and these help to deter potential predators and also serve as fixing points for the nests.

Distribution: Ranges widely across Africa south of the Sahara Desert, eastwards to Sudan and Ethiopia and south to northern South Africa and Angola.
Size: 13cm (5in).
Habitat: Often close to reed beds.
Nest: Made of grasses.
Eggs: 2–4, pale blue.
Food: Seeds and invertebrates.

Identification: Both sexes have brown and black streaked plumage outside the nesting season. Cocks in breeding colour have a black mask, with pinkish plumage on the head extending across the underparts. Dark brown and black wings. Tail feathers are dark.

WRENS, TITS, NUTHATCHES AND WARBLERS

These relatively small birds are most likely to be spotted in gardens during the winter months, when the absence of leaves on trees makes them more conspicuous. Tits, in particular, are also frequent visitors to bird feeders and tables during colder weather. They can prove to be very resourceful when seeking food, clearly displaying their skill in aerobatics as they dart about and hang upside down to feed.

Wren

Troglodytes troglodytes

Although the wren's small size makes these tiny birds difficult to spot, their song is loud for their size and will betray their presence. Wrens are often found in areas where there is plenty of cover, such as ivy-clad walls, where they hunt for food, scurrying under the vegetation in search of spiders and similar prey. During the winter, when their small size could make them vulnerable to hypothermia, these wrens huddle together in roosts overnight to keep warm. In the spring, the hen chooses one of several nests that the male has constructed, lining it with feathers to form a soft base for her eggs. Wrens are surprisingly common, although not always conspicuous, with the British population alone made up of an estimated ten million birds. Populations are often badly affected by prolonged spells of severe weather.

Identification: Reddish-brown back and wings with barring visible. Lighter brown underparts and a narrow eye stripe. Short tail, often held vertically, which is greyish on its underside. Bill is long and relatively narrow. Sexes alike.

Distribution: Resident throughout Europe, apart from Scandinavia and neighbouring parts of Russia during the winter. Wrens in Europe move south in the winter. Present in North Africa.
Size: 10cm (4in).
Habitat: Overgrown gardens and woodland.
Nest: Ball-shaped.
Eggs: 5–6, white with reddish-brown markings.
Food: Mainly invertebrates.

Eurasian nuthatch

Sitta europaea

Distribution: Found throughout most of Europe, apart from Ireland, northern England, Scotland and much of Scandinavia. Occurs in North Africa opposite the Strait of Gibraltar.
Size: 14cm (5.5in).
Habitat: Gardens and parks with mature trees.
Nest: In a secluded spot.
Eggs: 6–9, white with heavy reddish-brown speckling.
Food: Invertebrates and seeds.

The relatively large, strong feet and powerful claws of the Eurasian nuthatch give a hint as to the behaviour of these birds. They are adept at scampering up and down tree trunks, hunting for invertebrates, which they extract with their narrow bills. Their compact and powerful beak also enables these birds to feed easily on nuts, which they first wedge into a suitable crevice in the bark. Nuthatches then hammer at the shell, breaking it open so they can extract the kernel. They also store nuts, which they can use when other food is in short supply. The bill is also a useful tool to help the birds plaster over the entrance to their nest hole in the spring. The small opening just allows the birds to squeeze in, helping to protect them from predators. These nuthatches are most likely to be encountered in areas with broad-leafed trees, as these provide food such as acorns and hazelnuts.

Identification: Bluish-grey upperparts from head to tail, with a black stripe running across the eyes. Underparts vary in colour, depending on the race, from white through to a rusty shade of buff. Dark reddish-brown vent area, more brightly coloured in cocks.

Blue tit

Parus caeruleus

Distribution: Throughout Europe except the far north of Scandinavia. Also present in north-western Africa.
Size: 12cm (5in).
Habitat: Wooded areas in parks and gardens.
Nest: Tree holes.
Eggs: 7–16, white with reddish-brown markings.
Food: Invertebrates, seeds and nuts.

A common visitor to bird tables, blue tits are lively, active birds by nature, and are welcomed by gardeners because they eat aphids. Their small size allows them to hop up the stems of thin plants and, hanging upside down, seek these pests under leaves. Blue tits are well adapted to garden life and readily adopt nest boxes supplied for them. Their young leave the nest before they are able to fly properly, and are vulnerable to predators such as cats at this time. Those that do survive the critical early weeks can be easily distinguished by the presence of yellow rather than white cheek patches.

Identification: Has a distinctive area of blue on the crown, edged with white, and narrow black stripe running across eyes. Cheeks are white. Underparts are yellowish. The back is a greyish-green. There is a whitish bar across the top of the blue wings. The tail is also blue. Sexes similar but hens duller.

Willow warbler

Phylloscopus trochilus

Distribution: Occurs in the summer from the British Isles right across northern Europe. Overwinters in Africa.
Size: 12cm (5in).
Habitat: Wooded areas.
Nest: Domed, built on the ground.
Eggs: 6–7, pale pink with reddish spotting.
Food: Small invertebrates.

The subdued coloration of these small birds is so effective that, in spite of being one of Europe's most common bird species, the willow warbler is relatively inconspicuous. They are quite difficult to observe in the wooded areas that they frequent, although their song, which heralds their arrival in the spring, will betray their presence. In the British Isles, the willow warbler is the most numerous warbler; the population is estimated to comprise three million pairs. These warblers are usually resident in Europe between April and September. The nest is well hidden in vegetation and features a low entry point. In late summer, willow warblers are often observed in loose association with various tits, before heading off to their wintering grounds.

Identification: Greyish-green upperparts, with a pale yellowish streak running across the eyes. Pale yellow throat and chest, with whitish underparts. The yellow plumage is much whiter in birds from more northern areas.

Long-tailed tit (*Aegithalos caudatus*): 15cm (6in)
Occurs throughout most of Europe, except for much of northern Scandinavia. Distinctive narrow, long tail feathers, up to 9cm (3.5in) long. Head predominantly white, with a variable black streak above the eyes. Reddish-brown patches on the upper part of the wings and the flanks. Back and wings are otherwise black.

Great tit (*Parus major*): 15cm (6in)
Present throughout Europe and extends to north-western Africa. Also occurs in eastern Asia. Prominent black head with white patches on the cheeks. Black stripe extending from the throat down the midline of the underparts, which is far more prominent in cocks than hens. The rest of the underparts are yellow. Greyish-green back, with a white wing bar and blue hues.

Coal tit (*Parus ater*): 11cm (4in)
Range extends throughout most of Europe, apart from the far north of Scandinavia. Also present in north-western Africa. Coal-black markings on the head, with a white area on the nape and cheeks. Brownish-white underparts. Olive-grey wings with white markings. North African race has yellow rather than white markings.

Blackcap warbler (*Sylvia atricapilla*): 15cm (6in)
Ranges over most of Europe in the summer, apart from northern Scandinavia. Moves south in winter and has a resident population restricted largely to southern parts of the British Isles (including Ireland), France, the Iberian Peninsula and Italy. Also resident in north-western Africa. Jet black area on the crown, extending just above the eye and bordered by grey above the bill. Remainder of the head and breast is greyish. Has white plumage under the throat. Back, wings and underparts are olive grey. Sexes alike. Young birds have a reddish brown cap.

FINCHES

By feeding mainly on seeds, but adopting different feeding strategies, finch species can exploit a wide variety of food sources without competing with each other. At one extreme, goldfinches, for example, can probe for and eat small seeds, whereas the stout-billed hawfinch can crack cherry seeds, exerting a force equivalent to 50kg (110lb) to reach the kernel within.

Chaffinch

Fringilla coelebs

The behaviour of the chaffinch changes significantly during the year. These birds can be seen in groups during the winter, but at the onset of spring, and the breeding season, cock birds become very territorial, driving away any rivals. While resident chaffinches remain in gardens and similar settings throughout the year, large groups of migrants seeking refuge from harsh winter weather associate as larger flocks in farmland areas. These birds usually prefer to feed on the ground, hopping and walking along in search of seeds. They seek invertebrates almost exclusively for rearing their chicks.

Identification: Has a black band above the bill with grey over the head and neck. The cheeks and underparts are pinkish. The back is brown with two distinctive white wing bars. Cocks are less brightly coloured in winter plumage. Hens have dull grey cheek patches and dark greyish-green upperparts. Their underparts are a buff shade of greyish white.

Distribution: Resident in the British Isles and western Europe, and a summer visitor to Scandinavia and eastern Europe. Also occurs in North Africa. Resident in the west of North Africa and at the south-western tip of Africa.
Size: 16cm (6in).
Habitat: Woodland in parks and gardens.
Nest: Cup-shaped in a tree fork.
Eggs: 4–5, light brown or blue with dark, often smudgy markings.
Food: Seeds and some invertebrates.

European goldfinch

Carduelis carduelis

The long, narrow bill of the goldfinch enables it to prise kernels out of seeds, and these birds often congregate in the winter to feed on stands of thistle heads and teasel. Alder cones are also a favoured food at this time of year. Goldfinches are very agile birds, capable of clinging on to narrow stems when feeding. They are social by nature, usually mixing in small flocks in areas where food is plentiful, although they are usually shy when feeding on the ground. They have a relatively loud, attractive, twittering song. Pairs usually prefer to build their nest in the fork of a tree rather than concealing it in a hedge.

Identification: Bright red face with black lores. Black area across the top of the crown that broadens to a collar on the neck. White extends around the throat, and a brown necklace separates the white on the throat from the paler underparts. Brown back and flanks; otherwise underparts are white. Bill is narrow and pointed. Wings are black with white spotting and yellow barring. Tail is black with white markings. Hens display duller coloration with less yellow apparent.

Distribution: Occurs throughout much of the British Isles and mainland Europe, including Denmark but confined to the extreme south of Scandinavia. Also present in North Africa.
Size: 13cm (5in).
Habitat: Woodland and more open areas.
Nest: Cup-shaped, made of vegetation.
Eggs: 5–6, bluish white with darker markings.
Food: Seeds and invertebrates.

Brambling (*Fringilla montifringilla*): 16cm (6in)
Breeds in the far north of Scandinavia. Overwinters in southern Europe and north-western Africa. In summer, cocks have a glossy, bluish-black head and back, and a black bill. Chest and vent are rusty orange with white underparts and dark grey speckling on the flanks. In the winter, black areas are broken by brown speckling and the bill turns yellow. Hens have greyish-brown plumage and a buff-coloured breast.

Common linnet (*Carduelis cannabina*):
14cm (5.5in)
Resident in western Europe and north-western Africa. Summer resident in the north-eastern areas; absent from much of Scandinavia. A red crown and grey head. Back and wings are brown. Sides of the chest are red, becoming paler on the flanks with a white area on the breast. Hens are much duller with a short grey bill.

Common redpoll (*Carduelis flammea*):
14cm (5.5in)
Occurs in northern Europe, including Iceland, moving south in winter. A crimson red cap and black lores, with streaked upperparts. Red chest fading into white on the steaked abdomen. White wing bar, yellowish bill. Hens lack the red on the chest.

Hawfinch (*Coccothraustes coccothraustes*):
18cm (7in)
Present in Europe, apart from Ireland and much of Scandinavia. Occurs in North Africa. Stout, triangular-shaped, blackish bill that turns yellowish brown in winter. Has black feathering around the eyes and throat. The head is rusty brown with a grey collar. The back is dark brown but the rump is a lighter colour. There is a white area on the wings and the underparts are buff. Hens have a grey area on the wings.

European greenfinch

Carduelis chloris

Greenfinches have stout bills that allow them to crack open seed casings easily and reach the edible kernels inside. They are most likely to be observed in areas where there are trees and bushes that provide nesting cover. In the winter, the European greenfinch visits bird tables, taking peanuts readily as well as foraging in gardens. Groups of greenfinches are also sighted in more open areas of countryside, such as farmland, searching for weed seeds and grains that may have been dropped during harvesting. Pairs often nest two or three times in succession during the summer, and invertebrates are consumed in larger quantities at this time when there are chicks in the nest.

Distribution: Throughout Europe and North Africa apart from the far north of Scandinavia.
Size: 16cm (6in).
Habitat: Edges of woodland and more open areas.
Nest: Bulky, cup-shaped.
Eggs: 4–6, whitish to pale blue with darker markings.
Food: Largely seeds and some invertebrates.

Identification: Greenish head, with greyer areas on the sides of the face and wings. Yellowish-green breast, with yellow also evident on the flight feathers. Relatively large, conical bill. Hen is duller, with greyer tone overall, brownish mantle and less yellow on the wings.

European serin

Serinus serinus

Although mainly confined to relatively southerly latitudes, these serins are occasionally seen in the British Isles and have even bred successfully in southern England. It appears that serins are slowly extending their northerly distribution. Ornithological records reveal they had spread to central Europe by 1875, and had started to colonize France within another 50 years. Serins often seek out stands of conifers, where they nest, although they also frequent citrus groves further south in their range. Young birds are quite different in appearance from adults, being predominantly brown and lacking any yellow in their plumage.

Identification: A bright yellow forehead, extending in a stripe above the eyes, encircling the cheeks down on to the breast. Back is yellow and streaked with brown, as are the white flanks. Hens are duller in coloration, with a pale yellow rump.

Distribution: Resident in coastal areas of France south through the Iberian Peninsula to North Africa and around the northern Mediterranean area. A summer visitor elsewhere in mainland Europe.
Size: 12cm (5in).
Habitat: Parks and gardens.
Nest: Cup-shaped in tree.
Eggs: 3–5, pale blue with darker markings.
Food: Seeds and some invertebrates.

AFRICAN FINCHES

Most of these finches are highly social and are often encountered in large flocks, which can inflict serious damage on ripening crops. Prolific when breeding, these birds are generally short-lived, and studies suggest that they typically have a life expectancy of less than two years. It is not just predators and human persecution that account for this short life span – drought, too, can result in heavy mortality.

Golden song sparrow

Passer luteus

In spite of their name, these birds are not talented songsters, even during the breeding season, uttering little more than a series of chirping notes. Cocks undergo an unusual change at this time, however, as their bills are transformed from a pinkish shade to black. The depth of yellow can vary, being paler in some cases than others and often reflecting slight regional variations. Although golden song sparrows tend not to feed in towns, they frequently roost there in large flocks. They are often nomadic when not breeding, with flocks typically made up of more than 100 birds wandering widely in search of favourable conditions. They breed communally too, and the young are reared primarily on invertebrates.

Identification: Has a yellow head and underparts. Chestnut coloured feathering runs over the back and wings, and merges with black. Hens are a dull brown, and have paler, buff-coloured underparts.

Distribution: Extends in a broad band from Mauritania in western Africa eastwards right across the continent to northern parts of Sudan and Ethiopia.
Size: 13cm (5in).
Habitat: Scrub, cropland and towns.
Nest: Bulky.
Eggs: 3–6, off-white with darker irregular markings.
Food: Seeds and some invertebrates.

Red-cheeked cordon bleu

Uraeginthus bengalus

Distribution: Ranges across Africa south of the Sahara Desert extending to parts of southern Zaire; also occurs in eastern Angola and Zambia. Believed to be present on the Cape Verde Islands.
Size: 13cm (5in).
Habitat: Gardens and grasslands.
Nest: Bulky oval or spherical structure.
Eggs: 4–5, white.
Food: Seeds and invertebrates.

The depth of blue coloration of the red-cheeked cordon bleu varies through its range, especially in the case of males. These colourful finches have adapted well to the spread of human settlement, and are often sighted in villages. They seek food primarily on the ground, hopping along in search of seeds as well as invertebrates, which are used to feed chicks in the nest. These so-called blue waxbills are also sufficiently agile to catch flying ants on occasion. When nesting, pairs are relatively solitary, but after the breeding season, they will reunite to form quite large flocks. The natural environment of these cordon bleus is open country, and although they may wander through their range, they are unlikely to be encountered in densely forested areas.

Identification: Greyish-brown plumage extends from the top of the bill down over the back and wings. The plumage around the eyes down on to the chest and flanks is sky blue, and the abdomen is light buff. Sexes similar except hens lack the dark red ear coverts and also have less blue on their underparts.

St Helena waxbill

Common waxbill *Estrilda astrild*

A highly adaptable species, these waxbills are not only encountered commonly in Africa, but also in other parts of the world, including the island of St Helena where they have been introduced. Other populations are also established on the islands of Rodriquez, Seychelles and Reunion, close to Africa, as well as further afield in locatities as diverse as Hawaii and Brazil. St Helena waxbills are most likely to be observed in flocks in areas where there are relatively tall grasses. Grass seeds feature prominently in their diet. The birds will often roost alongside each other, as well as grasping onto the stems and feeding from ripening seedheads. They rarely stray very far from water. While in proximity to people, whether in gardens or villages, they can become quite tame.

Distribution: Occurs across much of Africa, south of the Sahara. Absent from heavily-forested areas
Size: 12cm (4^1/$_2$in).
Habitat: Grassland areas and gardens.
Nest: Bulky, pear-shaped structure.
Eggs: 4–8, pink.
Food: Seeds, invertebrates.

Identification: Brown forehead and prominent red eye stripes. They have a pale chest, dark brown, barred wings and heavy barring on the underparts, including the flanks, with slight red markings in the centre of the abdomen. Sexes are alike.

Orange-eared waxbill (*Estrilda melpoda*): 10cm (4in)
From Senegal in western Africa on to the Congo, Zaire, Angola and Zambia. Large, orange cheek patches. Surrounding plumage is greyish but the head is darker. Wings are chestnut brown. The rump is reddish. Sexes generally alike, although hens may be slightly paler.

Silverbill (*Lonchura cantans*): 10cm (4in)
Extends in a broad band across Africa south of the Sahara from Mauritania in western Africa eastwards to Somalia and Tanzania. Also ranges from Saudi Arabia to Oman. The top of the head is dark brown and this continues down over the back and wings. The chest and cheeks are pale buff, but become darker on the abdomen. Silvery bill and black rump. Sexes are similar, but hens may be a little smaller.

Purple grenadier (*Uraeginthus ianthinogaster*): 14cm (5.5in)
Ranges in eastern Africa from Sudan, Ethiopia and Somalia south to parts of Uganda, Kenya and Tanzania. Has a purple area above and below the eyes, and another extensive area of purple on the lower breast over the abdomen and rump. The remainder of the plumage is reddish brown. Hens are much duller with whitish-purple plumage around the eyes and purple elsewhere essentially confined to the rump. Has whitish scalloping on the flanks.

Magpie mannikin

Lonchura fringilloides

Mannikins as a group are relatively dull in colour, with black, brown and white coloration predominating in their plumage. The magpie mannikin is no different in this respect from Asiatic members of the group. It lives in small flocks, but is not especially common through much of its range if compared to other African mannikins overlapping its area of distribution. Tall grasses, reeds and bamboos are favoured roosting, feeding and breeding areas, whether in close proximity to human settlement or further afield. Magpie mannikins seek out ripening seeds, and use their spindly claws to anchor themselves on to narrow stems to obtain food.

Distribution: Ranges from Senegal in western Africa eastwards to southern Sudan and south to Gabon and eastern South Africa.
Size: 13cm (5in).
Habitat: Grassland and woodland clearings.
Nest: Ball of dried grass and similar material.
Eggs: 5–6, white.
Food: Seeds and invertebrates.

Identification: Glossy bluish-black head, and powerful, conical greyish-black bill. Underparts entirely white aside from black and brown barring on the flanks. Back and wings are dark brown, broken by some lighter markings, especially on the back. Rump and tail are black. Sexes alike.

THRUSHES

Various members of this group of birds are excellent songsters, although overall they are not brightly coloured. Their long, powerful bills allow them to prey on a range of invertebrates, and they also feed on berries and fruit. Some thrushes are migratory, either moving within Europe or flying further afield before winter, descending in large numbers in some areas when the weather is unfavourable elsewhere.

Robin

Erithacus rubecula

The robin's colourful appearance belies its strong aggressive streak, for these birds are highly territorial. In the garden, robins can become very tame, regularly hopping down alongside the gardener's fork or spade to grab invertebrates such as earthworms as they come to the surface. Young, recently fledged robins look very different from mature individuals – they are almost entirely brown with dense spotting on the head and chest. Robins are not musical birds, and their calls consist largely of a tick-like call note that is often drawn out and repeated, particularly if they are alarmed by the presence of a nearby predator such as a cat. Since they often feed on the ground, robins can be very vulnerable to these predators.

Identification: Bright orange plumage extends just above the bill, around the eyes and down over virtually the entire breast. Lower underparts are whitish grey, becoming browner on the flanks. Top of the head and wings are brown, with a pale wing bar. Sexes are alike.

Distribution: Resident in the British Isles, western Europe and parts of North Africa. Scandinavian and eastern European populations are migratory, overwintering further south.
Size: 14cm (5.5in).
Habitat: Gardens, parks and woodland areas.
Nest: Under cover, often near the ground.
Eggs: 5–7, bluish white with red markings.
Food: Invertebrates, berries, fruit and seeds.

Song thrush

Turdus philomelos

The song of these thrushes is both powerful and musical. It is heard particularly in the spring at the start of the breeding season and usually uttered from a relatively high branch. Song thrushes are welcomed by gardeners, as they readily hunt and eat snails and other garden pests on the ground. Having grabbed a snail, the birds choose special sites, known as anvils, where they batter the snail against a rock to break the shell and dislodge the mollusc within. Song thrushes can run effectively, which allows them to pursue quarry such as leather-jackets (the larvae of certain species of cranefly). When breeding, they build a typical cup-shaped nest, and the hen is mainly, or even solely, responsible for construction.

Identification: Has brown back and wings, with some black areas evident, and a yellow-buff area across the chest. Dark markings that extend over the chest and abdomen are shaped like arrows, rather than circular. Sexes alike. Young birds have smaller spots and these are likely to be less numerous on their underparts.

Distribution: Ranges widely throughout Europe. Eastern populations head south to the Mediterranean region for the winter. Also in North Africa, even as far south as the Sudan.
Size: 22cm (8.5in).
Habitat: Woodlands and gardens.
Nest: Cup-shaped.
Eggs: 5–6, greenish blue with reddish-brown markings.
Food: Invertebrates and berries.

Common blackbird

Turdus merula

Blackbirds frequently descend to feed on lawns, seeking invertebrates. After rain, earthworms, which often feature prominently in blackbirds' diet, are most likely to be drawn to the surface, and slugs and snails also emerge in wet conditions. In the 19th century, blackbirds were rarely seen in gardens, but today they have become commonplace. They utter a variety of calls and are quite vocal. Cocks are talented songsters, and both sexes will utter an urgent, harsh alarm call. Although blackbirds do not associate together in flocks, pairs are seen foraging together on occasion. As with other thrushes, their tails are surprisingly flexible and can be raised or lowered at will. It is not unusual to see pied blackbirds occasionally, with variable amounts of white feathering among the black plumage. The majority of these birds, especially those with the most extensive white areas, are cocks.

Distribution: Resident throughout most of Europe and North Africa. The majority of Scandinavian and eastern European populations are migratory.
Size: 29cm (11.5in).
Habitat: Woodland, gardens and parkland.
Nest: Well-hidden cup-shaped nest.
Eggs: 3–5, greenish blue with reddish-brown markings.
Food: Invertebrates, fruit and berries

Identification: Plumage is a magnificent jet black, contrasting with the bright yellow bill, which becomes a deeper shade during the winter. Hens are drab in comparison, being brownish overall with some streaking, notably on the breast, and with a darker bill.

Left: The hen alone is usually responsible for incubating the eggs, although very occasionally the cock may share the task.

Common redstart (*Phoenicurus phoenicurus*): 14cm (5.5in)
Breeds throughout most of the British Isles (except Ireland) and western Europe eastwards into Scandinavia, as well as in North Africa. Overwinters further south in Africa. Has a chestnut-red breast and a black face with a white stripe above. Crown, back and wings are greyish. Has chestnut tail feathers. Hens have greyish-brown upperparts and buff-white underparts.

Mistle thrush (*Turdus viscivorus*): 29cm (11.5in)
Resident throughout most of western Europe south to North Africa. Breeds as far north as Scandinavia and also further east. Relatively large with white underparts, often smudged with an area of grey on the upper breast and displaying a variable black spotted patterning. Pale sides to the head. Grey back and wings. Sexes alike.

Fieldfare (*Turdus pilaris*): 27cm (10.5in)
Occurs in central parts of Europe, overwintering in the British Isles and south to the northern Mediterranean. Has a white eye stripe and grey on the sides of the head. Brown band joins the wings across the back. The rump is grey. Rusty yellow band across the breast with darker markings, especially on the flanks. Underparts otherwise white. Sexes are alike.

Common nightingale

Erithacus megarhynchos

It is often surprisingly difficult to spot the common nightingale, although they often utter their musical calls towards dusk and even after dark on moonlit nights. Their relatively large eyes indicate the fact that these members of the thrush family are crepuscular, becoming active at dusk. Their subdued coloration enables them to blend easily into the dense vegetation, either woodland or shrubbery, that they favour. The common nightingale is only present in Europe from April to September, when it breeds before heading back to southern parts of Africa for the winter. The nightingale repeats the journey north and its arrival is seen as heralding the start of spring.

Distribution: Southern England and mainland Europe on similar latitude. South into north-western Africa. Overwinters further south in Africa.
Size: 16cm (6in).
Habitat: Woodlands, gardens.
Nest: Cup-shaped.
Eggs: 4–5 greyish-green to reddish-buff.
Food: Mainly invertebrates.

Identification: Brown plumage extends from above the bill down over the back of the head and wings, becoming reddish brown on the rump and tail. A sandy buff area extends across the breast, while the lower underparts are whitish. Eyes are large and dark and highlighted by a light eye ring. Sexes alike.

STARLINGS AND SUNBIRDS

These two unrelated groups often show iridescence in their feathering, although not always. In the case of sunbirds, it tends to be confined to cock birds. The iridescence makes the plumage shimmer in the light, revealing otherwise hidden colours. It is thought that the iridescence is linked to the birds' reproductive behaviour, especially as various sunbirds display iridescence only in their breeding plumage.

Purple glossy starling

Lamprotornis purpureus

Like most starlings, the purple glossy is very adaptable in its habits, feeding both in trees and on the ground. They descend to find food in areas after grassland fires, and even grab retreating invertebrates from in front of the flames. Although the traditional nest site of these birds is a tree hole, they have adapted to nesting under the roofs of buildings and even use drainpipes. The hen incubates alone, but the cock bird helps to rear the chicks, which are fed mainly on invertebrates in the early stages after hatching. Invertebrates in the diet help to meet the chicks' need for protein in order to grow rapidly. Outside the breeding season in particular, these starlings can be seen in large groups, made up of as many as several thousand individuals. In such numbers, they readily drive off solitary birds of prey drawn to the colony.

Identification: Upperparts are bluish green. Sides of the face and the underparts are deep purple. Iridescence is most marked on the wings and in the vicinity of the neck. Tail feathers are purple. Iris of adults is bright yellow; grey in young birds. Sexes alike.

Distribution: Extends across Africa south of the Sahara, from Senegal in the west eastwards to parts of Sudan, Kenya and Uganda.
Size: 27cm (10.5in).
Habitat: Light woodland and parkland.
Nest: Sticks in a tree hole.
Eggs: 3–4, blue-green with darker markings.
Food: Invertebrates, fruit and berries.

Splendid starling

Superb starling *Spreo superbus*

Like other birds from this part of Africa, splendid starlings roost quietly during the heat of the day, and this means that they are hard to spot in spite of their bright colour. They are most easily observed either early in the morning or late afternoon, often near water. However, these starlings have recognized that tourists are a likely source of food, and they frequent safari camps in some areas. Few birds are more adaptable in their nesting requirements. Pairs may even build in the thatched roofs of village huts or take over the nests of weaver birds, often adding thorny branches around the entrance to give increased protection from predators while the nest is occupied.

Distribution: Occurs in eastern Africa from southern Ethiopia, Kenya, Somalia and western Uganda southwards into Tanzania.
Size: 18cm (7in).
Habitat: Open country.
Nest: Large self-built or lines a tree hole.
Eggs: 4, dark blue.
Food: Invertebrates, fruits and berries.

Identification: Glossy blackish head merging into shiny blue nape and breast. Distinctive white band extends across breast. Belly is chestnut, and vent and undertail coverts are white. Wings are metallic bluish green. Iris is pale yellowish white. Sexes alike.

-Common starling (European starling, *Sturnus vulgaris*): 22cm (8.5in)
Ranges throughout Europe and North Africa. The Scandinavian and eastern European populations migrate south in the winter. Glossy in appearance with purplish-black plumage on the head. Has a greenish hue on the body overlaid with spots, particularly on the neck, back and vent. Dark brown wings and tail. Hens are similar, but their spotting is larger and they have a pinkish rather than blue base to the bill. This distinguishes them from cocks in breeding condition. Young birds are much duller, lacking the iridescence of the adults, and are brownish with a dark bill.

Spotless starling (*Sturnus unicolor*): 22cm (8.5in)
Ranges throughout the Iberian Peninsula and adjacent areas of North Africa. Also found on Sicily, Corsica and Sardinia. Predominantly glossy black with long feathers on the throat when in breeding plumage. During the winter, fine white spotting appears over the head and extends down on to the chest. The bill is yellow but becomes darker in the winter, when the plumage itself becomes greyer. Hens are similar to cocks in breeding plumage, but have shorter neck feathering and are less glossy overall.

Scarlet-chested sunbird (*Nectarinia senegalensis*): 15cm (6in)
Widely distributed through western Africa from Senegal and the Gambia east to Cameroon and the Central African Republic. Has an iridescent green crown and chin and scarlet-red plumage on the throat and breast. The remainder of the plumage is blackish brown and often a lighter shade on the wings. Hens are duller. They have a mottled dark brown throat with yellowish underparts and are brown elsewhere.

Scarlet-tufted malachite sunbird

Nectarinia johnstoni

These distinctive sunbirds are found in mountainous areas of Africa such as Mount Kilimanjaro in Tanzania. Although close to the Equator, the temperature drops considerably at night here. These birds seek flowering plants, which provide them with nectar in open country, and are often seen near flowering protea bushes. They usually occur in pairs or small parties, although cock birds are often aggressive towards each other, particularly when in breeding plumage. The nest may be constructed from a wide variety of materials, and is lined with feathers and bound together using silk from cobwebs.

Distribution: Ranges in eastern Africa from parts of Kenya, Uganda and Tanzania south to Malawi and Zambia.
Size: Cock 30cm (12in); hen 15cm (6in).
Habitat: Open country.
Nest: Bulky, suspended in bushes.
Eggs: 2–3, cream with dark streaks.
Food: Nectar and small invertebrates.

Identification: A rich shade of dark green, with red pectoral tufts at the highest point of the wing. In non-breeding plumage, the cock's body feathers are blackish brown. The tail is square, with two much longer narrow tail plumes extending beyond it, accounting for half the sunbird's total length. Hens are dark brown in colour, paler in the centre of their bellies, with red pectoral tufts. They lack the long tail feathers.

Eastern double-collared sunbird

Nectarinia mediocris

There are several different species of double-collared sunbird whose distributions overlap. For this reason, it can be difficult to tell them apart, but much depends on the altitude at which sightings are made. The eastern double-collared sunbird is seen only at relatively high altitudes, above 1,500m (5,000ft), so that it is quite locally distributed through its range. Like other sunbirds, eastern double-collared sunbirds allow a relatively close approach when they are feeding, especially in flower gardens, which they visit regularly. Red flowers hold a particular appeal for them, especially the blooms of red hot pokers (*Kniphofia* species), which are native to Africa.

Identification: Iridescent green plumage on the head, chest and back. The rump is blue. The lower chest is scarlet and has a yellow edging to longer feathers (known as pectoral tufts). The remainder of the underparts are olive. The wings and tail are dark and the bill is relatively short and narrow, curving down at its tip. Hens are a dusky shade of olive green.

Distribution: Ranges in eastern Africa through parts of Kenya and Tanzania south into Malawi and Zambia.
Size: 10cm (4in).
Habitat: Forest and gardens.
Nest: Bulky, built off a branch.
Eggs: 2, pale greenish-white with darker markings.
Food: Nectar and small invertebrates.

BIRDS OF ASIA, AUSTRALIA AND NEW ZEALAND

Nowhere else in the world is there such a striking division between avian distributions as there is in this region. Although some of the birds occurring on the Asiatic mainland are also found further west in Europe, there is a very clear split in avian distributions off the coast of the Asian continent. Many of the species that inhabit the islands to the east and south, such as cockatoos, are restricted to this region, and do not occur on the mainland. There can be seasonal movements to some of these islands, however, with birds migrating southwards in Asia. The avifauna of New Zealand is particularly unusual, as birds have evolved here in the absence of mammalian predators over the course of many millions of years. While the dominant avian group – the giant moas – is now extinct, a number of other bizarre birds, such as the flightless kiwi, are still to be found on these islands.

Above from left: Rainbow lorikeet (Trichoglossus haematodus), *sulphur-crested cockatoo* (Cacatua sulphurea), *great hornbill* (Buceros bicornis).

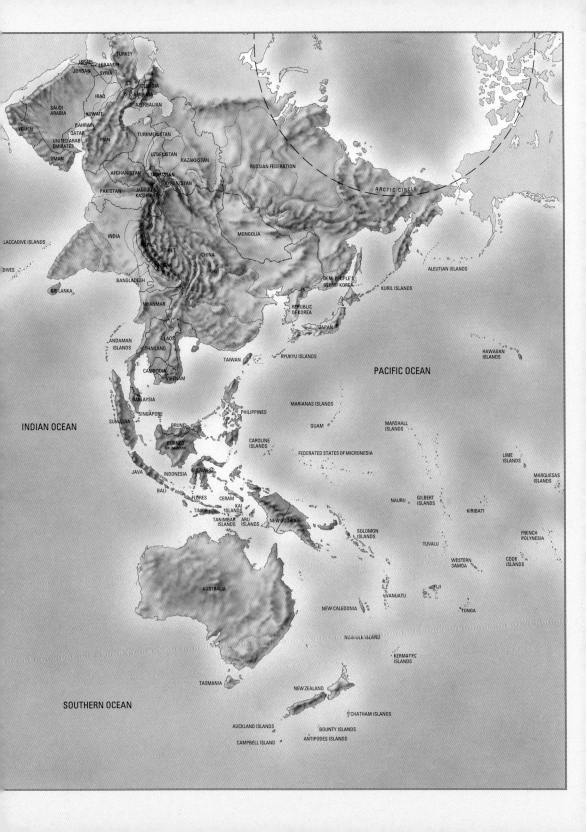

SEABIRDS

Many of the seabirds found in Asiatic and Australian waters have a wide distribution, which can be pan-global, often extending around the southern oceans and sometimes even further afield. Birds such as albatrosses are well adapted to spending virtually their entire lives on the wing, even to the extent of scooping their food from the surface of the sea and sleeping on the wing as they glide.

Red-billed tropic bird

Phaethon aethereus

These sleek, elegant birds swoop down from their cliff-top roosts and out over the oceans, catching their food by diving into the sea. The red-billed is the largest of the tropic birds. Their elegant, long, streaming white tail distinguishes them from the red-tailed tropic bird (*P. rubricauda*) which ranges further across the Indo-Pacific ocean to the south and also has paler, whitish wings. The bill of the Indian Ocean population of these tropic birds is less brightly coloured, serving to distinguish them from others of the species occurring elsewhere in the world. Islands rather than mainland areas are favoured breeding sites, as their position means that the birds will be in less danger from their predators.

Above: Red-billed tropic birds nest in crevices in the ground.

Identification: Predominantly white with a black streak running through the eyes. Black is clearly visible on the primary flight feathers at the ends of the wings. Black streaking runs over the back and rump down to the base of the tail. Tail streamers are longer in the cock bird than the hen. Bill reddish-orange with black edging.

Distribution: Ranges widely through the Red Sea, the Gulf of Aden and the Persian Gulf. Other populations occur in the Caribbean as well as the southern Atlantic and the eastern Pacific oceans.
Size: 105cm (41in), including streamers up to 55cm (22in) in length.
Habitat: Tropical and subtropical seas.
Nest: Rocky crevice or hollow on the ground.
Eggs: 1, pinkish with darker markings.
Food: Fish and squid. Agile enough to catch flying fish.

Masked booby

Blue-faced booby *Sula dactylatra*

Distribution: This bird is pan-tropical – both north and south of the Equator – as it is found right around northern Australia.
Size: 92cm (36in).
Habitat: Sea.
Nest: On the ground or a cliff.
Eggs: 2, bluish white.
Food: Mainly fish.

Island habitats are favoured by the masked booby, allowing these birds to fly long distances out over the sea in search of prey, stopping off to rest on the islands as they do so. They catch fish by plunging into the middle of a shoal, swimming well underwater to achieve a catch. Apart from fish, other marine creatures, such as squid, feature less prominently in their diet. They live in colonies and individuals may sometimes be badly harried by frigate birds (*Fregata* species), which rob the masked boobies of their catch before they reach land. They lay their eggs on bare rock, and although two chicks may hatch, only one is likely to be reared successfully, unless food is freely available.

Identification: Large, white head, back and underparts. Dark areas around the eyes and the base of the bill. Black areas on the wings are apparent at rest and in flight. Tail feathers are black. The bill is yellowish in cock birds and greenish in hens. Legs and feet are greyish.

Wilson's storm petrel (*Oceanites oceanicus*):
19cm (7.5in)
Extends from Antarctica throughout the
southern oceans into northern latitudes.
Brownish overall, with a prominent white rump.
Paler buff barring on the upper and underwing
coverts. Sexes alike.

Sooty albatross (*Phoebetria fusca*):
89cm (35in)
Ranges across oceans from the west coast
of Tasmania westwards almost as far as the
Falkland Islands. A distinctive uniform shade of
sooty black with a black bill. Its wings are long
and pointed. Tail feathers are long and wedge-
shaped. Sexes alike.

Fairy prion (*Pachyptila turtur*): 28cm (11in)
Found in three separate colonies in the southern
oceans: one extends from south-east Australia to
New Zealand. Grey crown, wings and back with
white underparts and a dark tip to the tail.
Blackish patterning across the wings. Sexes alike.

Streaked shearwater (white-fronted shearwater,
Calonectris leucomelas): 48cm (19in)
Extends from eastern Asia from the Ryuku Islands
and north-eastern Japan to Korea. Migrates south
to Australia via New Guinea. Whitish underparts.
Brown mottling on the sides of the head. Brown
edging to the undersides of the wings. Upperparts are brown. Bill is silvery grey. Sexes alike.

Southern giant petrel

Macronectes giganteus

These aerial giants, with a wingspan
of more than 2m (78in) and weighing
as much as 5kg (11lb), can cover huge
distances over the oceans around the
southern hemisphere. They feed on the
carcasses of marine mammals, such as
seals, left on the shoreline, as well
as dead seabirds. They may be sighted
close to trawlers, seeking offal and
fish thrown overboard,
which they scoop up
from the sea's surface.
These petrels nest on
grassy islands in colonies of up
to 300 pairs. The single chick
develops slowly and may not
fledge until it is nearly 20 weeks
old. It is unlikely to breed for the
first time until it is seven years old.

Identification: Brownish overall although
darker on the lower underparts towards the
vent. Paler greyish-brown head and neck.
Bill yellow. The white morph of this
species displays odd speckled
brownish feathering on a white
background. Hens smaller.

Distribution: Circumpolar in
the southern ocean, occurring
off the southern half of the
Australian coastline and right
around New Zealand.
Size: 99cm (39in).
Habitat: Sea.
Nest: Grassy mound or pile
of stones.
Eggs: 1, white.
Food: Carrion.

Wandering albatross

Snowy albatross *Diomedea exulans*

Distribution: The range is
circumpolar, extending from
southern parts of Australia
and New Zealand south-
wards. Also occurs on
numerous smaller islands,
such as Antipodes Island, all
south-east of New Zealand.
Size: 135cm (53in).
Habitat: Sea.
Nest: Piles of mud and grass.
Eggs: 1, white with reddish-
brown speckling.
Food: Mainly squid, but also
fish, crustaceans and carrion.

As their name suggests, these albatrosses range widely over
the southern oceans, often following ships and scavenging
on galley scraps thrown overboard. They are also active
hunters, however, scooping squid from the sea
after dark, when these cephalopods come
closer to the surface. Pairs separate at
the end of the breeding period, but
then some will reunite later on the
breeding grounds. They breed
only every second year because
it takes nearly 40 weeks for a
newly hatched chick to grow
large enough to leave the nest.

Identification: Predominantly white. Black
areas over much of the wings, although
the areas closest to the body have only
a black edging. There is often a pinkish
area near the ear coverts, and there
may be a greyish area on the crown.
Bill is pink with a yellowish, hooked
tip. Hens are slightly smaller, and may
display a light greyish band around the chest
and black on the edges of the tail feathers.

PENGUINS, PELICANS AND OTHER COASTAL BIRDS

Although these birds are not closely related, they all depend on the marine environment for food in the form of fish or marine invertebrates. While some groups, such as plovers, have a broad distribution around the world, penguins in particular are confined to relatively cold areas of the southern hemisphere.

Rockhopper penguin

Eudyptes crysocome

Distribution: One population occurs in the southern ocean between Africa and Australia; one extends south from the southern coast of Australia; the third is on the eastern side of South America.
Size: 62cm (24.5in).
Habitat: Sea and close to the shoreline.
Nest: Made of grass and other available materials.
Eggs: 2, bluish white.
Food: Mainly krill. Some fish.

These penguins are so called because of the way they hop across land instead of walking. They live communally in rookeries, using their sharp bills to ward off gulls and other predatory birds that may land in their midst. Despite its relatively small size, the rockhopper is the most aggressive of all penguins. It is also one of the most adaptable, being found even in temperate areas. These penguins feed underwater, using their wings like flippers to steer themselves. If danger threatens, they swim towards the shore and leap out of the water on to the land with considerable force.

Identification: White underparts. Black head, flippers and tail although the ear coverts appear slightly paler. The bill is red, as are the irises. A line of golden plumage forms a crest towards the rear on each side of the head. Hens are smaller and have less stout bills.

Above: These ungainly hopping penguins are elegant swimmers.

Spot-billed pelican

Grey pelican *Pelecanus philippensis*

This particular species is thought to be the rarest member of the pelican family and its range is now greatly reduced. Indeed, it is extinct in the Philippines despite also being known as the Philippine pelican. The use of pesticides may have contributed to this decline, along with habitat changes. These large birds weigh about 5kg (11lb) and need to catch roughly a fifth of their body weight in food every day, so easy access to food is imperative to their survival. Widespread destruction of forests is also believed to have had an adverse effect on their numbers, as these pelicans require large trees in which to build their nests.

Above: These pelicans fish by trawling the water with their bills.

Identification: Predominantly a silvery-grey colour. Darker over the wings. A short, brownish crest extends down the neck. The bill and pouch are pinkish with darker blotching. Greyish legs and feet. Sexes are alike.

Distribution: South-east India and Sri Lanka east to Myanmar (Burma) and south-eastern parts of China. Overwinters further south reaching Sumatra and Java.
Size: 150cm (59in).
Habitat: Ranges from coastal bays to lakes.
Nest: Made of vegetation.
Eggs: 2–3, chalky white.
Food: Fish.

Greater frigate bird

Fregata minor

The frigate bird is an aerial hunter, scooping up its prey from the surface of the ocean, and is attracted by shoals of flying fish, and squid too. These birds are opportunistic when feeding, however, and will swoop over beaches where turtles nest to catch and eat the hatchling reptiles as they try to make for the relative safety of the sea. Frigate birds will also harry other sea-birds, causing them to drop their catches, which they then take themselves. The frigate bird breeds in colonies on remote islands. Their chicks develop very slowly and are cared for by both their parents for up to a year and a half after birth.

Above: The greater frigate bird inflates the throat sac for display purposes.

Identification: Dark overall with a bright red throat sac. Abdomen is black. Has a long, hooked bill and a streaming tail. Brownish wing bars on the upper side of the wings. An angular wing posture is evident in flight. The black areas of plumage have a glossy green suffusion when the light catches them. Sexes are similar but the hens are larger with a greyish white throat and white chest.

Distribution: Mainly in the Pacific, from the west coast of South America to the northern coast of Australia and southern Asia to East Africa. A smaller population also occurs in the south Atlantic.
Size: 105cm (41in).
Habitat: Islands and mangroves.
Nest: Platform of sticks.
Eggs: 1, chalky white.
Food: Mainly fish, some squid and carrion occasionally.

Royal penguin (*Eudyptes schlegeli*): 76cm (30in)
Distribution centred on Mocker Island, south of New Zealand and Campbell Island. Sometimes found on the southern coast of New Zealand. Crested, but with a distinctive white face. Black plumage on the crown, back and wings. Under-parts are white. Has a greyish band across the throat. Hens smaller, with a less robust bill.

King penguin (*Aptenodytes patagonicus*): 95cm (37in)
This penguin is almost circumpolar, breeding on sub-Antarctic and Antarctic islands. Has a black head with a relatively narrow orange collar around the side of the head. Upperparts are greyish. On the upper chest, underparts are white with an orange suffusion. Long bill which is pale red near the base of the lower mandible. Sexes are alike. These large penguins weigh up to 15kg (33lb).

Little penguin (fairy penguin) (*Eudyptula minor*): 45cm (18in)
Found on southern coasts of Australia, extending from Perth and east to Tasmania, New Zealand and the Chatham Islands. Has dark greyish-black upperparts and white underparts. Dull pinkish black bill. Pink feet. Sexes alike. Weighing barely 1kg (2.2lb), this is the smallest of the penguins.

Crab plover (*Dromas ardeola*): 40cm (16in)
Confined to the Indian Ocean coastline. White body with areas of black feathering on the top and edges of the wing. Legs are greyish. Large, heavy, blackish bill is used for crushing crabs. Sexes alike. It is the only wader that nests in underground tunnels over 1.5m (5ft) in length.

Milky stork

Mycteria cinerea (E)

The name of these storks originates from the milky white shade of their plumage when they are in breeding condition. Milky storks have become much rarer through their range for a variety of reasons, which include habitat destruction. In Vietnam, the widespread use of defoliant chemicals in mangrove swamps during the Vietnam War is thought to have affected their numbers to the extent that there is only a single breeding colony left in the country. The largest remaining population occurs on the eastern part of the Indonesian island of Sumatra. There is some movement of these storks after breeding, which takes place during the dry season. They use their long bill to probe for food in often muddy water, grabbing fish and small vertebrates that come within reach.

Identification: Predominantly white, but has a bald, reddish area of skin over much of the face and a black patch by the base of the bill. The edge of the wings are blackish. Legs and feet are red and the bill is straw-coloured. Young birds have more extensive feathering on their heads and their bare skin is yellowish. Sexes alike.

Distribution: Scattered localities through South-east Asia, notably Vietnam, Malaysia, Sumatra, Java and Sulawesi.
Size: 100cm (39in).
Habitat: Coastal mudflats and mangroves.
Nest: Platform of sticks in a tree.
Eggs: 1-4, whitish.
Food: Fish and other vertebrates.

KINGFISHERS, CORMORANTS AND OTHER FISH-EATERS

The hunting strategies of this group of birds differ widely, but they are all well adapted to their environments. The way in which they have evolved in this respect is perhaps best illustrated by the collared kingfisher, which occurs in a huge number of different forms through its wide range.

Collared kingfisher

Mangrove kingfisher *Halycon chloris*

More than 50 distinctive races of the collared kingfisher are recognized across its extensive distribution. Many of the most distinctive evolved in relative isolation on remote Pacific islands, such as New Britain – their white areas are heavily suffused with an orange shade. On the southern Mariana islands, however, the white plumage is more extensive, covering virtually the entire head apart from bluish-green stripes behind the eyes. The diet of these birds is equally variable, ranging from crabs to cicadas, snails and even small snakes. When nesting, the collared kingfisher is highly territorial although pairs will drive away intruders at any time of the year.

Identification: Highly variable appearance depending on the subspecies, although the wings are invariably greenish blue with bright blue edges. Underparts are generally white and the collar is white as well. Many races have a greenish-blue crown with a black stripe running through the eyes. The beak is black, with a distinct paler base to the lower bill. Sexes are alike.

Distribution: Extends over a huge area from the Red sea across southern Asia and the small Pacific islands on to northern and eastern Australia.
Size: 25cm (11in).
Habitat: Coastal areas. Sometimes inland.
Nest: Tree hole or an arboreal termite mound.
Eggs: 2–5, white.
Food: Invertebrates, crustaceans and small vertebrates.

Little pied cormorant

Phalacrocorax melanoleucos

Distribution: Extends from eastern Indonesia to the Solomon Islands and New Caledonia, and south to Australia and New Zealand.
Size: 65cm (26in).
Habitat: Coastal areas and inland waters.
Nest: Platform of sticks usually with trees nearby, which will be used for nesting purposes.
Eggs: 3–5, pale bluish.
Food: Fish and other aquatic creatures.

The appearance of these cormorants varies noticeably through the range. The New Zealand race (*P. m. brevirostris*), for example, displays a variable amount of white plumage on the underparts. These cormorants obtain their food by diving, seeking not just fish but also amphibians, crustaceans and other invertebrates, with the prey varying according to the cormorant's habitat. Although they are occasionally seen in loose groups, little pied cormorants tend to fish independently and may even take up residence in public parks where they feed heavily on goldfish in the ponds.

Identification: Distinctive appearance. Has a predominantly white head with black plumage to the crown area that extends down the back of the neck. Underparts may be entirely white or black, depending on the race. Has a long black tail and a small crest on the head. The bill is yellowish. Feet and legs are black. Sexes alike.

Brown booby

White-bellied booby *Sula leucogaster*

These boobies hunt a variety of fish relatively close to the shoreline, so usually they dive into the water from a low height, hitting the surface at an angle rather than entering vertically. This means that they penetrate the water less deeply. They are effective underwater swimmers, using their webbed feet and their wings to help them. The brown booby has an interesting relationship with its masked relative (*S. dactylatra*) when their distribution overlaps. They sometimes harry masked boobies for food in flight, stealing their catch. Rare mixed pairings between these two species have given rise to hybrid offspring.

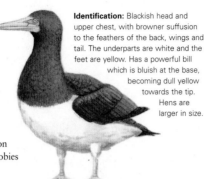

Identification: Blackish head and upper chest, with browner suffusion to the feathers of the back, wings and tail. The underparts are white and the feet are yellow. Has a powerful bill which is bluish at the base, becoming dull yellow towards the tip. Hens are larger in size.

Distribution: Extends from the western Pacific to the east coast of Africa. Also present in the Atlantic, the Caribbean, and the western coast of Central America.
Size: 74cm (29in).
Habitat: Inshore waters.
Nest: Hollow on the ground.
Eggs: 2, bluish white.
Food: Fish.

Silver gull (*Larus novaehollandiae*): 43cm (17in)
Extends from the coast of Ethiopia around the Asiatic coastline south to mainland Australia and Tasmania. Also occurs as far east as New Caledonia. Has a predominantly white and silvery-grey back, with black evident on the flight feathers. Orange-red ring around the eyes. Bill red, as are the legs. Sexes alike.

Whiskered tern (*Chlidonias hybrida*): 27cm (11in)
Widely distributed on shores from southern Africa to Asia, including the Indonesian islands and New Guinea, south to Australia. It is sometimes seen as a vagrant in Tasmania. Cocks in breeding condition have a black cap on the head and the rest of their body is grey apart from white areas on the sides of the face. Cap becomes speckled outside the breeding season, when underparts are white. Wings are grey. Sexes are alike.

Black-naped tern (*Sterna sumatrana*): 35cm (14in)
Found on islands and coastal areas throughout the Indian and Pacific Oceans south to northern Australia. Predominantly white, with a strongly forked tail and a black area extending back from the eyes around the nape. Has silvery wings and a black bill. Sexes are alike.

Little black shag (*Phalacrocorax sulcirostris*): 65cm (26in)
Ranges from New Guinea westwards to Indonesia and then southwards to Australia, including Tasmania, and on to New Zealand. Occurs both in coastal and inland areas. Has black plumage, a black bill and black feet. Traces of white feathering above the eye are only evident during the breeding season. Sexes are alike.

Mangrove heron

Green-backed heron *Butorides striatus*

The great variation in the appearance of the mangrove heron has led to more than 30 distinctive races being recognized by taxonomists. It is not just differences in coloration that sets them apart, but also their size because the Australian races are larger than those from elsewhere. These herons are equally at home in saltwater areas, such as mangroves, as well as fresh-water lakes, although they prefer areas where there is dense cover as this enables them to keep their presence hidden. Their shy nature is also reflected in their feeding habits. The mangrove heron often prefers to seek food at night, if the tide is favourable.

Identification: Very variable, even between members of the same race. Blackish plumage on the crown. Underparts are often pinkish greyish with a white stripe down the centre of the body, but can range from light brown to grey. Usually a bare area of yellow skin is most conspicuous in front of the eyes. Wings dark. Sexes are generally alike.

Distribution: Pan-global: ranges from the Indian subcontinent through Southeast Asia to northern and eastern parts of Australia.
Size: 48cm (19in).
Habitat: Shallow water.
Nest: Built of twigs in a tree or bush.
Eggs: 2–5, pale blue.
Food: Fish and other aquatic life, reptiles and mice.

WADING BIRDS

These birds are well equipped to forage in wetland areas, with their long legs enabling them to wade through the shallows easily, while also giving them a good field of vision to detect possible prey. A sharp bill and rapid reflexes make them formidable hunters of small aquatic creatures. They may also be encountered in fields close to stretches of water.

White-necked heron

Pacific heron *Ardea pacific*

The main distribution of these herons is centred on Australia. Although less common here, they also congregate in areas such as Irian Jaya in New Guinea. Following prolonged periods of rainfall, flooding means that these herons have greater feeding opportunities so populations can shift quite widely in search of flooded areas. They may be seen in coastal areas but prefer freshwater localities. White-necked herons breed in colonies of 20 or so pairs, building their nests in trees at least 15m (49ft) off the ground. Occasionally, much larger groups of as many as 150 pairs have been observed. They often nest in trees with other birds, such as spoonbills. Juvenile birds can be distinguished by greyish, rather than white, plumage on their head and neck.

Identification: The head and neck are white, and have slight black streaking in the centre of the lower throat and upper breast when out of breeding condition. Wings are blackish with a grey overlay. The underparts are blackish with white streaking. The bill, legs and feet are dark. Sexes alike.

Distribution: Found in southern New Guinea. Also present throughout Australia, apart from the central area.
Size: 106cm (41in).
Habitat: Shallow waters.
Nest: Platform of sticks.
Eggs: 3–4, pale blue.
Food: Small fish, vertebrates.

Cattle egret

Bubulcus ibis

Distribution: Exceedingly wide pan-global distribution. Asiatic race extends from southern and eastern parts of Asia into parts of Australia and New Zealand.
Size: 56cm (22in).
Habitat: Shallow waters and even relatively dry areas.
Nest: Sometimes in reedbeds, often on a platform above the ground.
Eggs: 2–5, pale blue.
Food: Invertebrates, amphibians and other small vertebrates.

The sharp bills of these egrets allow them to catch their quarry easily, although in urban areas they can often be seen scavenging around markets and in rubbish dumps. The Asiatic race (*B. i. coromandus*) is the largest and tallest of the three subspecies found worldwide. Banding studies have revealed that cattle egrets will fly long distances, with those birds occurring in north-eastern Asia moving south in the winter. Ringed birds have turned up as far afield as the Philippines. This tendency to roam widely has allowed these egrets to colonize many of the more remote islands in the Pacific. Indeed, distinct seasonal movements have even been recorded in Australia.

Below: The egret's buff plumage is replaced largely by white during the breeding period for display purposes.

Identification: Pale buff coloration on the head and throat, extending down to the breast; also on the back and rump. The remainder of the plumage is white. There may be traces of white plumage around the yellow bill. The legs and feet are also yellow. Sexes alike.

Sarus crane

Grus antigone

These large, long-lived birds pair for life, which can be for 30 years or more. They are easily spotted from some distance away in open, wet countryside, usually in pairs. In areas where food is plentiful, however, larger numbers of sarus cranes may occasionally gather together, with as many as 60 individuals recorded in one locality. These cranes are relatively fearless, often stalking among cattle in fields to pounce on small animals, such as frogs, that have been disturbed by the herd. In common with other species of cranes, their courtship involves a spectacular dancing ritual which is accompanied by loud calls.

Identification: Grey plumage, with a characteristic red head and long neck. Has an area of black plumage on the wings. The tertiaries drooping over the grey tail are pale, verging on white. Straight greenish, horn-coloured bill that tapers to a point. Legs are reddish and very long. Sexes alike.

Distribution: Ranges from the Indian subcontinent east and south across Cambodia and Laos, Vietnam as far as north-eastern Australia.
Size: 152cm (60in).
Habitat: Wetland areas, including paddy fields.
Nest: Platform of vegetation on the ground.
Eggs: 2, pinkish-white. May have brown markings.
Food: Invertebrates, fish, frogs, and some vegetable matter.

Plumed egret (*Egretta intermedia*): 72cm (28in)
Extends from New Guinea to eastern Indonesia and south to Australia. White body, with delicate plumes over the back and on the chest. The bill and the area around the eyes are yellow in the Asiatic race (*E. i. plumifera*). Top part of the legs are yellowish. The feet are greyish. Sexes alike.

Australasian bittern (brown bittern, *Botaurus poiciloptilus*): 76cm (30in)
Found in south-west and south-east Australia, including Tasmania, plus New Zealand, New Caledonia and the Loyalty Islands. Has white plumage on the throat and running down on to the neck. Brownish elsewhere but with black markings. The depth of coloration varies among individuals. Pale stripe above the eye. The bill and legs are pale yellow.

Black-necked stork (*Ephippiorhynchus asiaticus*): 137cm (54in)
Two populations: one is confined essentially to India; the other is in northern and eastern Australia. Glossy black plumage on the head and neck. The body is white apart from prominent black areas on the wings. Strong, powerful black bill. Legs and feet are red.

Straw-necked ibis (*Threskiornis spinicollis*): 76cm (30in)
Found in New Guinea and Australia apart from central and central-southern areas. Bare black head with white collar over much of the neck and buff area beneath. Rest of the upper breast area, back and wings are all greenish. Underparts white. Legs are red. Hens smaller.

Glossy ibis

Plegadis falcinellus

Groups of these ibises can be encountered in a wide range of environments, from rice fields to river estuaries, and they will often undertake extensive seasonal movements. They tend to feed by probing into the mud with the tips of their sensitive bills, enabling them to grab prey easily even if the water is muddy. They occasionally dip their heads under water when feeding, too. These birds may also use their long legs to pursue prey, such as snakes, on the ground. Pairs nest colonially. The nest site is located low over the water, so fledglings sometimes fall victim to crocodiles lurking nearby as they leave the nest.

Distribution: Wide. Extends from the Red Sea via northern India to the eastern coast of Asia. Also present in Australia, the Philippines and Indonesia.
Size: 66cm (26in).
Habitat: Shallow areas of water.
Nest: Platform of sticks, built above water.
Eggs: 2–6, deep green to blue.
Food: Invertebrates, plus crustaceans and small vertebrates.

Identification: Dark brown overall but with some white streaking on the head. The wings and rump are green. Legs and bill are dark. When not in breeding condition, they are a duller colour. Sexes are alike.

RAILS, CRAKES, AND SIMILAR BIRDS

Although shy by nature, some members of this group are seen in cultivated areas. Their large toes help to prevent them sinking into marshy ground. Sadly, the flightless nature of some rails from this region, such as the Tahiti rail (Gallirallus pacificus) has left them vulnerable to introduced predators, especially feral cats, and a number of the most distinctive Pacific island species, including this species, are now extinct.

Tasmanian native hen

Gallinula mortierii

Distribution: Confined to Tasmania and smaller offshore islands.
Size: 51cm (20in).
Habitat: Wetland areas with vegetative cover nearby.
Nest: Large, cup-shaped.
Eggs: 3–9, yellowish-buff with brownish markings.
Food: Mainly seeds and plants.

These large rails are flightless, and it is believed that the Australian mainland population died out as a result of hunting by dingoes less than 5,000 years ago. Their main defence is to run quickly away from danger. They are capable of reaching speeds equivalent to 48kph (30mph) over short distances. These birds sometimes graze in agricultural areas, even taking fruit from orchards. They live in groups, and when conflict breaks out with newcomers, the combatants jump into the air up to 1.5m (5ft), lashing out with their powerful feet until the weaker individual backs down.

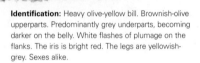

Identification: Heavy olive-yellow bill. Brownish-olive upperparts. Predominantly grey underparts, becoming darker on the belly. White flashes of plumage on the flanks. The iris is bright red. The legs are yellowish-grey. Sexes alike.

Watercock

Kora *Gallicrex cinerea*

In much of their range, these rails move south during the winter when they are mainly found on the island of Sumatra. Watercocks are most active at twilight, hiding away during the daytime, although in recently planted rice paddies they will often remain quite conspicuous until the plants grow larger and conceal their presence. They have characteristically jerky tail movements, that highlight their buff undertail coverts. Pairs call loudly for up to 30 minutes at a time during the breeding period but are quieter during the rest of the year.

Identification: The cock in breeding condition has an unmistakable upright red horn extending back over the eyes, with mainly blackish plumage and scalloping over the wings. The iris, legs and feet are red. It resembles the adult hen for the remainder of the year, but is larger in size. The hen is predominantly brown, with a dark area on the head and scalloping on the wings. Dark barring to the plumage on the underparts.

Distribution: Across southern Asia from Pakistan and India east to China, Japan and the Philippines. Then south through South-east Asia to Sumatra and other islands.
Size: Cock birds up to 43cm (17in); hens 36cm (14in).
Habitat: Swampland, including rice paddies.
Nest: Cup-shaped mass of vegetation.
Eggs: 3–6, varying from whitish through yellowish to pink with darker spots.
Food: Mainly vegetation, including rice. Also invertebrates.

Dusky moorhen (black moorhen)
(*Gallinula tenebrosa*) Australian birds up to 40cm
(16in); New Guinea birds as small as 25cm (10in).
Extends from Sumatra, Borneo, Sulawesi and
New Guinea to Australia. Breeding birds have a
bright red beak and shield with a yellow tip.
Greyish-black plumage. Joints of the orangish
legs and feet are dark. Outside the breeding
period, the bill is olive as are the legs and feet.

Malaysian banded crake (red-legged crake,
Rallina fasciata): 25cm (10in)
Present in South-east Asia from north-eastern
India south via Malaysia to Sumatra, Java,
Borneo and neighbouring islands. Has reddish-
chestnut plumage on the head, neck and breast.
Browner on the back with black and white
barring on the wings and underparts. Legs and
feet red. Hens have a more cinnamon shade of
feathering on the head and narrower black barring
on underparts.

Slaty-breasted rail (*Gallirallus striatus*):
30cm (12in)
Ranges eastwards from India to China and across
South-east Asia to the Sunda islands and the
Philippines. Chestnut-brown feathering runs from
the head to the base of the neck. Underparts
from the chin to the lower belly are a dark slate-
grey. The rest of the plumage is dark brown with
white stripes. Mainland birds tend to be much
paler overall than the nominate race, which is
found in eastern parts of the species' range.

White-breasted waterhen

White-breasted swamphen
Amaurornis phoenicurus

These wide-ranging crakes show a regional
variation in size, with island races exhibiting
the greatest diversity. It is not uncommon for
island birds to have irregular white patches
of feathering in areas that would normally
be dark. This characteristic is described as
partial albinism. These waterhens show little
fear of human contact and can be seen in
irrigation canals and similar stretches of
water. They are not very strong flyers, but
can swim and dive for food.

Distribution: From Pakistan
and India to China and Japan.
Present on Sri Lanka and
through South-east Asia to
the Sundas and other islands,
including the Philippines.
Size: 30cm (12in).
Habitat: Swampland, sides
of lakes and similar water.
Nest: Cup-shaped pad of
vegetation.
Eggs: 3–9, cream to pinkish-
white with darker markings.
Food: Mainly invertebrates
and small fish.

Identification: White extends
down over the chest and upper
abdomen. Flanks are black. The
upperparts are dark slate-grey,
although browner over the rump.
Has a red area on the top of the
yellowish bill. Reddish plumage
extends from near the vent to the
undertail coverts. Sexes alike, but
hens have a more olive tone to bill.

Pheasant-tailed jacana

Hydrophasianus chirurgus

The very long toes of these birds may not actually enable them to walk on water, but by
distributing their weight effectively in this way, they can walk on mats of vegetation and
the leaves of aquatic plants such as water lilies and lotuses, which is why they are also
known as lily-trotters. They can swim if necessary, however, and dive on occasions, too.
When breeding, cock birds incubate on their own, rearing the resulting
chicks, while the hen moves on to seek another mate and lay again.

Identification: White plumage on the head down
to the upper breast with white also on the sides
of the wing. A black area runs down the back of
the head and a broad yellow band runs on
top of this. Underparts are dark brown,
but lighter in colour on the back. The
long, blackish tail is missing outside the
breeding season. The underparts are
white apart from a greyish band on the
breast, while the upperparts are much
paler. Distinctive long toes. Sexes alike.

Distribution: Runs eastwards
from India as far as China and
south through South-east Asia
to the Greater Sundas via
Sumatra, Java and Borneo.
Present in the Philippines.
Size: 30cm (12in).
Habitat: Areas of still or
slow-flowing water, such as
marshes and ponds.
Nest: Pad of vegetation.
Eggs: 2–5, pale brown with
darker markings.
Food: Invertebrates and
vegetation.

WATERFOWL

This group of birds has diversified to occupy a wide range of habitats and has adopted a correspondingly broad range of lifestyles, from grazing wetland areas to an almost entirely aquatic existence. Breeding habits vary, too, with some members of the group preferring to breed on the ground, while others choose the relative safety of tree hollows for their nest site.

Cape Barren goose

Cereopsis goose *Surpasses novaehollandiae*

Distribution: Found in parts of southern Australia, including Tasmania. Breeds in four main areas: the Furneaux islands, Spencer Gulf islands, islands of the Recherche Archipelago and off Wilson's Promontory.
Size: 99cm (39in).
Habitat: Pasture and open country.
Nest: Made of vegetation, built on the ground.
Eggs: 3–6, white.
Food: Grasses and sedges.

These geese live almost entirely on land, only taking to water as a last resort when danger threatens, or when, during the moult, they are unable to fly for a period. They breed on small islands, where they are relatively safe from disturbance, nesting among the tufts of grass and other vegetation which they browse using their strong bills. Male birds have a much louder call than hens, whose vocalisations have been described as pig-like grunts. They weigh up to 5.3kg (12lb) but are still powerful in flight, their wing beats being both shallow and fast.

Above: Cape Barren geese graze in flocks on grass: they are highly sociable birds by nature.

Identification: A distinctive grey colour with a paler whitish area on the head. Tail is black. Some irregular darker spotting on the wings, most pronounced in young birds. Reddish legs with black feet. Greatly enlarged greenish-yellow cere encompassing the nostrils. Bill is black. Hens are smaller in size.

Cotton pygmy goose

White pygmy goose *Nettapus coromandelianus*

These geese spend most of their time on the water, frequently favouring deep areas. They are most commonly observed in pairs or small groups, although they occasionally congregate in much greater numbers outside the breeding season. These geese feed by dabbling under the water, only diving down occasionally, and often choosing vegetation growing above the water's surface. When flushed out, they fly quite low and generally not very far. The breeding season begins at the onset of the rainy season. Pairs nest individually and tend to remain close to the water. In some parts of their range, most notably in Australia, the numbers of cotton pygmy geese have declined as the result of wetland drainage.

Identification: A black stripe runs from the bill over the top of the head. A black collar runs around the upper breast and this is intersected with an area of white plumage. Underparts are mainly pale grey and the wings are blackish. Female is duller: mainly grey with black eye stripe. When not in breeding plumage, cock birds resemble hens, apart from a larger, white area on the wing.

Distribution: India eastwards across Asia. Also in Indonesia and eastern Australia.
Size: 37cm (14in).
Habitat: Deep water with plant growth.
Nest: Tree hollows lined with down.
Eggs: 6–16, ivory white.
Food: Aquatic plants and invertebrates.

White-eyed duck

Australian hardhead *Aythya australis*

Although these pochards are usually only encountered in Australia, they do irrupt on occasion and can then be seen much further afield in countries as far apart as Java and New Zealand. It is thought that such behaviour is usually triggered by severe droughts. It is believed that the remote population on Banks Island originated as a result of an irruption of this kind, rather than from a deliberate human introduction, and these immigrants have successfully established a separate breeding population. In Australia, there has been a decline in the number of white-eyed ducks over recent years as a by-product of drainage schemes.

Identification: A rich chocolate-brown colour with white lower breast and belly. Has white plumage around the vent. Bill is greyish, with a light band and a black tip. Iris is whitish. Females are very similar, but have dark eyes and may be slightly lighter and browner overall. There is no eclipse plumage. Juvenile birds resemble females but have russet-brown feathering on the abdomen.

Distribution: Australia, apart from central and central-southern parts. Isolated colony on Banks Island.
Size: 59cm (23in).
Habitat: Large, well-vegetated lakes and marshes.
Nest: Platform of vegetation.
Eggs: 9–13, greenish-grey.
Food: Mainly plant matter, some invertebrates.

Chestnut-breasted shelduck (Australian shelduck, *Tadorna tadornoides*): 72cm (28in) Occurs mainly in western and south-eastern parts of Australia, including Tasmania, in shallow stretches of water. Drakes have glossy dark green head and neck with a narrow white collar separating this area from the chestnut breast. The remainder of the body, apart from the chestnut rump, is dark. The broad white area in the wing is most visible in flight. Ducks are recognizable by white edging around the base of the bill and eyes. They have greyish-brown bodies in eclipse plumage.

Pacific black duck (*Anas superciliosa*):
61cm (24in)
Found in Indonesia, New Guinea and islands to the east, as well as Australia, New Zealand and neighbouring islands. The basic coloration varies from brown to black, with lighter scalloping on the feathers. Has green speculum in the wing. Dark crown, and an eye stripe with buff lines is evident on the face as well. The bill is greyish and the legs and feet are a yellowish-grey. Hens tend to have browner plumage on the upperparts of the body.

Magpie goose (*Anseranas semipalmata*):
85cm (34in)
Present in southern New Guinea and northern Australia and extending down the east coast. The body is white apart from glossy, blackish plumage on the head and rear of the body. There is a swollen area on the crown of the head. The bare facial skin is reddish. The legs are a golden yellow. Hens are smaller, and the swollen area is less pronounced.

Lesser tree duck

Lesser whistling duck *Dendrocygna javanica*

This is the smallest of the tree ducks, and like other members of the group, it prefers to roost in trees at night rather than on the water. The breeding habits of the lesser tree duck are unusual because although it does sometimes nest on the ground, it usually prefers to choose a site in a suitable tree. Pairs tend to either adopt a tree hollow for this purpose or to take over an abandoned platform nest made from sticks that would have been constructed originally by herons or a bird of prey. Only at the northern edge of their current distribution do these birds head south in the winter. They used to occur in Japan, but, sadly, they were hunted to extinction in the early 20th century.

Distribution: From India and Pakistan eastwards across mainland Asia to China. Wide distribution across South-east Asia. Also south to Indonesian islands, including Java and Sumatra, and the island of Borneo.
Size: 40cm (16in).
Habitat: Shallow water edged with trees.
Nest: Either on the ground or in trees.
Eggs: 7–12, creamy white.
Food: Plant matter and aquatic snails.

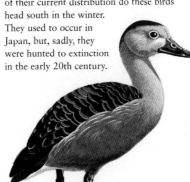

Identification: Brownish, with a darker streak across the top of the head. Underparts are slightly pinkish. White area around the vent. Dark brown back and wings with lighter scalloping. Grey bill, legs and feet. Sexes alike.

FROGMOUTHS AND OWLS

These hunting birds are all cryptically coloured, with none of them displaying the bright plumage seen in the case of some woodland birds. Their hearing and keen vision help to alert them to the presence of possible prey. In spite of their popular image, however, not all owls are nocturnal hunters, with some being seen on the wing throughout the day rather than solely becoming active at dusk.

Large frogmouth

Batrachostomus auritus

These frogmouths seem to be rare on the Asiatic mainland, and so relatively little is known about their habits. What we do know is that they hunt off a perch, seeking invertebrates, such as grasshoppers or cicadas, which they swoop down on and seize in their bill. Large frogmouths have a very wide gape that allows them to feed easily. They are nocturnal creatures, hunting from dusk onwards. They are reminiscent of owls, in terms of cryptic coloration and calls.

Identification: These birds are much larger than other frogmouths. They have dark rufous-brown upperparts amd white spotting forms a collar around the back of the neck. There are both white spots on the wings and buff barring on the flight feathers. The throat and breast are similar in shade to the upperparts, with white spotting on the breast and buff plumage on the belly. Forward-pointing bristles mask the bill. The eyes are relatively large. Hens are duller in colour and smaller overall.

Distribution: Ranges from peninsular Thailand and through Malaysia to Sumatra and Borneo.
Size: 41cm (16in), making this species twice as large as other frogmouths.
Habitat: Lowland forest.
Nest: Pad of down on a tree.
Eggs: 1, white.
Food: Invertebrates.

Collared owlet

Glaucidium brodiei

These owlets are unusual members of the owl family in that they hunt during the day, and may be seen in the vicinity of open clearings. Their vocalizations are unusual too, consisting of a series of quite musical call notes. In spite of their small size, these birds are aggressive hunters, and can take birds and even lizards as large as themselves. Their strong feet and fearsome-looking talons enable them to hold down their prey with ease as they kill it with their strong bill. It is not unusual for these owlets to be mobbed by groups of other birds. The disturbance that results from the driving mob can provide a means of identifying the owlets' presence in an area.

Above: The spots on the back of the collared owlet's head resemble eyes. This serves to detract possible predators.

Identification: Greyish-brown barred plumage. Has lemon-yellow eyes and white eyebrows and throat area. The underparts are also whitish. Greenish-yellow feet. Hens larger in size.

Distribution: Ranges from the Himalayan region east to China and southwards through much of the Malay Peninsula, then on to parts of Sumatra and Borneo.
Size: 15cm (6in).
Habitat: Hill and mountain forests with clearings, ranging up to an altitude of around 3,200m (10,500ft).
Nest: Tree hollow. The owl either uses a natural hole or takes over a chamber created by a woodpecker or barbet.
Eggs: 3–5, white.
Food: Large invertebrates and small vertebrates.

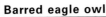

Barred eagle owl

Malay eagle owl *Bubo sumatranus*

Hard to spot during the daytime, barred eagle owls frequently choose to roost in a concealed locality out of sight, well disguised by foliage, with their barred pattern of markings helping to provide them with additional camouflage. They are also not especially common, simply because pairs occupy large territories. These owls are thought to pair for life and will return annually to the same nest site, with pairs occurring in Sumatra and Java not infrequently choosing a large bird's nest fern (*Asplenium*), rather than a tree hollow.

Identification: Large, fairly horizontal tufts of feathers on the top of the head, directed to the sides, with white streaks above dark brown eyes. Barred blackish-brown and buff plumage, with a finer pattern of barring across the breast. Underparts whiter overall, but still with distinct barring. Bill and feet are a pale yellow. Hens may be larger.

Distribution: From southern Myanmar (Burma) and Thailand across the Malay Peninsula to Borneo, Sumatra, Java, Bali and adjacent islands.
Size: 46cm (18in).
Habitat: Tropical forests up to 1,600m (5,250ft).
Nest: Tree holes and ferns.
Eggs: 1, white.
Food: Invertebrates and smaller vertebrates.

Spotted wood owl (*Strix seloputo*): 47cm (18.5in)
Found across South-east Asia over the Malay Peninsula to coastal areas of Java. Also present on Palawan in the Philippines and may occur on Sumatra. Rufous-buff facial disc. No ear tufts. Brownish barring on the underparts, may have areas that are whitish to more definite shades of buff. Eyes brown. Bill greyish. Hens larger.

Brown hawk owl (*Ninox scutulata*): 32cm (13in)
Extends from the Indian subcontinent and South-east Asia to some Indonesian islands, Japan and the Philippines, then via the mainland to eastern Siberia. White underparts with brown streaking. Some subspecies may have underparts of lighter brown than the streaking. Brownish back and wings. Greyish-black bill. Hens are usually smaller.

Oriental bay owl (*Phodilus badius*): 33cm (13in)
Ranges across South-east Asia to Indonesia. Also present on Samar in the Philippines. An isolated population exists in south-west India and on Sri Lanka. Whitish facial disc, resembling a mask, with a speckled collar beneath. The wings are reddish-brown with speckling; underparts paler. A distinctive v-shaped frontal shield extends from between the eyes to the base of the yellow bill. Females are usually bigger.

Buffy fish owl (*Bubo ketupu*): 48cm (19in)
Extends from southern Myanmar (Burma) into Thailand, through the Malay Peninsula to various Indonesian islands. Predominantly brown back and wings. The underparts are a pale yellowish-brown. Unfeathered, pale yellowish legs. Yellow eyes and black bill. Females larger.

Mountain scops owl

Spotted scops owl *Otus spilocephalus*

Inhabiting relatively inaccessible areas such as deep ravines, these owls become active at dusk when they begin to hunt their invertebrate prey. Males occupy relatively small territories and sing regularly, even outside the breeding period, with their calls sounding like a double whistle. Hens call far less often with their single note being heard in response to that of the cock bird, before merging into it. Although little has been recorded about their hunting habits, it is thought these scops owls obtain at least some of their prey on the wing, with moths as well as beetles featuring significantly in their diet.

Identification: Quite a small size compared to other owls. Some regional variation in colour. White feathering runs along the upper part of each wing. Underparts are brownish and have white areas crossed by black marks that are said to resemble arrowheads. Bristles are apparent on the face. Yellow eyes. The bill is cream. Sexes are alike.

Distribution: Indian Himalayan region, parts of Nepal, Pakistan and Myanmar (Burma), to south-eastern China, Taiwan and south through the Malay Peninsula to Sumatra and Borneo.
Size: 18cm (7in).
Habitat: Humid upland areas of forest.
Nest: Tree holes, sometimes excavated by other birds.
Eggs: 2–5, white.
Food: Invertebrates.

WOODPECKERS, CUCKOOS AND BEE-EATERS

These birds all hunt invertebrates but they have evolved very different techniques for this purpose. While bee-eaters often target flying insects, woodpeckers prefer to hunt those that hide out of sight, using their bills to expose and then capture them. Cuckoos, on the other hand, have no specialized feeding strategy but eat whatever they are able to catch, locating their prey by keen observation.

Oriental cuckoo

Himalayan cuckoo *Cuculus saturatus*

Distribution: Migratory races breed in northern parts of eastern Russia, Japan and the Himalayan region, before moving to South-east Asia in the winter. Resident populations are found on the Greater Sundas.
Size: 26cm (10.5in).
Habitat: Forest.
Nest: Those of other birds.
Eggs: 1 per nest, the colour of the egg corresponds to those of the foster species.
Food: Invertebrates.

Resident and migratory populations of these birds appear not to mix very much, with the migratory cuckoos often encountered at lower altitudes. It is actually said to be possible to distinguish between the non-migratory and migratory types of this cuckoo by their calls: the former will repeatedly utter a four- rather than three-note call. During the breeding season, the cuckoo utters its call more frequently so that it is easier to locate in the forest canopy. In northern parts of their range, these cuckoos frequent coniferous forests. In Asia, nests of the chestnut-crowned warbler (*Seicercus castaniceps*) are often parasitized by the oriental cuckoo.

Left: These cuckoos fly long distances and overwinter widely through Indonesia.

Identification: Has grey head and wings. Grey barring on white underparts, with a bare area of bright yellow skin around the eyes. Hens tend to be indistinguishable, but occasionally they are predominantly brownish with black barring in place of the grey areas. These are sometimes described as hepatic (liver-coloured) females and are a very rare sight.

Speckled piculet

Picumnus innominatus

These tiny woodpeckers are similar in habits to their larger relatives, using their bills to probe stems and branches for food. They are also sufficiently nimble in flight to feed on the wing, and can swoop down on spiders moving across bark. Speckled piculets are often observed foraging for food in the company of other birds, including various flycatchers and babblers, fire-tufted barbets and drongos. It is thought that the movements of these other birds help to stir up invertebrates, so making them easier for the piculets to catch. The nesting chamber excavated by speckled piculets is very small, measuring just 15cm (6in) in height and 6cm (2.5in) in width and depth. They often prefer to nest in rotten timber as this is easier to bore into with their bills. When breeding, these small piculets are most likely to be located by their persistent tapping rather than actually seen.

Distribution: From northern Pakistan and India east to southern China and down across the Malay Peninsula to Sumatra and Borneo. An isolated population exists in India's Western Ghats region.
Size: 10cm (4in).
Habitat: Trees, shrubs and stands of bamboo.
Nest: Hole excavated in bamboo or tree.
Eggs: 2–4, white.
Food: Insect larvae, spiders and other invertebrates.

Identification: Olive back, with a short tail. Has characteristic black and white spotted underparts. Black plumage runs through the eyes and is bordered by white streaks top and bottom. Cocks can be easily distinguished from hens by the orange patch on their forehead.

Brush cuckoo (*Cacomantis variolosus*):
24cm (9.5in)
Widely-distributed across Thailand and the Malay Peninsula, across the Sundas, south to Australia and east to the Philippines and the Solomon Islands. Head and upperparts are brownish-grey. Rufous underparts, with greyish tone to the throat and upper breast. Yellow eye ring. Sexes alike.

Chestnut-winged cuckoo (*Clamator coromandus*): 45cm (18in)
Distribution extends from east India to southern China and across South-east Asia to the Greater Sundas, Sulawesi and the Greater Sundas. Has a black head and a spectacular tufted crest. The collar is whitish and there is chestnut on the wings. The breast is a buff colour and there are grey underparts. The back and wings are blackish. Sexes are alike.

Great slaty woodpecker (*Mulleripicus pulverulentus*): 50cm (20in)
Extensive distribution from northern central parts of India through Nepal east to south-west China. Also occurs in Vietnam, Thailand and Malaysia. Present in western Indonesia east to Borneo and Palawan. Slaty-grey underparts. Paler edging to the feathers, forming white spots on the neck. Red flashes below the eyes only apparent in cock birds. Buff plumage on the throat.

Bamboo woodpecker (*Gecinulus viridis*):
28cm (11in)
Extends from Myanmar (Burma) eastwards to parts of Thailand, northern Laos and Malaysia. Cocks are predominantly greenish with a large crimson area on the head. The rump too is red. Bill greyish. Hens lack the red area on the head.

Greater yellow-naped woodpecker

Picus flavinucha

During the breeding season, the distinctive crest of these woodpeckers is used as part of their display. The sound of drumming can be heard at this time as the cock bird taps quickly and repeatedly on the side of a tree to attract a mate. Both parents help to construct a breeding chamber, which is located 2–6m (6.5–20ft) off the ground. Both also actively incubate the eggs and feed the chicks. After fledging, the young will call loudly and repeatedly if they become separated from the family group. It is quite common to encounter these woodpeckers foraging in small parties. These birds find food largely by probing in rotting vegetation rather than excavating holes in the bark. They rarely descend to ground level.

Distribution: From the Himalayan region of north-west India through Nepal to Myanmar (Burma) across South-east Asia to China. Also isolated distribution through the Malay Peninsula to Sumatra.
Size: 34cm (13in).
Habitat: Forested foothills and mountain slopes.
Nest: Rotten tree.
Eggs: 3–4, white.
Food: Wide range of invertebrates and even frogs.

Identification:
Predominantly green body, with a black tail and brown and black barring on the flight feathers. Distinctive yellow crest at the back of the head. Yellowish plumage on the throat with white spots beneath. Hens have more streaking on the throat.

Red-bearded bee-eater

Nyctyornis athertoni

These bee-eaters are more likely to be seen in the middle and upper parts of the forest canopy, rather than in the darker undergrowth. Here they catch a wide variety of invertebrates in flight, preying not just on bees but also beetles, wasps and ants. They rest quietly on a chosen branch, waiting for their quarry to come within range, then fly fast and with great agility to capture it. Trees adjacent to clearings are often favoured, as these breaks in the forest provide an open area to capture prey. When breeding, the bee-eaters excavate tunnels, which can extend back 1.2m (4ft) into cliff faces and similar localities.

Identification: Pink plumage extends from in front of the eyes up over the crown. A red area beneath the bill leads down on to the chest. Yellow underside to the tail with black tips. The remainder of the body is green. The bill is dark and curves downwards at its tip. Hens have less pink plumage on the head.

Distribution: Through the Malay peninsula, apart from the southern tip, to Sumatra and Borneo.
Size: 30cm (12in).
Habitat: Lowland forested areas.
Nest: Hole in a vertical bank.
Eggs: 3–5, white.
Food: Invertebrates, including bees.

HONEYGUIDES, HORNBILLS AND BARBETS

The hornbills include some of the most magnificent birds found in the forests of Asia, not so much for their bright coloration but rather for their spectacular size and incredible bills. Barbets may be smaller, but they too have stocky bills, which in this case are used to bore into rotten wood, although they are not as talented in this respect as woodpeckers.

Malaysian honeyguide

Indicator archipelagicus

The Malaysian honeyguide is an Asian representative of a family whose members are more commonly distributed in Africa. Honeyguides have a zygodactyl perching grip, which means that their toes are arranged in a 2:2 perching configuration. They are hard to spot in the canopy, thanks both to their dull coloration and small size, and are normally solitary by nature, so very little has been documented about their habits. They do have a distinctive call, however, that consists of two notes: the first resembles the miaowing of a cat, and this is closely followed by a rattling noise. Honeyguides feed on bees as they emerge from their nests. This helps people pinpoint the nests of wild bees and find honey, which is how these birds acquired their name.

Identification: Dark olive-brown upperparts, with red irises and grey bill. Underparts greyish-white, becoming increasingly white on the lower underparts, with dark blackish streaking on the flanks. Hens lack the narrow yellow shoulder patch.

Below: The honeyguide feeds on bees, snatched from the air as they emerge from their nests.

Distribution: Ranges over the Malay Peninsula south to Sumatra and Borneo.
Size: 18cm (7in).
Habitat: Forested areas, typically in the lowlands up to an altitude of 1,000m (3,300ft).
Nest: Tree holes.
Eggs: Presently unrecorded.
Food: Bees and wasps.

Rhinoceros hornbill

Buceros rhinoceros

Distribution: In South-east Asia south through the Malay peninsula to Sumatra, Java and Borneo.
Size: 110 cm (43in).
Habitat: Lowland and hill forests.
Nest: Tree hollow.
Eggs: 2, white.
Food: Fruit and smaller vertebrates.

Right: The distinctive, long bill of this hornbill helps them to pluck fruit from otherwise inaccessible places.

The upturned casque on the top of the bill of these hornbills resembles the horn of a rhinoceros, which is, of course, why they got their name. They are most likely to be seen close by fruiting figs, which are one of their favourite foods. Deforestation of the areas inhabited by these large birds is a serious threat to their future, especially as they do not live at high densities. Individual pairs will roam over wide areas and depend on large trees for nesting purposes. As with related species, the male rhinoceros hornbill incarcerates his mate in the nest chamber, sealing the entrance with mud. He returns here regularly to feed her and their brood until the family are ready to break out of the chamber. This barrier is believed to guard against would-be predators, such as snakes.

Identification: Has a black head, breast, back and wings with a white abdomen. The tail is also white, but with a broad black band. Bill is yellowish, redder at the base with a distinctive horn-like casque above. Cock birds have a red iris, but this can range from whitish to blue in hens. Otherwise, sexes are alike.

Bushy-crested hornbill (*Anorrhinus galeritus*): 70cm (28in)
Ranges from the Malay Peninsula to Sumatra, Borneo and north Natuna. Predominantly black in colour with a loose crest at the back of the head. Has a greyish-brown tail with a black band at the base. Blue areas of skin present on the throat and around the eye. Cock birds have red irises and black bills while hens have black irises and whitish bills.

Asian black hornbill (*Anthracoceros malayanus*): 75cm (29.5in)
Found across the Malay Peninsula south to islands, including Sumatra and Borneo. Body is entirely black apart from white edging to the tail feathers. The bill and casque are whitish and the iris is red. Hens have greyish bills and pinkish skin surrounding the eyes.

Wreathed hornbill (*Aceros undulatus*): 100cm (39in)
Ranges from eastern India to south-west China, through South-east Asia and on across the Malay Peninsula to Sumatra, Java, Bali and Borneo. Has a cream-coloured head, with a reddish stripe extending from the nape. The back, wings and underparts are black. There is an unfeathered yellow gular pouch on the throat. Hens have black upperparts, a blue gular pouch and small casque.

Yellow-crowned barbet (*Megalaima henricii*): 21cm (8.5in)
Extends from the Malay Peninsula to Sumatra and Borneo. Mainly green, but darker on the wings. Has a prominent yellow forehead that extends back over the eyes. Blue plumage is present on the throat and at the back of the head. A black stripe passes through the eyes, and reddish spots are present on the nape and at the sides of the neck. Sexes alike.

Great hornbill

Buceros bicornis (E)

There is some variation in size through the extensive range of these hornbills. Mainland populations tend to be slightly smaller than their counterparts occurring on the islands. Great hornbills are most likely to be seen flying over the forest, as their large size and rather noisy flight means they are more obvious. They may also be spotted feeding in the canopy, jumping from branch to branch as they do so. Their loud call sounds rather like the barking of a small dog.

Right: The cock bird finds food and brings it to the nest for its young.

Distribution: Range extends from India to South-east Asia, across the Malay Peninsula to Sumatra.
Size: 125cm (49in).
Habitat: Forested areas.
Nest: Tree hollow.
Eggs: 2, white.
Food: Fruit and small vertebrates.

Identification: A black band encircles the face and base of the lower bill, with a cream area behind that runs down on to the upper breast. Wings predominantly black, with a white band across. White also apparent across the tips of the flight feathers when the wing is closed. Lower underparts white, as is the tail apart from a broad black band relatively close to the rounded tip. Bill yellowish, with flat-topped casque above. Cocks have red irises while hens have cream-coloured irises. Sexes are otherwise alike.

Fire-tufted barbet

Psilopogon pyrolophus

The relatively long tail and short bill of these barbets sets them apart from other species occurring in Asia. They are noisy and active by nature, often hopping from one branch to another, and occurring in small groups where food is plentiful. If danger threatens, however, fire-tufted barbets are likely to freeze, which makes them hard to observe. When roosting, they often perch with their long tails held in a vertical position. This stance allows them to roost and breed in quite small nesting chambers, which they excavate using their powerful bills.

Identification: Predominantly green, although darker on the wings and lighter on the underparts. Has a black collar around the chest with an area of yellow plumage above. Areas of black, grey and green plumage are also present on the head, with brown extending down the back of the head. Has prominent forward-pointing bristles with reddish tips evident above the upper bill. The beak itself is greenish-yellow, with two black spots on each side. Sexes alike.

Distribution: Confined to the Malay Peninsula and Sumatra.
Size: 26cm (10.5in).
Habitat: Forested areas up to 1,500m (4,900ft).
Nest: Tree holes.
Eggs: Presently unrecorded.
Food: Mainly fruit and invertebrates.

PITTAS AND TROGONS

These brightly coloured woodland birds are surprisingly hard to spot in their natural habitat, not just because they are often shy, but also because they merge into the background thanks to the various shades and markings on their bodies. Pittas spend much of their time on or near the forest floor, while trogons tend to occupy the lower reaches, too, with the shafts of light helping to obscure their presence.

Giant pitta

Great blue pitta *Pitta caerulea*

The large, powerful bill of the giant pitta is used to feed mainly on snails, which are broken on particular stones in the pitta's territory. Cock birds maintain and defend their own areas vigorously. Earthworms are also a favoured food and occasionally they catch small snakes. These birds turn over leaf litter on the forest floor where they feed, seeking edible items. They build their nest quite close to the forest floor, usually in the fork of a suitable tree. Pairs tend to stay together throughout the year, but they can be hard to observe, as they hop away through the undergrowth at the slightest hint of danger.

Identification: A distinctive blue back, wings and tail, with pale buff underparts. The head has a blackish stripe down the centre, another extending back from the eyes and a black collar around the back of the neck. The remainder of facial plumage is a greyish colour but with some black edging. The hens have a blue tail but the rest of the plumage on the back is chestnut brown rather than blue. Their head is brownish rather than grey.

Distribution: Extends from Myanmar (Burma) and Thailand through the Malay Peninsula to Sumatra and Borneo.
Size: 30cm (12in).
Habitat: Lowland and hill forests.
Nest: Dome-shaped, with entrance at the front.
Eggs: 2, whitish with brown speckling.
Food: Mainly invertebrates, and some small vertebrates.

Hooded pitta

Green-breasted pitta *Pitta sordida*

There are approximately a dozen recognized subspecies of hooded pitta, resulting in a considerable variation in appearance through these birds' wide range. Hooded pittas tend to be solitary by nature, seeking out food on the ground, although they will sometimes perch at least 7m (23ft) off the ground. Both members of the pair are involved in nest-building, and use a variety of vegetation to create a dome shape. The nest is well concealed on the ground, with access to the interior via a side-opening. In some parts of their range, hooded pittas are migratory by nature, and can travel long distances, often flying at night. At the onset of the rainy season they will call after dark.

Identification: Generally has a black head, with green wings and a whitish blue flash on each wing. There is a variable crimson area around the vent, which travels up to the centre of the abdomen. An area of black plumage may appear on the front. White wing patches are sometimes evident. Sexes alike.

Distribution: Sporadic distribution from the foothills of the Himalayas through the Malay Peninsula to Indonesia, New Guinea, the Philippines and other islands in the region.
Size: 30cm (12in).
Habitat: Forested areas.
Nest: Dome-shaped mass of vegetation.
Eggs: 3–5, white with darker, often brownish spots and markings.
Food: Invertebrates.

Blue-winged pitta (*Pitta moluccensis*): 20cm (8in)
Migratory in northern parts of its range, with these birds overwintering in more southerly localities. Occurs in China, Myanmar
(Burma), Vietnam, Laos, Cambodia, Thailand and then south
through the Malay Peninsula to Sumatra, Borneo and neighbouring
islands, occuring at lower altitudes. Has a black crown and black
stripe running through the eye that are separated by a brown
band. White throat. Green on the back and wings. The underparts
are buff but become crimson around the vent. Has violet-blue
wing coverts and rump, with a white area present here. Very
short tail. Sexes alike.

Banded pitta (*Pitta guajana*): 24cm (9.5in)
Found in Thailand and the Malay Peninsula south to Java, Sumatra
and Borneo, but does not apparently appear in Singapore. Has a
yellow to orange stripe above the eyes, with black plumage below,
running across the sides of the face. Some white on the throat.
Upperparts are chestnut-brown and the tail is a rich shade of blue.
The underparts are barred in hens but violet-blue in most cock
birds. The pitta's appearance is exceedingly variable, to the extent
that some taxonomists believe that this species should be split
into two separate species.

Red-naped trogon (*Harpactes kasumba*): 33cm (13in)
Ranges from the Malay Peninsula down to Sumatra and Borneo.
Black head, with a white collar across the chest and red plumage
beneath. There is also a red collar around the nape of the neck.
The bill and bare skin around the eyes are bluish. The underside of
the long tail is whitish. The back is brown. Hens are much paler,
with a greyish head, and buff collar and underparts.

Orange-breasted trogon (*Harpactes oreskios*): 25cm (10in)
Ranges from southern China and across South-east Asia down
to Sumatra, Java and Borneo. Has an olive head, brown back and
tail, The underparts are orange with yellow around the vent. The
wings are black and there is some white barring. Hens have grey
heads and breast, with yellowish-brown underparts. The barring
on their wings is black.

Garnet pitta

Red-headed scarlet pitta *Pitta granatina*

These stunningly beautiful birds tend to be well concealed
in their forest habitat, where their presence is likely to be
revealed initially by their song. This sounds like a whistle
that becomes louder and then stops suddenly. It can carry
over quite a distance. Having once located the presence
of a garnet pitta, it is usually possible to get quite close
without scaring the bird away, as
they are not really very shy.
They often disappear from
tracks in the forest, preferring
instead to hunt for food in
the undergrowth.

Distribution: From Thailand
through the Malay Peninsula
to northern parts of Sumatra
and Borneo.
Size: 15cm (6in).
Habitat: Lowland forests.
Nest: Domed cup of
vegetation.
Eggs: 2, glossy-white with
reddish-brown spots.
Food: Mainly invertebrates.

Identification: Some regional
variation in the markings, with
more black on the head of the
Bornean race. In common, they
have a fiery red area of plumage
on the head, the rest of which
is black apart from a pale bluish
streak on the side of the head.
This separates the two colours.
Purplish chest and back, with rich
crimson underparts. Lighter blue
area on the wings. Sexes alike.

Red-headed trogon

Harpactes erythrocephalus

These trogons tend to occupy the
lower levels of the thick forest
in which they live. They hunt a
variety of invertebrates, using
a suitable perch as a watchout
point before swooping down
on their quarry. Like other
trogons, these have the 2:2
zygodactyl perching grip,
where two toes are directed
forwards and two provide
support behind the perch.
When breeding, these birds
seek out tree hollows, which
may be natural spaces or
created by other birds such
as woodpeckers.

Identification: A bright
red head contrasts with
the bluish bill and blue,
bare skin around
the eyes. A white
stripe across the
breast separates
the more pinkish
plumage on the
underparts from the
red head. Wings and
tail are brown, with
black edging around
the upper tail feathers.
Barring is present on
the edge of the wings.
Hens have brownish
rather than red heads,
that merge into the
colour on the back.

Distribution: Ranges widely
from the Himalayas across
Asia to southern China and
south via the Malay Peninsula
to Sumatra.
Size: 30cm (12in).
Habitat: Hill forest.
Nest: Tree holes.
Eggs: 2–3, buff.
Food: Invertebrates.

PHEASANTS AND OTHER SIMILAR BIRDS

This group of forest-dwelling birds are all likely to be encountered on or certainly near ground level. Some, such as the lyrebird and great argus, have difficulty in flying any distance because of their ornate plumage, whereas the brown kiwi, like others of its kind, has lost the ability to fly. Its closest relatives are actually much larger ratites such as emus and ostriches.

Superb lyrebird

Queen Victoria's lyrebird *Menura novaehollandiae*

The lyrebird resembles a pheasant and is sometimes known, misleadingly, as the native pheasant. Lyrebirds are shy and hard to spot, but the lyrebird is a talented songbird and the cock's powerful, far-carrying and lyrical song will often reveal his presence. The hens, though, have a quieter call. These birds are most likely to be glimpsed as they scurry across roads and open ground, although they can fly. They seek food on the ground, raking over leaf litter with their powerful feet. The cock bird also uses its feet to scrape up soil to form his display mounds.

Above: The lyrebird's tail feathers are more than 60cm (2ft) in length.

Identification: Dark, brownish upperparts with a coppery hue on the wings. Underparts are greyish. Adult cock birds have a distinctive train of lacy tail plumes with two long outer feathers, known as lyrates, that measure at least 60cm (24in). The tails are made up of seven pairs of feathers, with the central pair the longest. The tail itself is usually carried horizontally. Hens have shorter, more pointed tails without the filamentous plumes.

Distribution: Found in eastern Australia, from southern Queensland to Victoria. Also introduced successfully to Tasmania.
Size: Cock 100cm (38in); hen 86cm (34in).
Habitat: Wooded terrain.
Nest: Large dome-shaped nest constructed from vegetable matter.
Eggs: 1, ranges from grey to purple-brown with dark grey markings.
Food: Invertebrates, including crustaceans.

Golden pheasant

Chrysolophus pictus

Distribution: Occurs naturally in central China. Introduced to a few localities elsewhere, most notably in eastern England.
Size: Cock 115cm (45in); hen 70cm (27.5in).
Habitat: Wooded areas with shrubs and bamboo.
Nest: A scrape on the ground.
Eggs: 5–12, buff.
Food: Vegetation and invertebrates.

Adult cock golden pheasants are naturally polygamous, living with two or three hens, but very little else has been documented about the habits of these birds in the wild. They occur in areas where there is dense vegetative cover, and because they live on the ground, observing them in these surroundings is difficult. They feed mainly on the leaves and shoots of a variety of plants, especially bamboo, as well as eating the flowers of rhododendrons.

Identification: Golden-yellow feathering on head, lower back and rump. The underparts are vibrant scarlet, merging into chestnut. The ruff or tippet on the neck is golden with black edging to the plumage and the upper back is green. Has long, mottled tail feathers. Hens in comparison are smaller and a duller colour, being essentially brown with mottling or barring on the feathers. Their tail feathers are pointed at the tips. Young birds resemble hens but have less pronounced markings.

Chestnut-breasted hill partridge (*Arborophila mandellii*): 28cm (11in)
Ranges from north-east India via Bhutan to south-eastern Tibet. Chestnut crown, paler on the sides of the face, with black speckling. A greyish streak extends back from the eyes. White band with narrow black stripe beneath lies above chestnut breast feathering. Rest of the body is greyish with chestnut speckling on the flanks. Wings browner with black scalloping. Sexes alike.

Crested wood partridge (roulroul, *Rollulus roulroul*): 26cm (10.5in)
Extends from southern Myanmar (Burma) and Thailand through the Malay Peninsula to islands including Sumatra and Borneo. Highly distinctive reddish crest, edged with white. Red skin around the eyes. The rest of the plumage is dark. Hens lack the crest, and are greenish with a greyish head and brownish wings.

Crested fireback (*Lophura ignita*): Cock 66cm (26in); hen 56cm (22in)
Ranges from South-east Asia to the islands of Borneo and Sumatra. Dark bluish crest, with lighter blue wattles around the eyes. Rump is reddish. Dark blue underparts are streaked white or orange. White or buff tail feathers, depending on subspecies. Hens are predominantly brown, even blackish, with blue facial markings. White scalloping to the feathering on the underparts.

Brown kiwi

Apteryx australis

Distribution: Confined to New Zealand and present on both North and South Island as well as Stewart Island and some smaller islands.
Size: 56cm (22in).
Habitat: Forest.
Nest: In a burrow.
Eggs: 1–2, white or greenish.
Food: Invertebrates and a little fruit.

Identification: The reddish-brown plumage with darker streaking, has a distinctive hair-like texture. Long yellowish bill with bristles at the base. Strong, powerful legs. Sexes alike, although hens are larger with a longer bill.

The kiwi has become New Zealand's national emblem. These highly unusual flightless birds are essentially nocturnal in their habits. They have sensitive nostrils at the end of their bill and locate their food by smell, which is handy in the dark. They also use their bills like levers to pull out worms found in the forest soil. Hens lay what is proportionately the largest egg in the avian world relative to body size, and the yolk is relatively bigger too. This helps to nourish the chick through what is a very long incubation period, typically lasting 12 weeks. The male carries out incubation duties. Young brown kiwis resemble the adult but are smaller.

Great argus

Argusianus argus

The magnificent train created by the tail feathers of the male great argus can be up to 1.2m (4ft) long. Unfortunately, they are shy, solitary birds by nature and, therefore, hard to observe. While hens can fly without difficulty, the enlarged flight feathers of the cock, coupled with its long train affects its ability to fly any distance at all. It is not until a young male is three years old that the elongated feathers start to develop, with their transformation occurring gradually over successive moults over the next four years. They are generally used for display purposes.

Identification: Head and neck are blue, with a short blackish crest at the back of the head. Has white spots over brown plumage on the body. Large eye-like markings called ocelli in the wings. Upper breast is rusty-red. Grey coloration on the central tail feathers. Hens are much smaller, with a paler blue head and barred markings on the short tail.

Distribution: The Malay Peninsula, but absent from the south. Also found on Sumatra and Borneo.
Size: Cock 200cm (79in); hen 76cm (30in).
Habitat: Primary and logged areas of forest.
Nest: Hollow lined with grass.
Eggs: 2, creamy white.
Food: Plant matter and ants.

Left: The final stage of the cock's display involves bowing to the hen with his magnificent tail feathers held erect.

BROADBILLS AND OTHER SMALLER WOODLAND-DWELLERS

A number of Asian birds have ornamental rackets at the tips of their tail feathers, which are attached by so-called shafts, which like the racket are a continuation of the feather and quite flexible. They tend to be used for display purposes, although other ornamentations of the plumage, such as crests and bright coloration, can be seen in many broadbills.

Green broadbill

Calyptomena viridis

Distribution: From Myanmar (Burma) and western Thailand to the Malay Peninsula, Sumatra and Borneo.
Size: 17cm (7in).
Habitat: Lower levels of rainforest. Very rarely encountered in forests that have been logged.
Nest: Made of plant fibres.
Eggs: 1–3, whitish.
Food: Fruit.

These broadbills are so-called because of the size of their gape, or mouth-opening, rather than the size of their bill. They feed by foraging for fruit and their wide gape allows them to eat it whole. Their bill is very weak and lacks a cutting edge so they can only eat soft fruits such as members of the fig family. The green broadbill helps to maintain structure and diversity within the rainforest, since their feeding habits mean that they help to distribute the indigestible seeds of such plants via their droppings as they move around the forest. Their nest is an elaborate construction, resembling a bottle gourd in shape. It is suspended from a very thin branch as this helps to protect the birds from possible predators.

Identification: Has dark green plumage with three black bars across the top of the wings. A black circular area lies behind each eye. The very short tail emphasizes the outline of the plump body. The crest above the bill is larger in males. Hens are green all over but it is a lighter shade than the cocks.

Lesser cuckoo shrike

Coracina fimbriata

Despite their name, these birds are related to neither cuckoos nor shrikes, but are actually a relative of the crow family, according to DNA studies. They are so-called because they resemble the cuckoos in shape and appearance, and yet are equipped with a strong, hooked bill like shrikes, which is used for seizing invertebrates. Lesser cuckoo shrikes are birds of the forest canopy. They even nest in the canopy and are most unlikely to be seen on the ground. These cuckoo shrike's young have very different colouring, with barring evident over what is primarily white plumage. These birds have relatively harsh calls which are most likely to be uttered when they are in a group, although individuals have been known to sing on occasion.

Identification: Mainly grey, although the sides of the face, wings and tail are blackish. There is white edging to the tips of the tail feathers. The eyes are dark brown. Hens are paler and have pale grey, rather than black, feathering on their face, plus some distinctive barring on underparts.

Distribution: Ranges across the Malay Peninsula to Java and Sumatra in the Greater Sunda islands. Also Borneo.
Size: 20cm (8in).
Habitat: Lowland and hill forest.
Nest: Cup-shaped, made of vegetation.
Eggs: 3 olive-green, with brown markings.
Food: Invertebrates.

Orange-bellied leafbird

Hardwick's fruitsucker *Chloropsis hardwickii*

The relatively long bills of these birds are used to search for invertebrates among the leaves, and to probe flowers in search of nectar. The eponymous coloration of the orange-bellied leafbird allows it to blend effectively into a background of vegetation. Young, recently fledged birds are entirely green. Their nests are well hidden in forks of trees. These leafbirds are solitary by nature, although they are more likely to be seen in pairs during the breeding season. They have quite loud, meliforous calls, with cocks singing more frequently during the breeding period. Leafbirds are also talented mimics and can master the song of other birds.

Identification: Mainly green upperparts with a black mask that extends from the cheeks down on to the chest. This is broken by a blue streak that runs down below the bill. Underparts are orange-yellow. There is some dark blue plumage in the wings. The tail is dark blue. Hens are essentially green with matching underparts but have lighter blue streaks on the sides of the long bill.

Distribution: Extends from the Himalayan region to southern China and south to areas of South-east Asia down to the Malay Peninsula.
Size: 20cm (8in).
Habitat: Hill forests.
Nest: Loose cup.
Eggs: 2–3, buff-cream with pale red markings.
Food: Mainly invertebrates. Also nectar and fruit.

Greater racket-tailed drongo

Dicrurus paradiseus

Distribution: Ranges from India eastwards through South-east Asia to China and down across the Malay Peninsula to the Greater Sundas. Is present on Sumatra, Java and Bali as well as Borneo.
Size: 36cm (14in).
Habitat: Lowland forest.
Nest: Cup-shaped, made from vegetation.
Eggs: 3–4, creamy-white with dark markings.
Food: Invertebrates.

Identification: Has bluish-black plumage, with a short crest above the bill. Sharply forked tail with narrow tail shafts that end in twisted enlargements known as rackets. During the moulting period, however, the rackets may be missing or simply not developed to their full extent. The sharp, pointed bill is black as are the legs and feet. Sexes alike.

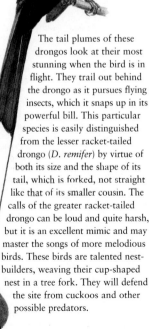

The tail plumes of these drongos look at their most stunning when the bird is in flight. They trail out behind the drongo as it pursues flying insects, which it snaps up in its powerful bill. This particular species is easily distinguished from the lesser racket-tailed drongo (*D. remifer*) by virtue of both its size and the shape of its tail, which is forked, not straight like that of its smaller cousin. The calls of the greater racket-tailed drongo can be loud and quite harsh, but it is an excellent mimic and may master the songs of more melodious birds. These birds are talented nest-builders, weaving their cup-shaped nest in a tree fork. They will defend the site from cuckoos and other possible predators.

Long-tailed broadbill (*Psarisomus dalhousiae*): 25cm (10in)
Sporadic distribution where suitable habitat is found from the eastern Himalayas across much of South-east Asia to Sumatra and Borneo. Black plumage on the top and rear of the head, with small blue and yellow areas. White collar around the neck. Greenish underparts and dark green over the back. Some blue on the wings. Blue tail. Hens may have faint yellow area on the nape.

Banded broadbill (purple-headed broadbill, *Eurylaimus javanicus*): 23cm (9in)
From Indo-China and Malaysia to Java, Sumatra and Borneo. Purple-maroon plumage on the head and underparts. Has an obvious black breast band that is absent in hens. Yellow markings on the back and wings, which are otherwise dark in colour. Bill pale blue and yellower at the tip.

Dusky broadbill (*Corydon sumatranus*): 25cm (10in)
Ranges from Indo-China down across the Malay Peninsula to Sumatra and Borneo. Pinkish-purple bill and bare skin around the eyes. The plumage is paler on the throat and blackish-brown else-where. Sexes alike.

Large wood shrike (hook-billed woodshrike, *Tephrodornis gularis*): 22cm (8.5in)
Found in western India, and from the Himalayas across South-east Asia to southern China and south through the Malay Peninsula to Java, Sumatra and Borneo. Eleven races recognized: larger birds with browner back in northern areas; smaller greyer populations in the south. Black stripe running through the eye. Rump whitish, as is the area under the throat. Underparts pale grey. Hens similar to cocks, but with browner tails.

PIGEONS AND DOVES

The diversity that exists within this group of birds can be seen at its greatest in the Australasian region,
which is home to some of the most bizarre and distinctive members of this widely distributed family
of birds. Vivid red, yellow and blue hues are apparent in the plumage of a number of species from
the area, especially in the case of the fruit doves forming the genus Ptilinopus.

Nicobar pigeon

Caloenas nicobarica

These highly distinctive pigeons are found on many islands,
particularly those least affected by human habitation.
They are largely terrestrial, although if disturbed on
the ground, they fly up noisily to branches close to the
forest canopy. Here, their dark coloration makes them
hard to spot. Nicobar pigeons have a particularly thick-
walled gizzard, which allows them to grind up and
digest large, heavily coated seeds without difficulty.
Inevitable food shortages on small islands mean that
these pigeons are often forced to forage further afield,
crossing the sea to nearby larger islands, particularly during
the breeding season when they are feeding their chicks.

Identification: Predominantly dark slaty-grey with green and coppery
iridescent tones evident over the wings. Trail of long, relatively narrow
feathers hanging down from the neck. White tail feathers and prominent
swelling, known as a caruncle, on the top of the bill. Sexes alike.

Distribution: Found on
islands in the Bay of Bengal
eastwards as far as Palau and
the Solomons. Larger
numbers on breeding islands.
Size: 34cm (13in).
Habitat: Coastal forest areas.
Nest: Loose platform of
twigs in a tree or bush.
Eggs: 1, white.
Food: Mainly seeds and fruit,
some invertebrates.

Victoria crowned pigeon

White-tipped crown pigeon *Goura victoria*

Distribution: Northern
New Guinea. Extends from
Geelvink Bay to Collingwood
Bay. Also found on a few
smaller offshore islands
here, such as Biak, Salawati
and Seram.
Size: 74cm (29in).
Habitat: Lowland forest
areas where the pigeons
spend much of their time
on the ground.
Nest: Platform of sticks, palm
leaves and other vegetation.
Eggs: 1, white.
Food: Fruits, seeds and
invertebrates.

This is one of three species of crowned pigeon occurring in
New Guinea. These birds are likely to be encountered
wandering in groups of up to ten individuals through
forested areas, although in recent years they have
become much scarcer near settlements as
the result of being heavily hunted. If
disturbed, crowned pigeons will fly
up on to branches. Pairs also nest off
the ground. The young bird is much
smaller than its parents on fledging.
It grows slowly, and will not be fully
independent until more than
three months old.

Identification: Has unique white
tips to the blue lacy fan-like crest
on the head. Remainder of the
body primarily pale bluish grey,
with a maroon breast and bluish
underparts. Area of maroon also
on the lower edges of the
wing, with pale blue wing bar
above. Lighter blue tip to the
tail. Black feathering extends
over the red irises. Sexes
alike. Some individuals
will display more
black areas in their
plumage than others.

Pied imperial pigeon (*Ducula bicolor*):
38cm (15in)
Found on islands across southern Asia down to
Australia. Frequently in coastal areas; scarce in
the Lesser Sundas. Creamy white with black flight
feathers and broad blackish area on the tail. Dark-
greyish bill and eyes. Some races have black
barring on the undertail coverts. Sexes alike.

Wedge-tailed green pigeon (*Treron sphenura*):
33cm (13in)
Ranges from Himalayan region to southern China,
across the Malay Peninsula to Sumatra, Java and
Lombok. Greenish, with claret areas on the wings
adjoining the shoulders. Pale blue wash and slight
orangish hue on the breast, depending on race.
Dark green barring on yellow undertail coverts.
Long, wedge-shaped tail. Hens are greener.

Jambu fruit dove (*Ptilinopus jambu*):
24cm (9.5in)
Ranges from southern peninsular Thailand to
Sumatra, western Java and Borneo. Red mask on
the face, with a paler breast and white plumage
on the lower underparts. Back of the head, wings
and tail are green. Undertail coverts are brown.
Hens are dark green overall, with a dull purple
area on the face and greyish tone to the breast.

Barred cuckoo dove (bar-tailed cuckoo dove,
Macropygia unchall): 37cm (14.5in)
Extends from Himalayan region to China, parts of
South-east Asia and the Malay Peninsula. On to
Java, Sumatra, Bali, Flores and Lombok. Greyish-
pink on the head and neck, greenish suffusion on
the neck. Black, with chestnut markings on the
back, wings and long tail. Barring on the chest.
Hens have black and chestnut underparts.

Wompoo fruit dove

Ptilinopus magnificus

Distribution: Present
throughout New Guinea,
except the central
mountainous region. Also
extends down the eastern
side of Australia.
Size: Races vary widely, from
29 to 48cm (11.5 to 19in).
Habitat: Mainly evergreen
rainforest.
Nest: Loose platform
constructed off the ground.
Eggs: 1, white.
Food: Fruit.

Identification: Pale greyish head,
with red eyes and a red bill with
a yellow tip. Back, wings and tail
are dark green, with a contrasting
yellow wing bar. Claret breast,
with the lower part of the body
and under-wing feathering bright
yellow. Greyish undertail coverts
are edged with yellow. Underside
of the flight feathers and tail are
greyish. Sexes alike.

Wompoo fruit
doves are so-
called because
of the sound of
their distinctive
calls. Living in
rainforest areas
means that there
will be sources
of fruit available to
these birds throughout the year, and they
have been documented as feeding on more
than 50 different types. Indigestible seeds
pass through their bodies and are deposited
elsewhere in the forest, and this helps to
maintain their food supply in the future.
Like other fruit pigeons, they have a very
wide gape, enabling them to swallow fruits
whole, as they are unable to bite into them
with their rather weak bills. Young chicks
grow very rapidly and will leave the nest at
just under two
weeks old.

*Left:
Although
both sexes
will share
incubation
duties, the
cock tends
to sit the
longest.*

Pheasant pigeon

Otidiphaps nobilis

Distribution: Much of New
Guinea and various small
islands.
Size: 46cm (18in).
Habitat: Hill forests.
Nest: Sticks on the ground in
a tree buttress.
Eggs: 1, white.
Food: Seeds and fruit.

These unusual pigeons
have no close relatives,
although they actually walk
a little like pheasants, with
their head held forwards and
their tail feathers moving
rhythmically. They are seen
on their own or in pairs. Being
both shy and alert by nature,
pheasant pigeons are very hard
to observe in the field, however,
unless the observer is well hidden.
When displaying during the breeding
period, males will swoop down from
a perch, flapping their short wings to
create an unusual sound that has
been likened to a gunshot.

Identification: Resembles a brightly coloured pheasant,
with a crest on the back of the head. although this is
more conspicuous in some races than others. Blackish
head and underparts with variable violet-blue sheen.
Chestnut back and wings. Feathering on the nape
may range in colour from white through grey
to green, with the latter colour present
on the breast of the Aru race (*O. n.
aruoncio*). Roddioh bill and eyes.
Long, broad tail. Sexes alike.

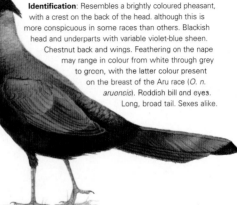

CORVIDS

Blackish plumage predominates in members of the crow family, although there are some spectacularly coloured members of the family found in the Australasian region, such as the vivid green hunting cissas. Corvids are an adaptable group of birds, found in a wide range of habitats, and are not easily overlooked, thanks often to their loud calls.

Forest raven

Tasmanian raven *Corvus tasmanicus*

These ravens are often seen in flocks, sometimes scavenging on rubbish tips for food. Pairs do not breed communally, preferring to seek out separate sites in tall trees, lining the inside of their nest with animal hair or wool. The colour of the eyes provides a means of aging these corvids. They are bluish grey prior to fledging and brownish by the time of fledging. It is not until they are three years old that the characteristic white coloration becomes evident.

Identification: Stocky outline with relatively short wings and tail. Glossy black coloration, with a purplish-blue, or greenish-blue, suffusion. The plumage on the abdomen tends to be held quite loosely rather than lying sleekly. Iris is whitish. Heavy, blackish bill and feet. Hens are slightly smaller.

Distribution: Tasmania and offshore islands, as well as the south-eastern corner of the Australian mainland.
Size: 52cm (21in).
Habitat: Most common in wooded areas.
Nest: Bulky cup of twigs and sticks.
Eggs: 3–6, greenish with darker markings.
Food: Carrion, invertebrates and vegetable matter.

Green magpie

Hunting cissa *Cissa chinensis*

The plumage of the green magpie can undergo an unusual but spectacular change, depending on its environmental conditions. When these birds live in relatively open country, the stronger sunlight actually bleaches their plumage. This results in the green areas becoming transformed into a light sky blue shade, while the chestnut patches change to a darker, duller shade of brown. The magpies usually occupy the lower reaches of the forest, searching in small parties through the shrubbery for invertebrates and will even eat carrion on occasions. Pairs breed on their own. The young birds have yellow bills and legs once they fledge.

Identification: Predominantly light green, with black bands running through the eyes. Broad chestnut areas cover the wings, with characteristic black and white barring where the wings meet. The undersides of the tail feathers are also black and white. Bill, legs and feet red. Sexes similar.

Distribution: Occurs over an extensive area from north-west India down to South-east Asia, as well as on the islands of Sumatra and Borneo.
Size: 39cm (15in).
Habitat: Edges of hill and lowland forests.
Nest: Cup-shaped platform of vegetation.
Eggs: 3–7, white through to pale green with darker markings.
Food: Invertebrates.

Slender-billed crow (*Corvus enca*):
47cm (18.5in)
Malay Peninsula and numerous offshore islands, including Sumatra, Java, Bali, Borneo, and the Sula islands. Entirely black plumage. Relatively slim bill shape. Culmen curves quite gently and is bare of feathers at its base. Sexes alike.

Large-billed crow (*Corvus macrorhynchos*):
43-59cm (17-23in)
From Himalayan region and eastern Asia to Siberia and China, through South-east Asia to the Malay Peninsula. Present on many islands, from Sumatra, Java and Borneo north to Japan and the Philippines. Entirely black but with arched and long bill. Broad wings. Hens are slightly smaller.

Brown-headed crow (*Corvus fuscicapillus*):
45cm (18in)
Found in northern New Guinea and neighbouring islands. Has a dark brown rather than blackish head and a short, square tail. The bill is large and distinctly curved. Sexes are alike, but young birds can be distinguished by their yellowish rather than black bills.

Grey crow (Bare-faced crow, *Corvus tristis*):
45cm (18in)
Widely-distributed through New Guinea. Variable coloration depends partly on age. Adults blackish, with browner tone to underparts. Patches of bare skin around pale blue eyes. Hens usually smaller. Young birds are greyer overall, paler on the head and underparts than the wings.

Crested jay

Platylophus galericulatus

Distribution: From Thailand and the Malay Peninsula south to Sumatra, Java and Borneo.
Size: 33cm (13.5in).
Habitat: Lowland forest areas.
Nest: Platform of twigs.
Eggs: Presently unrecorded.
Food: Invertebrates.

Identification: Highly distinctive tail and reasonably broad crest. Adults vary from a shade bordering on black to reddish-brown, depending on the race. In all cases, a broad white area is evident on the side of the neck. Bill and legs are blackish. Sexes are alike. Juvenile birds display barred plumage on their underparts.

With their distinctive crest, these jays are instantly recognizable, but relatively little is known about their habits through their wide range. They are quite bold by nature and not instinctively given to flying away from people, especially when searching in the branches for food. They move their crest feathers up and down readily, and call quite loudly as well, uttering notes that have been likened to a rattle. The most distinctive of these races (*P. g. coronatus*) is found on Borneo and Sumatra. It is a reddish-brown overall, which is not dissimilar to the basic colour of young birds from other races.

Hooded racket-tailed treepie

Crypsirina cucullata

These particular treepies are thought to have become much rarer over recent years as a direct result of the deforestation of their natural habitat. These birds hunt their prey in vegetation rather than on the ground. They may sometimes be seen in small parties, but pairs will breed on their own rather than in colonies. The nest itself is often partly covered with a dome made of spiny branches, which offers increased protection against nest-raiders. Young birds can be identified for a year or so after fledging by the orange skin inside their mouths. This turns yellow during their second year and finally black. Their plumage is darker than an adult bird's.

Identification: Mainly pale grey with a narrow white band below the black head. Has black wings and central tail feathers enlarged at their tips. Other tail feathers are fawn grey. The irises are dark. Sexes alike.

Distribution: Exclusively present in Myanmar (Burma), but particularly observed in central areas.
Size: 30cm (12in).
Habitat: Lowland forest.
Nest: Cup-shaped, made from vegetation.
Eggs: 2–4, creamy to greenish white with dark markings.
Food: Invertebrates, and some berries.

BIRDS OF PARADISE AND BOWERBIRDS

The magnificent appearance of mature cock birds of these species is totally unique. There are
approximately 43 distinct species of birds of paradise and 18 recognized species of bowerbird. Their
distribution is centred on New Guinea, extending to neighbouring islands, south as far as Australia.
Hens in contrast are much duller, as are their offspring who take several years to reach adult coloration.

Golden bowerbird

Newton's bowerbird *Prionodura newtoniana*

Cock birds are quite flamboyantly coloured, with
their longer crest feathers being erected for display
purposes. They are so-called because the males
construct ornate structures called bowers, which
are used to attract would-be mates. These bowers
are carefully built from twigs and other
vegetation, and well-maintained. The golden
bowerbird may be the smallest of all
bowerbirds, but it constructs the largest
bower, up to 3m (10ft) in height. The eggs
are laid in a separate site by the hen.

Identification: Cock bird has a yellow-olive head,
with a short yellow crest. Wings are olive, with the
underparts a rich, glistening golden shade, extending to
the tail feathers. Hens have much duller coloration, with
olive-brown upperparts. Underparts are greyish, with slight
streaking on the throat and breast. Hens are also smaller in size.

Distribution: North-eastern
Queensland, Australia
Size: 25cm (10in).
Habitat: mountain rainforest
Nest: Cup-shaped, made of
vegetation.
Eggs: 2, creamy white.
Food: Fruit such as wild figs,
plus insects.

Red bird of paradise

Paradisaea rubra

Hard to spot against a forest background,
in spite of their striking appearance, these
birds of paradise are most likely to reveal
their presence by their shrill calls, which
echo through the trees. Cock birds live
in groups, separate from hens, and
will gather at specific
trees traditionally used
for display purposes.
Red birds of paradise
tend to call down
from branches
in the canopy
and their calls
are uttered
rapidly –
about once
every second.
They forage
up and down
tree trunks.

Distribution: Western
Papuan islands of Batanta,
Waigeu and Saonek.
Size: 33cm (13in).
Habitat: Dense tropical
forest.
Nest: Cup-shaped.
Eggs: 1, creamy with darker
streaks.
Food: Predominantly fruit and
also invertebrates.

Identification: Long, delicate red
feathering on the flanks. Green
plumage extends over the top of
the head. Unusual curled, ribbon-
like tail wires, which can be as
long as 59cm (23in) when
extended. Hens are less bright
but have a yellow nuchal collar.

Great bowerbird (Queensland bowerbird, *Chlamydera nuchalis*): 37.5cm (15in)
Present in northern Australia from Broome in the west of the area to the coast of Queensland. The cock has grey on the underparts, mottled upperparts and a whitish edging to the brownish plumage over the wing and rump. A striking lilac crest is apparent on the nape of the neck. Hens may lack this crest feathering and are paler with less mottling.

Arfak astrapia (black astrapia, *Astrapia nigra*): 76cm (30in)
Restricted to the Arfak mountains of Vogelkop, north-western New Guinea. Cock has a broad purplish tail, bluish-green coloration on the throat and a blackish chest area with a copper-coloured surround. Head and wings dark, with back and underparts being green. Hens are greyish-brown, with barring on their tail and underparts.

King bird of paradise (*Cicinnurus regius*): 15cm (6in)
New Guinea and nearby islands. Cock bird has red upperparts and white underparts. Very short tail, with two wires terminating in green discs. Bill yellowish. Both sexes have blue legs. Hens are mainly brownish-greyish, with barred underparts.

Wilson's bird of paradise (*Cicinnurus respublica*): 17cm (7in)
Solely confined to the Western Papuan islands of Waigeo and Batanta. Cock birds have a blue cap on the head, yellow mantle, red back and wings. The underparts are green. The short tail is black and the tail wires spiral. Hens also have a blue cap and a black area over the rest of the head, but the wings and back are greyish brown, and the underparts are heavily barred.

Magnificent riflebird

Ptiloris magnificus

The distinctive display of the cock bird involves puffing out its chest feathering and stretching out its wings. Tall trees, often covered in vines and other creepers, are favoured as display sites. The sudden explosive calls of cock birds resemble the sound of a rifle firing, although distinctive regional dialects exist in the two separate New Guinea populations. The magnificent riflebirds found in the east – in Sepik, for example – make a more guttural noise than the westerly populations. These birds are sometimes seen foraging on trees in the company of babblers and pitohuis, seeking out invertebrates that have been disturbed by their companions.

Identification: Cocks dark with short tails and a long bill, and an iridescent bluish area on the crown and breast. Females also have a long elongated bill, but are basically brown in colour, with barring on their underparts.

Distribution: Parts of New Guinea and Queensland, Australia.
Size: 37cm (14.5in).
Habitat: Forested, usually upland areas.
Nest: Deep cup-shaped nest, often built in a palm.
Eggs: 2, creamy with some darker markings.
Food: Fruit and invertebrates.

Black-billed sicklebill

Buff-tailed sicklebill *Drepanornis albertisii*

Distribution: North-west, central and east New Guinea.
Size: 35cm (14in).
Habitat: Mountain forests.
Nest: Broad cup-shape.
Eggs: 1, pinky cream with red and grey blotching.
Food: Fruit and invertebrates.

It is thought that the long, narrow curved bill of these birds probably helps them to feed. Although not rare, very little is known about the black-billed sicklebill's habits and this is partly because they usually occur in the upper branches of the tallest trees, making them hard to observe. In addition, their coloration enables them to blend into their surroundings very effectively. It is thought that they feed in a woodpecker-like fashion on tree bark, using their long bills to probe for invertebrates that might be lurking in holes in the trunk or under loose bark. Their distribution does not appear to be consistent throughout their range, even in areas of apparently identical habitat. On occasions, the powerful musical call of a cock bird may be heard.

Identification: The stunning beauty of the cock bird is most apparent during the display, when the tufted areas of feathering on the sides of the body are held erect. Hens lack these fan tufts, and are brownish with mottled plumage on the underparts and also have longer, more pointed tail feathers, which are darker in colour than those of cocks.

CASSOWARIES AND PARROTS

These birds include not just one of the largest birds of the world, in the guise of the double-wattled cassowary, but also a representative of the group of smallest parrots in the world, which are appropriately known as pygmy parrots. They represent two extremes within the avian order that can be encountered within the forest environment in the Australasian region.

Double-wattled cassowary

Casuarius casuarius

Distribution: New Guinea, apart from northern-central region and the central highlands. Also on the Aru Islands. Two separate Australian populations found in north-eastern Queensland.
Size: 130–170cm (51–67in).
Habitat: Rainforest areas.
Nest: Depression on the ground.
Eggs: 3–5, pale to dark green.
Food: Mainly fruit, some animal matter.

These gigantic birds of the forest are quite able to kill a person if cornered, disembowelling them with a blow from the long inner claw present on their feet. The colour of the bare skin on the cassowary's head and neck changes with mood, becoming more brightly coloured when the bird is excited or angry. Hens mate with a number of different cock birds, leaving the male to hatch and rear the chicks on their own. The young cassowaries stay with the male for up to nine months.

Identification: Massive, predominantly black flightless bird with immensely powerful feet. Has a large blade-like casque on the head and a powerful bill. Head tends to be bluish overall with two striking reddish wattles hanging down the neck. Hens have a larger casque and are also much heavier, weighing up to 58kg (128lb), whereas males rarely exceed 34kg (75lb).

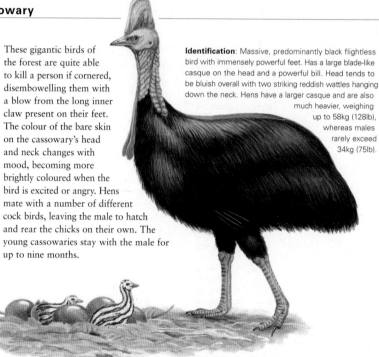

Red-breasted pygmy parrot

Mountain pygmy parrot *Micropsitta bruijnii*

As their name suggests, the pygmy parrots are the smallest of all parrots, with their distribution confined to islands off South-east Asia. This particular species is found at higher altitudes than are other pygmy parrots, and also uses trees rather than arboreal termite nests as breeding sites. They have jerky movements, rather reminiscent of nuthatches (*Sitta* species), and cling close to the bark as they search for the lichens growing on trees, which form the major part of their diet.

Identification: Has a buff-red crown, becoming bluish-purple at the back of the neck. The throat and cheeks are also buff-red and become yellowish around the bill. The remainder of the underparts are red while the back and wings are mainly dark green. Hens have a blue crown with buff orange cheeks, although these areas are a paler shade than in the cock.

Distribution: Buru, Seram and central New Guinea east to the Bismarck Archipelago and the Solomon Islands.
Size: 8cm (3in).
Habitat: Forest areas.
Nest: Tree holes.
Eggs: 3, white.
Food: Plant matter.

Edwards's fig parrot

Psittaculirostris edwardsii

These chunky parrots are very agile when feeding, being able to eat without difficulty when hanging upside down from a branch. As their name suggests, figs form an important part of their diet, and hundreds of these parrots may congregate in an area where fruit is freely available. More commonly, however, they live in pairs or small groups, and can be hard to spot in the canopy where they feed, because of their small size, even though they are not especially shy by nature.

Distribution: Restricted to north-eastern area of New Guinea.
Size: 18cm (7in).
Habitat: Lowland forest.
Nest: Tree holes.
Eggs: 2–3, white.
Food: Fruit and some invertebrates.

Identification: Cock birds have a green crown with a narrow black stripe extending behind the eye. Yellow area beneath eye, along with some sky blue feathering, while the cheeks, breast and abdomen are scarlet, broken with variable violet markings across the throat. Hens are duller in colour, with green rather than red plumage below the collar. Young birds of both sexes resemble the hen, although their ear coverts are of a more greenish-yellow shade.

Brehm's tiger parrot (*Psittacella brehmii*): 24cm (9.5in)
Three distinct populations: central highlands of New Guinea; north-east Huon Peninsula; and Vogelkop, where they live in areas of mountain forest. Cock has olive-brown head, partial yellow collar at the sides of the head, green underparts, red undertail coverts. Green feathering on the back is edged with black. Hens similar but display barring on the breast and lack any yellow plumage on the neck.

Pesquet's parrot (vulturine parrot, *Psittrichas fulgidus*): 46cm (18in)
Two distinct populations on New Guinea. One confined to the Vogelkop, the other extending through the central area towards the Huon Peninsula and the south-east. Unmistakable with bare skin on the head, predominantly black plumage with barring on the chest and brilliant scarlet red areas on the wings and underparts. Looks more like a vulture in flight than a parrot, soaring readily above the forest. Sexes alike.

Papuan king parrot (green-winged king parrot, *Alisterus chloropterus*): 38cm (15in)
Found in northern, central and south-eastern parts of New Guinea. Cocks have a red head and underparts, green wings with distinctive yellow-green barring and purple over the back, which may be darker than the wings, depending on the race. They also have a long dark tail. Hens are duller in colour, with a green head, breast and wings, except in the case of the northern race (*A. c. moszkowskii*), which resembles the cock but with a green mantle.

Timor crimson-wing parakeet (*Aprosmictus jonquillaceus*): 35cm (14in)
Ranges up to altitudes of 2,600m (8,500ft) on the Indonesian islands of Timor, Weta and Roti. Predominantly green, but with blue suffusion on the back that is absent in hens. Characteristic crimson red coloration apparent on the wing coverts. Turquoise-blue rump. Broad green tail. Bill reddish.

Eclectus parrot

Eclectus roratus

This species represents the most extreme example of sexual dimorphism among all parrots. It was thought for many years following their discovery that the cock and hen were actually two separate species. There are around ten distinct races, and it is the appearance of the hen birds that differs most markedly. The feeding habits of these parrots are such that they are often seen in agricultural areas, readily feeding on crops ranging from bananas to maize. They are dependent on mature trees as nest sites however, choosing chambers that may be up to 6m (20ft) in depth.

Identification: Thick-set, with quite short, broad tails. Mostly green, with a yellowish upper bill and a red patch on the flanks. Hens have black bills. They are bright red, typically with purplish markings on the underparts, although these markings depend on the race. You can determine a juvenile's sex in the nest, from the colour of its plumage.

Distribution: Centred on New Guinea, but extends widely, to islands to both the west and east. A small population is also present on the Cape York peninsula, Australia.
Size: 35cm (14in).
Habitat: Lowland forests, often in coastal regions. Also in mangroves.
Nest: Tree hollow.
Eggs: 2, white.
Food: Fruit, buds and seeds.

LORIKEETS AND OTHER PSITTACINES

Cockatoos, with their distinctive crest feathers that can be raised when an individual is alarmed or excited, are confined to islands off South-east Asia, extending as far as Australia. Their plumage differs significantly from that of other parrots in another, less obvious way, however, in that it lacks the so-called blue layer. As a result, cockatoos tend to be either black or white.

Papuan lorikeet

Charmosyna papou

The beautiful, active and agile lorikeets are likely to be encountered in groups in the vicinity of flowering trees. They tend to bound from branch to branch, rather than flying. Their long tongues are specially adapted, as in the case of other lories and lorikeets, with special brush-like papillae that can be raised to sweep tiny pollen granules into the mouth. The melanistic form occurs in those populations, such as Stella's lorikeet (*C. p. stellae*), that are found in the eastern part of their range. Such birds tend to be found at higher altitudes. They interbreed freely with their red-coloured cousins, and both forms can be present in the same nest.

Identification: Four different races exist, all of which have long, narrow tail streamers. Predominantly red with a violet and black area on the back of the head. Has violet-blue underparts. Green wings and tail, which is yellowish at the tip. Hens distinguished by yellow rump. Also occurs in a melanistic form, with black replacing the red plumage, except on the back and under the tail.

Left: The melanistic form of the papuan lorikeet is a naturally occuring mutation of the species.

Distribution: Confined to New Guinea, with populations in Vogelkop, central areas and down to the south-east. Also occurs in isolation on the Huon Peninsula.
Size: 42cm (16.5in) including tail plumes.
Habitat: Woodland areas from 1,500–3,500m (5,000–11,500ft.)
Nest: Tree hollow.
Eggs: 2–3, white.
Food: Mainly nectar, pollen and fruit.

Palm cockatoo

Goliath cockatoo *Probosciger aterrimus*

Distribution: Found through much of New Guinea, aside from the central region. Also present on western Papuan and neighbouring islands, and the northern tip of the Cape York peninsula of Australia.
Size: 64cm (25in).
Habitat: Forest areas, especially edges of rainforest.
Nest: Hollow tree.
Eggs: 1, white.
Food: Nuts, seeds and fruit.

The very distinctive appearance of these cockatoos sets them apart from other species. They call frequently and loudly, with their calls having been likened to the braying of a donkey, when heard from some distance away. Their powerful bills allow them to crack the thick-shelled nuts of forest trees with little difficulty. Male birds often drum with a piece of stick, using this to bang rhythmically on the side of a tree trunk during the nesting period, as part of a territorial display. Unlike other cockatoos, they also line their chosen nesting cavity with a platform of sticks. It is thought this behaviour may help to prevent either the egg or chick being lost as a result of flooding during heavy rains.

Identification: Predominantly black, with a large, distinctive, erectile crest. Bare patch of reddish facial skin. Massive, powerful bill, which is smaller in hens. Sexes are otherwise alike. Juvenile birds have a paler patch of facial skin, and the skin around their eyes is whitish.

Yellow-streaked lorikeet

Chalcopsitta sintillata

These lories are adaptable in terms of the countryside where they can be observed, seeking out the flowering trees on which they depend for their food. They may subsequently invade orchards, in search of ripening fruit, and can sometimes be spotted feeding in the company of other lorikeets. Yellow-streaked lorikeets are quite social by nature, and so they are often observed flying in small flocks, calling out noisily at the same time. Even when perched, they often reveal their presence by their calls, which sound like persistent squealing. Young birds may be harder to recognize, due to the lack of red plumage on the forehead.

Identification: Has a bright red area above the bill. The head is blackish, becoming browner on the breast with lighter streaking. Wings, back and underparts are mainly green, but have yellowish streaking on the abdomen. Thighs are red. Bill black, legs and feet are grey. Sexes alike.

Distribution: The southern part of New Guinea from Triton Bay and Geelvink Bay in the west to Port Moresby in the east. Also occurs on the Aru islands.
Size: 31cm (12.5in).
Habitat: Forested areas, including coconut plantations.
Nest: Tree holes.
Eggs: 2–3, white.
Food: Nectar, pollen and fruit.

Papuan hanging parrot (orange-fronted hanging parrot, *Loriculus aurantiifrons*): 10cm (4in)
Occurs through much of New Guinea, especially lowland areas, with the notable exception of the south-central region and small offshore islands. Predominantly green. Has a yellow crown and an orangish area on the throat. The rump is red with a yellow border. Hens lack the yellow crown. They have green heads with a bluish tinge to their cheeks and their bill is black. These parrots are so-called because of their habit of roosting upside down.

Fairy lorikeet (little red lorikeet, *Charmosyna pulchella*): 19cm (7.5in)
Found in central parts of New Guinea. Relatively small, with a mainly red head. The breast is red and streaked with a row of yellow feathers. Has a black area on the back of the head, with violet on the back and sides. The long tail is reddish on its upperparts. Hens display yellow plumage on the rump and the adjacent area of the back.

Red-cheeked parrot (Geoffroy's song parrot, *Geoffroyus geoffroyi*): 21cm (8.5in)
Found on various islands from Lombok and the Moluccas eastward via New Guinea to Rossel, which is part of the Louisiade Archipelago. Also present on Australia's Cape York peninsula. Predominantly bright green, often with a red shoulder patch. Plum-coloured head with violet crown and nape. Broad and short-tailed. Blue visible under the wings. Hens have brown heads with black bills.

Whiskered lorikeet (plum-faced lorikeet, *Oreopsittacus arfaki*): 15cm (6in)
Three separate populations in the mountainous areas of New Guinea. Predominantly green. Bright red area on the top of the head. White streaks below the eyes are on a mauve background and edged with black. Reddish underside to the tail. Hens have a green, rather than red, area on top of the head. Sexes otherwise alike.

Great-billed parrot

Tanygnathus megalorhynchos

These parrots frequently move between smaller islands, although their fractured distribution means that eight different races have been identified through their range, each varying slightly in terms of plumage. Great-billed parrots move in search of food, congregating in relatively large numbers at favoured feeding sites. They may even be encountered in mangroves. In flight their large bill and short tail means that they can be identified quite easily. Their strong bills enable them to crack nuts with ease.

Distribution: Present in the Moluccas, the western Papuan, Lesser Sunda and Tanimbar islands, as well as islands around Sulawesi. Thought to have been introduced to Balut in the Philippines.
Size: 41cm (16in).
Habitat: Forested coastal areas and foothills.
Nest: Tree hollow.
Eggs: 2–3, white.
Food: Nuts and fruit.

Identification: Massive reddish bill. Bright green head and greenish-yellow underparts. Has a bluish suffusion over the back and a black area on the shoulders. Golden edging is most apparent on the feathers on the upper part of the wing. Lower feathers are a dull green and the rump is light blue. The relatively short tail is green with a yellowish tip. Sexes are alike.

BIRDS OF PREY

Although dense stretches of woodland may not appear to represent the best hunting possibilities for birds of prey, it is remarkable how these predatory birds have adapted to this environment. This is also reflected by the way in which a number of species have become highly specialized in their hunting habits, such as the crested honey buzzard.

Blyth's hawk eagle

Spizaetus alboniger

These strong aerial hunters seize their prey in the upper levels of the forest, taking not just birds but also lizards, bats and other mammals. They are watchful hunters, like other hawk eagles, often swooping on their quarry from a favoured perch that affords good visibility of any movements in the canopy. On occasions, these eagles are mobbed by groups of smaller birds, such as drongos, seeking to drive the bigger birds away, and the resulting disturbance draws attention to the birds' presence. These hawk eagles may also be seen circling and soaring over the forest. They are quite rare through their range, occurring at low population densities.

Identification: Darkish coloration on the head and back, with a long crest at the back of the head. Throat is white. Black barring on the breast and white barring to the dark feathers on the underparts. Has a greyer, broad band on the tail. Sexes alike.

Distribution: From southern Myanmar (Burma) through the Malay Peninsula to Sumatra and small nearby islands. Also present in north Borneo.
Size: 58cm (23in).
Habitat: Upland forest areas.
Nest: Bulky nest built at the top of a tree.
Eggs: 1, whitish with darker markings.
Food: Vertebrates.

New Guinea harpy eagle

Kapul eagle *Harpyopsis novaeguineae*

These forest eagles are formidable hunters, taking a wide range of prey, including tree kangaroos and wallabies and even domestic animals such as puppies. The distinctive ruff of feathers around the face helps them trace the source of sounds, and these birds also have keen eyesight. In addition to swooping down on their quarry, these eagles run and bound over the ground for short distances using their long legs. Breeding pairs return to the same site every year, choosing a tree with no lower branches and amassing a large platform of sticks near the crown at a height of 20m (66ft).

Right: Barred markings can be seen under the wings when the bird is in flight.

Distribution: Confined to the island of New Guinea.
Size: 90cm (35in).
Habitat: Rainforest up to 3,200m (10,500ft).
Nest: Platform of sticks.
Eggs: 1, white with darker markings.
Food: Vertebrates.

Identification: Brown upperparts with darker barring across the tail, which ends in a dark tip. The breast is brown and the underparts white. Long unfeathered legs with yellow feet. Has a crest that can be raised at the back of the head, and a pronounced ruff of feathers around the face. Hens are larger, but otherwise alike.

Crested serpent eagle

Spilornis cheela

There is a considerable variation in the size of these eagles through their wide range. The largest examples occur in northern India and Nepal and the smallest individuals are found further south on the Nicobar islands, off India's coast. Their name partly derives from the snakes that are a regular feature of their diet. The crested serpent eagle is likely to be observed soaring over the forest, although when hunting it usually rests on a perch, swooping down to grab snakes or lizards from either trees or the ground. Crested serpent eagles will sometimes prey on other vertebrates, including aquatic species such as eels, and have also been observed catching crabs.

Identification: Blackish brown upperparts, but has more variable underparts that range from reddish to dark brown and broken by white markings. The bill is blackish at the tip and yellow at its base. Broad greyish bar across the tail feathers. Sexes alike.

Distribution: India and Sri Lanka eastwards to China. Across South-east Asia and the Malay Peninsula south to Sumatra, Java and Borneo.
Size: 41–75cm (16–29.5in).
Habitat: Wooded areas, but not dense forest.
Nest: Small cup-shaped with grass lining.
Eggs: 1, whitish with darker markings.
Food: Primarily reptiles.

Lesser fish eagle (*Ichthyophaga humilis*): 60cm (24in)
Extends from Kashmir through the Himalayas into Myanmar (Burma) and Hainan, then south through the Malay Peninsula to Sumatra, Borneo, Sulawesi and neighbouring islands. Cock has a greyish head and neck, with brown back, wings and tail. White underparts. Greyish hooked bill and legs. Sexes are alike.

Long-tailed buzzard (*Henicopernis longicauda*): 60cm (24in)
Found on the west Papuan islands, Aru islands and New Guinea. Light and darker brown barring on the wings and tail. The head is brown with lighter chestnut ear patches. Whitish streaking around the neck and down on to the breast. The abdomen has a buff rather than whitish tone. Hens are larger.

Little eagle (*Hieraaetus morphnoides*): 55cm (22in)
Present all over New Guinea apart from the central mountainous region, and throughout Australia apart from Tasmania. These eagles occur in both a light and a dark form. The darker morphs are a deeper shade of brown, especially on the head and underparts. Lighter individuals have whitish areas on the greater wing coverts. Hens are larger.

Doria's hawk (*Megatriorchis doriae*): 69cm (27in)
Present on New Guinea and neighbouring Batanta Island. Light brown with black barring on the upperparts. Grey tail with black banding. White underparts with dark streaking, which is most pronounced on the chest. Hens are larger.

Crested honey buzzard

Pernis ptilorhynchus

The far-north Asiatic population of the crested honey buzzard winters in the far south of the species' range on the Greater Sundas. It is possible to distinguish between these birds and the resident population, however, thanks to the former's lack of a pronounced crest. The feeding habits of these buzzards are highly distinctive, since they attack the nests of wild bees and wasps, eating not just the insects and their larvae but also the honeycomb. Although crested honey buzzards prefer to raid tree nests, they are quite able to use their strong feet to dig out nests on the ground. They also prey on other social insects such as ants and termites.

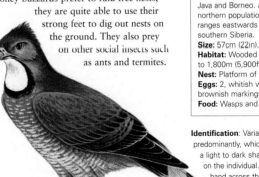

Distribution: Across India and South-east Asia, south across the Malay Peninsula to islands including Sumatra, Java and Borneo. Also a northern population, which ranges eastwards through southern Siberia.
Size: 57cm (22in).
Habitat: Wooded areas up to 1,800m (5,900ft).
Nest: Platform of twigs.
Eggs: 2, whitish with brownish markings.
Food: Wasps and bees.

Identification: Variable. Brown predominantly, which ranges from a light to dark shade depending on the individual. Broad greyish band across the tail feathers. Has white markings in the vicinity of the neck and on the underparts. Crest may be evident on the back of the neck. The bill is grey. Legs and feet are yellow. Sexes are alike.

CHATS AND OTHER INSECTIVOROUS BIRDS

All these birds, ranging from the tiny emu-wren to the pied currawong, hunt invertebrates, although they adopt very different feeding strategies. The savanna nightjar hunts on the wing and is a nocturnal hunter, whereas the fairy martin also hunts on the wing but during the hours of daylight. Others, such as the chats, prefer to look for their food on the ground.

Rufous-crowned emu-wren

Stipiturus ruficeps

Distribution: Extends from western Australia east to Queensland. Separate population in the south-east.
Size: 14.5cm (5.5in).
Habitat: Dry, treeless country.
Nest: Oval structure made from vegetation.
Eggs: 2–3, white with brownish blotching.
Food: Invertebrates, and occasionally seeds.

The habitat requirements of these birds appear to be precise as they are found in areas of spinifex and porcupine grass, especially where there are isolated shrubs. Their small size makes it difficult to track their exact distribution, particularly as they skulk in the vegetation for long periods, although they sometimes reveal their presence by high-pitched calls. If disturbed, they fly a short distance before returning to the grass. Emu-wrens get their name from their tail feathers, which are long and stiff, resembling those of emus. They are unique in having just six tail plumes, fewer than any other bird in the world.

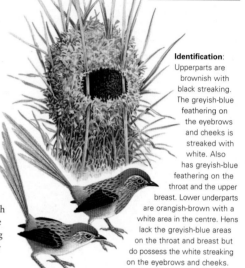

Identification: Upperparts are brownish with black streaking. The greyish-blue feathering on the eyebrows and cheeks is streaked with white. Also has greyish-blue feathering on the throat and the upper breast. Lower underparts are orangish-brown with a white area in the centre. Hens lack the greyish-blue areas on the throat and breast but do possess the white streaking on the eyebrows and cheeks.

Savanna nightjar

Allied nightjar *Caprimulgus affinis*

Nocturnal by nature as their name suggests, the persistent vocalizations of these nightjars helps to reveal their presence. They will call almost constantly for approximately half an hour, both at dusk and dawn, uttering a distinctive and repetitive cheeping sound. During the day, these nightjars rest in a relatively secure location on the ground, where their cryptic coloration helps to conceal their presence. They have also adapted well to urban living, however, and are not averse to resting out of sight on the roofs of buildings. The savanna nightjar is also drawn to hunt around electric lights, such as street lamps, as these attract night-flying invertebrates such as moths.

Identification: Short tail. Dark brown and black overall with barring on the tail and body. Has white outer tail feathers. Small bill is surrounded by bristle-like feathers. The white throat band is split into two. Hens lack the white outer tail feathers and have a more rufous-brown coloration.

Distribution: Extends eastwards from India to southern China south across South-east Asia to the Sunda islands, Sulawesi and the Philippines.
Size: 22cm (9in).
Habitat: Dry, open coastal areas.
Nest: Scrape on the ground.
Eggs: 2, buff with darker markings.
Food: Invertebrates.

Desert chat

Gibberbird *Ashbyia lovensis*

These chats are most likely to be observed on the ground, where their upright gait helps them to run fast if necessary. When flying short distances, they flutter low across the ground but they can fly strongly too, as befits a nomadic species that moves from one area to another in search of favourable conditions. The desert chat lines a scrape on the ground with vegetation to disguise its presence. It is not uncommon to see pairs together, although they are easily overlooked as they are well concealed on the ground. Occasionally, flocks of up to 20 individuals may be spotted, and often pairs choose to nest quite close together.

Identification: Brownish-black, mottled upperparts, with white tip to the black tail. Yellowish underparts, although the rump is a more orangish colour. Narrow, pointed, black bill. Dark eyes. Hens are similar but duller in appearance. Both sexes adopt an upright pose when standing.

Distribution: Southern-central parts of Australia near border areas between New South Wales, Queensland, Northern Territory and South Australia, although the precise range is not well known.
Size: 12.5cm (5in).
Habitat: Arid areas.
Nest: Scrape on the ground.
Eggs: 3, white with reddish-brown markings.
Food: Invertebrates.

Long-tailed shrike (black-capped shrike, *Lanius schach*): 25cm (10in)
Extensive range from Iraq and India east to China, and south across the Malay Peninsula to the Greater Sundas and other islands, including the Philippines and New Guinea. Has either a black and grey or black head depending on the race. Mainly white underparts, with a rufous-brown mantle, back and flanks. Wings are black with a white area. Has a long tail and black on its upperparts. Sexes are alike.

Fairy martin (cliff swallow, *Hirundo ariel*): 12.5cm (5in)
Widely distributed across Australia apart from the south-western corner and the northern part of the Cape York peninsula. Normally absent from Tasmania. Has a pale rust-red colour to the crown and whitish underparts. Wings and tail are blackish. The rump is white. Sexes alike.

Pied currawong (pied bell-magpie, *Strepera graculina*): 49cm (19in)
Occurs down the entire eastern side of mainland Australia. Predominantly black, with a long, black, powerful bill and striking yellow eyes. There are white areas on the flight feathers, as well as at the base of the tail and in the vicinity of the vent. The tip of the tail is also white. Sexes are alike.

Pied butcherbird (black-throated butcherbird, *Cracticus nigrogularis*): 37.5cm (15in)
Occurs all over Australia apart from the south-west corner and the south-east coastal region. Black head, Black areas on the wings and tail. The rest of the body is white. The sexes are alike. Young birds have brownish rather than black coloration.

Crimson chat

Ephthianura tricolor

These smallish birds are one of Australia's most nomadic species and travel across huge distances of inhospitable territory. They survive even when invertebrates are scarce. As these form the bulk of their diet, the crimson chat feeds instead on nectar gathered from desert plants. Remarkably, these plants can produce large amounts of nectar and this encourages the chat to fertilize their flowers by transferring pollen between the blooms as they feed on them. Probably correlating with flowering times, crimson chats are sometimes seen in quite large numbers where they have not occurred before, and then disappear as suddenly as they came.

Distribution: Across the interior of Australia from the west coast, although generally absent from other coastal areas.
Size: 12cm (5.5in).
Habitat: Shrubland and open country.
Nest: Cup-shaped, located just off the ground.
Eggs: 3–4, white with darker spots.
Food: Invertebrates and nectar.

Identification: Crimson cap. Has blackish-brown sides to the face that extend over the mantle and back, although the wing feathers have paler edges. The throat is white; the underparts are crimson. Hens are easily distinguished by the light brown colour of their crown, and the red patches on their white underparts.

AUSTRALIAN PARAKEETS

Although grass parakeets are smaller than rosellas, both have comparable habits, having evolved to feed primarily on the ground, searching out grass seeds and other similar titbits. Members of both groups occur widely through Australia. Rosellas are easily distinguished from parakeets of similar size by means of the scalloping on their back and wings.

Bourke's grass parakeet

Neophema bourkii

The relatively large eyes of these parakeets are an indication that they are most active at dusk and daybreak, resting when the sun is at its hottest, and have been known to fly after dark. They feed on the ground, moving on to new localities if a shortage of food or water threatens. Although these birds are usually encountered in small groups, much larger congregations, of up to a thousand birds, have been observed at larger waterholes in times of drought. Where conditions are favourable, they rear two rounds of chicks in succession: the first-round offspring disperse rather than stay near the nest site.

Identification: Has unusual coloration with brownish upperparts that often have a slightly rosy hue. The underparts are very pinkish, especially the abdomen. Has blue plumage on forehead, white around the eye and flecking on the face. Has violet-blue flight feathers and paler blue undertail coverts. Sexes are similar, although hens do not have the blue forehead-plumage.

Distribution: Interior of Australia, from Geraldton in Western Australia eastwards to South Australia. Separate population in south-west Queensland and the adjacent area of New South Wales.
Size: 20cm (8in).
Habitat: Scrubland and lightly wooded areas.
Nest: Tree hole.
Eggs: 3–6, white.
Food: Grass seeds and other vegetation.

Splendid grass parakeet

Scarlet-chested parakeet *Neophema splendida*

Distribution: Southern-central parts of Australia and western and south Australia.
Size: 22cm (9in).
Habitat: Semi-desert areas.
Nest: Hollow tree.
Eggs: 3–6, white.
Food: Grass seeds and other vegetation.

These nomadic parakeets move readily from the Great Victoria Desert region into neighbouring areas. These irruptions are triggered by a search for more favourable conditions. They can survive quite well without ready access to drinking water, however, as succulent plants help to meet much of their fluid requirement. They feed mainly on grass seeds and are most commonly sighted in areas of spinifex. Splendid grass parakeets have developed clever feeding techniques whereby they hold down seed heads with one foot and prise the seeds out with their bill.

Identification: Scarlet plumage on the breast and yellow lower under-parts distinguishes the cock bird from all other grass parakeets. The facial area is blue, becoming paler around the eyes. Crown, neck, back and wings are green, apart from blue areas on the edge of the wing. Hens are similar but duller, with a green breast and paler blue face.

Adelaide rosella

Platycercus adelaidae

Some ornithologists believe that this bird is a naturally occurring hybrid between the crimson rosella (*P. elegans*) and the yellow rosella (*P. flaveolus*). Even so, these parakeets breed true, and it is estimated that they have a population of more than 50,000. There is certainly not a significant overlap between the distributions of the two suggested ancestral species today.

Distribution: Southern Australia, being present in the Mount Lofty and southern Flinders ranges.
Size: 36cm (14in).
Habitat: Lightly wooded areas.
Nest: Tree holes.
Eggs: 4–5, white.
Food: Mainly seeds and fruit.

Identification: Variable coloration but appearing an orange-red colour overall. Often a little lighter at the top of the wings, with the scalloped patterning here both yellow and orange, depending on the individual. Wings are mauvish in the vicinity of the flight feathers and the tail. Sexes alike. Young birds are less colourful and do not acquire adult plumage until their second year.

Turquoisine grass parakeet (*Neophema pulchella*): 20cm (8in)
Found in eastern Australia, from Queensland south via eastern New South Wales into Victoria. Blue area surrounding the black bill, extending back to the eyes. Yellowish underparts, but more orange on the breast. Crown, back, wings and tail are green, apart from the red bar and the prominent areas of blue on the wings. Hens lack the red plumage on the wings and have whitish lores, which help to distinguish them from hen scarlet-chested parakeets.

Blue-winged grass parakeet (*Neophema chrysostoma*): 20cm (8in)
Often migrates across the Bass strait to breed on Tasmania, returning to overwinter on mainland Australia and can be found as far north as Queensland. Yellow area around the bill, with a dark and light band of blue above, connecting the eyes. Olive-green upperparts and chest, with yellow abdomen. Prominent areas of dark blue on the wings. Hens are less brightly coloured.

Pale-headed rosella (mealy rosella, *Platycercus adscitus*): 30cm (12in)
Found in north-eastern Australia, from the Cape York peninsula down to northern New South Wales. Yellowish plumage on the top of the head and white on the sides. Has blue cheek marking (depending on the race) and underparts. Red undertail coverts. Yellowish-white scalloping to the black feathers on the back, with blue on the wing. Sexes are alike.

Eastern rosella

Platycercus eximius

Distribution: From south-eastern Queensland, continuing southwards along the coast into the south-eastern part of South Australia. Also found on Tasmania.
Size: 33cm (13in).
Habitat: Grassland to wooded areas.
Nest: Tree hole.
Eggs: 4–9, white.
Food: Seeds and fruit.

Rosellas form part of the 'broadtail' group of parakeets, so-called because their tail feathers do not taper to a point unlike those of many other parakeets. The eastern rosella is a highly adaptable species. Small introduced populations are now established in New Zealand, where it has successfully adapted to living in pine forests. Eastern rosellas often feed on the ground and can be seen hunting for seeds on roadside verges, especially early in the morning. They then roost quietly through the warmer hours of the day. The hen incubates the eggs alone, although the cock bird may join her in the nest.

Identification: Bright red head with white cheek patches. Has yellowish-green underparts that become green towards the vent and red undertail coverts. The scalloped edging on the back varies from yellow to green, depending on the race. The rump is green. The tail feathers become bluish at their tips. The red is slightly duller in hens and the white cheek patches are not so clearly defined.

BUDGERIGARS AND OTHER AUSTRALIAN PSITTACINES

Although the budgerigar is the best-known of all Australia's psittacines, this is a large group of birds which display a considerable diversity in appearance. In Australia, the terms 'parrot' and 'parakeet' tend to be used almost interchangeably. Elsewhere, however, the description of 'parakeet' is usually applied to psittacines with long tails.

Princess of Wales' parakeet

Queen Alexandra's parakeet *Polytelis alexandrae*

Distribution: Australian interior, from the Great Sandy Desert of Western Australia east to the Northern Territory via Alice Springs and as far as the extreme west of Queensland.
Size: 46cm (18in).
Habitat: Arid country.
Nest: Tree hollow.
Eggs: 4–6, white.
Food: Mainly seeds.

Very little is known about these enigmatic parakeets, which turn up unexpectedly in a region and then disappear again for many years. It used to be thought they were truly nomadic, but recent studies suggest the centre of their distribution is in the vicinity of Lake Tobin, from where they irrupt at intervals to other parts of their range. These parakeets are opportunistic when breeding, with pairs usually choosing to nest when food is plentiful. They seek their food on the ground.

Identification: Delicate pastel shades predominate in the plumage. Pale blue is evident on the crown and a pinkish hue on the throat. Has bright green plumage across the back and a bright blue rump. Hens lack the pale blue crown and their back is duller in tone.

Barraband parakeet

Superb parrot *Polytelis swainsonii*

There is some seasonal movement of these parakeets as they often move further north at the approach of winter. During the breeding season, small flocks of male barraband parakeets often forage for food alone. Pairs may nest in a loose colonial system of as many as six pairs, so hens are in the neighbourhood at this time. Barraband parakeets are quite opportunistic when seeking food, and they are not averse to feeding in agricultural areas, often descending into fields to pick up any seeds remaining after the harvest. These birds generally prefer feeding on the ground, although they will forage in the trees as well.

Identification: Stunning yellow face, with a red band separating it from the breast. The remainder of the plumage is bright green apart from the tip of the tail and the flight feathers which are a bluish-black. The bill is red. Hens lack the bright yellow facial colouring and instead have a blue tinge to their green facial plumage and at the bend of the wing.

Distribution: Mainly confined to the Australian state of New South Wales, but also found to the south just across the border in northern Victoria.
Size: 42cm (16.5in).
Habitat: Open woodland.
Nest: Suitable hole in a tree.
Eggs: 4–6, white.
Food: Seeds, fruit and vegetation.

Cockatiel

Nymphicus hollandicus

Distribution: Occurs over most of Australia, although generally not in coastal areas, and absent from central-southern parts. Not present on Tasmania.
Size: 30cm (12in).
Habitat: Mainly arid areas.
Nest: Tree hollow.
Eggs: 4–7, white.
Food: Seeds and fruit.

These elegant relatives of the cockatoo live in flocks and are relatively nomadic by nature. Their whistling calls are much quieter than the cockatoos', and cock birds vocalize more than hens. Large flocks, hundreds of birds in size, may be seen in agricultural areas. Cockatiels often prefer to feed on the ground, with some flock members acting as sentinels, warning of the approach of possible danger. Once alerted, the whole flock will wheel away, so it can be quite difficult to approach these cockatiels closely.

Identification: Grey overall with white areas on the wings. Crest feathers are yellow with yellow sides to the face and orange ear coverts. Dark grey tail. Hens are duller. They have a greyish-yellow colour on the head. Their tails are barred on the underside with yellow and this also occurs on the underside of the wings in flight.

Regent parakeet (rock pebbler, *Polytelis anthopeplus*): 41cm (16in)
There are two widely separated populations on Australia: one is found in the south-west of Western Australia, while the other extends east across the South Australian border. Yellowish with a green mantle and reddish area on the wing. Bluish-black flight feathers and tail. Hens are greener, with a greyer tone to their underparts.

Port Lincoln parakeet (*Barnardius zonarius*): 44cm (17in)
Ranges from western to central parts of Australia, mainly across the southern part of the continent. Has a blackish head, dark blue cheek patches and a yellow collar around the neck. The remainder of the body is mainly green, with a yellower abdomen, depending on the race. There may be a red frontal band. Hens are duller in colour.

Blue bonnet (*Northiella haematogaster*): 30cm (12in)
There are four distinct populations present in the southern half of Australia and these range from the western side of the continent to Queensland. Has a prominent dark blue area on the face. The rest of the plumage has greyish tones, apart from the abdomen which is pale yellow with reddish markings. Undertail coverts may be red, depending on race. Blue area on the sides of the wings. Hens are less blue on the face.

Budgerigar

Melopsittacus undulatus

Distribution: Ranges over most of Australia, apart from coastal areas. Not present on Tasmania.
Size: 18cm (7in).
Habitat: Arid country.
Nest: Tree holes.
Eggs: 4–8, white.
Food: Mainly grass seeds.

Wild budgerigars are much smaller, more streamlined birds than their domesticated cousins, with the garish, domestic colour variants virtually unknown in wild flocks. When flocks are harried by a bird of prey, the budgerigars fly in tight formation, making it hard for the would-be predator to target an individual unless there is a straggler. Budgerigars are vulnerable to water shortages and so in times of drought, their numbers may plummet, although thanks to their free-breeding nature, their population recovers quickly when conditions are more favourable.

Identification: Facial area is mainly yellow with some spots evident. The underparts are light green. Black and yellow barring extends down over the back and there is scalloping over the wings. Tail feathers are bluish-green. Uniquely among psittacines, the budgerigar can be sexed by the colour of its cere, which is blue in cocks and brownish in hens.

AUSTRALIAN PARROTS AND PARAKEETS

*Some of the most unusual parrots in the world are found in Australia and New Zealand, such as
the ground parrot, which has evolved in the relative absence of predators. In part, the diversity in
appearance and lifestyles reflects the harsh environments in which the birds occur, ranging from
the searing heat of the Australian desert to the mountainous areas of New Zealand.*

Golden-shouldered parakeet

Psephotus chrysopterygius (E)

These beautiful parakeets have a very restricted range, and the entire
wild population is made up of no more than around 500 birds.
Habitat changes have contributed to their decline, as changes in
the grazing patterns of sheep have restricted the availability of
grass seeds which form the basis of their diet. Unusually, the
golden-shouldered parakeets nest in termite mounds, rather
than adopting tree holes like most parrots. They prefer
conical-shaped mounds, excavating an entrance
which leads via a tunnel to a rounded chamber,
around 25cm (10in) in diameter.

Identification: Yellow band on the
forehead, with a black cap behind,
extending down the back of the head.
Greyish mantle and wings. Has an
extensive golden yellow area at the
shoulder. Sides of the face are bluish-
green. The abdomen is orangish-red
on a pale yellow background. Hens are
mainly yellowish-green, with reddish
markings on the abdomen.

Distribution: Four distinct
populations are present on
the Cape York peninsula in
northern Queensland, north-
east Australia.
Size: 27cm (11in).
Habitat: Lightly wooded
grassland areas.
Nest: Terrestrial termite
mounds, hence occasionally
known as the ant bed parrot.
Eggs: 5–7, white.
Food: Grass seeds.

Night parrot

Geopsittacus occidentalis (E)

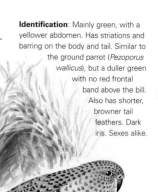

Distribution: Arid central
area of Australia. Absent from
coastal regions.
Size: 25cm (10in).
Habitat: Arid scrubland near
lakes.
Nest: Tunnel lined with sticks
within a tussock of spinifex
grass.
Eggs: 4–5, white.
Food: Spinifex grass seeds
and other vegetation.

These parrots are very hard to observe, thanks to their
cryptic coloration, nomadic nature and nocturnal habits.
There were suggestions that they had become extinct,
but during the 1990s, sightings to the south
of Cloncurry confirmed their continued
survival. Night parrots are most likely
to be encountered among patches
of marsh samphire in dried-up
lake areas, and in spinifex grass,
where they construct a tunnel
lined with sticks as a nest site.
As their name suggests, night
parrots are active after dark
when the desert cools down.
These birds have few natural
predators, but their numbers
may have suffered because of
introduced mammals such
as cats and foxes.

Identification: Mainly green, with a
yellower abdomen. Has striations and
barring on the body and tail. Similar to
the ground parrot (*Pezoporus
wallicus*), but a duller green
with no red frontal
band above the bill.
Also has shorter,
browner tail
feathers. Dark
iris. Sexes alike.

Sulphur-crested cockatoo

Cacatua galerita

These raucous cockatoos can often be heard screeching from some distance away as they fly overhead, particularly in the early morning and then again towards dusk. They are highly adaptable and found in a wide range of terrain. They are not even averse to attacking agricultural crops, particularly as these are ripening. A close approach is difficult, especially in areas where they are persecuted. Several of the flock members watch for danger while their companions feed, emitting a harsh alarm call as warning which results in the entire party flying off. Pairs may often rest in trees during the heat of the day, and this is when they preen each other.

Identification: Large white body. Has prominent yellow crest feathers which can be erected if the bird is excited or alarmed. Tail is relatively short. Some yellowish suffusion under the wings. Powerful black bill. Greyish-black legs. Has a white eye ring, but this is pale blue in some races. Iris is black in cock birds and appears reddish-brown in a good light in hens.

Distribution: From the eastern Moluccas, through much of New Guinea (apart from the central region), and offshore islands south to northern and eastern Australia, the south-eastern corner, and Tasmania. Introduced to New Zealand.
Size: 51cm (20in).
Habitat: Open country to woodland.
Nest: Tree hollow.
Eggs: 2, white.
Food: Seeds, nuts and fruit.

Kea (mountain parrot) (*Nestor notabilis*): 46cm (18in)
Occurs in mountainous areas of North Island, New Zealand – frequently above the treeline. Predominantly olive brown, with darker edges to the individual feathers and a reddish-brown rump. Dark band on the tail. Elongated black upper bill. Hens are smaller. Young birds have yellow not black ceres. Keas have been heavily persecuted in the past for scavenging on sheep carcasses, giving these birds an unjustified reputation as sheep killers.

Galah cockatoo (roseate cockatoo, *Eolophus roseicapillus*): 38cm (15in)
One of the most common and widely distributed cockatoos, occurring over virtually the whole of Australia. Less common on Tasmania, and are scarce in the Western Desert area. Has grey upperparts with rose-pink underparts and a compact, pinkish-white crest. Some variation in depth of coloration may be apparent, and on rare occasions, galah cockatoos with white rather then grey upperparts have been recorded in flocks. Hens have a reddish-brown iris.

Long-billed corella (*Cacatua tenuirostris*): 41cm (16in)
Found in south-eastern Australia, in the Murray-Darling area. Predominantly white in colour, with pronounced pinkish suffusion in the vicinity of the eyes and on the upper breast. Blue skin around the eyes. Has a distinctive long upper bill which is often used for digging up roots. A yellowish hue can be seen on the underside of the wings and tail in flight. Has a short, broad white crest. Sexes are alike.

Ground parrot

Swamp parrot *Pezoporus wallicus*

As their name suggests, ground parrots are largely terrestrial in their habits, but they can fly in a zig-zag pattern after being flushed, and then dip back down into cover. Their presence is most likely to be revealed by their whistling calls. These are typically uttered just before sunrise and at sunset, although they may be heard during the day. Cocks croak rather like frogs near the nest, and this is well concealed with a tunnel-like entrance on the ground. Their distribution in heathland areas will suffer when the ground is swept by fire. Once the diversity of vegetation has been restored, it is likely to take four years until pairs start breeding successfully again.

Identification: Similar to, but more brightly coloured than the night parrot (*Geopsittacus occidentalis*). Distinctive wingbar and a long, tapering tail which can measure up to 20cm (8in) overall. Red frontal band present in adult birds. Sexes alike.

Distribution: Narrow coastal strips in eastern, south-eastern and south-western Australia. Also present on Tasmania.
Size: 33cm (13.5in).
Habitat: Heathland and sedge.
Nest: Cup of vegetation on the ground.
Eggs: 2–6, white.
Food: Seeds and some invertebrates.

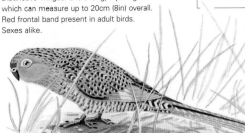

PIGEONS AND DOVES

This group of birds are highly adaptable, as reflected by their reproductive habits. They breed quickly under favourable conditions, often nesting repeatedly in suitable surroundings. This in turn means that they can survive well in fairly inhospitable conditions, such as Australia's arid interior, taking advantage of the unpredictable rains that trigger a resurgence in the plant life.

Diamond dove

Geopelia cuneata

Distribution: Most of Australia, apart from southern and eastern coastal regions.
Size: 20cm (8in).
Habitat: Lightly wooded areas and grassland. Commonly encountered in the outback.
Nest: Loose platform of twigs and vegetation.
Eggs: 2, white.
Food: Mainly small seeds.

These doves live in small parties and usually tolerate quite a close approach, even when walking on the ground. They spend long periods here, seeking seeds and other edible items. When displaying, the cock bird bows in front of the hen and fans his long tail feathers, cooing loudly. The eye ring of the cock becomes more prominent during the breeding season. Pairs tend to be opportunistic breeders, and nest whenever conditions are favourable. In common with many members of this family, incubation duties are shared, with the cock bird sitting for much of the day. The chicks grow rapidly and leave the nest as young as 12 days old, even before they are able to fly well. Diamond doves have been known to spread occasionally outside the usual area of distribution.

Identification: Predominantly greyish brown, with white spots dotted irregularly over the wings. Has chestnut flight feathers. White underside to the tail. Prominent crimson eye ring, especially in cocks during the breeding season. Otherwise sexes alike. Young birds are brownish and lack the white spotting.

Left: The diamond dove's eye ring is a distinctive characteristic.

Crested pigeon

Ocyphaps lophotes

These large pigeons are usually seen in flocks, which may consist of more than 100 individuals, frequently foraging for food on the ground. They have benefited from the spread of agriculture in Australia, not simply because of the increase in crops but also the provision of waterholes for livestock on ranches in more remote areas. Crested pigeons are very adaptable, able to forage for native seeds or cereals and other crops. If disturbed, these pigeons fly up to a nearby tree, often jerking their tails vertically when they land on a branch. They often seek out the protection of a thorn bush or similar shrub when nesting, particularly in the more treeless parts of their range. The colourful areas on the wing form part of the cock bird's display.

Identification: Prominent narrow crest on the top of the head. The underparts are pinkish-grey. The back and wings are brownish and show black barring. Purplish areas are evident towards the rear of the wing. Sexes are similar.

Distribution: Australia, apart from north of the Northern Territory, Cape York peninsula, and the south-east region.
Size: 33cm (13in).
Habitat: Lightly wooded and open areas of country.
Nest: Platform of twigs in a bush.
Eggs: 2, white.
Food: Seeds, other plant matter and invertebrates.

Flock pigeon (harlequin bronzewing, *Phaps histrionica*): 30cm (12in)
Found in northern parts of Australia away from the coastal zone. Highly nomadic by nature. Chestnut mantle, wings, back, tail and lower abdomen. The head is black with a white forehead and a C-shaped marking extending to the cheek from the eye. Also has a white patch on the upper chest and breast. The upper abdomen is greyish. Hen is dark brown. The grey on the throat is surrounded by a white area extending up above the bill. Has greyer underparts.

Squatter pigeon (*Geophaps scripta*): 28cm (11in)
Present in eastern Australia where it ranges north as far as the central area of the Cape York peninsula and south as far as north-eastern New South Wales. Predominantly brown on the upper chest, back and wings with white breast and flanks. Has black and white patterning on the sides of the face. The skin around the eye is red in northern populations. Sexes are alike.

Partridge pigeon (*Geophaps smithii*): 27cm (10.5in)
Found in northern Western Australia, with a separate population in the tip of the Northern Territory. Also present on Melville Island. Mainly brown with a white area extending from the shoulder region and down the sides of the flanks. Some slight barring across the upper breast. Bare area of reddish or orange orbital skin with white area below, bordered by black. Sexes are alike.

Red turtle dove

Red collared dove
Streptopelia tranquebarica

These doves are usually spotted in pairs but may also be seen feeding in the company of other related birds such as the laughing dove (*S. senegalensis*) in the east of their range. They tend to feed on the ground, and are especially numerous in agricultural areas where cereals are cultivated.
Red turtle doves are not sedentary throughout their range, however, and leave the northerly parts of their range such as Taiwan during the winter months to head further south. Breeding in warmer climates can take place at any stage during the year, although the fragile nature of this dove's nest – a platform of twigs – means that it may sometimes collapse, resulting in the loss of both eggs and chicks.

Identification: Greyish head, becoming darker on the crown, with a prominent black collar across the back of the neck. Underparts are vinous-pink. Wings are brick red. Flight feathers are black and the tail is grey. Hens are brown and more buff-coloured than pink on the underparts. They also have a black collar.

Distribution: Extends across the Indian subcontinent east as far as China and offshore islands, including the Philippines, and south across South-east Asia. Has recently occurred on Java.
Size: 23cm (9in).
Habitat: Open countryside.
Nest: Platform of twigs.
Eggs: 2, whitish.
Food: Seeds.

Distribution: Three distinct populations in northern Australia. Chestnut-bellied form occur in north-west; the white-bellied form in northern-central region and southern part of Cape York peninsula.
Size: 20cm (8in).
Habitat: Arid areas, where spinifex grass predominates.
Nest: Scrape concealed on the ground.
Eggs: 2, whitish.
Food: Seeds, some invertebrates.

Spinifex pigeon

Plumed rock pigeon *Geophaps plumifera*

Despite inhabiting the arid interior of the Australian continent, these pigeons rarely stray far from water. They favour areas where there are rocky outcrops, often breeding in this terrain and concealing their nest close to a rock. Spinifex pigeons spend much of their time on the ground, where they are encountered much of the time in groups. When they do take to the wing, they fly with their long crest lying back over the neck. If not directly threatened, these pigeons often prefer to run off and only fly away as a last resort. When displaying, cocks will bow and spread their tail feathers in front of a hen. This behaviour is also used as a threatening gesture to other males.

Identification: Rich chestnut, with black barring on the wings and neck area. Long narrow crest on top of the head. Greyish forehead and grey on sides of the face. White area under the throat. Bare reddish skin around the eyes is bordered by black. Whitish area on the belly, depending on the race. Hens may have shorter crests.

EMUS, MALLEE FOWL AND FINCHES

Birds have evolved a number of different breeding strategies, but surely one of the strangest is that of the mallee fowl, whose eggs are hatched entirely by artificial means. This is in distinct contrast to the breeding cycle of the emu, which results in the cock bird remaining constantly with the eggs until they hatch weeks later, often going without food and water for much of this time.

Emu

Dromaius novaehollandiae

These flightless birds are well-adapted for running to escape danger and are capable of sprinting at speeds equivalent to 48kph (30mph) over short distances. They usually walk with little effort at a speed of about 7kph (4mph) and are able to cover more than 2.7m (9ft) in a single stride. When resting, emus lie down on their haunches in the open. They cool themselves by holding out their rudimentary wings, so that heat can be dissipated from the veins flowing close to the skin. After hatching their eggs, the cock rears the chicks on his own, although the group remains together for at least eight months.

Distribution: Most of Australia, apart from desert areas in the interior and some parts of the south-east. Not present on Tasmania.
Size: 190cm (75in).
Habitat: Plains and open woodland areas.
Nest: Scrape on the ground.
Eggs: 5–24, dark green, almost blackish.
Food: Omnivorous.

Identification: Very large. Brownish and shaggy-feathered with long legs and three toes on each foot. Black feathering on the face and down the back of the neck. The sides of the neck are bluish in colour. Has a black bill and reddish eyes. Hens are heavier, weighing up to 55kg (121lb) with deep blue coloration on the face and black feathering on the throat. Young birds have prominently brown-and-white striped backs.

Mallee fowl

Leipoa ocellata

Distribution: Australia. Western coast up to Northern Territory and east to New South Wales.
Size: 60cm (24in).
Habitat: Mallee and other scrubland.
Nest: Mound.
Eggs: 16–33, pinkish.
Food: Omnivorous.

The condition of the soil is very important to mallee fowl, which favour areas of sandy soil that they can excavate easily. Pairs construct a natural incubator for their eggs, in the shape of a massive mound up to 1m (3ft) high and 5m (16ft) in diameter. A hole is dug which is filled with vegetation and left over the winter before being covered with sand. The female then lays her eggs and buries them in the mound where the heat from the decomposing vegetation keeps them warm, at 33°C (91°F). The cock adjusts the temperature by moving the sand. Seven weeks later, the newly hatched chicks dig themselves out.

Identification: Head and neck greyish, with an inconspicuous black crest. Has barred wings, and a blackish line runs down the centre of the breast. Heavily-barred upper-parts, with brown, black, grey and white markings. Sexes similar but cocks have a booming call and hens crow.

Right: Chicks emerging from the incubation mound.

Zebra finch

Poephila guttata

Living in flocks, these noisy finches are a common sight. Their calls are likened to the sound of toy trumpets. They often perch in the open, on fences, and can be spotted on the ground alongside roads, hopping along and searching for grass seeds. If necessary, they can fly with some agility, catching insects on the wing. Their nest is relatively large and untidy, with extra material often added through the incubation period. Pairs tend to breed repeatedly when conditions are favourable. The nest itself is sited in a variety of localities, ranging from inside the eaves of agricultural buildings to hollow trees.

Identification: Light grey head. Prominent chestnut-orange ear coverts, with a black stripe in front. Has fine zebra-like barring on the chest. The underparts are white and white-spotted chestnut areas extend down the flanks. The back is brownish. The tail is black and white. Hens are much duller, with a brownish-grey head and chest and creamy underparts. Bill is paler than that of the cock and they lack orange ear coverts.

Distribution: Lesser Sunda Islands of Indonesia and most of Australia apart from the far north and the east coast.
Size: 10cm (4in).
Habitat: Scrub, plains, open woodland.
Nest: Made of vegetation.
Eggs: 3–7, pale blue.
Food: Grass seeds and some invertebrates.

Painted firetail (painted finch, *Emblema picta*): 11cm (4.5in) Extends from western and central parts of Australia to western Queensland. Red face, back, rump and belly. The head, mantle, wings and tip of the tail are brown. Has a black area on the breast and flanks which is broken by white spots. Hens have virtually no red feathering on the underparts and feature a greatly reduced red area on the face.

Star finch (*Neochmia ruficauda*): 10cm (4in) Widely distributed across northern parts of Australia but is more localized around the Cape York peninsula. Bright red plumage on the sides of the face extends to just behind the eye and down around the throat and is broken by fine white speckling. The breast and flanks are greyish with larger spots. The underparts are whitish. The back and wings are olive-green and the tail is reddish. Hens have a much more restricted area of red on the face, from the bill to the eyes, and are a duller shade overall.

Chestnut-breasted mannikin (chestnut-breasted munia, *Lonchura castaneothorax*): 10cm (4in) Present on New Guinea and northern and eastern Australia. Also found on some Pacific islands. Has a prominent chestnut area on the breast, with a black border beneath. Underparts are mainly white and there is black barring on the flanks. Undertail coverts are black. There are black areas with paler streaking on the sides of the face, with grey above, and these extend down to the nape. Brown mantle and wings. Golden-yellow rump and tail. Sexes are alike but the hen may be slightly duller in colour.

Spicebird (spotted munia, scaly-breasted munia, *Lonchura punctulata*): 10cm (4in) Extends from the Indian subcontinent east to China, through South-east Asia and the Malay Peninsula to the Greater Sundas, Sulawesi and other islands. Introduced in some areas. Head and upperparts are rich brown, with black or dark brown crescent-shaped patterning on the white of the underparts. Spotted rump and yellowish tail. Sexes are alike.

Gouldian finch

Chloebia gouldiae

The gouldian ranks as one of the most stunningly-coloured finches in the world. Unfortunately, its numbers are in a severe decline. This appears to be at least in part due to a tiny parasite which spreads to nestlings via their parents and invades their airways. This leads to severe breathing difficulty and, frequently, premature death. The head coloration of this finch naturally varies – most often it is black or deep red, while, less commonly, it is an orangish yellow. These are not separate subspecies, but rather they are naturally occurring colour variants within a flock due to free interbreeding among these colourful birds.

Identification: The colour of the head is variable but the rest of the finch's body is consistent in colour. Has a bright blue collar around the head. Mantle and wings are green. Has a purple area on the breast. The underparts are yellow and the rump is blue. Pointed tail. Hens are duller with a shorter tail.

Distribution: Northern parts of Australia.
Size: 13.5cm (5in).
Habitat: Grassy plains with some trees.
Nest: Ball-like, often located in a hollow tree.
Eggs: 4–8, white.
Food: Mainly grass seeds and some invertebrates.

BIRDS OF PREY

Keen vision, fast flight and agility allow many birds of prey to hunt effectively, but those that feed primarily on carrion, in the form of dead animals, require a different strategy, as exemplified by vultures. While acute vision is also vital for them, they need to stay airborne with minimum effort, covering large distances while searching for the carcass of a large herbivore on the ground below.

Little falcon

Australian hobby *Falco longipennis*

These small, adaptable falcons may be seen flying during the day, and through into the night, particularly where there are artificial lights which attract insects, moths and similar invertebrates after dark. They catch their prey in flight, and are agile enough to take fast-flying quarry such as swallows. Farmers often welcome their presence because they feed on sparrows. Little falcons will build their nest in a tree, although other less conventional sites such as electricity poles may sometimes be used, especially in areas where alternatives are not readily available. After nesting, hens, especially, migrate north, leaving Australia for the winter. Populations elsewhere, in the Lesser Sundas for example, are sedentary.

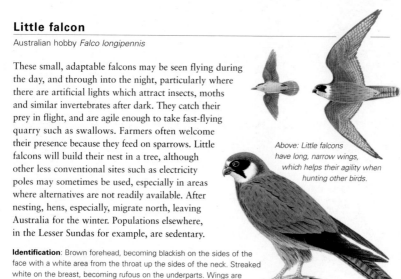

Above: Little falcons have long, narrow wings, which helps their agility when hunting other birds.

Identification: Brown forehead, becoming blackish on the sides of the face with a white area from the throat up the sides of the neck. Streaked white on the breast, becoming rufous on the underparts. Wings are slate-grey with lighter edging. Barred tail has a white tip. Hens larger.

Distribution: Australia including Tasmania, ranging to New Guinea, New Britain and the Moluccas outside the breeding period. Also occurs on the Lesser Sundas.
Size: 35cm (14in).
Habitat: Open and wooded areas.
Nest: Platform made of sticks.
Eggs: 2–4, white with reddish-brown markings.
Food: Small birds, bats and invertebrates.

Grey-faced buzzard

Frog hawk *Butastur indicus*

These buzzards are frequently seen in areas close to water, where they hunt amphibians, which form a significant part of their diet. The grey-faced buzzard seeks a good vantage point and then uses its keen eyesight to pinpoint its prey before swooping down to seize it. These birds come together to form massive flocks, which may number thousands of birds when on migration. The migration routes may stretch along the Pacific coastline of Japan to the Philippines, with a separate route via Korea on the Asiatic mainland.

When migrating in such numbers, grey-faced buzzards are vulnerable to being shot by hunters, and certainly in some areas, they are declining in numbers because of this threat.

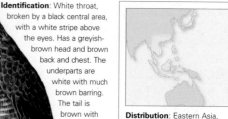

Identification: White throat, broken by a black central area, with a white stripe above the eyes. Has a greyish-brown head and brown back and chest. The underparts are white with much brown barring. The tail is brown with black barring. Has long wings. Yellow legs and feet. Young birds less colourful. Sexes alike.

Distribution: Eastern Asia, Japan and the Philippines. Widely distributed through South-east Asia, down across the Malay Peninsula to the Greater Sundas, Sulawesi and neighbouring islands.
Size: 46cm (18in).
Habitat: Open country with nearby wooded areas.
Nest: Small platform of twigs in a tree.
Eggs: 2–4, white.
Food: Frogs, reptiles and rodents.

Himalayan griffon vulture

Gyps himalayensis

These massive vultures glide almost effortlessly over long distances, relying primarily on their keen eyesight to locate the carcasses of large herbivores and other creatures on the ground. The size of this vulture means that it can drive off other smaller relatives at feeding sites, with the exception of the more assertive Eurasian black vulture (*Aegypius monachus*). Large numbers are drawn to a suitable feeding site, where they rip the flesh off the carcass quickly and efficiently using their powerful hooked bills. Their largely bald heads mean they can feed without their plumage becoming matted with blood.

Identification: Variable, whitish-buff. Bare purplish-pink skin at the base of the neck. Greyish face. Wings and tail dark brown. Sexes alike. Young birds are darker in colour than adults.

Distribution: Himalayan region, from Pakistan to western and central parts of China.
Size: 115–150cm (45–59in).
Habitat: Mountainous regions, from 900–5,000m (3,000–16,500ft).
Nest: Sticks on cliff-face.
Eggs: 1, white with traces of red markings.
Food: Carrion.

Black falcon (*Falco subniger*):
56cm (22in)
Found in central and eastern Australia. Black with light edging on back and wing feathers and a white tip to the tail. Black bill and cere. Looks broad-winged in flight. Hens are larger.

Spotted harrier (*Circus assimilis*):
61cm (24in)
Present on Sulawesi, the Sula Islands, and mainland Australia. Has white spotting on the underparts and pale grey markings over the wings. Chestnut face, with greyish collar. The tail is barred. Hens are larger.

Black-breasted kite (black-breasted buzzard, *Hamirostra melanosternon*):
61cm (24in)
Found in northern and western areas of Australia. Blackish crown, face, breast and back. Chestnut-orange plumage on the back of the head and neck and on the underparts. White areas on the wings. Dark tail. Powerful, greyish bill with dark tip. Hens are larger.

Long-billed vulture (*Gyps indicus*):
80-100cm (32-39in)
Ranges from south-eastern Pakistan and all India (apart from the extreme south) into Indo-China and the northern Malay Peninsula. Has a bare greyish head with white plumage at the base of the neck. The wings are brown, but become blackish on the flight feathers and tail. Underparts are buff-brown. The bill is more slender than in related species. Sexes are alike.

Swamp harrier

Western marsh-harrier *Circus aeruginosus*

Unlike many birds of prey, this harrier is a truly opportunistic hunter. It raids the nests of other birds, as well as catching the birds themselves, and also hunts mammals, such as rabbits, by swooping on them in the open. Its food varies, partly depending on its range, and may change throughout the year. During the winter, even the carcasses of dead whales washed ashore in coastal areas may feature in its diet. In Asia, these birds tend to migrate southwards at this time of year. Pairs regularly return to the same nest site in the following spring.

Identification: Plumage varies according to the race. Head is brownish with white streaks. Darker streaking on a buff chest. The abdomen is entirely brown. Wings are brown with rufous edging to the feathers. White and grey areas are also apparent. Tail is pale greyish. Hens are larger, with a yellowish-cream suffusion on the head, throat and shoulder. Young birds resemble hens but have darker shoulder markings.

Distribution: Extensive, being found in Africa and Europe as well as western Asia, where one population is centred across the entire Indian subcontinent and Sri Lanka. Further north, the species extends from Asia Minor eastwards to Mongolia.
Size: 48–56 cm (19–22in).
Habitat: Marshland and nearby open country.
Nest: Pile of reeds in a secluded reedbed.
Eggs: 2–7, pale bluish-white.
Food: Birds, plus other small vertebrates.

NECTAR-FEEDERS AND SEED-EATERS

*Within the parrot family, some members of the group feed mainly on seeds, whereas others such as the
lorikeets rely on their specially adapted tongues to feed on nectar. Small birds, notably sunbirds, also feed
on nectar, but use their long, narrow bills to reach it. While this restricts their distribution largely to the
tropics, other species such as pigeons and doves have more adaptable feeding habits.*

Crimson rosella

Pennant's parakeet *Platycercus elegans*

Inhabiting a variety of localities, these
colourful parakeets can become really
quite tame. Although they prefer to feed
on the ground, they will take food such
as seed placed on bird tables readily and
visit gardens on a regular basis. Their presence there
is not always welcomed, however, as they may also
strip off branches and eat blossoms, attacking fruit
crops as well on occasion. The immature plumage
is surprisingly variable, with birds from northern
areas tending to have more red plumage than
those in southern populations, which are
mainly green on fledging. It takes the
crimson rosella up to 15 months
to attain its adult plumage.

Identification: Crimson
head and underparts. Has
black scalloped patterning
over the wings. Prominent
blue cheek patches. Has blue
on the edge of the wings as well
as on the tail. Sexes alike. Young
birds are often predominantly
green on fledging.

Distribution: Two distinct
populations in coastal parts
of eastern and south-eastern
Australia. Introduced to New
Zealand.
Size: 37cm (15in).
Habitat: Woodland,
agricultural areas and gardens.
Nest: Tree hollow.
Eggs: 5–8, white.
Food: Seeds and other plant
matter.

Rainbow lorikeet

Trichoglossus haematodus

There is considerable diversity in the appearance of these
lorikeets, and approximately 21 different races have been
identified over the islands where they occur. The variation is
mainly in the colour of the neck and breast plumage, giving
rise to local names such as the green-naped lorikeet (*T. h.
haematodus*). Rainbow lorikeets are conspicuous, noisy
birds with bold natures. In some parts of eastern Australia,
wild flocks regularly visit campsites, where they are a major
tourist attraction, feeding on trays of sponge cake soaked in
honey water held up for them by visitors.
They are more active during the early
morning and late afternoon and
tend to roost quietly when
the sun is at its hottest.

*Above: The tip of the rainbow
lorikeet's tongue is covered with
tiny papillae, which effectively
sweep up the pollen grain as it
feeds on flowers.*

Identification: Dark bluish head
and green back and wings. Often
has barring on the underparts.
Breast is yellow to red, with a
variable amount of scalloping.
Collar varies from green through
yellow to red, depending on the
individual. Sexes are alike.

Distribution: Islands from
Bali eastwards through the
Moluccas and New Guinea
to the Solomon Islands and
New Caledonia. Occurs in
Australia south from the Cape
York Peninsula along the east,
south-east and south coasts
to the Eyre Peninsula. They
also move between islands.
Size: 26cm (10in).
Habitat: Woodland, farmland
and gardens.
Nest: Tree hollow.
Eggs: 2–3, white.
Food: Nectar, pollen, fruit and
some seeds.

Spotted turtle dove (*Streptopelia chinensis*):
31cm (12¹/₂in)
Wide distribution from eastern Afghanistan across southern parts of Asia to China and offshore islands. South through the Malay Peninsula to the Sundas and the Philippines. Introduced to numerous areas, including parts of Australia and New Zealand. Has a distinctive black neck patch that is spotted with white markings. Greyish head. Has pinkish-buff underparts. The wings, back and tail are a brownish shade, often with darker markings apparent. Sexes alike.

Bar-shouldered dove (*Geopelia humeralis*):
29cm (11¹/₂in)
Northern and eastern parts of Australia and southern New Guinea. Has a copper-coloured patch on the neck and black barring over much of the brown upperparts. The forehead and sides of the face, as well as the breast, are greyish. The underparts are predominantly pink-buff. Sexes alike.

Black-capped white-eye (*Zosterops atricapilla*):
11cm (4¹/₂in)
Extends through the Malay Peninsula to Sumatra and Borneo. Has distinctive blackish feathering on the front and sides of the face and a white eye ring. The upperparts are olive green. The underparts are yellowish with grey flanks. The tail is also dark. Sexes alike.

Purple-throated sunbird (*Nectarinia sperata*):
14cm (5¹/₂in)
Extends from eastern Pakistan, mainly through coastal parts of South-east Asia, east to the Philippines then south to the Sunda islands and Sulawesi. Cocks may appear almost entirely black but have a purplish throat with crimson on the belly and upper abdomen. Hens have a characteristic greenish-yellow belly and undertail coverts, with dark olive upperparts and a black tail.

Oriental white-eye

Zosterops palpebrosa

The relatively narrow yet stocky and slightly curved bill of this bird is used not only to probe flowers for nectar, but also to grab invertebrates. The bill is not especially powerful, however, and this results in oriental white-eyes tending to stab at fruit rather than biting off chunks. White-eyes are seen in loose flocks, often foraging through vegetation in the company of other birds. These birds are very active and extremely agile and can be observed hopping from branch to branch. They call frequently to other members of the group, with their calls consisting of a series of twittering notes, combined when necessary with sharper alarm calls. When breeding, pairs of these birds build compact, well-constructed nests that are usually hidden and supported in the fork of a tree.

Distribution: From northern India eastwards to southern China. Present across South-east Asia and the Malay Peninsula to the Greater Sunda islands.
Size: 11cm (4¹/₂in).
Habitat: Vegetation in lowland areas.
Nest: Cup-shaped in vegetation.
Eggs: 2, pale blue.
Food: Invertebrates, nectar and fruit.

Identification: Yellowish-green upperparts with a characteristic narrow, white ring of plumage around the eyes. Underparts may be entirely yellow or the flanks may be greyish, depending on the subspecies. Sexes are alike.

Yellow-breasted sunbird

Olive-backed sunbird *Nectarinia jugularis*

Although sunbirds are quite common on mainland Asia, the yellow-breasted variety is the only species present on Australia. They use their long bills to obtain nectar from plants, and also hunt invertebrates, with spiders being a favoured food. In spite of its small size, the yellow-breasted sunbird is quite bold, even to the extent of siting its nests under the roofs of verandas and porches and in the vicinity of other outbuildings. It uses the gossamer threads of spiders' webs rather like cotton to bind the nest fibres together, frequently incorporating a trailing tail beneath as part of the design. The internal area of the nest is lined with softer materials such as down feathers. The young in the nest are reared almost exclusively on insects.

Identification: Brownish-green upperparts and bright yellow underparts. Adult cocks easily identified by a dark purplish metallic area on the throat, which is more extensive in breeding plumage. Narrow black bill. Short tail. Young birds resemble adult hens.

Distribution: From China across South-east Asia and the Malay Peninsula to parts of Indonesia and New Guinea. Extends south to north-eastern coastal region of Australia.
Size: 11cm (4¹/₂in).
Habitat: Areas where there are trees in the vicinity.
Nest: Pendulous, made of vegetation.
Eggs: 2–3, grey-green with mottling.
Food: Nectar, invertebrates.

HONEYEATERS, FAIRY WRENS AND OTHER AUSTRALASIAN SPECIES

There is a clear divide between birds found in Australia and New Guinea, and those occurring on the mainland of Asia and the Greater Sunda chain of islands. This division in distribution was first identified by the Victorian zoologist William Wallace, after whom the Wallace line is named, which marks the border between the Asiatic and Australasian zones. This border runs between the islands of Bali and Lombok.

Plain honeyeater

Nondescript honeyeater *Pycnopygius ixoides*

Its drab plumage means that the plain honeyeater is easily overlooked, especially when it occurs in the company of other related species. It is quiet by nature, which presents a further difficulty in assessing its numbers with any accuracy. Some ornithologists suggest that these honeyeaters are quite rare, although others think that they are in fact quite common but are not easily observed. When these honeyeaters feeds on flowers that produce large amounts of pollen, the pollen may stain their heads temporarily, giving them a yellowish hue. Honeyeaters as a group have a very important role in pollinating flowers as they feed, not just from pollen transferred on their heads, but also from pollen on their brush-like tongue.

Identification: Corresponds well to the name of nondescript honeyeater, in that its plumage is plain, drab brown with no instantly recognizable features, apart from a greyer tone to the plumage on the head. Its bill is quite small compared with related species. Brown irises. Sexes alike.

Distribution: All of New Guinea, apart from the southern Trans-fly region.
Size: 18cm (7in).
Habitat: Lowland areas, but has been known to extend up into the hills.
Nest: Cup-shaped.
Eggs: 2, pinkish with darker spotting.
Food: Fruit, nectar and invertebrates.

Little wattlebird

Brush mockingbird *Anthochaera chrysoptera*

In spite of its name, and unlike its close relative the red wattlebird (*A. carunculata*), this species has no fleshy swellings, or wattle, on its neck. The heavily streaked plumage on the little wattlebird's body helps to conceal its presence well when it is seeking food among its favourite shrub, the banksia. Little wattlebirds tend to be rather bold by nature, especially in areas such as gardens, and will allow a relatively close approach. They are also quite noisy and have a varied repertoire of calls. They raise their tails when they are excited, and will rattle their bills without actually giving voice. Their nest is concealed in a shrub and is usually lined with a soft material such as loose bark stripped from eucalyptus trees.

Identification: Heavily streaked plumage with lighter underparts. The silvery streaking is most apparent on the sides of the head and neck. Rufous patches on the wings are apparent in flight. White tip to the relatively long tail feathers. Black pointed bill. Sexes alike.

Distribution: South-western and south-eastern parts of mainland Australia. Also present on Tasmania.
Size: 30cm (12in).
Habitat: Woodlands, parks and gardens.
Nest: Cup-shaped, made of twigs.
Eggs: 1–2, salmon-pink with darker reddish spots.
Food: Invertebrates, fruit and nectar.

Left: Invertebrates features prominently in the diet of young little wattlebirds.

Superb blue wren

Malurus cyaneus

Despite their small size, superb blue wrens are notoriously aggressive and territorial when nesting, even to the point of both sexes attacking their reflections in a window or a car hubcap parked by a verge. After the breeding period, the family stays together, although hens leave the group in the spring. Young cocks remain and help to feed the first round of chicks in the following year, and this allows the adults to build a new nest and breed again very quickly. These blue wrens have adapted well to garden life, searching out invertebrates in the plants.

Identification: Cock bird in breeding plumage has a bright blue head, extending back along the sides of the neck to the mantle. Has a blackish intervening area. Breast is a characteristic bluish-black, with whitish underparts. Long, dark blue tail. Wings brownish. Hen is brown with a whitish throat, while the underparts are fawn-white in colour. Tail is brown with a bluish wash. Reddish-brown feathers around the eye and similar-coloured bill distinguish hens from out-of-colour cock birds, whose bills are black.

Distribution: Eastern and south-eastern Australia, including Tasmania.
Size: 14cm (5¹/₂in).
Habitat: Dense, low vegetation.
Nest: Domed structure made of plant fibres.
Eggs: 3–4, pinkish-white.
Food: Mostly small invertebrates.

Noisy friarbird (*Philemon corniculatus*): 35cm (14in)
Found down the eastern side of Australia, although not in the extreme north or the far south. Brownish back, wings and tail with a ruff of creamy feathers around the neck and long silvery plumes on the upper part of the breast. Underparts greyish-white. Head bare and black with a swelling on the upper bill close to the base. White tips to the tail prominent in flight. Sexes alike.

Striated pardalote (*Pardalotus striatus*): 11.5cm (4¹/₂in)
Present in various forms through much of Australia including Tasmania and other islands. Variable appearance, depending on race. Blackish crown with white markings. Greyish back with pale orange to red streak above the eyes. Grey and yellow evident on the underparts. Short blackish tail. White edging to the flight feathers. Hens are duller in overall coloration.

Figbird (banana bird, *Sphecotheres viridis*): 30cm (12in)
Present on the eastern Lesser Sundas, New Guinea, Kai Islands and others in the Torres Strait south to Australia, being present in the north and eastern coastal areas as far as New South Wales. Has black plumage over much of the head, and bare area of red skin around the eyes. Green wing and rump, with black tail. Underparts vary from green to yellow, depending on the race. Whiter around the vent region. Hens have speckled underparts with brown or greenish back, wings and tail.

Pallid cuckoo (*Cuculus pallidus*): 33cm (13¹/₂in)
Found over much of Australia, including Tasmania. Undertakes seasonal movements and is occasionally seen in the Moluccas and New Guinea over the winter. Has a dark area around the eyes, a white area on the nape and white markings on the wings and flight feathers. The underparts are relatively pale. The long tail has whitish edging. Sexes are alike.

Flame robin

Bank robin *Petroica phoenicea*

These birds are unusual among the many robins found in Australia and Tasmania, simply because they form flocks outside the breeding season, with hens usually predominating in these groups. When nesting, these birds occur in wooded areas, before moving into more open countryside for the rest of the year. Although the flame robins are more conspicuous in the open, the hens' dull-coloured plumage means that it can prove difficult to identify them correctly. The site chosen for the cup-shaped nest is variable, ranging from a fork in a tree to a cavity in the trunk, and may even be situated beneath a rocky overhang. The construction process usually takes at least two weeks. The nest is bound using the thread from a spider's web.

Distribution: South-eastern Australia including Tasmania
Size: 14cm (5¹/₂in).
Habitat: Wooded and open country.
Nest: Bulky, cup-shaped.
Eggs: 3–4, greenish-white with dark markings.
Food: Invertebrates.

Identification: The head, wings and tail are dark grey apart from a prominent white area above the bill and white wing patches. Throat area is brownish too. Has buff and white markings across the wings and orange-red underparts. Hens have greyish-brown upperparts and white underparts.

STARLINGS, MYNAHS, SPIDERHUNTERS AND LAUGHING THRUSHES

The starling family Sturnidae is well represented both in Asia and Australia, where the European starling (Sturnus vulgaris) has been introduced alongside native species. Mynahs are a distinct grouping within the starling family, with this description being applied to large, short-tailed species with iridescent black plumage. Laughing thrushes, however, are found only in Asia, and have an attractive song in many cases.

Singing starling

Aplonis cantoroides

Distribution: New Guinea and neighbouring islands extending to the Bismarck Archipelago and the Solomon Islands.
Size: 19cm (7¹/₂in).
Habitat: Mainly open country.
Nest: Cavity in a tree hole or elsewhere.
Eggs: 2–3, pale blue with brown and violet spotting.
Food: Mainly fruit but also eats invertebrates.

During the breeding season, singing starlings are likely to be observed in pairs or even singly, but after the chicks have fledged, they join up to form large flocks comprised of both adult and juvenile birds. Perhaps surprisingly, in spite of their name, singing starlings are not talented songsters, although their calls are less harsh than those of many starlings. These starlings are seen predominantly in coastal lowland areas, and are a common sight in towns there. They have even been known to nest in buildings on occasions.

Identification: Predominantly black in colour with a marked green-metallic iridescence, depending on the light. Plumage on the back of the head and neck is elongated, forming hackles. The square, short tail is blackish. Iris is a bright contrasting orange-red. Bill and legs are black. Sexes alike. Young birds very different, having brown wings with some greenish suffusion, while the underparts are whitish with brown streaking. Iris brown.

Yellow-faced mynah

Papuan mynah *Mino dumontii*

Studies have revealed how these mynahs have different dialects in parts of their range. Those living in the vicinity of New Guinea's main town – Port Moresby – have call notes consisting primarily of two syllables, whereas in mynahs living elsewhere through their range, three or more distinct notes running together can be identified. Yellow-faced mynahs are believed to pair for life, even though they may congregate in large flocks comprised of hundreds of individuals at times. When nesting, a pair may be assisted by members of their previous brood. Once the chicks have hatched, insects and even small vertebrates assume greater importance in their diet to provide protein.

Identification: Stocky in stature. Predominantly glossy black. White rump and undertail coverts, and a white wing bar too. Large area of bright orange skin encircling the eyes, with an orange throat and an orange area on the abdomen as well. Yellow bill and legs. Sexes alike. The orange facial skin is paler in young birds.

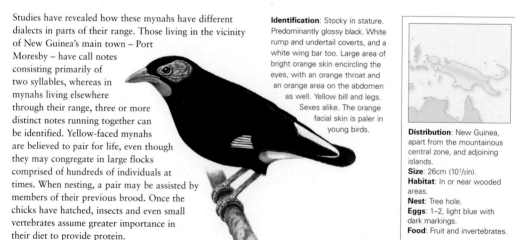

Distribution: New Guinea, apart from the mountainous central zone, and adjoining islands.
Size: 26cm (10¹/₂in).
Habitat: In or near wooded areas.
Nest: Tree hole.
Eggs: 1–2, light blue with dark markings.
Food: Fruit and invertebrates.

Common mynah

House mynah *Acridotheres tristis*

Distribution: Extends from south-eastern Iran and Afghanistan across central and southern Asia. Range is extending in some areas and the common mynah has been introduced to many islands around the world from Madagascar to Hawaii, Australia and New Zealand
Size: 25cm (10in)
Habitat: Open country.
Nest: Usually built in a cavity
Eggs: 2–6, bluish
Food: Fruit, invertebrates

Identification: Black head with broad yellowish bare patch of skin around the eyes. Wings and body brownish with a white patch on the wings, white undertail coverts and a white tip to the tail. Yellow bill. Sexes alike.

As their name suggests, these mynahs are a common sight through much of their range, in agricultural areas as well as in towns and cities. They are very adaptable and this is reflected in their choice of nest sites. Common mynahs have been recorded breeding in lamp posts, under the eaves of houses, in old machinery and even in air-conditioning units. An equally wide range of materials, from grass and leaves to pieces of plastic and paper, may be used in the construction. Common mynahs are often seen in pairs, frequently foraging on the ground in parks and gardens for invertebrates. This is one of just a few avian species that have actively benefited from changes in the landscape arising from human development.

Chestnut-cheeked starling (violet-backed starling, *Sturnia philippensis*): 18cm (7in) Breeding grounds are centred in northern and central parts of Japan, with overwintering occurring further south, in Borneo, southern Sulu islands, parts of the Philippines and elsewhere, although the exact range has yet to be defined. Rarely seen on the Asiatic mainland in China. Cock bird has pale chestnut-coloured patches on the cheeks, greyish underparts, white wing bar and violet back. Hens by comparison are brownish-grey overall with paler underparts. A wing bar is also apparent.

Crested mynah (Chinese jungle mynah, *Acridotheres cristatellus*): 26cm (10½in) Occurs in central and south-eastern China, extending to northern Indo-China. Also occurs on Hainan and Taiwan, and sometimes seen in western parts of Japan. Black, with a low crest extending back from the bill towards the eyes. Distinctive ivory bill. White patch on the wing and yellow iris. Sexes alike.

Hwamei (melodious laughing thrush, *Garrulax canorus*) : 21.5cm (8½in) Occurs in northern Indo-China and southern parts of China, including Hong Kong, as well as Hainan and Taiwan. Predominantly brown, with darker wings and tail. The tail is barred. Has dark streaking on the head and breast. The white plumage around the eye extends back to form a stripe running down each side of the neck. Has a "hwamei", which translates as "beautiful eyebrow". Sexes alike.

Spectacled spiderhunter

Greater yellow-eared spiderhunter *Arachnothera flavigaster*

Distribution: Extends from western Myanmar (Burma) through southern Thailand and the Malay Peninsula to Sumatra, Java and Borneo.
Size: 21cm (8in).
Habitat: Open forests and scrub.
Nest: Suspended structure.
Eggs: 2–3, pinkish with dark markings.
Food: Invertebrates, nectar.

Flowers that are red or orange in colour and shaped like trumpets tend to attract these nectar-feeding birds, which are members of the sunbird family in spite of the lack of iridescence in their plumage. They can be very aggressive, particularly during the breeding season, with an established cock bird chasing rivals away without any hesitation. At this time, the long, pointed bill of these birds is used rather like a needle to sew the nest in place, using gossamer threads of spiders' webs for this purpose. Spiderhunters are very bold birds by nature, and can often be seen in the open, particularly during the morning and later part of the afternoon, searching for food.

Identification: Relatively large spiderhunter. Predominantly olive green, darker in colour on the head, back and wings. There is a yellow suffusion to the plumage of the underparts. Yellow circles resembling spectacles encircle the eyes, and there are adjoining yellow ear patches. Narrow, long, down-curving black bill. Sexes alike.

BULBULS AND OTHER GARDEN BIRDS

*There is a wide range of birds that may be encountered in garden surroundings, and they can be quite
bold in this type of environment. A number are valuable allies of people, catching invertebrates that
would otherwise become pests, particularly in tropical areas, although they also inflict damage on
crops in some regions, especially when these are maturing.*

Red-whiskered bulbul

Pycnonotus jocusus

These lively bulbuls are quite conspicuous through their range,
occurring in small groups. They sing for quite long periods from
the same perch, especially at the start of the breeding season,
although the crest may not always be clearly
visible at this stage. Sometimes they may be seen
on branches but they will also perch on telephone
cables in the open. Red-whiskered bulbuls are
rarely seen on the ground, preferring to seek their
food in trees. They are also sufficiently agile to be able
to catch invertebrates in flight. When breeding, their nest
is typically constructed up to 3m (10ft) off the ground in
a bush or tree, being made of plant matter and lined with
smaller plant fibres.

Identification: Head black, with a tall crest extending back towards the
rear. Red patch behind the eyes, with white cheeks and throat broken
by thin black lines. The wings and back are brownish. The underparts
are buff in colour, apart from the vent area, which is red. Sexes alike.

Distribution: Extends from
India eastwards to China and
South-east Asia. Introduced
in various localities including
Australia.
Size: 20cm (8in).
Habitat: Open wooded areas
and villages.
Nest: Cup-shaped, made of
vegetation.
Eggs: 2–4, pinkish white with
darker markings.
Food: Fruit and invertebrates.

Edible-nest swiftlet

Collocalia unicolor

Distribution: Found on many
offshore islands, including the
Andamans, Nicobars and the
Sundas. Also present on
parts of the South-east Asian
mainland at lower altitudes,
including Myanmar (Burma),
Thailand and the Malay
Peninsula.
Size: 13cm (5in).
Habitat: Scrubland and
towns.
Nest: Made entirely of
saliva.
Eggs: 2, white.
Food: Invertebrates.

Although they fly in daylight, edible-nest swiftlets also rely
on echolocation, rather like bats, which enables them to
fly around caves in darkness. The rattling sounds that they
utter reverberate off nearby objects, allowing them to fly
without hitting any obstructions. The nests made by these
swiftlets are constructed from saliva, and are traditionally
harvested as the key ingredient of birds' nest soup. Over-
collection of these nests and the resulting disruption of
long-standing breeding colonies has led
to a decline in the populations of
edible-nest swiftlets at a number
of localities through their range.

Identification: Upperparts blackish-
brown, with brown underparts. Rump
colour is variable, depending on the
distribution. It is palest, bordering on
white, in the case of birds originating
from Singapore, and much darker in
those found further north.

*Right: These swiftlets breed
communally in caves used
over several generations.*

Straw-headed bulbul (yellow-crowned bulbul, *Pycnonotus zeylanicus*): 28cm (11in)
Extends through the Malay Peninsula down to the Greater Sunda islands. This is one of the larger bulbuls. It has a straw-yellow head and a white throat. Black lines run through the eyes and extend backwards from the side of the bill. Has a greyish chest with white streaking. This becomes grey on the belly and has a yellow vent. Olive-brown back, with whitish streaking near the neck. Sexes alike.

Collared finchbill (*Spizixos semitorques*): 23cm (9in)
Found in central, eastern and southern parts of China and Taiwan. Has olive-green upperparts with the underparts a more golden-olive shade. The bill is short and thick and less pointed than in other bulbuls. Has a low, rounded crest on a black head. Has white streaking on the sides of the face, white lores and a white collar. The tail has a black tip. Sexes alike.

House crow (Indian crow, *Corvus splendens*): 43cm (17in)
Occurs mainly in Asia from India eastwards to the western parts of South-east Asia, but also present in localities in the Middle East and Africa. Lighter greyish neck, back and underparts than other crows but with a jet black face, crown and throat. Sexes alike.

Coppersmith barbet

Crimson-breasted barbet *Megalaima haemacephala*

The monotonous, repetitive calls of the coppersmith barbet resemble the sound of hammering on metal, which accounts for its unusual name. Their calls can be repeated as frequently as 100 times or more per minute, and this behaviour has led to them becoming known less flatteringly as "brainfever birds". They can also use their stout bills just like a hammer to tap away at rotten wood to create a suitable nesting cavity, which may be used for roosting purposes as well. In common with other barbets, the coppersmith displays the characteristic outward-curving longer feathers around the base of its bill, which are responsible for the common name of this group of birds ("barbet" actually means "bearded").

Distribution: Ranges from western Pakistan across Asia to south-western China, and through the Malay Peninsula to Sumatra and Java. Occurs on some Philippine islands.
Size: 15cm (6in).
Habitat: Wooded areas, often in cities and gardens.
Nest: Tree cavity.
Egg: 2–3, white.
Food: Fruit and invertebrates.

Identification: Red area above stocky, dark bill and across the breast, separated by pale yellow, which is also present above and below the eyes. Crown and lower part of the cheeks are black. Lower underparts light greyish with dark green streaks, while the upperparts are olive green. Legs reddish. Sexes alike.

Java sparrow

Rice bird *Lonchura oryzivora*

These members of the munia group are drawn to areas where cereals are ripening and flocks can inflict considerable damage on rice crops at this stage, especially when they descend in large numbers. Java sparrows are quite conspicuous finches, thanks to their large size and unusual coloration. Groups often settle in the evening on top of buildings before heading to their roosting sites. They frequently engage in a behaviour known as "clumping" when resting for any length of time, with the birds perching against each other. Pairs may nest under the eaves of buildings, although often they will use tree cavities for this purpose.

Identification: Black head with white cheek patches, grey chest and back with pinkish belly and white undertail coverts. Rump and tail above are black. Prominent reddish ring around the eyes. The large bill is pinkish. Both the eye ring and the bill may appear slightly enlarged in cock birds during the breeding season. Sexes are otherwise alike.

Distribution: Naturally found on Bali, Java and Kangean (part of the Greater Sunda islands) but introduced elsewhere both in the region – on Lombok, for example – and further afield in Venezuela and Puerto Rico, among other localities.
Size: 13cm (5in).
Habitat: Cultivated. grasslands and gardens.
Nest: Domed nest with side entrance.
Eggs: 3–8, white.
Food: Cereal seeds such as rice, plus invertebrates.

CLASSIFICATION

The way in which different birds are grouped is known as classification. This is not only helpful in terms of distinguishing individual species and those that are closely related, but it also enables wider assessments of relationships between larger groups to be made.

Interest in how best to group birds into distinct categories is nothing new. It dates back nearly 2,500 years to the ancient Greeks, when an early method of classification was developed by the philosopher Aristole. He sought to group living creatures on the basis of differences in their lifestyles, rather than on the basis of anatomical distinctions, which are favoured today. The first modern attempt to trace relationships between birds was made by Sir Francis Willoughby, in a book entitled *Ornithologia,* which was published in 1676. Willoughby saw the need for what was essentially an identification key that would enable readers to find an unknown bird by means of special tables devised for this purpose.

Willoughby's work concentrated solely on birds, but it was actually a Swedish botanist, Carl von Linné (also known as Linnaeus), who devised the universal system of classification that

Above: The so-called nominate subspecies of the African grey parrot – Psittacus erithacus erithacus.

Below: This is the timneh subspecies of the grey parrot, known scientifically as Psittacus erithacus timneh.

is now known as the Linnean System. Linnaeus relied primarily on the physical similarities between living organisms as the basis for grouping them, laying the foundations for the science of classification, which is now known as systematics. Linnaeus refined this approach through a series of new editions of his classic work *Systema Naturae,* which was originally published in 1735 for the first time.

Linnaeus's system operates through a series of ranks, creating what is sometimes described as a hierarchal method. Starting from a very general base, the ranks become increasingly specific, splitting into smaller groups, until finally, individual types of birds can be identified. One advantage of this system is that when a new species is discovered, it can be fitted easily into this existing framework.

New advances

While Linnaeus and successive generations of taxonomists relied on physical similarities, the use of DNA analysis is currently transforming our understanding of the natural world. By comparing sequences of the genetic material DNA, it is possible for ornithologists to investigate which birds share DNA sequences that suggest a close relationship. This method of study is set to revolutionize taxonomy and is already leading to numerous revisions of the existing classification of birds.

How the system works

As animals, birds belong to the Kingdom Animalia, and having backbones, they are members of the phylum Chordata, which includes all vertebrates. The class Aves is the first division at which birds are separated from other vertebrates such as mammals. Birds alone comprise this major grouping, which is subdivided

Above: In the case of the African race of (Psittacula krameri krameri), the green coloration is of a more yellowish shade, while the bill is darker.

into smaller categories called orders. It is then a matter of tracking an individual species down through the various ranks of classification. For example, the classificatory breakdown of the grey parrot is as follows:

Order: Psittaciformes
Family: Psittacidae
Genus: *Psittacus*
Species: *Psittacus erithacus*
Subspecies: *Psittacus erithacus erithacus, Psittacus erithacus timneh*

If you are unsure where you are in the ranking, the way in which the names are written gives a clear indication. The names of orders end in "-formes", while family names terminate with "-idae". At or below genus level, all names are italicized, with the genus comprising one or more species. The scientific name of species always consist of two descriptions, with the genus names being written first. Species are the basic fundamental level in the taxonomic tree, enabling particular types of birds to be named individually. Members of a particular

species generally identify with each other and do not normally interbreed with other species. However, if interbreeding does occur, the resulting offspring are know as hybrids.

At the most specific level of the taxonomic tree are subspecies: closely related forms of the same species that are nevertheless distinctive enough to be identified separately. These are often defined on the basis of their size, although also because of distinct differences in coloration. In the case of the grey parrot (*Psittacus erithacus*) given above, the so-called nominate form, which is the first form to have been recognized, is *Psittacus erithacus erithacus*, as indicated by a repetition of the so-called trivial name *erithacus*. The subspecies timneh (which can be written in an abbreviated form *P. e. timneh* in the context of the nominate subspecies) is recognizable in this instance because of its smaller size, significantly darker grey coloration and maroon rather than red tail feathers.

It was Linnaeus himself who devised this method of distinguishing between such closely related individuals, first describing it in 1758. His method is

sometimes known as the trinomial system, thanks to its use of three names in these cases.

What's in a name?

Even the choice of scientific names is not random. They can give an insight into a bird's appearance or distribution, often based on Latin. The name *flavinucha,* for example, indicates yellow plumage around the neck; the description *peruviana* in the case of the parrot-billed seed eater (*Sporophila peruviana*) indicates the bird's distribution in South America. In a few instances, the species' description features a person's name, for example *Chloebia gouldiae* – the Gouldian finch – which the noted naturalist and explorer John Gould named after his wife Elizabeth, because of its beauty. In order to be recognized as a species, an example of the bird concerned, known as the "type specimen", has to be held in a museum collection, enabling a detailed description to be written up as part of the identification process.

Below: Subtle but consistent differences in appearance allow subspecies to be distinguished. The Indian race of the ringnecked parakeet (Psittacula krameri manillensis) is seen here.

GLOSSARY

anvil: A rock or hard object against which certain species batter prey such as snails, to break the shell.

avifauna: The birds of a specified region or period of time.

breeding plumage: The often brightly coloured plumage that the cock birds of some species adopt before the breeding season. Also known as summer or alternate plumage.

carpal: The area of plumage at the top of the leading edge of the wings, corresponding to the wrist.

carrion-eaters: Birds such as vultures that feed on the carcasses of dead creatures that they themselves have not killed.

cere: The fleshy area encompassing the nostrils located above the bill. Often especially prominent in parrots.

cline: A gradual change in a characteristic of a species, such as size, or the frequency of a characteristic, over a geographical area.

clumping: The way in which small birds such as the common wren (*Troglodytes troglodytes*) come together and roost collectively to retain body heat.

cob: A male swan.

columbiforms: The group of birds that comprises doves and pigeons.

contour feathers: The smaller feathers covering the head and body.

corvid: A member of the Corvidae family, such as crows, ravens and jays.

coverts: The specific contour feathers covering the wings, and also present at the base of the tail.

cryptic: Refers to coloration or formation that conceals or camouflages.

culmen: The central ridge of the bill.

down: Plumage that primarily serves to conserve body heat, and has a loose texture.

eclipse plumage: A transitional plumage seen, for example, in the drakes of some species of duck, occurring after they have moulted their breeding plumage, usually being much duller and resembling that of a female. Also seen in some weavers and other birds.

Above: Greater racket-tailed drongo (Dicrurus paradiseus)

frugivore: A species that eats mainly fruit.

irruption: An unpredictable movement of large numbers of birds, typically in search of food outside their normal range.

lek: An area where the male birds of certain species, such as the capercaillie (*Tetrao urogallus*), gather to perform their courtship displays.

lores: The area between the bill and the eyes on each side of the face.

mantle: The plumage on the back and folded wings of certain birds when it is the same colour.

melanistic: A dominance of black pigment in the plumage, such as in a particular colour phase of some species.

migrant: A bird that undertakes regular seasonal movements, breeding in one locality and overwintering in another.

moustachial: An area of plumage, usually a stripe, running from the bill under the eye, resembling a moustache in appearance, as seen in the Inca tern (*Larosterna inca*).

munias: A group of estrildid finches, also sometimes known as mannikins, typically but not exclusively belonging to the genus *Lonchura*.

nidicolous: Refers to the chicks of species that remain in the nest for some time after hatching.

nidifugous: Describes the chicks of species that leave the nest almost immediately after hatching.

nuchal: The plumage at the nape of the neck.

orbital: The skin around the eye.

pectoral: Of or located on the breast.

precocial: Refers to newly hatched young that are covered with down and fully active, able to run around at this stage.

race: A geographically isolated population below the level of species, which differs slightly, typically in size or colour, from other races of the same species.

racket/racquet: Enlargements at the tips of otherwise bare shafts of tail feathers, as in the hooded racket-tailed treepie (*Crypsirina cucullata*).

raptor: A bird of prey that actively hunts its food.

ratite: Any of the large, flightless birds, such as the emu (*Dromaius novaehollandiae*), that have a flat breastbone without the keel-like ridge of flying birds.

scapular: Of or on the shoulder.

spatule: Spoon-shaped or spatula-shaped feathers, on the wing or the tail.

speculum: A distinctive patch of colour evident in the flight feathers of certain birds, particularly ducks and parrots.

syrinx: The voice organ of birds, located at the base of the trachea (windpipe).

tarsal: Refers to the area at or below the ankle in birds, as in tarsal spur.

torpidity: A state of dormancy, usually undertaken to conserve energy and combat possible starvation in the face of adverse environmental conditions.

tousling: Territorial behaviour by pairs during the breeding period, in which the pair attacks the chicks of other birds, or even their own chicks, if they venture too close.

wattle: A wrinkled, fleshy, often brightly coloured piece of skin that hangs from the throat or chin of certain birds, such as the long-wattled umbrellabird (*Cephalopterus penduliger*), or may be present elsewhere on the head, as with the hill mynah (*Gracula religiosa*).

zygodactyl: The 2:2 perching grip, with two toes holding the perch at the front and two at the back.

Below: Parrots have a zygodactyl perching grip.

SELECTED BIBLIOGRAPHY

Alderton, David (1992) *Parrots*, Whittet Books, London, UK.

Brudenell-Bruce, P.G.C. (1975) *The Birds of New Providence and the Bahama Islands*, Collins, London, UK.

Byers, Clive; Olsson, Urban & Curson, Jon (1995) *Buntings and Sparrows: A Guide to the Buntings and North American Sparrows*, Pica Press, Robertsbridge, East Sussex, UK.

Cramp, Stanley (series editor) (1977–94) *Birds of the Western Palearctic: Handbook of the Birds of Europe, the Middle East and North Africa* Vols 1–9, Oxford University Press, Oxford, UK.

De Schauensee, Rodolphe Meyer (1984) *The Birds of China*, Smithsonian Institution Press, Washington DC, USA.

Dorst, Jean (1974) *The Life of Birds*, two volumes, Weidenfeld & Nicolson, London, UK.

Fjeldsa, Jon & Krabbe, Niels (1990) *Birds of the High Andes*, Zoological Museum, University of Copenhagen and Apollo Books, Svendborg, Denmark.

Forshaw, Joseph & Cooper, William T. (1969) *Australian Parrots*, Lansdowne Press, Melbourne, Australia.

Forshaw, Joseph & Cooper, William T. (1989) *Parrots of the World*, Blandford Press, London, UK.

Fry, C. Hilary; Fry, Kathie & Harris, Alan (1992) *Kingfishers, Bee-eaters & Rollers*, Christopher Helm, London, UK.

Gibbs, David; Barnes, Eustace & Cox, John (2001) *Pigeons and Doves*, Pica Press, Robertsbridge, East Sussex, UK.

Harris, Tony & Franklin, Kim (2000) *Shrikes & Bush-Shrikes*, Christopher Helm, London, UK.

Harrap, Simon & Quinn, David (1996) *Tits, Nuthatches & Treecreepers*, Christopher Helm, London, UK.

Hayman, Peter; Marchant, John & Prater, Tony (1986) *Shorebirds*, Christopher Helm, London, UK.

Heinzel, H., Fitter, R. & Parslow, J. (1972) *The Birds of Britain & Europe with North Africa and the Middle East*, Collins, London, UK.

Hilty, Steven L. & Brown, William L. (1986) *A Guide to the Birds of Colombia*, Princeton University Press, NJ, USA.

Hoyo, Josep del; Elliott, Andrew & Sargatal, Jordi (series editors) (1992–) *Handbook of Birds of the World Vols 1–7*, Lynx Edicions, Barcelona, Spain.

Jeyarajasingam, Allen & Pearson, Alan (1999) *A Field Guide to the Birds of West Malaysia & Singapore*, Oxford University Press, Oxford, UK.

Johnsgard, Paul A. (1983) *The Hummingbirds of North America*, Smithsonian Institution Press, Washington DC, USA.

King, Ben; Woodcock, Martin & Dickinson, E.C. (1975) *A Field Guide to the Birds of South-east Asia*, Collins, London, UK.

Lambert, Frank & Woodcock, Martin (1996) *Pittas, Broadbills and Asitites*, Pica Press, Robertsbridge, East Sussex, UK.

Lewington, I., Alstrom, P., & Colston, Peter (1991) *A Field Guide to the Rare Birds of Britain & Europe*, HarperCollins, London, UK.

MacKinnon, John & Phillipps, Karen (1993) *A Field Guide to the Birds of Borneo, Sumatra, Java and Bali*, Oxford University Press, Oxford, UK.

Madge, Steve & Burn, Hilary (1988) *Wildfowl*,

Above: Greater frigate bird (Fregata minor).

Christopher Helm, London, UK.

Marchant, S. & Higgins, P.J. (series editors) (1996–) *Handbook of Australian, New Zealand and Antarctic Birds*, Oxford University Press, Melbourne, Australia.

Ogilvie, Malcolm & Carol (1986) *Flamingos*, Alan Sutton Publishing, Gloucester, UK.

Peterson, Roger T. (1961) *Peterson Field Guides: Western Birds*, Houghton Mifflin Co., Boston, USA.

Peterson, Roger T. (1980) *Peterson Field Guides: Eastern Birds*, Houghton Mifflin Co., Boston, USA.

Pratt, H.D.; Bruner, P.L. & Berrett, D.G. (1987) *A Field Guide to The Birds of Hawaii and the Tropical Pacific*, Princeton University Press, Princeton, NJ, USA.

Sparks, John & Soper, Tony (1987) *Penguins*, David & Charles, Devon, UK.

Urban, E.K.; Fry, C.H. & Keith, S. (series editors) (1986–) *The Birds of Africa*, Academic Press, London, UK.

PICTURE ACKNOWLEDGEMENTS

The Publishers would like to thank the following agencies for permission to reproduce their photographs in this book. Jacket photographs are credited on page 4.

Key: l = left, r = right, t = top, m = middle, b = bottom, E = endpaper.

Dennis Avon: 246b, 247t, 247b.

Ardea: 2, 7, 13hr, 14r, 15t, 15h, 19l, 19hr, 20, 21br, 22bl, 23tl, 23tr, 23b, 24b, 25b, 26t, 27t, 29t, 29b, 31tl, 31tr, 31b, 32t, 32b, 33tl, 35b, 36t, 36b, 37t, 37m, 38, 39t, 39m, 40t, 48bl, 50tl, 50b, 52t, 52b, 54t, 56b, 58m, 60t, 62b, 63tr, 66tm, 66tr, 126tl, 126tm, 126tr, 186tl, 186tm, 186tr

Oxford Scientific Films: 6b, 6t, 8/9, 11, 13tl, 13tr, 13ml, 13mr, 13bl, 14l, 16t, 17tl, 17ml, 18t, 18b, 21bl, 24t, 25tl, 25tr, 26bl, 26br, 27b, 28t, 28b, 30t, 33tr, 33b, 35t, 37b, 39b, 40b, 41t, 41b, 43t, 43b, 44t, 44m, 44b, 46t, 48t, 48br, 50tr, 54b, 56t, 58t, 58b, 60b, 62t, 63tl, 63b, 66tl, 246t, E.

Illustrations were provided by:

Peter Barrett: 60, 68, 69, 70, 71, 72, 73, 74, 75, 76, 77, 78, 79, 80, 81, 82, 83, 84, 86, 87, 88, 89, 90, 91, 92, 93, 94, 95, 96, 97, 98, 99, 100, 101, 102, 103, 104, 106, 106, 107, 108, 109, 110, 112, 113, 114, 115, 116, 117, 118, 119, 120, 121, 122, 125, 125, 129, 130, 132, 133, 148, 149, 154, 155, 156, 157, 158, 159, 164, 165, 173, 174, 175, 160, 161, 162, 163, 164, 168, 169, 181, 180, 181, 188, 189, 192, 193, 194, 198, 199, 200, 2020, 203, 204, 205, 206, 207, 208, 209, 210, 211, 212, 213, 214, 215, 216, 217, 218, 219, 220, 233, 234, 240.

Anna Childs: 134, 135, 182, 183.

Anthony Duke: 42, all location maps, pp68-245.

Studio Galante: 90, 91, 106, 107, 110, 111, 122, 123, 130, 131, 162, 166, 167, 172, 173.

Martin Knowelden: 10, 11, 12, 13, 17, 19, 20, 21, 22, 28, 28, 30, 34, 38, 45, 47, 49, 51, 53, 55, 57, 59, 61, 64.

Janos Marffy: 66, 126, 186.

Andrew Robinson: 00, 01, 102, 150, 200, 239, 244, 245.

Tim Thackeray: 128, 129, 136, 137, 138, 139, 140, 141, 142, 143, 144, 145, 146, 147, 150, 151, 170, 171, 176, 177, 178, 179, 184, 185, 188, 189, 190, 191, 194, 195, 196, 197, 198, 199, 200, 201, 220, 221, 222, 223, 224, 225, 226, 227, 228, 229, 230, 231, 232, 233, 234, 235, 236, 237, 240, 241, 242, 243.

WEBSITES OF INTEREST

UK ORGANIZATIONS
British Birds Rarities Committee
http://dspace.dial.pipex.com/town/terrace/
yrr86/bbrc.htm

British Ornithologists' Club
Email: mbcasement@aol.com.uk

British Ornithologists' Union
http://www.bou.org/

British Trust for Ornithology
http://www.bto.org.uk

Rare Breeding Birds Panel
http://www.indaal.demon.co.uk/rbbp.html

Royal Society for the Protection of Birds
http://www.rspb.org.uk

Wildfowl & Wetlands Trust
http://www.wwt.org.uk

NORTH AMERICAN ORGANIZATIONS
American Birding Association
Email: member@aba.org

American Ornithologists' Union
http://www.aou.org

Cornell Laboratory of Ornithology
http://birds.cornell.edu/

National Audubon Society
http://www.audubon.org/

Wilson Ornithological Society
http://www.ummz.lsa.umich.edu/birds/
wos.html

AUSTRALIAN & NEW ZEALAND ORGANIZATIONS
Barren Ground Bird Observatory
http://www.users.bigpond.com/barren.
grounds

Bird Observers Club of Australia
http://www.birdobservers.org.au

Birding NSW (NSW Field Ornithologists
Club Inc)

http://members.ozemail.com.au/~nswbirds/

Birds Australia
Website: www.birdsaustralia.com.au

Cumberland Bird Observers Club Inc.
http://www.cboc.org.au

Eyre Bird Observatory
Email: eyrebirdobs@bigpond.com

The Avicultural Society of New South
Wales
http://www.aviculturalsocietynsw.org

SOME MISCELLANEOUS WEBSITES
African Bird Club
http://www.africanbirdclub.org

Bird On
http://www.birdcare.com/birdon

BirdLife International
http://www.birdlife.net/

Disabled Birders Association (UK)
http://www.disabledbirdersassociation.org.
uk/DBAindex.htm

Edward Grey Institute of Field Ornithology
http://www.zoo.ac.uk/orniandbehav/egi.html

European Ornithologists' Union
http://www.eou.at

Fat Birder
http://www.fatbirder.com

Gay Birders Club
http://dspace.dial.pipex.com/gay.birders/
index.shtml

Global Ringing and Banding Internet Links
Database
http://www.birdsinthe.net

Hawk & Owl Trust
http://www.hawkandowl.co.uk

Hawk Conservancy
http://www.hawk-conservancy.org/

Above: American goldfinch
(Carduelis tristis)

International Ornithological Committee
http://www.nmnh.si.edu/BIRDNET/IOC/
index.html

National Bird-Feeding Society (US-based)
http://www.birdfeeding.org/

Neotropical Bird Club
http://www.neotropicalbirdclub.org/

Oriental Bird Club
http://www.orientalbirdclub.org

Ornithological Societies of North America
http://www.nmnh.si.edu/BIRDNET/OSNA/

Ornithological Society of the Middle East
http://www.osme.org/

Pacific Seabird Group
http://www.pacificseabirdgroup.org/

Percy Fitzpatrick Institute of African
Ornithology
http://www.uct.ac.za/depts/fitzpatrick

Rare Birds of the World
http://www.geocities.com/RainForest/Vines/
2408/critical.html

Working Group on International Waderbird
and Wetland Research
http://www.wiwo-international.org/

World Bird Count
http://eco.goo.ne.jp/wbc/wbc_e/index.html

INDEX

NOTES

NOTES

Notes

NOTES

NOTES

NOTES

NOTES

NOTES